Theater and Integrity

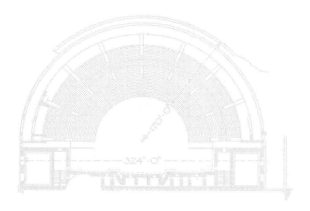

Theater and Integrity

Emptying Selves in Drama, Ethics, and Religion

Larry D. Bouchard

NORTHWESTERN UNIVERSITY PRESS
EVANSTON, ILLINOIS

Northwestern University Press
www.nupress.northwestern.edu

Printed in the United States of America

10   9   8   7   6   5   4   3   2   1

Library of Congress Cataloging-in-Publication Data

Bouchard, Larry D., 1952–
   Theater and integrity : emptying selves in drama, ethics, and religion / Larry D.
Bouchard.
     p. cm.
   Includes bibliographical references and index.
   ISBN 978-0-8101-2562-9 (cloth : alk. paper)
   ISBN 978-0-8101-2563-6 (pbk. : alk. paper)
   1. Integrity in literature. 2. Self in literature. 3. Religion and drama.
   4. Drama—History and criticism. 5. Drama—Moral and ethical aspects. I. Title.
PN1650.I58B68 2011
809.2'9384—dc22

                                         2011009508

For Margaret Galloway

Contents

Preface

THERE ARE SCENES in the 2006 film *The Lives of Others* that help identify this book's themes and counterthemes.[1] They concern the possibilities of integrity that appear when selves perform *as, with, among,* or *for* others.

In 1984 Hauptmann Wiesler, an officer in the East German Stasi, is spying on playwright Georg Dreyman and his lover, actress Christa-Maria Sieland. Dreyman has never challenged the regime's authorities, but now seems to be suspected of subversion. In fact, he is being bugged because Christa-Maria is an insecure drug abuser, who is secretly trapped in a liaison with a grotesque party official, who in turn would like to separate her from Dreyman. For his part, Dreyman is chagrined he has taken no political risks, as have other artists he knows; so he sets out to publish an article exposing the East's high suicide rate. All this Wiesler has been taping. He arranges for Georg to discover his lover's affair, and thereafter in shame she leaves him.

But Wiesler enjoys the theater and has seen Christa-Maria perform in Georg's plays. Incredibly, as Wiesler listens to their private lives through his headset, he begins to take a compassionate interest in the couple. He seeks her out in a bar, wins her trust, and tells her that he knows her as she truly is, onstage, and that she is a very fine actress. And we get the impression he genuinely means it. Christa-Maria is moved by his words and returns to Georg, who forgives her. When Wiesler monitors their reconciliation scene, he is pleased—in fact, he is now dangerously switching his allegiances—so touched has he been by their love and artistry, in contrast to his own loveless life and brutal vocation as a secret audience, an official voyeur.

What are we to make of the idea that Christa-Maria is her truest self when acting in Dreyman's plays? Or that she is least "her own" in her private roles as lover, mistress, addict, and self-loathing self? The film turns over many sides of these questions. Wiesler must relinquish his role in the Stasi. Dreyman must renew his role as a conscientious writer, while Christa-Maria is tragically lost among the parts she plays. Are her weaknesses thematically necessary to the story, or do they reflect an anti-theatrical prejudice? None of the characters entirely negotiates the public/private ambiguities of his or her life. Sometimes we might attribute integrity to them, sometimes not. Hence, my themes and counterthemes:

Themes: There is the odd, though quite old, idea that integrity is better found in the "parts we play" or "masks we wear," as we perform with others, than in what we "really are behind our masks." Most of us know what it means to be doubtful about ourselves until we can play parts that give a pattern to our living. And many of us, caught up in some new complex of relations, responsibilities, or insights, know what it is for minds or hearts to change. Do we find or do we lose our integrity on such occasions?

Counterthemes: But is it not counterintuitive to say that integrity comes with wearing masks and playing parts? Integrity connotes being "whole," "true to oneself," "committed to moral principles," or being honest, self-consistent, reliable, sincere, mature, authentic. Playing roles often connotes "bad faith." To attack someone's integrity can mean "unmasking" what they "really are." As long as there has been theater, playacting has been a figure for pretense or hypocrisy. And yet we will see how these themes and counterthemes can be mutually implicated in surprising ways.

Integrity can mean coherence, but integrity-talk is not very coherent. Does it mean first being true to oneself and personal commitments, or first being true to moral principles? Can one have personal integrity without moral integrity, or vice versa? If integrity means being constant, reliable, or sincere in one's convictions, can it ever entail serious compromise or real change? Integrity seems inconsistent with being self-deceived, but are there times when strong commitment requires self-deception? And if integrity means "whole" or "all of one piece," what about lives that suffer fragmentation? Can they have integrity? Is supererogation—acting beyond the call of duty—required by integrity, or is it optional? Is integrity a "secondary virtue"? Is it more an inward property, or outward? If inward, how can we recognize it? If outward, how can we trust it?

For a long time the idea of integrity was in eclipse in moral philosophy, and popular uses and abuses of the term might caution it should remain so. Yet the meanings associated with integrity are unavoidable, and the gaps among them—their real or apparent inconsistencies and indeterminacies—may offer space for constructive interpretation. Integrity may name a heuristic quality, *one for which to have it is to be searching for it and so, paradoxically, not yet to have it.* Patterns of integrity are realized in, but also unsettled by: contingent intersections with other lives, desires and commitments, moral principles and ethical visions of the good, traditions and histories, and uncertain futures. Thus, patterns of integrity may appear to us more as contingent gifts than secure possessions.

These studies will explore how qualities associated with integrity can be *discovered in and illuminated by theatrical drama,* which is an art that perennially reflects, criticizes, and reconstitutes understandings of self and identity. Questions and possibilities of integrity can, as well, *illuminate dramatic works and performances.* Most of this book is devoted to theater, and I hope the chapters on drama and performance can be enjoyed independently of the more theoretical introduction and the four preludes and postlude. But all of these essays argue by exposition and exemplification that theater not only reflects upon the *emptying* of selves into others, with others and for others—the movement that is here termed *kenosis*—but theater may also *occasion or create* these relations of self-emptying and self-reception: for readers, performers, and audiences.

This last point signals how these studies follow a certain trajectory. Both the motif of *playing a part* and the motif of the *self emptying into the forms of others and receiving the self-emptying of others,* both in joy and suffering, provide a paradigm for reenvisioning integrity. I explore this under the heading "kenotic integrity," after a Greek word that has found new uses by philosophers, critics, ethicists, and theologians. *Kenosis*—emptying—illuminates and allows us to assess the *emptying self* as a feature of theatrical art and of the personal, ethical life.

Acknowledgments

I OWE MUCH of my postgraduate learning in theater-and-religion to two books by Max Harris, whom I came to know at the University of Virginia, *Theater and Incarnation* and *The Dialogical Theatre: Dramatizations of the Conquest of Mexico and the Question of the Other*. I am particularly indebted to his application of Mikhail Bakhtin for an understanding of what it means to perform another's texts and scripts, with openness to new understandings and to the subversion of oppressive structures. His work is also invaluable for exploring the logic of incarnation as it occurs in theater and the logic of embodied drama as it occurs in scripture.

Every time I embark on these waters I rediscover two very different theologians and culture critics who sailed here before: Hans Urs von Balthasar and Tom F. Driver. The first volume of Balthasar's *Theo-Drama: Theological Dramatic Theory* is a rich commentary on dramatics through the mid-twentieth century as well as the prolegomena to a trinitarian theology. I am indebted to his exposing the problem of "transition from role to mission." However, I situate my own concerns in ethics (broadly viewed), before approaching issues in theology (e.g., kenosis), rather than vice versa; also, some readers may ask if my sense of person, self, and identity is perhaps "weaker" or more fluid than Balthasar's.

Driver traces relations between realism and meaning in *Romantic Quest and Modern Query: A History of the Modern Theatre*. This trajectory, moving from drama as *quest for* reality to drama as *questioning of* reality, is invaluable. Modern, realistic theater reaches an impasse; as it holds a mirror to reality it also in effect holds a mirror to itself, and its powers of disclosure vanish into a point of infinite self-reflection. While I am not as pessimistic about the future of realistic drama as Driver, we both regard mutuality and participation as necessary correlatives to mimesis—if we are to grasp how this hybrid art can criticize us and delight us.

Mutuality and participation are also categories that govern the creation of this book. I am grateful to many ensembles of persons and institutions, so many in fact that naming them all is impossible. But the book's composition began at the Center of Theological Inquiry in Princeton, 2001–2. Margaret Galloway and our children, Micah, Austin, and Katherine, and our cats agreed to move me to New Jersey and were of constant assistance during that historically painful yet personally satisfying year. Peggy has ensured that I see plays and films I might not otherwise see, many of which figure throughout these pages.

Along with CTI's support, its mentors, Wallace Alston and Robert Jenson, were unfailingly encouraging, as were the scholars in residence that year; so too have been those I met through CTI's Pastor-Theologian program. I was also upheld by other groups. Good advice on *Pygmalion* and kenosis came from the Association of Disciples for Theological Discussion, which also considered my thoughts on *Philoctetes*.

Conversations with the Disciples Divinity House Board of Trustees were helpful; indeed, my travels to Chicago for DDH, under its dean, Kristine Culp, have indirectly funded my theater explorations there. The Princeton year was also funded through the generosity of the University of Virginia, and my research began with a UVA Sesquicentennial sabbatical fellowship. For these and other considerations I acknowledge the Dean of the College of Arts and Sciences and the Vice President for Research and Graduate Studies. I am also grateful to four chairs of the Religious Studies department, James Childress, Harry Gamble, Paul Groner, and Kevin Hart, who in addition to extensive substantive help may have stretched the meaning of "departmental travel" during my research of plays and performances.

Many others have read parts of the work and thereby contributed, wittingly or unwittingly, to these matters—especially students at UVA in my courses in religion, literature, and drama over the years. Recently, Howard Pickett examined my arguments, annotated the chapters, and made invaluable observations and suggestions. Among those helping with the whole manuscript are my mother, Sherry Bouchard, Frank Burch Brown, Henry Carrigan, Margaret Galloway, Frederick Rolf, Richard Rosengarten, and also Heather Antti and readers for Northwestern University Press. Others who commented on parts of the work and were helpful at different stages include Jacqueline Bussie, James F. Childress, Marcia Day Childress, Kristine Culp, Jason Danner, Jennifer Geddes, Mary Gerhart, Martien Halvorson-Taylor, Max Harris, Kevin Hart, Paul Daffyd Jones, Stephen Kepnes, Charles Mathewes, Esther Menn, Ann Mongoven, Daniel Moseley, Steve Neumeister, Peter Ochs, Vanessa Ochs, Brett Patterson, Benjamin Ray, Eugene Rogers, Robert Scharlemann, Nathan A. Scott Jr., Tom Siegfried, Anthony C. Yu, and Eric Ziolkowski. For these readers, and for important conversations with and insights from countless others, I will always be indebted.

Theater and Integrity

Introduction

Integrity, in Personal and Theatrical Terms

HAMLET: What players are they?
ROSENCRANTZ: Even those you were wont to take delight in, the
tragedians of the city.

—SHAKESPEARE, *Hamlet*

I'm a respectable girl. . . . They'll take away my character. . . . I'm a
good girl, I am.

—ELIZA DOOLITTLE, IN BERNARD SHAW, *Pygmalion*

Attention, attention must finally be paid to such a person.

—MRS. LOMAN, IN ARTHUR MILLER, *Death of a Salesman*

AGAINST A TIME when it was rarely treated in philosophy, ethics, and
religion, the problem of integrity has come out of eclipse for a number
of reasons:

Suspicions that modern moral thought, in the contrasting heritages
of John Stuart Mill and Immanuel Kant, fails to acknowledge the
particularity of persons
The crises of identity that can occur when frameworks of cultural
and religious meaning are disrupted by changing worldviews or by
historical moral catastrophes
Proposals that classical ethics of virtue can provide new understandings
of the moral life that may be needed in late modernity
Postmodern interests in the ethics of responsibility, otherness, and
relationality, which envision the person as constituted, or brought
into being, in encounters with other persons, cultural and spiritual
traditions, and with the natural environment

In these contexts, we may seek integrity as an "integrative" value or virtue. There is a rhetoric that asserts integrity to be a quality all should be able to recognize—in persons, in art, in nature—even across cultural and ideological differences.[1] However, as a term of common reference, *integrity* may be a slogan more than an idea, a compliment of last resort when we eulogize the unremarkable, inept, or tiresomely stubborn. As invective, accusing a foe of lacking integrity is always handy. It can be a reason for not compromising in religious, political, and cultural conflicts. In episodes of genocide, preserving national or racial integrity has provided horrible rationalizations. And the word offers refuge for the shamed, as when an accused official huffs and puffs, "I won't stand by while you attack my integrity!" Here, integrity seems both a *private, inward* possession yet also something *outward,* like the radiance of interior beauty, which others should be able to see.

Limits in the Language of Integrity

That last example indicates how the language of integrity embraces a complex and question-laden phenomenon. Consider the contrasting views of Gabriele Taylor and Raimond Gaita.[2] Taylor makes the case for *wholeness:* a person of integrity "keeps his inmost self intact." The lives of such persons are "of a piece," their selves are "whole and integrated." Whoever "lacks integrity is corrupt in the sense that his self is disintegrated." Taylor tends toward a pristine view of integrity, since any disruption of a unitary whole negates its wholeness, just as a fraction cannot be an integer. So there would be a kind of purity to integrity.[3] Not only would those who feign commitments lack it, so too the self-deceived or the weak-willed who have commitments but cannot keep them. Moreover, if I lose touch with my past, I lose integrity. Or if I am deeply confused about my basic principles, much less violate them, I will dissolve. "It is easy to see how this point leads to the conviction that the person of integrity has his own defense against chaos." Taylor articulates the intuition that having *personal integrity* is a shield against losing *moral integrity.*

Yet such a fragile, crystalline structure of wholeness may give us pause. Gaita, in response, imagines a person suffering from a mental illness, one who is terribly confused about his past:

> So severe is this confusion that one could say he had lost his past and with it his self-understanding. He struggles to regain his past by seeing

it under some pattern of sense, to see people and events in his past justly and compassionately; "struggles" because he has lost his confidence in that without which he cannot regain his sanity—his judgment, and because his fantasies and delusions periodically lay waste to whatever he had patiently and painfully achieved in understanding. Each time that happens, he has to begin again. He does. What has to be emphasized is not merely that he tries to restore order to his life, but that he does so in an uncompromising spirit of truthfulness.

Gaita wants to ascribe integrity to this person's uncompromising truthfulness, a form of *moral* integrity. But he doubts whether such a life can be said to be of one piece. Another example: A boy is raised in two cultures, where the conflict between cultures is the source of both his strengths and weaknesses. Sometimes he seems to himself rootless, "unlocated, vacillating and wasted." Nonetheless he approaches "his life in a spirit of truthfulness," and Gaita asks if we should really want him to be otherwise. No, for that would "wish him to be someone else." Is the boy all of one piece? Perhaps not. Is he a person of integrity? Perhaps so.[4] Notice that as Gaita casts doubt upon *wholeness,* two other traits of integrity come into play: an *uncompromising* spirit of *truthfulness.* When can persons of integrity compromise in respect to truthfulness? Is compromise *always* or only *sometimes* inconsistent with truth? Must truth, and hence integrity, always be so pristine?

These questions are not exhaustive, but they allow me to draw the first lines in a sketch of integrity discourse. At least since Bernard Williams and others began examining integrity in light of modern moral thought, one response has been simply to rest on the distinction between personal and moral integrity. However, some will ask if one is prior to the other, and others will want integrity to be all of one piece. But can we have, conceptually, what we desire? There are many facets to the problem of integrity; they make for an ambiguous yet compelling area of discourse fraught with ambiguities and limits, which give rise nonetheless to crucial life questions.

Personal Integrity as Wholeness

Integrity's connection with being whole or unimpaired relates to embodiment, an issue I will return to. Personal integrity as wholeness is also associated with *sincerity, authenticity, self-consistency, wholeheartedness, autonomy, constancy, reliability,* and with such *commitments* as to provide for identity and integrated selfhood. But while crucial to any account of integrity, these traits are not always commensurate. Also, some observers divide the topic of personal integrity between those who see it in terms of commitments that ground *identity* and those who see it in terms of relations and narratives that secure an *integrated self in community*.[5]

Critics of integrity as personal or communal wholeness often notice a formal lack of moral content. Thus, a devoted segregationist with a consistent commitment to white supremacy, or an egoistic hedonist committed to maximizing pleasure for oneself and one's friends, might be said to possess whole and committed selfhood. To be sure, admits John Rawls, the very formality of personal integrity can become attractive when there is no consensus about morality. At such times, "there is a tendency to fall back on the virtues of integrity: truthfulness and sincerity, lucidity and commitment, or, as some say, authenticity." However, "it is impossible to construct a moral view from these virtues alone; being virtues of form they are in a sense *secondary*. But *joined* to the appropriate conception of justice, one that allows for autonomy and objectivity correctly understood, they come into their own."[6] The question will be one of "joining."

Moral and Ethical Integrity

We also attribute integrity to persons conformed to virtues such as honesty or who are committed to rights, duties, and principles. Further, we often attribute integrity to those who display such moral commitments with impartiality and in the face of adversity.[7] And some consider moral integrity to require, as well, purity or "clean hands." Jody L. Graham views integrity as an interior trustworthiness few can really be said to have; most of us only have "integrity in the making."[8] Yet others contend that moral integrity may sometimes require dirtying one's hands, especially in life and death conflicts. Still others observe how the principles that moral integrity is often joined with, such as *justice* or *care,* may vary in relation to particularities, such as gender.[9] In the prelude to part I, we will see how Paul Ricoeur distinguishes *the moral* (concerning the *right*) from *the ethical* (concerning the *good*); here the ethical, or what Iris Murdoch calls "the sovereignty of good,"[10] might be more embracing of personal integrity in community than the moral. However, other questions about moral integrity need to be broached now.

Morality entails burdens of obligation that in certain vistas are both unrealistic and infinitely great. A follower of Martin Luther would find moral integrity ultimately impossible. We can never account for all our obligations and failures, given the circumstances bearing upon us and our shattered capacity to love self and others as God loves, without self-ish corruption. Luther knew he could never confess *all* his sins (or those of communities or nations). We are, at best, *simul justus et peccator*—at once counted as righteous yet sinful—implying integrity is at best my confession of its absence. In different doctrinal ways, Luther, Calvin, and also Catholics believe that the integration of wholeness and rightness requires mediations of grace: forgiving, sanctifying, or repairing grace. In Judaism and Islam, the grace of divine law—Torah, Sharia—affirms the joining of personal and moral integrity as a human possibility and obligation. So also would many nonreligious humanists.

But besides our inherent fallibility, our finitude also pulls us up short. The unending suffering around me calls me to *infinite* responsibility, which confounds my *finite* capacities both to act morally and pursue my personal abilities and interests. In fact, Susan Wolf regards the "moral saint" as an undesirable image for ethics; while she admires Mother Theresa, she would rather her daughter emulate Katharine Hepburn![11] Infinite responsibility makes the ethics of Emmanuel Levinas—for whom the other's suffering is the primary moral fact—vulnerable to suspicion that his hyperbole of being "hostage" to another's suffering unwittingly imputes violence to the other as a hostage taker.[12] To such concerns, John Caputo, in *Against Ethics* says simply, "obligations happen." What he is against is domesticating obligation in the safety nets of ethical systems or in religious resignation. Edith Wyschograd depicts the moral saint's exuberant and interesting "desire on behalf of the Other" as an image for reimagining ethics.[13]

What Williams brings to this story is how moral integrity can be as formalist as personal integrity. Universal principles (e.g., doing justice, respecting persons as persons, caring for the general welfare, avoiding harm) may elide actual lives. For Williams, personal integrity refers to one's commitment to a "ground project" that secures a sense of identity. His notorious example is Paul Gauguin, who abandoned his family and moved to Tahiti for the sake of his art. Only the particulars of his life, his work, and the "moral luck"[14] that his paintings turned out well, allow us to evaluate his choices and neglects. Even more familiar ground projects, such as a couple's desire to have a large family in an overcrowded world, or another's not to have children at all, may be eclipsed by universalizing morality. Williams thinks this is clearly true of utilitarianism—where maximizing general welfare is paramount—and even of Kantian deontological morality—where impartial respect for persons as ends, and not as means only, would override every particular, partial concern. These theories, he thinks, would obliterate the values and passions that make a particular life seem to itself worth living, that endow it with integrity, identity, and *a reason to be*.[15] At very least, Williams identifies how morality can become inarticulate about personal particularity.

Alasdair MacIntyre makes the analogous, communitarian claim that integrity requires particular cultural narratives of virtue, which modernity has largely forgotten.[16] He would no doubt regard the Rawls quote above as exemplifying the problem. Advocates of moral integrity, however, can reply to Williams and MacIntyre that if particular ground projects or cultural identities override universal principles, then to grant the integrity of communal pirates, committed segregationists, or hedonists-with-traditions would hardly seem avoidable.

Relational Views of Personal and Moral Integrity

Perhaps the split between the personal and the moral could be overcome by appealing to the *relational* dimension of individuals and others, so as to achieve a thicker account of integrity. For Cheshire Calhoun, life's bewildering complications cast doubt on pristine views of identity or integrated selves. Her innovation is to regard integrity as a social virtue, in which one "stands for something." Standing for something, before witnesses, challenges others to recognize that you have deliberated on what you stand for and believe others should "endorse" your stance. *Standing for* can also imply *standing by* others,[17] creating social solidarity. This picture still remains susceptible to the pirates-with-integrity critique, for a society's endorsements (say, of antebellum slavery) may later be impossible to justify. Nonetheless, Calhoun's treatments of deliberation, self-transcendence, and embodied action (*standing for/by*) illuminate common usage, where personal is not separate from moral integrity.

A relational view also helps us understand why integrity's opposite is not immorality per se but is often thought to be *hypocrisy*. Ruth W. Grant, however, argues that at least in politics, some hypocrisy is necessary, as opposed to two sorts of moral integrity: the flexible moderate (a Machiavelli-with-principles) and the purist (Rousseau). The moderate is susceptible to the vice of indifference, the purist to fanaticism. While moderation and purity can both be forms of integrity, they are not easily reconciled and neither easily recognizes the integrity of the other. Moreover, neither fares well in politics, where Grant thinks hypocrisy is the rule. "Hypocrisy" generally connotes a disconnection between one's stated values and one's actions, and there are different types of hypocrisy (e.g., conscious vs. unconscious, public vs. private, sometimes motivated by power and sometimes from weakness). But Grant thinks that at root, hypocrisy results from being *dependent on* or beholden to others, while integrity is rooted in personal *autonomy*. If politics is all about being dependent—cutting deals, compromising, relying on others, keeping promises—then being either a purist or an indifferent moderate is politically naive. Kantian respect for the individual's intrinsic autonomy, while essential in personal relations, is likely to harm a body politic. Grant thinks there are legitimate forms of hypocrisy, implying a kind of necessary, principled hypocrisy.[18]

If so, then what principles? And why call it *hypocrisy*? Clearly, for Grant, reasonable and effective politics requires willingness to dirty one's hands. Yet that would imply that *in the contextual realm of politics* the naive purist would be the hypocrite (only pretending to be a prudent politician). And further, if politics must relinquish some personal autonomy before the realities of dependency and fallibility, then necessary hypocrisy might better be called practical wisdom, which weighs principles and values beside the practical contingencies at hand.[19] In such deliberation, the paradigms of performance, improvisation, and enacting parts might inform rather than contradict how we might imagine the political requirements of integrity.

But who gets to improvise, and on what basis? Those questions underlie Margaret Urban Walker's account of relational moral integrity, which understands that we negotiate multiple commitments, responsibilities, and especially narratives: narratives of *identity*, of *relations with others*, and of *values and principles*. None of these is primary; different narratives make different claims upon us as circumstances and patterns of life change. Walker doubts that philosophy can find an "all-purpose solution" to how we arrange or change our multiple commitments or make compromises among them. She also prefers virtues such as *sturdiness*, *dependability*, and *reliability* to "global wholeness" or "true selves." Integrity means *reliable* and *collaborative* accountability to "a moving horizon of commitments and adjustments."[20] But she does ask, with Williams, whether all this creates a burden of obligation every bit just as problematic as paramount principles.

> Could a life responsive along these lines exhibit the commitments and concerns distinctive of the one who lives it? How could a person make,

or keep, this life her or his own? Responsibility ethics might seem to defeat personally meaningful life-ordering by visiting a veritable plague of commitments on each of us. It might even be claimed that such a view ignores, thwarts, or threatens a person's *integrity*.[21]

Walker's answer is that a flexible ethic of responsibility can hold the distinctive interests of individual lives "in tandem with reasonable reliability." This phrase makes her account congenial to what I want to call the "juxtaposition" of the personal and the moral. "It's the coherence of the three narratives, and connections among them, that makes a distinctive moral life out of what would otherwise be an odd lot of disparate parts." While no principle determines the proportions of coherence, consistency, and continuity that integrity requires, integrity does entail a "moral reliability" that those traits make possible.[22] *But again, who gets to improvise?* Each of us does, assuming luck and historical-political circumstances do not interfere—significant caveats. *And on what basis?* Walker implies *autonomy,* a notion as problematic as it is necessary to moral discourse. When autonomy means respecting personal agents as such, it seems indispensable; as an ultimate ground of reason and morality, it is troubling. Are appeals to autonomy finally appeals to power? This is a question that my notion of "kenotic integrity" will also need to address.

The importance of flexibility and willingness to revise values and commitments is articulated in a recent assessment of integrity theory by Damian Cox, Marguerite La Caze, and Michael P. Levine. For them, integrity should be ascribed to selves "always in process," capable of continually "remaking" itself in response to changing moral circumstances. Integrity is

> a complex and thick virtue term. It stands as a *mean* to various excesses: on the one side, conformity, arrogance, dogmatism, fanaticism . . . on the other side, capriciousness, wantonness, triviality. . . . The person of integrity lives in a fragile balance between every one of these all-too-human traits.
>
> Over and above these virtuous characteristics, integrity appears to . . . presuppose fundamental moral decency. Grossly immoral people, for example, do not even seem candidates for integrity.[23]

Their view resists the formalism of personal integrity as "well-functioning" wholeness, and also resists modernist moral integrity's obliviousness to actual persons. It avoids pure and essential selves and recognizes that integrity entails discernment and dynamic openness. It can make trenchant criticisms of other views of integrity, showing the ambiguities characterizing integrity discourse generally. And it affirms that insofar as openness to change can be *cultivated,* integrity would be a primary virtue that integrates other virtues.

Yet this definition also has its own formality. What is the "fragile balance" among those all-too-human traits that otherwise lead to fanaticism or indifference, unless it is "fundamental moral decency," as opposed to "grossly immoral people." *Decency* suggests a range of questions, as when the authors deny integrity to those living in "egocentric oblivion."[24] To be sure, kenotic integrity is likely the very opposite of egocentrism. Yet some Romantic geniuses arguably lived in egocentric oblivion, and their value of authenticity became an integrity paradigm. Moreover, some epistemological skeptics would urge that if we think we can easily avoid egocentric oblivion, we are self-deceived. As to what is grossly immoral, I would so regard hate speech—while numerous Americans regard it as a free speech option. Gay marriage remains for many an indecent oxymoron, just as not long ago did interracial marriage. Our current debates about decency and grotesquery touch on abortion, capitalism, war on terror, culture war, torture, capital punishment, universal health care, eating meat, the income tax, evangelical missionaries, illegal immigration, nudity onstage, and French painters who abandon their families to make art and love on exotic strands. Are Cox, La Caze, and Levine wrong to appeal to a moral consensus?

Not necessarily. Jeffrey Stout argues that my debate-list obscures how much consensus about democratic values there actually is in America. We *do* recognize that *most* of us are decent, even as we debate about the consensus or its lack. A real danger, thinks Stout, is that by neglecting to articulate our shared commitments to the tradition of democracy we may well lose it.[25] However, this consensus is indeed fragile and contested, meaning that integrity cannot be understood by *uncomplicated* appeals to common morality. Nor do I think integrity lends itself to clear and distinct concepts. We need other approaches, though integrity may turn out to entail relations that intrinsically resist claims to clarity and completeness.

Utopian-Transforming Practices of Integrity

Susan E. Babbitt worries that even progressive accounts of relational integrity can be oppressive. When narrativists such as Martha Nussbaum hold that we all need knowledge of myths and paradigms from many cultures, histories, and life situations, Babbitt gives qualified assent. But somewhat like Plato, she worries that exposure to a plurality of story traditions will not *unify moral agency*—which she sees as an aim of integrity—but may fragment it. Shattered selves in oppressive societies require *new stories and new kinds of unity,* unity that requires us to imagine transformed and transforming future communities.[26] Cuba is her example, with its achievements in literacy and health care. Babbitt also looks to fiction. But in contrast to Nussbaum, Babbitt valorizes stories of oppression and transformation, in which normal sorts of integrity are impossible. The integrity of Sethe in Toni Morrison's *Beloved*—who kills her daughter to keep her from being returned to slavery—*anticipates a good society Sethe can begin to imagine* but cannot yet realize, where her children will be nurtured as "full human beings."[27]

I term this view of integrity "utopian," not pejoratively but because such a regulative vision of the good can transform the present only from a future *scene,* as Jürgen Habermas calls it, of unencumbered discourse among all voices in society.[28] By itself, an ideal is but an abstraction; only in practice can an ideal affect practice; yet past ideals are liable to be (from this perspective) sources of distortion. Only an imagined future practice can transform the present. What mediates this normative scene is what Babbitt calls "moral imagination," entailing narrative, speculation, and construction.[29] Of moral imagination, I would add, there are varieties. Marx imagined a classless society, Kant a kingdom of moral ends, Plato a city ruled by philosophers, Jesus a kingdom of God. Nussbaum's and Ricoeur's visions of "human flourishing" and "the ethical aim" are, in a sense, also utopian scenes. Precisely because such futures are as yet real in "no place," their arrivals from the future must be imaginatively realized or concretized in "this place."[30] Thus, relational integrity must transcend personal and historical pasts and reconnect selves with others and the cosmos.[31]

Babbitt's celebrations of Guevara and Castro caution that social transformation may entail revolutionary power and violence, which may become state violence. An alternative picture of integrity-as-transforming might imagine the future via a committed pacifism, working to mitigate coercion in personality and society and denying that personality and culture are inherently violent. However, in both pacifist and just war perspectives we face questions of integrity in social-political practice, where utilitarian implications of violence are sometimes hidden, sometimes overt. We must later ask whether kenotic integrity intrinsically resists the reduction of life to will-to-power.

Integrity and Metaphors of Embodiment

While traits or family resemblances in the language of integrity resist capture in clear and distinct propositions, they do lend themselves to metaphoric forms of discourse. Indeed, one advantage of *integrity*—and a reason not to abandon it—is that the word lends itself to metaphors and predications: it joins things, and moves in numerous directions. So a person or an institution can have "organic integrity," as can a sonata or play. We often qualify integrity with the connective *as:* "*As* a merchant, she has integrity." A phrase I frequently employ, "patterns of integrity," is indicative of how even conceptual language is pervasively metaphorical,[32] both relying on explicit metaphors and holding conceptual meanings in tensive patterns, such as part and whole.

The wholeness of integrity is often expressed in metaphors of embodiment. Bodily integrity, in fact, is less a model of integrity than a dimension of most of the views of integrity I have sketched. The Latin *integer* and *integritas* indicate wholeness and the sense of being "untouched." Integrity also can translate the Hebrew *tam,* which connotes completeness and unbrokenness, especially in the senses of unimpaired or unblemished. In Wisdom literature, *tam*-related words are paired with opposites meaning crooked or perverse, and so *tam* can connote being whole, straight, or standing upright beside a norm, and for the well-being of the community.[33] We "stand for" and also "walk with" integrity.[34] In these ways, integrity can signal a pivotal or religious value, as when Job is said to "persist in his integrity," though thwarted by God and Satan (2:3).[35] Aside from the excellences of character (*aretai*), perhaps no one Greek word has the relational and bodily range of "integrity."[36] Since for Aristotle virtues are means between opposites, the relationality of integrity may be ingredient in each virtue as well as among them. And perhaps *dikaiosunē* (justice, "harmony of the soul") in Plato's *Republic* would integrate aspects of the psyche with the polis and, indeed, the spheres of nature in economic and ecological relation to the good.[37]

The relational character of integrity leads some translators to prefer it to "sincerity" for translating the Chinese *cheng.*[38] Like *tam* and *integritas, cheng* has connotations of wholeness and completeness, particularly in respect to ordering. Confucian sages who exemplify the way of *cheng* are well ordered in their intentions and ideas and are not self-deceived or double-minded. Since an individual's inward order is mutually implicated with society and heaven, the word can mean social and sacred ordering as well as personal[39] and can have resonating effects on the *cheng* of others. The integrity of virtuous persons is performative: as they express order in speech or rituals, they create an expectation of order and humaneness in those about them. In *Hamlet,* Polonius counsels Laertes, "This above all—to thine own self be true. . . . Thou canst not then be false to any man." Had he been Confucian, he might have said: If you are manifestly true to yourself, you not only will be false to no one, but others will be true to themselves in relation to you. The performance of integrity would draw others into its performance.[40]

Thus, integrity can convey a sense of wholeness-in-plurality, as in "integral" and "integrate." As a conceptual metaphor, integrity plays on how parts make a whole, where "parts" and "making whole" can be ideas in tension. The conceptual tension is in turn predicated with other matters, such as of personality or attributions of goodness or rightness.[41] Although integrity discourse rarely takes the classic metaphorical form *a is b* ("Senator Goodenough *is* Mr. Integrity"), it often implies possession ("Senator Goodenough *has*—or *has lost*—his integrity") or a quality manifested through enactment ("Senator Goodenough showed integrity when he voted No").

Ricoeur distinguishes "living metaphors" from idiomatic or dead metaphors, such as "table leg" or "eye of the storm."[42] But even idioms retain a dormant force that can reemerge, often as questions. To be told that "medicine fights disease with an arsenal of modern weapons" may lead us to raise counterquestions, such as when should medicine seek mainly to care rather than cure.[43] If we define metaphor simply as speaking of one thing in terms suggestive of something else,[44] then there may be tensions as well as resemblances between the juxtaposed fields of meaning (e.g., healing and warfare). The fields may contradict, qualify, or animate one another, thereby producing new meanings.[45] Metaphors might teach us *to see* in new ways, or else *raise doubt* about the matter being seen. For instance, integrity is often inclusive of honesty and risk; these different traits may relate to each other coherently or incoherently, and may invite us to explore patterns of integrity more critically. My sense is that to say "Senator Goodenough is Mr. Integrity" inevitably raises the question "Is he really?" Integrity discourse is *heuristic:* it invites exploration and discovery.

Narrative or Theatrical Drama?

For Ricoeur, narrative is extended metaphor, and many would understand integrity and the moral life in narrative terms. By narrative, I mean the *structures* of action, time, and character unfolding in a story and also the *mode of representing* such structures from the perspective of a narrator or an "implied author." Postmodernity has been defined both by its suspicion of grand metanarratives—such as of Christian redemption or modern enlightenment—and by its attentions to local narratives of communities and persons. Local narratives, historical or fictional, are said to discern how particularity, contingency, and even contradiction are inherent aspects of personal and communal life. However, Adam Zachary Newton warns that some narratives so privilege the coherence of plot, character, and perception as to lead ethics to *assume rather than interrogate* the wholeness of human lives. He worries that emphasis on narrative order and continuity may elide matters of contingency and suffering, which may be signaled by stylistic discontinuity.[46] This worry, in part, also prompts my studies. I argue that dramatic literature and performance are, in addition to narrative, sources for exploring both continuity and discontinuity in patterns of integrity.

Now, consider how when Polonius advises, "to thine own self be true," it may sound like he is affirming an inward possession of a wholeness and rightness within ourselves. And *if* we think of integrity as mainly such an interior relationship of self to itself, akin to authenticity, then narrative may at first seem to have an easier time than performed drama in depicting integrity or its lack. For narrative—unless it constrains itself—can peer into states of consciousness and unconsciousness, deception and self-deception, desire and despair. It can report finely textured perceptions and emotions, secret intentions, hidden histories, cultural assumptions, remote complications, all of which constitute what MacIntyre calls the dramatic narrative[47] of a person's life.

But another meaning of dramatic is pertinent to how patterns of integrity are constituted and recognized, namely, drama as *dramatized*. Performance plays to the sensorium: to our seeing and hearing and our felt sense of matter, space, and time. When we enjoy a narrative, what is usually *before us* is a text, and sometimes its author or an oral reader (and then it takes on a theatrical dimension). Theater includes narrative modes, but is distinctive in that what is directly before us is usually an ensemble of *persons* whose bodies are visible, while their interiors are invisible. Drama, as performed, realizes the physicality of personal presence with great perceptual intensity. As a hybrid form, it is narrative—with plots, characters, allusive sign structures, authorial viewpoints—and other than narrative, insofar as it makes meaning through living performers and audiences.

Critics of drama typically divide between interpreters of scripts and interpreters of performances, which can make the study of drama awkward. What shall we examine, the inadequate text or the ephemeral performance? In fact, this division need not be so strict.[48] Works of dramatic literature typically anticipate and reflect their realization in theatrical performance. Nonetheless, if dramatic literature is to be a medium for ethical inquiry, we must imagine the implications of the players' bodies being visibly before us, while their interiority (and that of the characters they play) is literally invisible. We see and hear *living* (i.e., feeling, thinking, and interpreting) bodies that move and speak in the immediacies and limits of shared space and time. Moreover, while our seeing may or may not be naive in the theater, our naïveté is resisted by the doubleness of what we see. Drama inherently offers its own critique of presence. The performer both is-and-is-not[49] "herself" and is-and-is-not the persona she plays, and so too the other players as we perceive and think of them. We should be asking what we believe about this hybrid presence of another. If Lysander and Hermia, Titania and Oberon, Puck and Bottom are "right before our eyes," we are also seeing an ensemble of persons interpreting *A Midsummer Night's Dream*. And we are aware that these persons need our interpretive responses to make the *Dream* appear.

So, as Peter Brook observes, if *stone* is a medium through which we see people in sculpture, then *people*—embodied, attending personalities—are a medium through which people see people in theater.[50] If seeing can be believing, and if integrity is primarily an interior self-relationship, then live theater might have to work much harder to succeed in representing the inwardness of integrity. And when it does succeed, it may succeed rather powerfully, for having surpassed the intrinsic limits of its form. We have, however, begun to see another possibility, *that integrity is not primarily an interior quality* of the self, but comprises relations the self performs with many others. It may encompass not only self-possession but the ways a person is at once singularly embodied yet smeared out in a nexus of heterogeneous relations. *If patterns of integrity are relational, as much exterior as interior, then they may lend themselves to theater's distinctive powers of exploration.*

Drama in live theater can recapitulate and interrogate how patterns of personal and moral integrity might emerge or change. Theater promotes the awareness that a person is a complex persona: not just a mask or social role, but an embodied being who—along with other such be-ings—creates, interprets, and performs *with* masks and *through* various parts, relationships, vocations, beliefs, and tasks. Theater also appreci-ates that persons are malleable or protean: they can be transformed by the parts offered them, even while remaining in fragile continuity with themselves. And while theater is aware of the dangers of distortion or harm, it regards the protean dimension of persons to be a good, to which we can respond with enjoyment and delight as well as with doubt. One of the questions of this book is how such delight can be "ethical."

This sense of delight is caught in two speeches from Peter Shaffer's play, *Amadeus,* in which the capacity of theater to reflect on life and on itself is celebrated and examined. Mozart has been defending his inten-tion to write operas, such as *The Marriage of Figaro,* about ordinary people. Although he distinguishes drama from opera, what Mozart loves about opera is in certain ways common to theater generally.[51] He imag-ines composing into a harmony the haughty attitudes of the courtiers he is arguing with, and is amazed that this ensemble of distinct, even op-posed voices could be perceived all together, as distinct yet combined. I would add that the performer's voice remains his or her own, yet it empties into the voice being performed, so that we hear both: we experi-ence even the individual as being herself an ensemble. Mozart likens this phenomenon to "how God hears the world," which is as much as to say that the phenomenon is "good."

But we may wonder whether this is only an aesthetic sense of the good; does it have anything to do with the ethical? One hesitates, because for centuries the tendency has been to keep these realms separate.[52] But con-sider how Salieri in *Amadeus* recalls the first performance of *Figaro.* "I saw a woman, dressed in her maid's clothes, hear her husband utter the first tender words he has offered to her in years, only because he thinks she is someone else. Could one catch a realer moment? And how, except in a net of pure artifice? The final reconciliation melted sight."[53] What will we make of the theatrical trick the wife has played? The ethical problem of disguise eliciting tenderness *may give us pause, just as we are being delighted.* And as we are recognizing the problem, it is resolved by forgiveness. And almost at the same moment, another ethical con-text emerges. Salieri is an alienated Christian and failed romantic; he is moved to tears only through the artifices of theater and music. Are his tears of theatrical delight ethically significant?

Delight in theatrical artifice has long been greeted with ambivalence, reflecting an "anti-theatrical" prejudice. I think we do have intuitions that the pleasure or intensified regard elicited by performed patterns of integrity is "good." *But we generally lack ordinary language or para-digms that well articulate this good* and so inform moral discourse.[54] One of my tasks will be to illuminate how plays and performances can help us articulate both this good and our ambivalence about it.

Theater and Integrity: Juxtapositions, and an Overture

The title "Theater and Integrity" can suggest several possibilities: (1) That some plays or performances *have* artistic or aesthetic integrity. (2) That theater can *depict and critically explore* relations, commitments, and forms of living suggested by traits such as *wholeness, steadfastness, right-ness, authenticity,* or their absence; that is, theatrical drama is a medium in which patterns of integrity can be investigated. (3) That some dramas or performances in life and in art may *create* patterns of integrity. While not my focus, the first possibility comes up when issues of aesthetic in-tegrity in a work such as *Hamlet* relate to how it examines integrity in life. The other possibilities are my focus. I follow a trajectory in which integrity may emerge as we perform parts with others and in encounters with persons, with circumstances, and with moral or sacred principles.

But how does any art form, and theater in particular, become a medium for ethical reflection? Consider how Nussbaum argues that some ethical issues *require* narrative modes of representation. First, she thinks that narrative forms can converge with certain ethical issues.[55] Love, friend-ship, emotion, temporality, the contingency of virtue, and the particular-ity of persons—philosophizing about these matters need not actually take a narrative form but needs to be affected by such forms. To speak with utter dispassion about passion would be a kind of contradiction. Narrative allows ethics to know more thoroughly and appropriately the complexities of circumstance, temporality, and emotion that it wants to conceptualize. A similar case may be made for theatrical drama, espe-cially if we recognize how certain attributes of integrity are performa-tive, that is, *happen in their performance.* Second, Nussbaum contends that ethics not only requires attention to narrative, but that some issues become finely tuned only by way of *specific* narratives. While we may dispute her choices (e.g., her taste for Henry James), this contention is as reasonable as saying some issues need certain specific arguments made by specific philosophers.

I cannot claim that every play examined here is essential for grasping all the problems of integrity, but I do hope they can keep us grounded in performative praxis. They are all more or less *metatheatrical,* in that each work reflects on performance in life and in its own art, and invites us to join in the reflection. They not only *mirror* ethical concerns and *engage* in ethical inquiry but, as A. Z. Newton formulates it, they *are* ethical relationships that seek to include us in them.[56]

So how does theater include us? Certainly, we are *there,* in proximity to a performance. But this sense of *shared space* is also a feature of a play's text, story, and relations with other works and performances. We can think of dramas, indeed all expressive works, as holistic arrangements of fragmentary materials (such as Aristotle's action, character, thought, spectacle, and elocution). The materials themselves are not complete, nor are the wholes they form. They are like a midrash, where fragments are held or juxtaposed, but not fused or synthesized.[57] Between the juxtaposed fragments are *spaces* (and in the temporal arts also *times,* since the fragments follow one other). Moreover, we usually experience works of art as juxtaposed, as in: "Last week I saw *The Tempest;* then I read *To the Lighthouse."* In the spaces and times created by juxtapositions, possibilities suggest themselves to our solitude and in our conversations. If we know our judgments of these works are not definitive, it is partly because we know we may later encounter them in new ways. In any case, within and between what is juxtaposed there are *gaps* or zones of liminality and receptivity,[58] inviting us into relations with the work and with others we may meet in such zones. We enter with our bodies, thoughts, feelings, and questions, and there we may hear such queries as: "What do I make of this? What do you make of it?" The finding and making of juxtapositions is the heuristic method of these chapters, which is really a way of sharing a common space—a stage—for further inquiry.

Part I begins narrowly, with the *moral integrity* of persons who associate, align, or in effect *attach their bodies to moral principles.* Such integrity can be performed, visibly, as a mode of assertion or persuasion in times of conflict. Thus, to perceive the body is to perceive the principles attached to it, and to harm the body is to risk harming the principles. To be sure, the instances of Antigone (chapter I), Thomas Becket (chapter II), and the Yoruba chief and his son (chapter III) include broader personal and cultural dimensions of integrity. These dimensions warn that before we would hazard to speak of anyone's integrity, we would need to explore the variegated complications of a whole and fragmented life. So might it not be more appropriate to begin with *personal integrity,* where the idea of "the personal" includes these complexities?

It might. However, insofar as integrity has normative meanings in tension with the personal, it may be clearer to start with the moral. Especially when considering plays that cross cultural boundaries, we may find that moral integrity is the more vivid place to begin. Not only do moral principles attempt to clarify conflicts, but dramas of moral integrity warn us that given the complexities of living and discerning, such clarity can only be provisional. I will be aided, here, by a distinction Ricoeur makes between *the moral*—or norms of obligation that address the question, "What should I, or we, do?"—and *the ethical*—or matters of identity and mutuality that ask, "What kind of people shall we be?" This distinction and its conflicts (between the "right" and the "good") are presented in the prelude to part I.

The chapters in part II explore the implication that *personal integrity,* in drama and in life, emerges as persons juxtapose—without necessarily synthesizing—the personal with the normative. Theatrical drama certainly cannot "solve" the problem of integrating norms with persons. But it can explore how inhabiting a pattern of integrity may require transformations of the personal and moral dimensions of integrity into new patterns with others, including aspects of wholeness and fragmentation. Just as sometimes integrity implies constancy, it can also imply an imperative of willingness to change, but with no certainty as to the ramifications of change.

Still, the rhetoric of integrity makes us cautious. Improvising "alignments" of bodies with causes can sound like relativism, not integrity, and can also seem grounded in nothing but power. There are few paradigms that articulate the good that may emerge as persons revise and play parts of others, with others. Moreover, playacting can be a trope for insincerity, as Shakespeare knew, although he also deployed other tropes affirming performance (chapter IV). Social roles can become prisons, which in turn are *mirrored* in the naturalism and expressionism of such playwrights as Chekhov, Ibsen, and Strindberg (chapter V). However, if the good of integrity does not always appear in *performance-as-mirroring,* it may yet appear in *performance-as-participation,* as examined in Bernard Shaw's *Pygmalion* and two related works: John Guare's *Six Degrees of Separation* and Willy Russell's *Educating Rita* (chapter VI).

The plays in part III return to how integrity is associated with *embodied* wholeness. Does the body secure the meaning of integrity? In Sophocles' *Philoctetes* (chapter VII), the abandoned hero's physical pain constricts his world of relations and responsibilities. Yet his suffering prompts a young foe, one who is playing out an elaborate deception, to change his intentions. He and Philoctetes undergo conversions toward one another. But if the suffering body can arouse compassion, it can also provoke revulsion and curiosity—as in Bernard Pomerance's *The Elephant Man*, Suzan-Lori Parks's *Venus*, and Margaret Edson's *Wit* (chapter VIII). Moreover, severe suffering—social or physical—can move us to imagine escaping our bodies. I explore motives for that possibility through Richard Schechner's and Mary Zimmerman's ways of transforming tales from Euripides and Ovid (chapter IX).

I return to my constructive thesis in part IV. The theatrical motif of playing a part with and for others and the scriptural/philosophical motif of kenosis, or of selves emptying into the forms of others, for others, suggest a new conceptual metaphor for reenvisioning integrity. *The gap between what is aligned or juxtaposed* can become *space into which selves empty into and receive the emptying of others.* Playing parts and emptying into others, for others, are motifs that appear together from time to time in theater, as in Denys Arcand's film about players, *Jesus of Montreal* (chapter X). Two comedies, Noel Coward's *Private Lives* and T. S. Eliot's *The Cocktail Party*, seek for patterns of self-with-others that disclose kenotic integrity (chapter XI), and Tony Kushner and Caryl Churchill explore its moral and political dimensions (chapter XII). A play by Robert Lepage and a film by Kristian Levring, juxtaposed with *King Lear* and *A Midsummer Night's Dream*, occasion an examination of kenotic integrity in terms of figures of "atonement" and "holding fragments" (chapter XIII).

How can self-emptying and holding fragments be images of integrity? In *Death of a Salesman*, Linda Loman is angered when her sons say their father has no character. "But he's a human being, and a terrible thing is happening to him. So attention must be paid."[59] She knows his fragmentation. Her anguish addresses those who would neither hold Willy's fragments nor allow him to hold theirs. Yes, play, like all human practices—even putative altruistic playing for others who suffer—can be a strategy of aggrandizement. But must play reduce to power and interest? Can we claim that prior to its myriad ways of distortion, play delights in and moves toward the play of others? Another question for kenotic integrity is whether it gives exclusive attention to the infinity of obligation. Can kenosis be emptying and receptive, particular and mutual, without becoming a self-serving exchange? Such questions course through *Six Degrees of Separation*, where an encounter is imagined briefly as "a new door opening to other worlds."

For Ricoeur, ethical life entails receptivity as well as solicitude. As deep as I can peer into myself, I discover no autonomous, self-authorizing voice but "attest" to language, dialogues, and witnesses that precede and address me. They give me trust, in the face of doubt, that I *am* and *can* respond; the voice of reason would be in voices heard, eliciting responses.[60] Does kenosis also entail the return of lives pouring in? Would the return be necessary, or contingent? If contingent, will we not have to await encounters with other persons, circumstances, and performances, which might arrive unlooked-for, and sometimes will not be apparent at all? Such a contingent, mutual emptying may imply a modest, kenotic ontology or a relatively negative theology, where the emptiness is not total or absolute but more like Brook's "empty space" of performance.[61] This analogy will be explored in part IV and in the postlude.

Personal and Theatrical Terms

Recurring in these chapters are groups of words with overlapping meanings. One group includes *person, self,* and *identity.* Another is *role, part,* and *character.* The last, *character,* could also be grouped with the first. In the second group are terms from drama that can speak of "life as theater" or "drama of life." My primary interest is not social theory,[62] and I hope not to begin with a theory of person, self, and identity and then define integrity with drama as illustrations. The meanings of these terms must always await the contingencies of the inquiry. However, I do generally use them in ways that can be provisionally described.

Person derives from Latin and Greek words meaning both face and mask, and connotes what we can immediately perceive of another's presence. We say *persons* to indicate embodied beings we meet, address, and answer with speech, touch, and reflection, for good or ill. The term has contrasting aspects: I cannot literally see through a person or behind a face, yet a person is not an unknowable, opaque monad but a fragile nexus. It is smeared out in its relations with others, nature, and culture—relations that change over time and space. A person expresses out of these relations and receives the expressions of others. In that sense, an embodied person is translucent. A person is also protean, as when we speak of personal transformation. But is *total* transformation thinkable, given the physical persistence of persons? Change and continuity are a paradox that drama and literature perennially explore.

Self derives from reflexive speech patterns, as in "he touched himself" or "she thought about herself." Thus, it considers the personal nexus from within, when one "looks into oneself." We can speak of the "world" of a self, in which its relations are structured, stratified, and fraught with meanings. We can also speak of historical discoveries of the self. One need not agree that in, say, Homer there is no trace of the self; we sense interiority when Achilles withdraws from the battle to brood and when Penelope weaves her "web full of sighs." But there are moments when the self is newly conceptualized, as arguably happens in Freud, Augustine, or Socrates. The self, while interior, still bears an objectivity that others discern. We speak of recognizing another's self, and we speak of aspects of other selves of which they are unaware. We recognize persons *as* selves, and persons may implicitly understand themselves to be social selves.

Identity is from the Latin for "the same," *idem,* as in "this is identical to that." But it is more helpful to define it in terms of what a person *identifies with* or that by which one is *named.* Such identifiers usually persist over time, meaning that identity is a mode of continuity-in-change.[63] Identity may prove the most important and troubling term in integrity discourse. It plays a crucial part in developmental theories, such as Erik Erikson's. But insecurity about identity, especially its ethnic and communal forms, is a crucial part of late modern discourse; those who perceive that a communal identity is threatened may play "identity politics." Identity as *identifying-with* refers to how the self is organized in relation to extrinsic yet internalized matters: traditions and families, tribes and nations, affiliations, vocations, missions, and so forth. Identity is part of how the self persists by being situated with meanings and relations that allow it to transcend itself. Naming symbolizes and helps to establish this persistence; in some cultures, when one's life situation changes, one may receive a new name.

The first three terms move from more overt to relatively hidden. I can literally see a person on the street or stage,[64] but not the person's self. I can figuratively see into my self more clearly than I can "see" my identity. Nonetheless, there are overt and hidden aspects to all three notions. For instance, a person's name and other signs allow us to apprehend her identity. So perhaps we should say these terms become progressively uncertain. If, say, in a jungle I meet a putative "wild child," I will probably assume she is a *person* even if I think she forages like a beast. But I may doubt that she has much of a *self* or *identity*—unless, to my surprise, she is wearing a mark or totem, meaning she is not so "wild" after all. However, even if *identity* and *self* have less verisimilitude than *person,* they remain crucial. My ease in perceiving a person in the forest, and my uncertainty in seeing her self and her identity, depend upon my self-understanding and the traditions and assumptions informing my discernment. Without a horizon of self and identity, my understanding of another could hardly begin, much less be corrected.[65]

All three terms have evaluative connotations. To be a person with a strong self or identity is typically *good,* implying that the terms have ethical content. Yet personal strengths may contribute to the identities of *bad* selves. We will later see how Ricoeur employs the concept of *the moral* to criticize and clarify the ethical life of persons in community and history.

Role and *part,* in sociology and common usage, are bridge terms between person, self, and identity.[66] So persons "play roles" that exist independently of themselves; selves are constituted by their multiple roles; persons "identify with social roles," or may find themselves "trapped" in them. Roles can be alienating, and playing a role can be synonymous with being inauthentic or insincere. Yet in the social sciences, roles and similar notions are the molecular forms of social life. Our ambivalence about roles might be relieved were we to think of them (1) as forms of life to inhabit, reflect upon, and redefine (and so not *only* imposed by circumstances) and (2) as being interconnected, overlapping, and not inevitably imprisoning. "Part" has fewer negative connotations. We typically say that it is good if "everyone has a part to play."

Character may be the most ambiguous of these terms. In English, if we say someone "*is* quite a character," and intend it as a compliment, we may mean only that she exudes a distinctive personality. If we are being critical, we likely mean she is histrionic, like a stage persona. But to say someone "*has* a lot of character" usually implies she is precisely *not* like someone onstage but exhibits virtues often associated with integrity. Character also implies "traits" in a neutral sense, which can be captured in a "character sketch." Hence, ethos-related words in Greek can mean custom or habit, accustomed place, the disposition of a person, one's facial expression, or the personae of a drama, whose dispositions were in part identifiable by masks. This sense of externality carries over subtly into common usage. We do not speak of our characters as much as we do of our own selves, but we do speak of the characters of others. So character implies qualities *we* attribute to the self that another presents. As we discern this other, we contribute to the creation of character; yet we know that the character we discern is really there. Character is another sign of the relational constitution of persons, selves, and identities.

Theatrical drama can disclose and criticize experiences of being and becoming persons, in part because it explores the ephemerae of personae, and in part because it is a hybrid and fluid art form. Again, some initial, orienting descriptions of theatrical drama's features may be useful.

Drama, theater, and *metatheater* are terms that overlap. The first refers more to action and dialogue, the second to performance before a live audience. *Metatheater,* brought to vogue by Lionel Abel,[67] is a pervasive aspect of drama. It most often refers to "plays within plays" or works aware of themselves as theater, as in Brecht, Pirandello, or avant-garde productions of the Living Theatre or Performance Group. I would distinguish three sorts of metatheater: (1) performances that refer to themselves or their own theatricality, as in Wilder's *Our Town;* (2) plays whose stories contain performances, such as the "Mousetrap" in *Hamlet* or the Tarantella dance in Ibsen's *A Doll House;* (3) drama that refers to performative or theater-like dimensions of life. *Oedipus the King* begins with a ceremony, in which a priest presents destitute subjects before the king. *Pygmalion* depicts efforts to prepare Eliza Doolittle for a performance.

Persons as media are the primary artistic material of theatrical drama. What we perceive in theater are persons shaping and being shaped into art, including bodily and vocal traits, their personalities, their many levels of intention and discernment, even their "real life" social contexts. Performers and their idiosyncrasies contribute their interpreting bodies, emotions, and minds to the material through which *Pygmalion* or *My Fair Lady* appear. As we see and hear Eliza, we also see and hear the players (e.g., Mrs. Patrick Campbell, Wendy Hiller, Julie Andrews, Audrey Hepburn, Marni Nixon), and we lend to them our own attentive selves.

Ensemble is even more fundamental to theater than "playing roles," especially as that phrase is too simply applied to life. Generally, theater entails creating parts, interpreting them through intensive work with others, in order to embody them, to give them life. Even in one-person shows, actors work with others to make their parts appear. Theatrical play entails *giving oneself to a part* (or being "played by" the persona) and *building the part* (or "playing" the persona). But what is usually missing in references to life as theater is that an actor's work occurs in ensembles, with and for particular others—as in the stormy cooperation of Shaw, Campbell, and Herbert Beerbohm Tree, who played Professor Higgins and also owned the theater.

Dialogical relations entail not only the discourses between characters but also subtle (or not so subtle) relations among performers and audiences. Such dialogical relations, we will see, make the different and problematic endings producers have added to *Pygmalion* more significant than whether or not they happened to be untrue to Shaw's wishes.

At issue is how actors and audiences both contribute to what is, in effect, a play's testing of cultural limits and possibilities.

Encounters structure the story of a play and the world appearing on-stage. When Eliza Doolittle first enters and collides with Freddy Eynsford Hill in Act I, we know nothing more about her than is provided by her body and environment (her grimy face and costume, her accent, the Covent Garden flower stalls). Upon subsequent entrances, we infer what has since transpired since her last exit. Of course actors, even when improvising, usually know pretty much what they are going to do and say. But in creating the spontaneity of encounter, they respond to the dynamics of each performance; in this respect, performers are always improvising. Theater then, with its entrances and exits, examines the hermeneutics of encounter in life, where persons attempt to understand one another with their various habits, idioms, and traditions.

Irony and *belief* also constitute theater, for we perceive the characters and we perceive the actor-persons interpreting the characters. This double awareness provokes reflection: we think about the play and its performance as we see it. The phrase "willing suspension of disbelief" is misleading if it implies that critical awareness is absent at a performance. We "lose ourselves" or become "caught up" in naive belief only to be, at other moments, cast back upon our selves in thought. Performers have a similar awareness. To believe, they must assess the performance as it transpires, as when in *Pygmalion* Higgins describes his letdown at the embassy party when realizing that Eliza was succeeding flawlessly. Performers may also enjoy ecstatic abandonment—as when in *My Fair Lady* Eliza sings, "I could have danced all night."

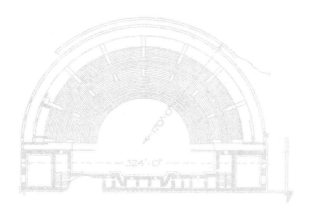

Part I

Patterns of Integrity

Moral Principles, Paradigms, and Ethical Dramas

> If we do not speak for Sophocles, then Sophocles is silent.
> If Sophocles is silent, Antigone never lived.
> If Antigone never lived, Creon rules unopposed.
>
> —BROCHURE FOR THE PEARL THEATRE, NEW YORK CITY

THESE UNUSUALLY GOOD lines of promotional copy were picked up in the lobby of a small theater company in East Greenwich Village. Since 1984, the Pearl Theatre has produced the Greeks, Shakespeare, and other "great standards and neglected treasures, the full spectrum of 2400 years of theatre." The brochure reflects a certain depth of understanding about the company's task.[1] It aspires to "present each play on the playwright's terms."

By itself, this phrase will raise eyebrows in a profession that tends to celebrate innovation over tradition and that doubts whether approximating the author's intention is possible or even desirable. Yet the brochure also understands that it is "we" who have to speak for Sophocles. We must lend him our own voices in order to borrow his "voice." For Sophocles to speak, there must be some meeting of horizons among translations, players, styles of performance, and audiences. Only in this way can the plays' questions and our questions meet across the distances of history, culture, language, psychology, and social setting. And what is the aim of staging the standards? The Pearl answers, "[I]t is important that a community comes together and experiences together the inherited wisdom and sensitivity of an ancestry."

The brochure, in short, is making a churchlike appeal to a complex kind of artistic integrity that has a strong moral resonance, moral in the general way Emil Durkheim used that term.[2] What the Pearl is doing is for the well-being of a larger community, whose ancestry is Western yet multicultural. And the "totem" (as Durkheim would call it) to which the brochure appeals is Antigone. For a large and diverse culture, of which the Pearl and its audiences constitute a tiny clan, Antigone is a paradigm. That is, her story serves as an exemplary model, simple but not without complexity, which can orient our understanding and actions. Moreover, she is, I submit, a paradigm of moral integrity, and her drama includes the variegated personal, communal, bodily, political, and religious dimensions I am concerned with in this book. As I will discuss in the next chapter, her becoming a moral paradigm has to do with how she aligns her *physical body* with a *moral or sacred principle that articulates a norm of obligation.*[3]

Antigone introduces, then, both the *moral* and the broader *ethical* dimensions of integrity. Since these terms are usually used interchangeably, some explanation is needed regarding their different meanings and their potentials for tragic conflict.

Ricoeur on the Moral and the Ethical

By the *moral*, following Paul Ricoeur and others, I mean norms of obligation taken to be binding on everyone.[4] These would be expressed in such principles as respecting personal autonomy, realizing justice, doing no harm, and offering care to those who are suffering. People to whom we attribute *moral integrity* would be committed to acting in accord with these or other such principles.[5] It may be objected, however, that this view of morality is too thin to account for the richness of the "moral life," that is, the broader and perhaps deeper realm that Ricoeur prefers to call "the ethical."

By *ethical*, Ricoeur means all the ways persons are mutually and dialogically constituted with others, and the ways their communities seek for one another the good of *eudaimonia*. This Greek philosophical term is commonly translated, "happiness." But that word has misleading, hedonistic connotations that lead some to prefer the translation "human flourishing" or simply "well-being." So conceived, the ethical deals not just with "What am I obliged to do?" but also with questions such as "Who am I?" "Who are we?" and "How and why should we live?" It concerns not just matters of action but also of character (what kinds of persons we are) and of vision (concerning what is good, true, or intrinsically valuable). To understand the ethical in its cultural and practical complexities requires "wisdom," thinks Ricoeur, of the sort that is mediated through traditions, including those of religion, philosophy, and the arts. And he thinks that universalizing principles of obligation—for example, "the Golden Rule"—are indeed found in various wisdom traditions; however, the purpose of such *moral* principles is to clarify or "test" the *ethical* life and lore in which they are rooted.

Do we need this difference between the moral and the ethical, when we have already distinguished *the moral* from *the personal* in matters of integrity? The moral integrity / personal integrity distinction provides a strong contrast between commitments to common principles and commitments to projects, relationships, and preferences of the kinds that give lives particular meaning. But to divide integrity this way is unsatisfying and unstable. We have already seen that what is ordinarily meant by integrity implies an entangled moral and personal dimension, which a simple separation does not capture. My guess is that when speaking of personal integrity, we usually mean moral integrity as well. Another reason to adjust, but not discard, the moral/personal distinction follows from how we are constituted *as persons* in relation to others in time and space. To regard persons as intrinsically relational and communal is already to relate *personal integrity* (i.e., being committed to purpose-giving projects and relations) to *the ethical*. However, *even within the ethical,* the personal and moral aspects of integrity may still be in conflict—even tragic conflict—as Ricoeur considers.

The Interpreting Self

Ricoeur's moral philosophy may be compared to his interpretation theory, which began as a "detour" in his life's work on philosophy of the will.[6] The detour results in a picture of an *interpreting self* for whom critical modes of reasoning, or *explanation,* clarify or correct activities of *understanding* and aim toward fuller, richer *post-critical understanding,* which he sometimes calls "second naïveté" and sometimes "appropriation and comprehension." The interpreting self emerges in dialogue with others and with its own works, projects, commitments, and relationships (including the texts and cultural forms it makes and receives). For Ricoeur, the wholeness of the self—like the meaning of a text—is not reducible to what is "behind" it. Its wholeness is dynamically "in front" of the self, as it envisions and enacts possibilities with others.[7] Clearly, Ricoeur thinks the interpreting self both *makes itself* and *finds itself* with others, in activities of speaking and writing, listening and reading, remembering and anticipating, and interpreting. For reasons related to those of Alasdair MacIntyre, Bernard Williams, Charles Taylor, and Martha Nussbaum, a self cannot be abstracted into a concept or algorithm. A self's identity is found more in its relationships to itself (*ipse*) and others in time, and less in its sameness (*idem*) over time.[8] So I suggest there can be no formula for a hypothetical paragon of integrity. But Ricoeur has reasons for saying a self can account for itself—and be accounted by others—through *narrative*.

(1) A self exists in time, and narrative is a mode of discourse that *unfolds in time even as it imitates time*. (2) Any particular self *exists only in relations to other selves in time,* and narrative can grasp these particular relationships by weaving them into stories. I myself identify with such narratives; by narratives, others identify me; thus, each of us enjoys what Ricoeur calls a "narrative identity." Narrative, then, is really an enlarged act of *naming* that answers the question, "Who?" (3) Larger historical and cultural narratives *name the good(s)* for which selves and communities aim and also *the ideas and beliefs* that guide them. (4) Finally, narrative mediates the *self-esteem* one enjoys when one realizes, *I can. I can* contribute to meaning-making. I also have *self-respect,* when I regard myself in relation to others who are also subject to rights and obligations. This dialectic of self-esteem and self-respect aims, in effect, to integrate the personal and the moral, and it culminates in one's having critical *convictions*.[9] So integrity, after Ricoeur, would arise (or fail to arise) in the working out of life narratives and could be understood by narrative modes (though aided by principles or concepts). A pattern of integrity would be a narrative improvisation of the moral and ethical, attempting to hold together personal aspirations with relations to others in history, nature, and language.

When Ricoeur differentiates between the moral and the ethical, he agrees with part of Williams's argument that universalizing principles are too thin to comprehend the life of any particular person. And he agrees with MacIntyre that we effectively know and practice norms in the context of languages, practices, and traditions, not simply as we are enlightened by naked rationality. But Ricoeur makes more room for universal principles than either of those thinkers. Again, we can grasp why he grants this room by comparing his moral/ethical distinction first with his hermeneutics, then with his view of tragedy.

In Ricoeur's hermeneutics, modes of *explaining* are to *moral* principles as dialogical *understanding* is to the *ethical aim* of life together. Explanation and understanding are dialectically related. Explanation (*erklären* in the German tradition Ricoeur revises) is a kind of testing rationality; it compares and clarifies meanings and is implicitly procedural.[10] Understanding (*verstehen*), in turn, is more intuitive and grasps meanings as they relate to my living in solitude and with others. This dialect is not static; rather, it moves. If explanation intervenes for the sake of critical understanding, it nonetheless begins in understanding and aims for richer understanding. Likewise, moral principles—such as respect for persons as such, and justice—"test" practices in the wider and deeper ethical realm. Yet they are rooted in the ethical, and they work to help realize the ethical intention: *"aiming at the 'good life' with and for others, in just institutions."*[11] This way of putting it shows how justice is a moral norm so dialectically related to the ethical that it cannot be avoided when defining the ethical aim. But more questions concern where moral principles "come from" and precisely why they are needed.

The first question has produced disagreement among Ricoeur's readers. Some see him trying to rescue the Kantian deontological tradition.[12] Moral principles—namely, the categorical imperative—would be forms of reason independent of traditions. Indeed, Ricoeur shows how the imperative appears implicitly in widely separated religious and cultural traditions and in Aristotle's view of friends-as-equals. Other readers, however, notice that Ricoeur subordinates Kant to Aristotle and shows how moral norms appear to be embedded in narratives of virtue, whose views of the good life guide the practices of communities.[13] (For Ricoeur, the good life would include rich comprehensions of others' meanings: through dialogue, written texts, arts, commerce, politics, etc.). The ethical aim, then, is not *derived from pure reason* so much as *attested to* or *witnessed by practical reason*. Moral norms and maxims, like versions of the Golden Rule, arise from communities' ethical recognition of others and possibilities of conflict.[14]

It is difficult to resolve these interpretations of Ricoeur. But when he says the moral is "irreducible" to the ethical, I think he has in mind the effects of the logical and semantic structure of sentences. The sense of the imperative phrase "Love your enemies" transcends its context and would bear on *all* who hear it, like a principle. But when he speaks of the moral as "subordinate" to the ethical, he has in mind the referential function of sentences. Moral discourse arises in real occasions with actual neighbors or enemies. My own point now is to notice that, in any case, moral principles are *found in discourse:* (1) we *encounter them* as *forms of expression* that require interpretation, and (2) they serve the ethical by helping us *test or clarify our practices and relations.* And so now we come to why principles are needed: because of conflict and violence.

Antigone and the Limits of Practical Wisdom

Aristotelians such as Nussbaum frequently take note of the contingency, plurality, and particularity of the various goods of human life. These goods (e.g., raising a child, playing a sonata, striving for social justice) are different in kind ("incommensurate"), and thus they can come into conflicts that are inherently difficult to resolve. Moreover, our capacities to realize these goods are affected by contingencies of circumstance, resources, physical means, and insight. We are also limited by human nature, including emotion. We cannot pursue personal projects or discern the good life with others apart from being emotionally involved in life. Few of us would want to be devoid of emotion—yet our passions often interfere with our discernment, which is another reason for conflict and suffering.[15]

Kantians, on the other hand, are more likely to attribute tragic suffering to the harming effects of moral culpability. That is, conflict arises less from the contingencies of our goods and finite capacities than from putting narrow or contradictory self-interests before the rights of all; thus, tragic suffering follows from the objective effects of sin and moral evil.

Ricoeur's own views of sin and tragedy are indebted to Aristotle, the Bible, Kant, and Kierkegaard, and they resonate with Barth, Reinhold Niebuhr, and a host of late modern theologians.[16] On this trajectory of thought (apart from Aristotle) sin precedes any given act of moral culpability—sin seems to presuppose itself.[17] How so? In its anxiety, the will imagines itself to be infinite or else resigns itself to being nothing at all, either way a kind of bondage. Yet the will also finds it is always already in bondage, as if inclined from the outset toward self-contradiction and deceit toward others. This account of our predicament plausibly reinterprets the Christian "myth" of original sin, thinks Niebuhr.[18] But it also resonates with Greek epic and tragic views of *hubris* (presumptuous violence), *atē* (delusion stemming from fate or divine powers), and Aristotle's *hamartia* (from archery, "a bad shot"), which could be culpable fault or an unlucky error, or both.[19] I have interpreted tragic experience as a variously proportioned *mix* of fault and contingency. The effects of *moral culpability* and *contingent circumstances,* in conflict and suffering, are intractably entangled but not always reducible one to the other.[20]

Moral norms of obligation, for Ricoeur—especially justice and respect for persons as such—are needed to assess conflicts and lessen violence within the ethical realm. These imperatives, while arising in the realm of relationship and dialogue, tend to speak across cultural and contextual differences. Take two commands of the Decalogue, *do not kill* and *honor father and mother.* Ricoeur observes how they retain traces of cultural and social particularity; thus we can debate whether the prohibition against killing applies only to "murdering" in specifiable senses, and we can examine the particulars of honoring parents in Hebraic, rabbinic Jewish, early Christian, and Islamic contexts. But the logical structures of these commands—which recognize the claim of respecting other individuals besides me—cut through a good deal of particularity, which is why they may bring clarity to complex conflicts and obligations.

They do not, however, bring perfect clarity. Among the reasons for subordinating the moral to the ethical is that moral norms themselves are also sources of conflict. In this, Ricoeur agrees with—as far as it goes—Hegel's reading of *Antigone,* noting how "the source of the conflict lies not only in the one-sidedness of the characters but also in the one-sidedness of the moral *principles* which themselves are confronted with the complexity of life."[21] At issue are duties—duties to blood ties or civic ties, or to the gods of kinship relations and of *polis*—which in the world of *Antigone* are being interpreted too narrowly. In life, such conflicts can impose moral dilemmas, wherein one finds oneself forced to do evil no matter which of two mutually exclusive yet unavoidable moral choices is made. Ricoeur also agrees that while Creon and Antigone *both* fail to acknowledge conflicts within their own causes, it is nonetheless Antigone who wins our sympathy by showing the limits of *all* human institutions.

> Creon's conception of his duties . . . does not take into account the variety and perhaps the heterogeneity of the tasks belonging to the city. For Creon . . . the opposition friend-enemy is confined to a narrow political category and admits of no nuance, no exception.

> [Antigone's] manner of distinguishing between *philos* and *ekthros* [friend and enemy] is no less rigid than Creon's. . . . Ultimately, only the dead relative is *philos.*

> In a sense, Antigone herself narrowed the unwritten laws [of the gods] down to funeral demands. But in invoking them to found her intimate conviction, she posited the limit that points up the human, all too human, character of every institution.
>
> The instruction of ethics by tragedy comes out of the recognition of this limit.[22]

Antigone, as a spectacle of poetic and theatrical art, answers a question some have posed of Ricoeur's distinction between the moral and the ethical realms. Given that both are fraught with conflict, would not yet another realm be required to mediate them?[23] Ricoeur appeals to the Greek idea of *phronesis* or practical wisdom, of which the play *Antigone* is itself an instance. Writing, performing, or attending *Antigone* may lead people to deliberate on how moral principles are interwoven with the various goods of citizenship and of kinship. To be sure, such interweaving of the moral right with the broader ethical good is inherently complex and often unstable. Thus, *Antigone* tells us that tragic moral conflict is less a problem to be "solved" than part of what life together entails. It takes artists or some equivalent of artists to enhance our capacities for *understanding by witnessing and living through* tragic conflict. Sometimes, Nussbaum observes, the poet's wisdom might help us avoid or wait out a tragic dilemma; at other times wise dramatists or poetic politicians may offer unexpected paradigms for action. The lore and practice of wisdom can help us relax some dilemmas, but not all. The criticism that Ricoeur leaves the distinction between the ethical and the moral incoherent may reflect a desire for settled coherence that practical wisdom knows it cannot offer.

John Caputo, in *Against Ethics,* similarly thinks we need poets of *phronesis* to respond to conflicts of obligation. In the absence of consensual narratives of God, the Good, or Autonomous Reason, it is only because obligations "happen" or "arrive"—and arrive *not* as formulae deciding matters in advance of conflicts—that there can be in modernity anything like "ethics." Caputo, like Levinas, sounds as if such obligations arrive with *the other.* But he also speaks of obligation as a language game, "not a game that we play but rather, as Gadamer shows, a game that plays us, that picks us up and carries us along by its momentum." This game precedes me and is "much older . . . than philosophy itself."[24] Caputo would be the last to identify obligations with moral principles. They are, rather, practical ligatures that happen to tie us to other persons, before we ever learn the names of these obligations or even of one another.

Aligning Bodies with Principles

However, I would urge that moral principles *also* have a happenstance, ad hoc, and unsettled coherence that bears upon us, in that they arrive *as forms of language*. Principles are like laconic voices and pithy texts—they are statements or mantras we encounter in experience or remember anew. On the road to Jericho, did the Samaritan *recall the principle* of loving one's neighbor or, rather, did he *hear the call* of the neighbor? The former would attest to his morality, the latter to his momentary sainthood—or could it be inseparably both? In any case, he aligns his body with the injured man, and wisdom has aligned his body with the principle of beneficence in the face of danger or rejection. The figure of Antigone is also a moral paradigm, both for the respect we owe the dead (related to "respect for persons") and the duty to resist authorities in the wrong. Our questions in part I concern how hers and similar stories become paradigms that lend themselves to theater. Antigone intends for Thebes to *see* her body aligned with a principle. The play intends for us to see, as well, the *limits of her alignment*. For if she places her body with the dead, where is there room—in this juxtaposition—for the living?

Chapter I

Why Does Antigone Matter to Us?

Yes, it was not Zeus that made the proclamation;
nor did Justice, which lives with those below, enact
such laws as that, for mankind. I did not believe
your proclamation had such power to enable
one who will someday die to override
God's ordinances, unwritten and secure.

—ANTIGONE TO CREON (LL. 450–55)

For our altars and our sacrificial hearths
are filled with the carrion meat of birds and dogs,
torn from the flesh of Oedipus' poor son.

—TEIRESIAS TO CREON (LL. 1016–18)

ANTIGONE ACCUSES CREON of violating a norm that she is upholding. We can set aside, for a moment, the personal and cultural complexities of this norm. What would make hers a "moral" claim is that she states a principle of obligation that is logically universal in comparable situations. While the claim has particular meanings for Antigone, it is not a preferential or partial claim only. She is not just saying that given who she is—daughter of King Oedipus (dead), sister of Ismene (alive), Eteocles (buried), and Polyneices (unburied, exposed)—it would be fitting to grant her wishes. She is also asserting a norm, binding on all, requiring that Polyneices be buried properly, so he can be at peace among the dead, the family at peace with its kin, and the city at peace with gods and cosmos. That is the *moral* pattern of her appeal.

What also gives her moral appeal a pattern of *integrity* is that she discovers the norm to be binding on herself in particular. If no one else will bury Polyneices, and if she can at least try, then it seems she must try, even in defiance of authority. She would not remain "who she is"—she would lose her integrity—were she to allow Polyneices to be scavenged by beasts. She must attempt what Creon has commanded the city not to do. How is her association with the normative principle accomplished? *By juxtaposing her embodied person with a moral and sacred norm.* But what are the limits of such bodily association as a paradigm of the self-in-relation-to-others? By what modes of demonstration and communication does her pattern of integrity become compelling to Thebes and even to us—assuming, of course, that it does?

Among Mercurial Norms: Antigone, Ismene, Creon

Ismene tells Antigone that, given how it is males who have authority, all she and her sister can really do is to beg forgiveness from the deities associated with kinship and the dead. "Extravagant action is not sensible," she warns (l. 68). While some theorists believe that integrity entails taking—or at least being willing to take—supererogatory risks in the face of adversity, others might agree with Ismene that integrity requires living or acting in accord with recognized moral obligations, *insofar as one is reasonably able.*[1] Views of what integrity requires in respect to risk are debatable; but for now, the pattern of integrity I wish to explore is that of a *particular person associating her body with a norm of obligation.* The extreme risk to Antigone in her drama of integrity may illuminate some of the textures of this pattern.

But Creon also claims to uphold a norm. Antigone's uncle and the brother of Jocaste (the late wife and mother of Oedipus), he has assumed power in Thebes after a war in which Eteocles and Polyneices died at each others' hands, vying for the throne. Significantly, even though Creon may seem to stand for civic as opposed to familial virtue, he also claims "kinship with the dead" (l. 174). He says he is performing the thankless duty of picking up the pieces—literally, burying the pieces of Eteocles and leaving to rot those of Polyneices. But his more serious moral claim is not that desecrating the bodies of enemies is good for Thebes, but that integrity requires rulers and citizens to transcend their partial interests, including those of kinship and friendship.

> It is impossible to know any man—
> I mean his soul, intelligence, and judgment—
> until he shows his skill in rule and law. (ll. 173–75)

If it so happens that the "supreme ruler of a city" neglects "the best counsel" for the people and,

> through some fear, keeps his tongue under lock and key,
> him I judge the worst of any;
> I have always judged so; and anyone thinking
> another man more a friend than his own county,
> I rate him nowhere. (ll. 180–84)

So Creon and Antigone both seem to be upholding orders of community: ties of kinship, of citizenship, even of cosmos.[2] Their conflict, as Hegel thought, would be in how they represent (even within themselves) true but not easily reconciled principles of civil and familial virtue; their story has long prompted reflection on how such dilemmas are possible. *Antigone* exposes uncertainty about how different norms interconnect, despite their universalizing force. But this uncertainty is perhaps less a matter of logicality than of palpability. The norms are invisible, untouchable—even if in an ideal sense they would be the most substantial of all realities.

Another uncertainty has to do with the invisible source of these norms. Do they issue from the gods or mortals, or are they prior to both? Are they rooted in reason, or in being itself? Or were they culturally constructed long ago and far away, and affect us now only through long, indirect, and mongrelized strands of history and culture? Moreover, how can we be sure that the universals to which Antigone and Creon appeal do not merely mirror their (or our) hopes, desires, and illusions? The Antigone paradigm makes such questions explicit, as when she appeals not just to divine "unwritten" laws but also to her own personal and familial peculiarities.

> ISMENE: Would you bury him, when it is forbidden the city?
> ANTIGONE: At least he is my brother—and yours too,
>   though you deny him. *I* will not prove false to him.
> ISMENE: You are so headstrong. Creon has forbidden it.
> ANTIGONE: It is not for him to keep me from my own. (ll. 44–48)

Structuralists who brood over these matters often find that the norms of family and city reflect different aspects of a complex system of symbols, myths, and ritual practices, in which there is arbitrariness and tension. Sometimes the characters invoke the Olympian gods, chief of whom is Zeus, associated with the sky and with overarching order. Creon says,

"I still reverence Zeus" (l. 304). Antigone also invokes Zeus, but she prominently appeals, as does Creon on occasion, to an older, Titanic order of deities that have claims in matters of blood and ancestry. They are associated with the sea, earth, and underworld. In Aeschylus's Oresteia trilogy, the third play (*Eumenides*) depicts an integration and demarcation of these jurisdictions, when Athena enlists the lower (or "chthonic") deities in enforcing justice against murderous violations of kinship.[3]

Recently, some feminist scholars have revisited the play in respect to Hegel's interpretation of tragedy as a conflict between compelling ideals. One concern has been to refute Hegel's associating women, or at least "pagan" women, with stereotypical immanent oneness with nature and with having little possibility for realizing self-transcendent identity. Patricia Jagentowicz Mills presents the following reading of Hegel's account of *Antigone:*[4]

Men, Hegel thought (as Mills explains), could achieve transcendent identity in city-states, in that the polis afforded very risky responsibilities (as in warfare) of the sort not usually found in families. However, Hegel also thought that in becoming self-transcendent as *particular* citizens, males became alienated from the laudable, immanent particularity afforded by kinship ties. And he thought that male sexual desire—which could not be integrated with self-transcendence—corrupted the immanence-in-nature of the family. The family was a realm in which women could thrive, *albeit without true consciousness.* Surprisingly, Hegel speculated that there was one relationship in the pagan world that approached the ideal of universalized individuality (or individualized universality), that of *sister and brother.* Both could benefit from their different relations to family and city, immanence and transcendence, without the taint of sexual desire. And this esteeming of the sister-brother bond would, at least for Hegel, illuminate why Antigone strangely tells Creon that losing an irreplaceable brother is worse than losing a husband. A new husband can be found, new children begotten.

> But when father and mother both were hidden in death
> no brother's life would bloom for me again.
> That is the law under which I gave you precedence,
> my dearest brother [dead Polyneices] . . . (ll. 911–14)

Mills observes how Hegel ignores some obvious problems. Close brother-sister relations occur in the family realm, not the polis; not everyone is blessed with siblings of the opposite sex; and in most cases brothers marry and become self-aware citizens, leaving their sisters behind to remain "unconscious," usually as wives and mothers. Mills also thinks Hegel ignores how Antigone *is* portrayed as a fully conscious person. She does enter the political realm, and she defies a tyrant in order to uphold a norm affirmed, finally, by everyone in the play. Her principal failure is blindness to another relationship that the play affirms (and Hegel ignores), *sister and sister.* When Ismene later begs to share in her sister's deed and fate, Antigone is wrong to refuse this offer of solidarity.[5] But otherwise, Mills thinks Antigone's pattern of moral integrity is fully conscious in respect to kinship and citizenship and is much less problematic than Hegel implies.[6]

Not so Judith Butler who, while congenial to Mills's critique of Hegel, deconstructs the norms of kinship and citizenship. These terms are mutually implicated in cultural structures that can never be stable. What Butler finds particularly troubling is that Antigone's "claim" is not rooted in nature or in kinship. Antigone and Ismene's familial bonds—with a father who is a brother, a mother who is a sister, an uncle who is also a brother—are as interesting as familial relations in our own time, given multiple partnerships, divorces, and same-sex parents. Rather, Antigone's claim is not *rooted-in* but rather is *borrowed-from* authoritarian power via authoritarian language. In other words, when she proclaims a law higher than that of the polis, Butler observes her to be mimicking the words of Creon, Eteocles, Polyneices, and finally Oedipus; in each case she appropriates the self-defeating rhetoric of the sovereign. Butler asks in her way—and Creon in his—whether Antigone's words of love for a "brother" can ever speak anything other than a love of death.

> Antigone does not achieve the effect of sovereignty she apparently seeks, and her action is not fully conscious. She is *propelled by the words that are upon her,* words of her father's that condemn the children of Oedipus to a life that ought not to have been lived. Between life and death, she is already living in the tomb prior to any banishment there. Her punishment precedes her crime, and her crime becomes the occasion for its literalization.[7]

Butler may also be saying, perhaps unwittingly, that Antigone, by mimicking, is *an actor,* and that histrionics is the reason she lacks the integrity of authenticity.

Should, then, Antigone remain a paradigm for us? The divine laws to which she appeals are mercurial. They transcend time ("not of today and yesterday") and are *"unwritten and secure. . . . They live for ever; none knows when they first were"* (ll. 454–56). In calling them "unwritten," she wants to underscore their ultimate origin and truth, as if writing were merely contingent, as in Plato. In other ancient traditions, the motif of writing the sacred laws underscores their substantiality. Moses receives "tablets of stone, written by the finger of God" (Exodus 31:18). Today, however, writing has become a postmodern trope for the fleeting status of meaning *and* a trope for all there fleetingly is. That law is as arbitrary as "writing" can imply that the "reality" of law is none other than marks, vowels, and glottal stops in their contingent cultural milieus. One does not have to grant that gender is a self-contradicting construction of power, as in Butler, or that linguistic reference is inherently indeterminate, as in Derrida, to sense what Antigone and Creon are on the edge of sensing. They employ rhetorical strategies for giving the laws palpable substantiation; but they implicitly wonder, how much substance is that?

A Postmodern Antigone?

This pathos about language, principles, bodies, and selves was anticipated by French playwright Jean Anouilh in his 1944 version of the play. A world-weary Creon asks Antigone if she really believes the nonsense about how the shade of Polyneices must "wander forever unless some dirt is tossed on his corpse, along with the formula of a priest." Creon expounds at length on the arbitrariness of maintaining the political and social order, and of how after the battle was finished the smashed bodies of the brothers were indistinguishable.

> CRÉON: I can't tell one from the other. And it's all the same to
>   me, I assure you.
> ANTIGONE: *after a long silence. . . .* Why have you told me this?
> CRÉON: Would it be worth your having to die for this wretched
>   story?
> ANTIGONE: Perhaps. To me—I believed. *Silence again.*[8]

As Anouilh portrays her, Antigone grants that her belief in religious burial is absurd. All she can really do is assert her identity, based on a family tradition of inquiry in the midst of despair. "We are those who pose questions until the end, until not even the smallest chance of hope remains. . . ." At the end, when Oedipus knew the truth of his identity and all his hope was gone, "suddenly he was calm, he could almost smile, he had become beautiful."[9] But in jail, dictating a letter for her fiancé Haemon, Creon's son, Antigone admits she has lost her conviction:

> "I no longer know why I am dying. . . . I am afraid. . . ." No. Erase all that. Better that no one ever know. It would be like seeing me naked and touching me when I was dead. Put only, "Forgive. . . . Forgive me, my dear. Without the little Antigone, your life would have been so very tranquil. I love you."[10]

The play is perhaps nihilistic. Not only is Creon cynical about corpses, but Antigone is left with only the *form* of civil disobedience, lacking confidence in any moral or sacred content to fill the form.[11] Anouilh apparently saw implications in Sophocles that postmodernists also see. One would be that any culture's system of norms is inherently unstable, as when some things are permitted as food, others forbidden, even though the differences seem utterly arbitrary to outsiders.[12] The system is an effect of a play of differences and contrasts. Sky gods are differentiated from those of the earth. The dead must be put *under* ground, not left *on* the boundaries between the dead and the living or between beasts and humans. Nor may the *living* dwell with the *dead*. The objection that these distinctions are not really clear in Greek tragedy (or any culture) is partly the point. To cross such boundaries is to *expose them as crossable*, erasable, mere lines in sand. Consider how Sophocles' Creon conflates citizenship with kinship (l. 174), and how Antigone mixes images of marriage and fraternity with images of death.

> ANTIGONE [to Ismene]: *I* myself will bury him. It will be good
>   To die, so doing. I shall lie by his side,
>   Loving him as he loved me. . . . (ll. 71–73)
> CREON: My enemy is still my enemy, even in death.
> ANTIGONE: My nature is to join in love, not hate.
> CREON: Go then to the world below, yourself, if you
>   must love. Love *them*. . . . (ll. 522–25)
> ANTIGONE: Hades who gives sleep to everyone
>   is leading me to the shores of Acheron,
>   though I have known nothing of marriage songs
>   nor the chant that brings the bride to bed.
>   My husband is to be the Lord of Death. (ll. 810–14)

> Tomb, bridal chamber, prison forever
> dug in rock, it is to you I am going
> to join my people. . . . (ll. 891–93)[13]

By associating mourning with nuptials, Antigone is attempting to re-integrate or pull around her body the disordered pieces of a normative frame. So too is Creon, when he rushes to bury Polyneices and release Antigone from the tomb—but it is too late to cover the undifferentiated chaos they both have exposed in the order of things.

Ismene's Head: Aligning Bodies with Principles

In order to harden her own and Thebes' impression of the unwritten, invisible norms, Antigone associates them with the actuality of her own body. If the normative idea or principle is by nature tenuous or contested, *then associating it with her body is how Antigone lends the principle her own palpable reality.* For the overt human body is not contestable in the way an idea is. So when she aligns *her body* with *the idea* that dead bodies must be buried, and then when we see or touch Antigone's body, we are in effect seeing or touching the idea, which she also uses Polyneices' body to enforce. The bodies, living and dead, lend the norm a felt reality.

Elaine Scarry calls this process, by which the physicality of bodies gives force to imagined or notional matters, "substantiation" or "ana-logical verification." Bodily substantiation follows from how pain gener-ally seems more real than "unanchored" issues or beliefs. In the case of war, Scarry argues that the *terms of the armistice* are substantiated by the *dead and injured bodies* that are implicitly or literally placed on view, *adjacent* to those terms. Bodies on both sides are gathered up and memo-rialized, and the injured return to their communities, where they are seen and remembered. Thus, it is upon harmed bodies, dispersed throughout society, that the peace is inscribed. As in the American Civil War, if the terms of the armistice are inscribed on enough bodies throughout the winning *and* the losing populations, then the settlement will probably hold. "What the body remembers is well remembered."[14] Cultures have found it hard to find substitutes for war, Scarry thinks, because it is hard to find peaceful ways to affect bodies in such numbers as to substantiate abstract ideas effectively. But in the Marshall Plan, the idea of feeding and rebuilding Europe was seized on by imaginative leaders and turned into the back-bending efforts of Americans and Europeans. The Marshall *idea* was substantiated into memory by the work of millions of hands and *bodies*.[15]

Something like bodily substantiation is going on, I suggest, when moral integrity is performed. One need not be as single-minded as Scarry (in holding that pain and pain relief are the primary human interests) to see that the facticity of the body is amazingly impressive to oneself and others. My body is the background and foreground of my sense of particularity, and it conditions my perception of the world and others, and no "presence" is quite so present to me as another embodied being. Bodies establish the nexus of person-and-culture in space, time, and culture.[16] So one feature of integrity we observe in Antigone *is that she lends her embodied person to the notions that her brother must be buried and that burial is owed to all.*

Indeed, one of the implicit threads of action in *Antigone* is her juxtaposing her body with ideas and with other bodies. With the play's first line, impossible to translate smoothly, Antigone literally establishes her relation to Ismene as to a body part.

> *Ō koinon autadelphon Ismēnēs kara,*
> "O kindred, own-sisterly head of Ismene . . ." (Nussbaum)[17]

Most translators absorb, as does David Grene, the reference to Ismene's head, *kara,* into the hyperbolic emphasis on kinship that continues in the speech:

> Ismene, my dear sister,
> whose father was my father, can you think of any
> of all the evils that stem from Oedipus
> that Zeus does not bring to pass for us, while we yet live?
> No pain, no ruin, no shame, and no dishonor
> but I have seen it in our mischiefs,
> yours and mine. (ll. 1–6)

Martha Nussbaum comments that Antigone addressing her sister's head is a gesture as distancing as it is intimate. If a modern actor playing an edgy Antigone were actually to grasp her sister's head while speaking these lines, many interpretive possibilities would resonate. It could intensify an impression of sororal love, even to the point of inordinate affection. It could at the same time signal a subtle violence toward Ismene, for soon Antigone will cruelly disavow this intimate sisterly relation.

The gesture could also hint of how the human body can be objectified or dismembered. Moreover, it could imply something about the protean and permeable nature of the body, as if it could attach itself to or absorb other bodies. Perhaps the gesture is histrionic, and a modern actor playing Antigone might address the *mask* of Ismene.[18] At this moment she is attempting to enlarge—or else narrow to a sharper focus—the nexus of selfhood, anticipating the task she must accomplish. As she urges Ismene to join her, she refers to herself in an oddly fragmented way: "Here is this hand [not "my hand" or "your hand"]. Will you help it [not "help me"] to lift the dead man?" (43). Lloyd-Jones's Loeb translation gives an impression of Antigone fusing her hand with the corpse: "Will you bury the dead man, together with this hand of mine?"

Thus begins Antigone's change from attachment with the living to attachment to the dead. When confronting Creon, she already is juxtaposing her body with that of her brother, with the ordinances of Zeus, and with chthonic orders of justice. "I shall lie by his side," she says,

> loving him as he loved me; I shall be
> a criminal—but a religious one.
> The time in which I must please those that are dead
> is longer than I must please those of this world.
> For there I shall lie forever. (ll. 73–77)

When she tells Creon—

> So for such as me, to face such a fate as this
> is pain that does not count. But if I dared to leave
> the dead man, my mother's son, dead and unburied,
> that would have been real pain. (ll. 463–67)

—she is asserting that her body has become an "integration" of person and principle. Thus, to harm the principle would be to harm her person and vice versa. Now she "is" the obligation to bury the dead. And Creon implicitly acknowledges this when he commands that she, though alive, be entombed. His and others' responses to her indicate yet another feature of this paradigm of moral integrity. It emerges in encounters with others, who act or do not act in reply: Ismene, Creon, Haemon, and the Chorus of elders. Burying Polyneices, while occurring secretly, will soon be for all to see. So it appears that integrity, in order to be, *must be perceived to be, and so must be dramatized.* Integrity requires a witness.

But there are problems with the idea of witnessing integrity, similar to that of witnessing pain. For Scarry, the fact that bodies suffer pain is, on the one hand, what we know best about each other and is a basis of sympathy and empathy. On the other hand, pain *as feeling* is what we might call an *interior exterior*—an interruption to my bodily horizon that only I directly perceive. Scarry asks us to imagine a migraine. There is no visible wound, but *to me* my pain is unproblematic; it is the most real thing there is. But *you,* my witness, have no certainty to begin with, for you cannot see or touch my headache. What is to me most real is to you a little less than real. My report of pain asks you *to believe,* to overcome a tinge of doubt, especially if you've never had migraines. Most of Scarry's analyses of torture, war, and cultural creation ramify from the premise that interiority (including pain and ideas) cannot be *directly* communicated. Pain to be perceived must be transferred to a visible object, such as an instrument or weapon or a visible wound. Then the pain can be put to use, as when a torturer uses instruments of pain to substantiate an impression of his power, or here, when Antigone aligns the vulnerability of her body—soon to be put in pain—with an idea.

As with invisible pain, when ideas—like norms and principles, or my commitment to them—are dramatized, something abstract is made visible by being adjoined to words, actions, and especially bodies. But moral integrity is unlike pain because my own commitment to norms is a matter that *I* may be uncertain about, just as you are. It is a matter of self-doubt as well as other-doubt. Antigone's alignment of her body with the norms may be an attempt both to communicate her commitment to others *and to convince herself* (as we might sense in her hyperbolic mixing of love, sister-brotherhood, and death, and, in Anouilh's version, when she tries to compose a letter to Haemon). In juxtaposing her body with principles, she would be *instantiating* moral integrity, implying the question: does moral integrity require the play and witnessing that comes of dramatization, including the inward witness of self-dramatization?

Haemon and Tereisias: Profusion of Body and Principle

Creon is asked to witness and recognize Antigone's performance of integrity. The most straightforward view of his story is that he hubristically ignores a principle (respect for the dead) clearly recognized in the end by all Thebes. This clarity extends to the audience as well. If we recognize that Antigone's is a *moral,* putatively universal claim, we should see that the claim is claiming us. In the play, however, the moral conflict is not often expressed clearly. Only once is the apparent dilemma made concise. The Chorus says, "There *is* a certain reverence for piety./But for him in authority, he cannot see that authority defied" (ll. 872–73). Clear enough, piety versus city; but more often we find that issues of kinship, politics, and ritual are thickly entangled.

Antigone appeals to "personal" and "universal" reasons for defying Creon. The muddle thickens when Haemon and Creon argue. Creon casts aspersions on Antigone's character and on women generally. When he says that nothing is worse for a city than to disobey authority (a moral principle), he also says, "we must not let people say that a woman beat us" (l. 680). For his part, Haemon begins his argument by prudently acknowledging paternal authority. Then, in reply to Creon's worry about being seen weaker than a woman, he says it would be wise to listen to the whispers that Antigone is being wrongfully executed. He warns that if Creon remains blinded by anger, he will rule nothing more than a desert. But as their antagonism inflames, Haemon never answers Creon's best argument. He never says, *If your concern is for a city torn apart by royal fratricide, you can only resolve the matter by appropriately disposing of the bodies on both sides.* Instead, his prudence disintegrates, he calls his father crazy, and says, "You will never again/set eyes upon my face" (ll. 761–62).

When the blind seer, Teiresias, does change Creon's mind he does so with appeals to embodiment that may at first seem bizarre, which entail how dead bodies mingle with the living. Teiresias is an augur. The screams and murderous flights of birds have aroused his suspicion, and so have the animal sacrifices on altars: their flesh and fat will not burn. Grene translates *empurōn egeuomen* (l. 1005) to mean that Teiresias also "tastes" as well as "tests" these sacrifices. The seer concludes that a god is interrupting the city's rites because the flesh of sacrifices has somehow come from the corpse of Polyneices.

> For our altars and our sacrificial hearths
> are filled with the carrion meat of birds and dogs,
> torn from the flesh of Oedipus' poor son. (ll. 1016–18)

The Thebans are unwittingly offering the deities what animals have eaten; the implication is that as the people consume animals that have consumed animals—whether or not they taste the offerings of alters—the people will also be consuming Polyneices. This profusion of the scavenged and scattered body throughout the society like the odor of death is, Teiresias says, the result of Creon's obstinate refusal to relax his "fine undeviating stand" (l. 1025). However, as this oracular argument does not yet strike home, Teiresias drives the point violently into Creon's own house: *Because you have put the living in the grave and left the dead on the ground, the Furies will take your son in exchange.* Then he brings the point back into the political realm:

> All the cities will stir in hatred
> against you, because their sons in mangled shreds
> receive their burial rites from dogs, from wild beasts
> or when some bird of the air brought a vile stink
> to each city that contained the hearths of the dead. (ll. 1080–83)

The violation will profuse and permeate. To be sure, this is uttered as a curse, which terrifies Creon into relenting. But the imagery of bodily profusion through consumption by beasts and birds has ethical import all should be able to grasp or intuit. The pollution of the dead cannot be isolated to one mangled corpse on one spot of earth, nor even many such corpses. It is everywhere, in "all the cities."[19] It is recognition that violence on others cannot be contained but returns through the very elements in which all live.

Participating at the Limits of Antigone's Integrity

Antigone's pattern of integrity requires an alignment of the human body with norms of obligation; however, her alignment is ambiguous. For Nussbaum and Mills, Antigone ignores interests of the city and diminishes her kinship with the living when she rejects Ismene's offer to join her. For Butler, she imitates the discourse of the hierarchy she opposes. Even so, Antigone upholds a norm the play also upholds and therefore is to be preferred over Creon. If she exaggerates or ignores familial or civic relationships, Creon threatens their very basis in society.

One way to acknowledge the limits of Antigone's paradigm of integrity is to say that her vision lacks the practical wisdom (*phronesis*) needed to flourish in the midst of contingency and ambiguity. The play may acknowledge this when it closes with the Chorus thinking that *phronesis* is the best part of happiness (l. 1348), a thought guiding Nussbaum's interpretation. Another way to criticize the Antigone paradigm is to recognize that the characters have stumbled into a realm where distinctions between nature and culture are unanchored or implicitly chaotic. René Girard, in turn, would view her as having been drawn into a scape-goating process. Her body is sacrificed in her society's effort to stop a vengeance cycle let loose by ritual failure.[20] Anouilh portrays her as a brooding romanticist Haemon would have been wiser to ignore.[21] All these observations, including this view of bodily substantiation, register how there something less than conventionally rational about lending one's material body to an abstract principle.

There is, however, another way to account for the limits of Antigone's paradigm. She is, in a sense, refuting Bernard Williams's critique of moral integrity and is at the same time proving him correct. She is align-ing her person with the principle that dead bodies should be respected, and this activity of alignment becomes her "ground project." But as a ground project—that is, as a reason to *live*—it has to some critics proven insufficient. We could say, then, that there is a *gap* or an *empty margin* between body and principle. The gap between the form of her commit-ment and its content may be why the story can both attract and unsettle us. *Moreover, if we are speaking of Antigone as a paradigm of moral integrity, we may wonder if this "gappiness" is more than a contingency of the story but part of the paradigm itself.* Moral integrity in others is frequently discomfiting. Even if we admire "moral saints" (as Susan Wolf calls them) we often want them to keep their distance. Beyond that, we might suspect the project of aligning the body with the norm is too nar-row, too much like a singular social "role" that is so confining as to bode ill or even destroy the person who tries to inhabit it.

However, to say there are problems with the paradigm of moral in-tegrity is not really a good reason to dismiss it, not if we agree with postmodernists (and a good many religious folk) that there is no option other than to be persons patterned of gaps and margins. The paradigm of moral integrity, with its limits, is a sign of human finitude, contin-gency, and fallibility—as when the moral saint is discovered to be at some moments weak, doubtful, slothful, or selfish yet still a moral saint. Moreover and more significantly, there remain all the ways in which the paradigm of integrity may enrich our lives, as well as disclose ambi-guities. That is, the "holes"—practical and conceptual—in integrity as moral wholeness may "allow room" for innovative modes in which we may enter, *to participate in another's pattern of integrity.*

We can see this latter possibility in the practices of conscientious ob-jectors and nonviolent resistors, which in part owe something to the Antigone paradigm. In a number of essays, James Childress describes how such persons often consider their integrity threatened by the authorities they oppose. In response to the threat, they in effect put themselves at risk by entrusting their persons to their opponents. Conscientious objectors and conscientious refusers[22] do this by showing how their own *consciences* are being put in *harm's way* by the authorities.[23] When Childress regards harm to conscience as a prima facie moral evil, he implicitly likens harm of conscience to personal and bodily harm. So if the law threatens to harm my conscience (as if it were part of my person and body), then it behooves the authorities to prove why it is exceptionally necessary for them to force me to choose between law and conscience.[24] Moreover, by showing how they are putting my conscience at risk, I am also showing them how they are putting their own consciences at risk. For if the principle "do no harm" applies to consciences, then the authorities may see that they are also doing something they should find impossible to live with. *They should find themselves sharing, or at least offered a share, in the objector's or refuser's crisis and pattern of integrity.*

Nonviolent resisters (as opposed to objectors and refusers) seek actively to alter the law by resisting the authorities. Their way of incorporating the integrity of their opponents into their own drama is even more dramatic, for now the body at risk is more literally at risk. Seventeenth-century Quakers, like twentieth-century followers of Gandhi and Martin Luther King, "put their lives in the hands of their opponents" *by risking bodily harm while not threatening bodily harm.*[25] In this way they sought to establish *a space of mutual trust* in which violence would not be resorted to, bodily integrity would not be jeopardized, and the authorities would restrain themselves. The resisters say: *You, the authority, can trust us to be nonviolent. As we oppose you, you can trust us not to cross certain bounds, and we trust you to so trust us.* Childress distinguishes between how the resisters "express" trust that their opponents will refrain from initiating (or cease continuing) violence, and how they also "evoke" such trust.[26] These encounters give patterns of integrity an embodied reality; the embodied reality, in turn, lends the principles the overt materiality of dramatization.

Antigone, however, does not express trust or elicit trust from Creon until it is too late to avoid violence. In Mary Whitlock Blundell's *Helping Friends and Harming Enemies*, "harming" turns out to be as binding an obligation in Hellenic culture as "helping." Through his play, Sophocles is asking: Who is friend, who is foe? Who must be helped, who must be harmed? Not only has Antigone's king/uncle become her enemy, so has her sister. And it seems that Antigone, who would defend the obligations of *philia*, has become harsh to all who are living.[27] By contrast, Childress's objectors and resisters act in a milieu in which the scriptural norm, "love your enemies," is not unknown and "do no harm" is generalized over all humanity. Even so, somewhat like the modern resister, Antigone's integrity begins to emerge as she aligns her body with a norm known to all in the city, including her enemy. Creon inadvertently recognizes her alignment when he entombs her. *If you, though alive, align yourself with the dead against me, then you shall be buried alive, with the dead.* And later he sees that in threatening her body he threatens a norm that bears on himself and everyone, in cities and families.

Does this matter to us? The easiest answer is that Antigone is morally right about burying the dead, irrespective of cultural practices and beliefs. That is, we know she is right because she touches a principle of respect for all human beings. Granted this affirmation, however, we have also seen that such principles are tenuous. If her integrity claims us, existentially and communally, it is not only because we recognize the logic of her cause, but also because we are "caught up" as witnesses in her embodied dramatization. Bodies matter, which may mean that we are invited to constitute her cause by lending it our bodies. But the fact remains that there is something arbitrary and isolating about the part she plays. *Bodies and principles may be aligned, but they remain to an extent incommensurable.* A gap remains, into which we may wish to enter, or may wish to avoid. As we watch Antigone sever her relations to living bodies on the way to the tomb that is her theater, we may want to shout, "Stop! Wait!" and look for other patterns of integrity. Our reticence does not guarantee that other patterns will be found, although they might be. On another day, might not Antigone find a way to align her body with Ismene's, and accept her sister's offer of hand and head in a kindred, dramatic cause?

Chapter II

Who Can See Thomas Becket's Integrity?

There is a gap in me where my honor ought to be.
—BECKET, IN JEAN ANOUILH's *Becket, or The Honor of God*

Now is the way clear, now is the meaning plain.
—THOMAS, IN T. S. ELIOT's *Murder in the Cathedral* (I.665)

THE INTEGRITY PARADIGM of Becket is similar to Antigone's. The twelfth-century archbishop aligns his body with a sacred cause in opposition to a king's civic cause. Becket's *body* must be seen to validate *principles*. This alignment arouses suspicions of aestheticism, in Jean Anouilh's version of the story, and of spiritual pride in T. S. Eliot's. Has Thomas really avoided "the greatest treason," as Eliot put it, "To do the right deed for the wrong reason" (I.665–66)? For both Antigone and Becket, the right reasons are elusive and seek material substantiation.

Anthropologist Victor Turner understood this substantiation by showing how the historical Becket negotiated a tricky, ritual-like passage through space filled with paradigms of sacrifice and martyrdom. Anouilh explores the "gap" in this alignment of Becket's person with principle. And Eliot, in a play whose theatrical possibilities are not now well appreciated, aims to draw the audience into the alignment. He dramatizes the emergence of Thomas Becket's integrity—and the integrity of the Women of Canterbury—into a pattern of "action and suffering." All three writers ask: how can *we perceive* (see and hear) integrity and the "design" in which the bishop and women become lost? Thus, the story of Becket is a place to examine how paradigms, norms, and principles are processes of embodiment, perhaps intrinsically dramatic and theatrical.

Becket's story also exemplifies how integrity's juxtaposition of body and idea is not without its limits and problems. Turner, Anouilh, Eliot, and Robert Bolt (whose treatment of Thomas More will be a coda for this chapter) lead us to contemplate the dangers of such alignments, when one becomes entrapped in an enclosure of moral integrity.

Becket of History

At least two problems keep the historical Becket intriguing. One is that unlike Antigone, the principles at stake are not now, nor were they in 1170, nearly as compelling as the obligation to respect the dead. Becket's "cause" (by some accounts he died with that word on his lips) consisted of matters about which reasonable bishops, not to mention royalists, disagreed. Among these were the church's independence in matters of appointment, taxation, and jurisprudence. Could, for instance, the church protect clerics, already convicted in ecclesiastical courts, from further punishment by the crown? When this dispute arose, so many people were "clerical" as to divide society into two bureaus of justice, which Henry found intolerable. He needed the English church to be a good, tax-paying vassal, not a separate entity, which is why he wanted to make his friend both chancellor and archbishop, an unprecedented arrangement. Today, Henry has strong supporters, and Christopher Fry's play *Curtmantle* (1961) depicts his reign sympathetically. Yet the principle of separating church and state arguably owes something both to Becket, who upheld the church's independence, and to Henry, whom Winston Churchill credited with laying "the foundations of English Common Law."[1]

Then there is the problem of Becket's personal integrity, which for some arises from his ability to exchange old allegiances for new. Thomas of Cheapside, London, was the brilliant son of a Norman merchant. After his father died, various mentors noticed him and made him their protégé. Henry was not the first to feel betrayed by his shifting loyalties. Archbishop Theobald had made him Archdeacon of Canterbury and later recommended him to the king. But nearing death, Theobald threatened to excommunicate Becket (now chancellor) for not continuing to consult with him. When in 1162 Henry forced the bishops to elect Becket archbishop (a man not even ordained a priest), their objections were not only that Becket had done Henry's bidding but also that, while chancellor, he had been a warrior whose bloody prowess exceeded that of the king's knights. When Becket surprised Henry by resigning upon swearing obedience to the pope, the king's vindictive disappointment was aroused and supposedly led, by 1170, to his hasty complaint about having to put up with mockery from "a low-born clerk."[2] Four barons took his words as a pretext to arrest and murder Becket.

Even to their supporters, the king's and archbishop's behaviors seemed extravagant. Henry accused his former chancellor of embezzlement, and Becket excommunicated several of Henry's allies. Were the two monstrously petty or merely using the tactics available? Anne Duggan argues the latter, in respect to Becket, while Frank Barlow thinks that, having once been the king's deputy, he was insecure and found it hard to compromise with his former patron.[3] When, under duress, Becket did verbally compromise at Clarendon in 1164, his fellow bishops objected. Becket then refused to sign the compromise, making a bad thing worse. His guilt over the debacle, Barlow thinks, exacerbated his intransigence. But no explanation can fully account for events that Becket's associates later found unfathomable. About the time pilgrimages began and hagiographies were written, some wrote to one another in bewildered awe about what had transpired with their erstwhile friend.[4] Given the limits of historical explanation, perhaps theater offers as "true" a way as any to understand Thomas Becket.[5]

Watching Thomas

My interest in drama and integrity began with the teaching of Eliot's 1935 play, a *locus classicus* in religion and drama.[6] In class, the issue often becomes how to appreciate its sacramental premises, with which many students are unfamiliar or oppose. Becket's death, after all, can be seen to legitimate sacrificial violence. His martyrdom can seem motivated by a self-destructive obsession. Eliot anticipated such reactions and wanted the play to jar or shift the orientations of a routinely secular audience. To bring us to a point of reflective sympathy, *the pattern of Thomas's self and the pattern of his religious/political vocation must be seen to coincide.*[7] Does *Murder in the Cathedral* bring us to such a point? Can we see and "believe in" Thomas's integrity?

Narrative writing, we have observed, has numerous devices for showing *internal action.* Theatrical drama has the more difficult task of dramatizing integrity without direct entrée into a person's interiority. As in life, we cannot literally see behind the "mask" of an actor's face and body into a character's mind, except through imported narrative methods such as prologues, soliloquies, and asides. So in theater, integrity as interior wholeness and rightness may be a matter in doubt, unless it becomes visible through the living bodies we perceive. And if it does, then we may ask whether integrity is not something far more extensive than interior action or an inward self-relationship.

Our belief in characters such as Antigone or Thomas will depend on *seeing* them *enact* the pattern of norms, vocational paradigms, and social relations that contribute to their identities. If we cannot see the pattern enacted, then the play may lack "integrity" as a dramatic imitation of action and character. That was a complaint about *Murder in the Cathedral* from neo-Aristotelian critic, Elder Olson: nothing happens. Henry is not even a character onstage. And Thomas does not really *do* anything to make us believe he has overcome his four temptations. Eliot's play, Olson objected, is not a play at all, but a long lyric poem to be recited in lovely period costumes. As a poem, the work is designed to provoke contemplation and feeling about its object, the story of Becket.[8] To grasp Olson's objection, and to see what answering it might reveal about the *action of paradigms or symbols* in drama, we need to consider what we do and do not see happening as the play begins.

What we see first is the Chorus, the Women of Canterbury, "living and partly living" (I.155), drawn to the cathedral by premonitions of danger. "For us, the poor, there is no action"—so far, Olson has a point—"But only to wait and to witness" (l. 49–50). Three Priests enter and provide less than helpful exposition. They do not know what Thomas has been up to during his long exile in France, but do say that in his absence raw power rules. One offers a glimpse of Thomas that is not encouraging: he is "isolated," "insecure," with "pride always feeding on his own virtues" (l. 118). A Messenger has announced that he is returning, "in pride and sorrow" (l. 86), still at odds with the king. The Women fear he is "bringing death into Canterbury" (l. 150) and hope he will go back to France. A Priest tells them to "put on pleasant faces"—when Thomas suddenly enters: "Peace. And let them be in their exaltation" (ll. 205–6). In eleven enigmatic lines he describes how the Women "know and do not know, what is to act and suffer." He speaks of their being "fixed/In an eternal action" in which to suffer and to will are also to consent, and of how "the wheel may turn and still/Be for ever still." But we know nothing of why he has returned or what situation confronts him. To the Priests he says, "All things prepare the event. Watch" (I.254). So we watch as the Tempters arrive.

Olson objected that the Tempters represent temptations Thomas has already overcome. They are merely voices in his mind, urging him to reconcile with the king, or take back the chancellorship for the sake of temporal power, or align with the barons, that is, with "the people." Thomas deflects the first three Tempters fairly easily. But the fourth surprises him with the promise of martyrdom and sainthood, "the way already chosen" (I.503), and so inflames his pride and also his despair of becoming a historical curiosity.[9] When this Tempter offers the opportunity to look down from heaven on the torment of his persecutors, Thomas reacts with agitation so great as to begin to refute Olson. "No!" he shouts, and later: "Is there no way, in my soul's sickness,/Does not lead to damnation in pride? . . . Can I neither act nor suffer/Without perdition?" (ll. 573, 584–90). In reply, the Tempter repeats the very phrases by which Thomas described the Women of Canterbury:

> You know and do not know, what it is to act or suffer,
> You know and do not know, that action is suffering,
> And suffering action. Neither does the agent suffer
> Nor the patient act. But both are fixed
> In an eternal action, an eternal patience
> To which all must consent that it may be willed. . . . (I.591–96)

The words are no less enigmatic than before, and for sixty-five lines Thomas says nothing.

During his silence, the Chorus, Tempters, and Priests speak, alternating in despair, accusation, and fear. The Women interpret the cosmos as losing its integrity: "God is leaving us, more pang, more pain than birth or death." They cry that Thomas save them, and "save us, save yourself that we may be saved;/Destroy yourself and we are destroyed" (I.655, 663–64). His long-delayed answer to their plea should mark the crux of whatever action is at stake in the play. If he has discovered an action that puts real temptation behind him, we should perceive this action, *now*.

> Now is my way clear, now is the meaning plain:
> Temptation shall not come in this kind again.
> The last temptation is the greatest treason:
> To do the right deed for the wrong reason. (I.665–68)

In question is not the deed, but the reason. Is anything *happening now* that visibly defeats the wrong reason (i.e., prideful spite in being righteous or moral)? Thomas is saying that in resisting the king, he has entered a new pattern of integrity, the "design of God." But is anything *making visible* this integrity as he claims, "I shall no longer act or suffer, to the sword's end" (l. 705)? What, in the structure of action and presentation, might be overcoming the skepticism Eliot knew would likely attend the Canterbury Festival of 1935, which commissioned this play?

Detour: Jean Anouilh's and Victor Turner's Liminal Becket

My skeptical students have found Anouilh's 1959 play more plausible, and it provides leverage for grasping certain semiotic and performative aspects of the story. Anouilh's Becket is an ironic, self-contained yet vulnerable, modern self. His personal and cultural center is divided, in part because the playwright used an erroneous source that said Becket was a Saxon, when in fact he was, like King Henry, Norman.[10] Anouilh's Henry is sardonic, boorish, pragmatic, yet also displaced and insecure even when asserting royal prerogative. The play is devoted mostly to private scenes of friendship and antagonism and, as with *Antigone*, Anouilh reduces the story to a romantic and existentialist form, almost but not quite empty of all religious and moral content. This reduction is signaled by a curious remark of Henry's, when he demands the favor of bedding Gwendolen, Becket's Welsh mistress.[11] "You can't tell a lie. . . ." the king says, not because of any moral consequences but because he thinks Becket merely considers lying "distasteful" or "inelegant." "What looks like morality in you," he concludes, "is nothing more than esthetics" (32). And what Henry means by "esthetic" is clarified by an earlier exchange, when he demands to know whether his friend is actually capable of loving—either him or Gwendolen—to which Becket replies enigmatically that "I am your servant," just as she "is my mistress." Exasperated, Henry asks him why he always employs "labels . . . to justify your feelings."

> BECKET: Because, without labels, the world would have no shape, my prince.
> KING: Is it so important for the world to have a shape?
> BECKET: It's essential, my prince, otherwise we can't know what we're doing. (17)

Anouilh thus portrays Becket as a modern individual who seeks order through arbitrary signs and is introspective about his lack of a personal center. He tells Gwendolen, "There is a gap in me where my honor ought to be" (*L'honneur est une lacune chez moi*). Theobald, the old archbishop, agrees: "He is as it were detached As if seeking his real self" (*Il y reste comme absent. Il se cherche*) (15). Although Becket is appalled when Henry brutalizes some Saxon peasants, he remains oddly loyal to, but cannot say he "loves," his king. Nor can he defend Gwendolyn; he is silent as Henry tells how she stabbed herself to death as he started to rape her.

So if the gap or *lacune* means he is not an integrated person, part of what makes this gap interesting is how Becket flourishes in *roles*—though without gaining a "real" self. Each time Henry bestows an office on Becket, the color drains from his face and he is terrified. But each time, he discovers an aesthetic pleasure and sense of purpose that comes with inhabiting the new part. After receiving the Seal of the Realm, making him chancellor—"My mother is England now," he says (13)—Becket becomes pleased to enforce Henry's taxes on the clergy. When Henry tells Becket is to be made archbishop, he turns "deathly pale," realizing "I could never serve both God and you" (61). But then he warms to his part and affirms a new sense of integrity, or what Bernard Williams calls a "ground project," as when he addresses his fellow bishops and admits he has been "a profligate," "a libertine," and "worldly man" who laughed at the externals of religious life and office.

> But you passed the burden onto me and now I have to carry it. I have rolled up my sleeves and taken it on my back and nothing will ever make me set it down again. (79)

And much later he tries to explain to Henry how he found his honor by enacting a role: "We must only do—absurdly—what we have been given to do—right to the end." He felt, at the ceremonial moment when Henry made him Archbishop, "for the first time that I was being entrusted with something. . . . I was a man without honor. And suddenly I found it—one I never imagined would ever become mine—the honor of God" (102), an honor he also considers to be "frail," "incomprehensible," and "vulnerable." One could say that while Becket does not fit the part of archbishop, the part is in effect *enacting him,* as if for the first time. He is now playing in what Victor Turner calls a "social drama."

Turner and Anouilh can help us see how paradigms can be both *models to imitate* (not to say "scripts," whose social connotations can seem too deterministic) and *agents.* Root paradigms are, for Turner, more fluid than the symbols Clifford Geertz likens to the grammar of a culture.[12] As paradigms interact with individuals and groups they can have unforeseen consequences. Citing their "metaphorical," "allusive," and "implicit" character, Turner speaks suggestively of "cultural root paradigms" being active "in the encounter of emotionally charged wills. . . . [They] *reach down* to irreducible life stances of individuals," taking "a fiduciary *hold* on what they sense to be axiomatic values, matters literally of life and death."[13] A Derridean injection of *différance* into paradigms need not confound Turner's analysis; the depths he asserts are patterns of possibility. As agents of possibility, such paradigms can be dramatized in "aesthetic dramas" precisely because they are active in social dramas. They would "charge" the will, even as receptive wills imitate their "charge" (consciously or unconsciously, paradigms being other than that psychological distinction). Turner avoids simple demarcations of freedom and destiny; these poles are mediated—and, I would infer, indeterminately mediated—by such paradigms. He implies a mutual receptivity of form and action and, indeed, a participatory mimetic view—hence a dramatic view—of language, feeling, and thought.

In his account of the social drama between Becket and Henry,[14] both men are receptive to the action of root paradigms in social and political life. Again, these paradigms arise in all sorts of forms, from folkways and beliefs to official practices or doctrines, and press into various political structures. They do not constitute a system so much as contribute to a "forest of symbols" (another phrase of Turner's), in which they are as dynamic as Tolkien's treelike Ents: you never know which paradigm in the forest might move and reach out and grab you, or allow you to grab it. Passing through the forest, so to speak, people of various groups and interests co-exist in a "field" of paradigms: for example, the king, the barons, peasants, and clerics. Also in this field are support structures, factions, roles, and social processes. Social dramas are close analogs to rites of passage: former identities are shed and new ones assumed in environments of *bounded nonidentity,* which Turner terms *liminality,* the situation of being "betwixt and between." In the liminal phase of a rite of passage, one's identity is protean and more liable to be shaped by new paradigms, which indeterminately become available for imitation and innovation. There is some flex and uncertainty about the outcome of a rite of passage. And conflicts in social dramas work themselves out in far riskier passages that involve entire communities. Turner outlines four phases of a social drama:

> An overt *breach* of norms governing relationships in a social structure (e.g., Becket resigns as chancellor and defends church prerogatives).

A mounting *crisis* between antagonists (Henry charges Becket with malfeasance).

Ritual or legal attempts at *redress or reconciliation,* wherein there may be liminal moments that deepen the crisis (Becket is tried at Northampton and flees to France).

A public *schism or reconciliation* between the parties (Becket's exile and murder, Henry's penance at Becket's tomb).

It is in the middle phases that things change. At the Council at North-ampton (October 1164), Becket had a kidney stone and was quartered in St. Andrew's Abbey, "a liminal place if there ever was one," writes Turner. He was all but spent in his fight against Henry. But in the ab-bey he gravitated toward symbols of martyrdom and the *via crucis.* His confessor prompted him to say the mass of St. Stephen, first martyr, in St. Stephen's chapel, and he is said to have wept. He carried a Host under his garments. He knew he had the support of the folk around Northampton. Anouilh, through a Page reporting these events to King Henry, offers a good account of what happened: the archbishop appeared before the council at the last possible moment, "sick, deathly pale, in full pontifical regalia and carrying his own heavy silver cross" down the long, crowded hall where no one dared rise to obstruct him. "[W]hen Robert Duke of Leicester, who was to read out his sentence, began the consecrated words, he stopped with a gesture and forbade him, in God's name, to pronounce sentence upon him, his spiritual Father." Becket then turned and left, as everyone "parted for him. . . . [H]is eyes were so cold, and so ironic—even though all he had in his hand was his episcopal crook— that one by one, they [the Barons] fell silent" (82, 83).

The cold irony that the Page notices may well be historical. Becket was among the most intelligent men in Henry's realm and was keen to the power of symbols,[15] and the king seems to have intuited what Becket was up to. Henry, Turner writes, "knew subliminally that the root paradigm of the martyr's *via crucis* was archetypically in control and he could only use direct force against him at the expense of giving him what he wanted. . . ." Indeed, the players in a social drama must implicitly recog-nize the paradigms in play; otherwise, there can be no crisis. So Henry, kneeling before Becket's tomb, is mistaken to ask, "Don't you think we'd have done better to understand each other?" (1). In effect, they did.

Becket's "honor," then, emerges in liminal moments of transformation, when certain paradigms capture him as much as he captures them. His *cause,* in Anouilh, is not what compels us. Rather, we respond to how he delights in a new sense of duty ("I have rolled up my sleeves," etc.). But although *principles* shape his emerging pattern of integrity—such as protecting the weak from the strong, a mix of *justice* and *care*—Anouilh portrays the pattern as being aesthetic rather than moral. Yet he is not entirely consistent about this. Yes, Becket implies that if lying has an ugly shape, truth telling has a more pleasing shape. But resting the moral upon the aesthetic may be another way of elevating the moral or the religious (to reverse Kierkegaard). As Becket tells Gwendolen, "Beauty is one of the few things which don't shake one's faith in God" (26). As to "the ethical" in Ricoeur's wider sense of the term, Anouilh tries to account for Becket's honor by having him identify with the Saxons. He tells Henry, "England will be fully built, my prince, on the day the Saxons are your sons as well" (20). Becket's honor is not utterly self-referential but connected with compassion for the poor, if not all the poor then at least the poor of Saxon blood.

Then there is the matter of God. Becket is "waiting for the honor of God and the honor of the realm to become one." He will be loyal to Henry, "in all save the honor of God." Henry asks, "Did you start to love God?" Becket replies, "I started to love the honor of God" (104). This may make God seem but a formula, one which Jean Anouilh—apparently an agnostic conservative to the right of Charles De Gaulle[16]—employed because of its totemic value. Yet Becket's prayers do sound as if he means them, as when he decides to end his exile and take up his cross, despite the suspicion that God was tempting him with the "diadem" as well as the "hair shirt." Under both,

> You discern the same pride, the same vanity, the same petty, complacent preoccupation with oneself. . . . I shall go back to my place, humbly, and let the world accuse me of pride, so that I may do what I believe is my life's work. (94)

Prayers, however, can be musings to oneself. In Act II, when he gives away his clothes, dons a monk's habit, and feeds the poor, does he pray to God or to himself? Do the apostrophe, "Farewell, Becket," and the second person pronoun immediately following—"I wish there had been something I regretted parting with, so I could offer it to You" (*pour vous l'offrir;* the capitalized You only in English)—suggest that Becket conflates himself with his paradigm? Only now does he turn to a crucifix, "Lord, are You sure You are not tempting me? It all seems far too easy" (64).

Perceiving the Design

With clues from Anouilh and Turner, we might now be able to reply to Olson. *Murder in the Cathedral* is drama if the paradigms are themselves quasi-agents that Thomas encounters, and if we can perceive this paradigmatic action playing out before us. However, the paradigms Eliot dramatizes are quite different from Anouilh's. Eliot wants us to consider that Thomas has conformed himself to, or been conformed, not by the "honor of God"—which would be an "absurd" formalism—but by the "design of God," which is to have material import. In his sermon, Thomas says the true martyr is neither accidental nor self-willed but is one "who has lost his will in the will of God, and who no longer desires anything for himself, not even the glory of being a martyr" (Interlude, ll. 68–70). The dramatic challenge is twofold: do we believe Thomas indeed "loses" his will, and does the motif of the "design of God" appear with theatrical and material substance?

Eliot's strategy was to build a drama both liturgical and modern.[17] *Liturgical,* because elements of worship are incorporated; *modern,* because we are to grasp its religious ideas not in spite of but *through* the covert and overt agnosticism of the times. This strategy has three meta-theatrical layers, which structure my analysis: (1) Eliot depicts a drama of vocation through a theatrical drama (as does Anouilh); (2) he employs techniques to make the audience recognize itself as participating in both *the theatrical event* and *the historic event;* and (3) he then uses our own palpable sense of participating in theater and history to assist in *bodily substantiating*[18] the "design of God." We should not have to share Eliot's theological idea to sense that Thomas may be viewed from an angle of vision other than the one from which we are assumed to start.

Drama of Vocation

Remembering that a shepherd is supposed to be for the welfare of his flock, consider again the sentence "Now is my way clear, now is the meaning plain." It should be viewed as Thomas's reply to the Women of Canterbury, which Francis Fergusson observes is crucial for his discovery of the right reason, charity or *agape* love.[19] This reason needs further elaboration. If in the past the Women of Canterbury were never utterly without hope, now they sense God forsaking them and "Lords of Hell" gathering around them. "Save us, save us, save yourself that we may be saved." And Thomas—who is frozen between acting and not acting—now grasps that what they truly need cannot be met by his fleeing again but by staying with them. The "right reason" is his accountability both to their perceived need for temporal security and their unwitting prayer for salvation. In their "living and partly living"—that is, in their suffering—he finds his "good angel," implying that temptation was, until now, quite real.

We can begin to "see" Thomas's integrity, then, if we see him being conformed to his vocation on behalf of the Women. Upon reflection, we still might speculate as to whether he is self-deceived in this. But to the extent we grasp the paradigm of priesthood, we are *seeing the work of one who inhabits the "habit" of a priest.* This impression is enlarged by the sermon, for to interpret a crisis with biblical texts is also part of a priest's work. If we can *see* these relations of identity, accountability, and work, then we have less reason for doubt when he says, "Now is my way clear." We have less need of an "inside view" (i.e., through his apparently private prayers and soliloquies, which may not convince us anyway). Theatrical and ritual forms of action are remaking him, *now,* before the eyes of the Chorus and the eyes of the audience.

Historic Participation

Becket and Henry played to their audiences, and Turner reports their antagonism can "still arouse fierce partisanship." Signified by camera-toting pilgrim-tourists to Canterbury, the Becket-event is an ongoing concern. Eliot invites audiences to recognize themselves as still being affected by the historic Becket. This invitation is implicit throughout the play, insofar as the Chorus links Becket's time with the mix of nominal Christians and cultured despisers in Eliot's audience. But the invitation to join with a lived sense of history (*Geschichte,* in German) is most explicit in the two moments when speakers address the audience directly.

The Christmas sermon in the Interlude between parts I and II is addressed to the Chorus. But E. Martin Browne (Eliot's first director) recalls that it "has always been the best remembered scene of the play." Why should this be so? It is a good sermon, both ritually and discursively. As *ritual,* it participates in what J. L. Austin calls "performative" speech, an utterance that realizes its referent by its being uttered. When one properly says, "I promise," a promissory situation comes into being; or when saying "bless you," a blessing happens. Here, the sermon can be read as a ritual instigating the promise of divine purpose and grace. As *discourse,* the homily explains the "right reason" and elicits understanding. Thomas asks us to "meditate on," "think for a moment," "reflect," "remember," and "consider." The first two-thirds of the sermon contain six interrogative sentences, creating the expectation of our response.

The sermon also exemplifies what Aristotle termed arguments primarily from "ethos" or character (as opposed to logic or emotion). Such an argument is created not by the audience's prior knowledge of the speaker but by how the speech itself embodies a tradition shared with the audience, in order to bring our perspective to a new place. The effect, suggests Jim Corder, is like a guide taking us up a mountain we know well, only to show us a vista we had not known.[20] The speaker's ethos is enlarged by the vista, which would in turn make the vista even more compelling or persuasive. Corder cites S. M. Halloran, who contrasts classical with modern rhetoric. For moderns, "ethos is generated by the seriousness and passion with which the speaker articulates his *own world,* the degree to which he is willing and able to make his world open to the other, and thus to the possibility of rupture."[21] In any case, Thomas would have us reflect on Christ, St. Stephen, and Canterbury's first martyr, St. Elphege—historic associations that will enlarge the Chorus's sense of the part Thomas is now playing and the person he is becoming.

In fact, Eliot here employs both modes of rhetoric. It wasn't simply that he knew his audience would be "serious people," who go to pious plays expecting to be bored.[22] Even the believers in the crowd would reflect the secularity of the times, and the agnostics will have been shaped in part by the Becket story. All will be partly understanding and misunderstanding. I think that Eliot implicitly sought to articulate his *own* idiosyncratic religious-aesthetic vision, in hopes that others might sense *another* vision interrupting their horizons. His audiences could not be expected to verify the "design of God," but they might begin to recognize themselves, with Thomas, in a pattern different from their expectations. (My suggestion, developing as we go through these chapters, is that the pattern is one of kenotic integrity.)

If the sermon prepares our habits of expectation to be ruptured, then the speeches of the Knights, immediately after they kill Thomas, force us to react to this rupture. In their "disinterested" rationalizations, they intend to speak *for us.* The Fourth Knight proposes that, in a psychological sense, Thomas was a suicide. The Second Knight reviews the political drama in a way that sounds like "the news" in any year we might happen to live:

> Unhappily, there are times when violence is the only way in which
> social justice can be secured. . . . [I]f you have now arrived at a just
> subordination of the pretensions of the Church to the welfare of the
> State, remember that it is we who took the first step. We have been in-
> strumental in bringing about the state of affairs that you approve. We
> have served your interests; we merit your applause; and if there is any
> guilt whatever in the matter, you must share it with us. (II.521–34)

Of course, Eliot would hope that the shock of recognition will prompt
us to reject the clichés that the Knights have lifted off our own tongues.[23]
His placement of their speeches invites us to invest ourselves in the event
the play is remembering. If now we further recognize Thomas's integrity,
it is not only because we may understand its priestly paradigms, but also
because we see ourselves in its historic pattern, which lends verisimilitude to the "design."

Substantiation

Eliot wants us to entertain and be entertained by the possibility that
we with the Chorus and Thomas are configured in the "design of God."
If this assent is to happen, even if only as a conceit to a premise, then
the burden finally rests not on liturgy[24] or shocking rhetoric, but on the
"action" of the Women responding to what they have seen. It is through
their suffering and seeing that we begin to see Thomas anew. We also
see them performing a ministry on *his* behalf, which confirms that the
Women of Canterbury are as large a role in the play as Thomas. This implies that we are to begin seeing ourselves in a pattern of ministry where
we, with the Women who are "acting and suffering," *are to contribute
our patterns of integrity to his.*

What the Women assumed at the outset was that integrity resides
only in the will to make something happen, to make history. Only the
powerful can pretend to such integrity. To the poor and forgotten, integrity would not be the *promise* but the ongoing *threat* of history,[25] which
is why the Women "do not wish for anything to happen." Thomas can
only be another will-to-power, and they fear he will prove insufficiently
powerful. Like Cassandra in Aeschylus's *Agamemnon,* they fear that
Thomas's return can only increase the perennial terror.

> Here is no continuing city, here is no abiding stay.
> Ill the wind, ill the time, uncertain the profit, certain the danger.

O late late late, late is the time, late too late, and rotten the year;
Evil the wind, and bitter the sea, and grey the sky, grey grey grey.
O Thomas return, Archbishop; return, return to France.
Return. Quickly. Quietly. Leave us to perish in quiet.
You come . . . bringing death into Canterbury.
A doom on the house, a doom on yourself, a doom on the world.
(I.144–51)

Thomas's words to the priests—"They speak better than they know, and beyond your understanding. . . . what it is to act or suffer" (ll. 207–8)—begin to reconfigure the meaning of integrity. Integrity is not the power of self-securing possession, not even of standing steadfastly in the right, but a "design" that both dispossesses and enlarges those who receive it. Yet if such a pattern is a gift, so to speak, then how is it that Thomas is tempted with his own good words? Because when removed from the plea of the Chorus, the theologically freighted words of his first speech—"Eternal patience," "the design of God," "the wheel that may turn and still / Be forever still"[26]—would be merely another idea, another exertion of the will to power. The presence of the Women contributes, then, to making these words part of an embodied pattern that would encompass suffering.

After the sermon, the Chorus speaks less fatalistically: of keeping "the peace of God" (II.14) and of how the defiled world needs to be "renewed" and "cleaned." But as they wait they have little expectation that the world will be cleaned; and if it is not, then the greening of the earth as winter turns to spring will only cover more wrongs. It is true that the Women, before the Knights intrude, express an understanding of evil, judgment, and separation: "behind the Judgement the Void, more horrid than active shapes of hell" (292). But their voices remain fearful and uncertain as they pray for intercession (ll. 302–9). Then as the Knights kill Thomas, they watch in frantic horror and their voices rise in a keening imperative.[27]

Clear the air! clean the sky! wash the wind! take stone from stone and wash them.
The land is foul, the water is foul, our beasts and ourselves defiled with blood. (ll. 397–98)

What they are now seeing is beyond their most fatalistic expectations: "But this, this is out of life, this is out of time." It is "an instant eternity of evil" and "a filth that we cannot clean." Now "supernatural vermin" defile the world (ll. 417–19). The Women continue . . .

> Clear the air! clean the sky! wash the wind! take stone from the stone,
>   take the skin from the arm, take the muscle from the bone, and wash
>   them. Wash the stone, wash the bone, wash the brain, wash the soul,
>   wash them wash them! (l. 422)

only to be interrupted by the First Knight's horrifyingly funny "We beg you to give us your attention for a few moments" (l. 423). Ironically, as they watch Thomas die, the Women witness and join an action by which the earth—in the "design of God"—*is* being cleaned.

Eliot of course knew the earth is *not* being cleansed, except when seen from a perspective of atonement toward which we, with the Women, would be shifted. Their final prayer (ll. 618–50) is dramatically earned, in that they were the ones who enabled Thomas to find himself in losing himself. I suggest it would be good if, in production, they—not the three Priests—could gather around Thomas's body as the *Te Deum* is sung.[28] Although they may or may not speak for us when they express gratitude for the blood of martyrs enriching the earth (l. 628) or beg forgiveness ("the sin of the world is upon our heads," l. 645), we would be disposed to consent to their ministrations to Thomas's body. If we have seen the alignment of his body with the "cause," and if the Women "are" now the materiality of that cause, and if they metatheatrically include the audience, then our bodies are being invited into the material substance of the pattern in which Thomas is lost. For his integrity is not affirmed, finally, apart from others' bodies. We may also resonate with how the Women correlate their praise with tangible images of creatures and nature: "In the snow, in the rain, in the wind, in the storm; in all of Thy creatures, both the hunters and the hunted. . . ." (l. 619).

> Even with the hand to the broom, the back bent in laying the fire, the
> knee bent in cleaning the hearth, we, the scrubbers and sweepers of
> Canterbury,
>   The back bent under toil, the knee bent under sin, the hands to the
> face under fear, the head bent under grief,
>   Even in us the voices of seasons, the snuffle of winter, the song of
> spring, the drone of summer, the voices of beasts and of birds, praise
> Thee. (ll. 625–27)

If the Women draw us into their doxology, then we might grasp a new pattern of integrity, of self-emptying integrity, because, for a moment, we may perceive that the pattern includes us as well.

Entrapping Integrity

Or we may not. Outside the theater or at some distance from the text, the complaints of the Knights linger. Did not Thomas imitate *the desire* for martyrdom? Did he not seek it out? Duggan thinks he had no reasonable options, but many have thought otherwise, giving weight to the Knights' objections.[29] There is no settling this dispute—it goes to how we assess "hidden" motivations—and there are other stories to juxtapose with Becket's. Stanley Hauerwas and Thomas Shaffer direct us to Lord Chancellor Thomas More's refusal to support King Henry VIII in the political and personal complexities of divorcing Catherine and rejecting papal authority.[30]

In reference to Robert Bolt's play *A Man for All Seasons* (1961), Hauerwas and Shaffer admire the ways in which More—who, perhaps unlike Barlow's Becket, had a clear, even "adamantine sense of his own self"[31]—attempted to avoid martyrdom. He was willing to parse official phrases to find wiggle room between his body and his principles. But alas, the gap would not open any wider, and More was "blithe" as he went to his execution. Hauerwas and Shaffer think his integrity included allegiance to faith, to be sure, but also to a plurality of civil law, the supremacy of conscience, and human wit—all of which gave More a certain room in which he sought to avoid moral entrapment by remaining silent as long as possible.

In Bolt's play, More tells Roper, his son-in-law, that he is not in fact denying the Act of Supremacy, because it affirms that the king is head of the church in England only "'so far as the law of God allows.' How far the law of God does allow it remains a matter of opinion, since the Act doesn't state it." When Roper asks just how much this "legal quibble" really allows for God, More answers evenly, "I'll keep my opinion to myself."[32] So Bolt treats More as a modern individual who finds himself drawn into an integrity trap and who looks everywhere for a way to juggle, or improvise, his obediences to church, law, crown, and especially his conscience; in the end, he cannot. Thus, the possibility that one can become *entrapped* in such a drama, unable to improvise, points to a danger of moral integrity as a singular model for living, a trap which More apparently attempted to avoid. He is shown to recognize that life and law afford legitimate chances to improvise upon public and private obligations, and he looks carefully for those chances. Only on seeing how all the chances to improvise have vanished does he speak his mind precisely as to the status of the king's marriage.

Improvisation would correlate with how we encounter moral claims in thick ethical contexts, which would make Hauerwas and Shaffer right to credit *A Man for All Seasons* with disclosing an expansive, less enclosing pattern of integrity. But if More could not find a way to improvise in the end, was it because the way had indeed closed? Or was it because More (*contra* Bolt) was less a modern than a feudal person?[33] While hagiographers remember the friend of Erasmus and author of *Utopia*, Peter Ackroyd reminds us that he was also a vehement opponent of Protestants and a blithe burner of heretics. Thomas More recognized and was *threatened* to see how, in Luther and William Tyndale, the invisible authority of conscience can effectively assert priority over visible authorities, and then attain visible power.[34] In opposing such a pattern of integrity (that of conscientious resistance), he was trapped in a pattern of zero-sum authority. By endorsing the execution of Tyndale and authorizing the burning of James Bainham, Richard Bayfield, John Tewkesbury, Thomas Drusgate, and others, More was playing Creon in a social drama similar to one that would later cost him his head.

It was similar not just because Henry VIII opened the way for Protestantism in England (a development which in most ways Henry himself despised) but also because More, when faced with a law he found illegitimate, could see no other choice but to assert the absolute priority of a singular principle and align that invisible principle with his embodied self.[35] If he saw the irony—that in opposing the king he had become a *new man,* his derogatory term for book smugglers and heretics who claimed the right of conscience—he apparently did not record it. Nor had he been troubled to notice, earlier, that when Church merges with State's power, it takes recourse to the violence always implicit in State power. More's irony, like that of Thomas Becket, can still arouse ire as well as admiration.

Chapter III

What If Your Integrity Repels Me?

Death and the King's Horseman
in the Theater of Understanding

> IYALOJA: I wish I could pity you.
> ELESIN: I need neither your pity nor the pity of the world. I need
> understanding. Even I need to understand. You were present at my
> defeat. You were part of the beginnings. You brought about the
> renewal of my tie to earth, you helped in the binding of the cord.
> —WOLE SOYINKA, *Death and the King's Horseman*

THE DRAMAS OF Antigone and Becket exemplify how integrity is valued
across various lines of cultural, religious, and political difference. Our
recognition of another's integrity depends, in part, on the phenomenon
of persons becoming attached to principles. Yet there are occasions when
another's integrity repels us, and this can be true whether or not we recognize the moral and cultural paradigms in play. Before exploring this
issue in Nigerian poet Wole Soyinka's *Death and the King's Horseman*
(1975), I want to take some more familiar bearings.

In *Keely and Du*[1] (1993), a woman is kidnapped from an abortion
clinic, having been raped by her ex-husband. Her abductors include Walter, a militant Christian minister, and an older woman, Du, who becomes
Keely's "nurse." They plan to hold her captive until she comes to term.
Despite its pro-choice orientation, this play is sometimes reviewed as
portraying both sides of the abortion debate; however, a production I saw
did not well articulate either the right to life or the principles of choice.
And any political dialogue it created could not transcend the fact that
Keely is, for much of the play, chained to a bed. What was reflected is

how there is very little dialogue in the abortion debate.[2] One community's "abomination" is another's "right." While Walter and Du appear to be breaking the Do No Harm principle common to most cultures, they would claim to be using extraordinary means to prevent harm; yet their violation of Keely is so gross that any insight into the integrity of "both sides" is lost.

By contrast, the happy resolution to Stanley Kramer's film *Guess Who's Coming to Dinner* (1967) depends on a father (Spencer Tracy) being nudged by his wife (Katharine Hepburn) to embrace the engagement of their daughter (Katharine Houghton) to a young African American doctor (Sidney Poitier). In accepting their marriage, Tracy's character enters a more expansive pattern of integrity, as do the parents of his future son-in-law (Roy Glenn and Beah Richards). Again, the story plays on the capacity of integrity to attract and repel. But it also relies on a common vocabulary of justice and respect, and on widely though not universally shared cultural paradigms, namely, romance and the liberty to marry whom one pleases. The film became a model for accepting interracial marriage—yet the story could have ended sadly. The fathers might not have changed their minds, given the complexities of their actual lives.

In the city of Oyo the tradition was that when the King (the *Oba* or *Alafin*) dies, his Horseman (the *Elesin*, an inherited chieftaincy of great status) accompanies the King to ensure his passage to the realm of the ancestors. So Elesin Oba waits in joyous equanimity for the right moment in the moon's journey to begin a trancelike dance of death, induced by chanting, drumming, and the power of his will. His community, whose cosmic security depends on his completing this dance, warns against complacency. They include Iyaloja, "mother" of the marketplace, and the Praise-Singer, whose chants will speak for the deceased Alafin and guide Elesin on his journey. But the dance is discovered by the District Officer, Simon Pilkings, who is repelled and resolved not to permit a ritual suicide while the British crown prince is visiting. For it is World War II, and H.R.H. has arrived to bolster colonial morale. Also arriving is Elesin's son, Olunde, a medical student in England. He has learned of the Alafin's death, and his coming to assume his father's heritage repels Simon's wife, the heretofore more "understanding" Jane Pilkings. Soyinka's play creates space to examine at least three integrity scenarios:

First, there is the violation of the Yoruba community, when Simon stops something a Westerner must regard as morally intolerable. Soyinka considers this the least significant aspect of the play. But from a perspective represented by the Pilkings, we are confronted with a moral dilemma between respecting persons and avoiding harm.

Second, there is an ethical crisis within the community, occasioned by Elesin's mixing of distinct paradigmatic roles. He desires to conceive a child just before his passage to the ancestors, thereby making his body a bridge to three metaphysical realms. He believes this conjoining will be auspicious, but his failure to complete the journey of death would threaten the community in its cosmos. Soyinka considers this failure to be the heart of the matter, in that it reveals the depth and power of the Yoruba worldview.[3]

Third, we are confronted with questions about the ethics of understanding. Are we obliged to understand an alien ethical horizon of meaning, when its logic would apparently threaten the integrity of our horizon? But irrespective of whether we are obliged to take seriously its moral implications, *how can we understand* another horizon if we cannot recognize the paradigms required for dialogue? Soyinka's invitation to enter another, for most of us alien, ethical world has led me to ponder a possible hermeneutical axiom, *that integrity is integrity only when complicated by alterity, by horizons or differences in which we are "pulled up short."*[4]

Metatheater and the "Clash of Cultures"

In 1979, I saw *DKH* under Soyinka's direction at Chicago's Goodman Theatre, and I retain but two impressions. First, bright color, owing to the cloth carried by the Yoruba women in Scene 1 and the *egungun* costumes in Scenes 2 and 4. But I cannot be sure, because color is about all I remember, color being a vector of knowing that bypassed my lack of understanding. Desire for understanding, my second impression. I left the theater knowing that while I had understood little, I had been affected. When much later I read the play, it struck me that my desire to understand had bumped into something Jane says to Olunde: "Your calm acceptance . . . can you explain that? It was so unnatural. I don't understand that at all. I feel I need to understand all I can" (56). And after the Women of the market fail to grasp why Elesin wants to sire a child on the eve of his death, Iyaloja says, "I dare not understand you yet Elesin" (21).

The play was opaque yet engaging when I saw it, and so was the Author's Note when I read it. The conflict is said to be "metaphysical" and is not comprehended by "clash of cultures." This would be "a prejudicial label which, quite apart from its frequent misapplication, presupposes a potential equality *in every given situation* of the alien culture and the indigenous, on the actual soil of the latter."[5] Thus, Soyinka discourages productions that would "make the District Officer the victim of a cruel dilemma." However, if *DKH* is not a clash of cultures, what is it? Soyinka contrasts his play with another version of the story, Duro Ladipo's Yoruba folk opera, *Oba Wàjà* (The King Is Dead). It refers to the same historical incident and treats more sympathetically the District Officer, who *is* being confronted with a moral dilemma. Against his better judgment, he is persuaded by his wife to arrest the Elesin and stop the suicide, to the horror of Oyo's elders and to the Elesin's shame. When the latter's son, a trader in Ghana, returns to find his father still alive, he stabs himself, whereupon the Elesin takes his own life as well. The District Officer then states his view of the tragic crux:

> I was trying to save a life—
> And I have caused a double death,
> Man only understands the good he does unto himself.
> When he acts for others,
> Good is turned into evil; evil is turned into good![6]

Ladipo's District Officer must choose between respecting another's set of norms and respecting his own. This dilemma remains implicit in *DKH*, especially in the encounter between Jane and Olunde. But Soyinka's Simon seems far less concerned about upholding moral principles than with keeping the Prince's visit from being spoiled.

Soyinka wants to avoid reducing his play to an anthropological equation. When the symbolic norms of each side are balanced or canceled out, we are left at best with an abstract insight into cultural relativity. Moreover, the irenic judgment that both systems are "equal" can only be made from some Archimedean point, upon which the adjudicator stands uncritically and which is probably closer to *the colonizer's* worldview. Soyinka wants to show how the Yoruba "metaphysical" side of this would-be equation illuminates reality far more profoundly than the colonialist side, which is only "catalytic." His Note insists that the play must illuminate "the universe of the Yoruba mind," which comprises "the world of the living, the dead and the unborn, and the numinous passage which links all: transition. *Death and the King's Horseman* can be fully realised only through an evocation of music from the abyss of transition."

If there is to be a place from which to comprehend the meaning of the conflict, it is the "abyss of transition," of which I will say more later.

Soyinka, then, is asking us to interpret the play for the knowledge of reality it may give. But the conflict of cultures is perhaps more than a catalyst here, because the play is written in the language of the colonists as well as in the cadences and imagery of Yoruba poetry. And it is offered to audiences likely to include former colonists as well as persons very familiar and very unfamiliar with the Yoruba cosmos. The *juxtaposition* of cultures—not "clash"—is built into the metatheatrical form of *DKH*. Whatever is meant by the metaphysics of transition, Soyinka means it to empty out into the witnessing audience. Hence, I want to continue for a while to approach the play as an unwitting member of the complex audience Soyinka addresses.[7]

By changing Elesin's son from a trader in Ghana to a medical student in England, an angle of vision is created that seems to hold out possibilities for understanding across horizons. In Ladipo's play, it was the wife of the District Officer who was the most ignorant, while her husband articulated tragic awareness. Soyinka reverses this, making Simon dismissive not only of Yoruba traditions but also those of his Catholic houseboy, Joseph, and his Muslim policeman, Amusa. The Pilkingses usually speak a British colonial idiom (Jane's name echoes Tarzan!), while the Elesin, the Praise-Singer, and the Women of the market speak in a high, proverbial style.[8] By shifting the action to the war,[9] Soyinka juxtaposes two cultures in crisis, contrasting a fragile Yoruba ethical world with an unassailable but vacuous British moral order. We become aware of this juxtaposition in scene 2, having moved from the Oyo market to the Pilkingses' veranda. Simon and Jane are preparing to attend a costume ball in honor of the visiting Prince. Their costumes—the Yoruba ancestral mask, or *egungun*, which covers the entire body—horrify Sgt. Amusa, who has come to warn Simon of the imminent ritual suicide. The metatheatrical ironies here are onstage and between the stage and the audience.

There is, first, the belief that the ancestral realm coexists with the realm of the living; the *egungun* masquerade ritually mediates the reality of the ancestors.[10] Sgt. Amusa (a Muslim policeman, servile and halfway assimilated) regards the ritual as being desecrated by the Pilkingses. He not only thinks they are being disrespectful of some "juju" he may still believe in, but also thinks they are behaving inappropriately to themselves. "Sir, it is a matter of death. How can man talk against death to person in uniform of death? Is like talking against government to person in uniform of police" (25).

Second, the play itself would occasion a clash with and within its audiences, both between Westerners and Africans, and possibly between contemporary Nigerian politics and Soyinka's version of the Yoruba worldview. *If* the Pilkingses are desecrating Yoruba signs, and *if* a Western audience perspective coincides momentarily with that of the Pilkingses, then will not the audience also be exposed as desecrators of the *egungun*?

However, the play creates this possibility only to transcend it. For if we *do* discover ourselves accountable to the desecration of the masquerade, we then are on the verge of encountering meanings *so important they can be desecrated.* These meanings are being substantiated—made concretely real to us—by the *egungun* forms attached to and animated by the bodies of the Pilkingses. In this surprising way, Soyinka is offering an invitation to understand these meanings and regard their realities, implying that this third relation of *irony* approaches *belief.* First, we may understand that whatever knowledge we are receiving is crucially entangled with our ignorance: we know *that* we do not know; we know *because* we do not know. But more substantively, we are invited to recognize an ethical, as opposed to moral, claim upon us, arising from a theatrical interpretation of the Yoruba cosmos. Soyinka means for the "clash of cultures" to give way to metaphysical awareness of the "abyss of transition."

Soyinka's Yoruba and Theatrical Paradigms

Let us turn away for a moment from the perspective of a less witting audience to that of the Yoruba world, as it informs the playwright's dramatic theory and practice. This world involves paradigms reflected in the play, but not always explicitly,[11] for unlike Eliot, Soyinka provides no sermonic interlude to explain the metaphysics of "transition."

In *DKH,* the import of transition, rather than cultural difference, is integral to the fiction and the dynamics of performance. The lines of actions are, first, Elesin's impulse to conceive a child right before his death; and, second, Simon's measures to prevent him from carrying out the ritual of death. These lines converge but do not meet, because Elesin's failure is irreducible to a single cause, even from the Yoruba vantage. The fading of his will at the crucial moment is attributed variously to *colonial interference, divine abandonment,* and *desire for his new bride,* and it results in loss of integration with his vocational task.[12] In the last scene, Elesin stands in a cell in the British Residency; he is in chains, shamed and bewildered, and makes several confessional interpretations of his failure—this one to the silent Bride who sits near him:

> First I blamed the white man, then I blamed the gods for deserting me. Now I feel I want to blame you for the mystery of the sapping of my will. But blame is a strange peace offering for a man to bring a world he has deeply wronged, and to its innocent dwellers. . . . I needed you as the abyss across which my body must be drawn, I filled it with earth and dropped my seed in it at the moment of preparedness for my crossing. . . . [M]y weakness came not merely from the abomination of the white man who came violently into my fading presence, there was also a weight of longing on my earth-held limbs. I would have shaken it off, already my foot had begun to lift but then, the white ghost entered and all was defiled. (65)

He also confesses to Iyaloja, who against her better judgment agreed to his marriage-before-dying; for he displaced her son, who had been betrothed to this girl. Iyaloja had agreed, hoping the union might further secure Elesin's journey and even enlarge its benefits, "as if the timelessness of the ancestor world and the unborn have joined [the ancestral] spirits to wring an issue of the elusive being of passage" (22).[13] But now concentrated in her voice is the contempt and resignation of the people of Oyo:

> IYALOJA: Who are you to open a new life when you dared not open the door to a new existence? I say who are you to make so bold? . . . Who are you to bring this abomination on us?
> ELESIN: My powers deserted me. My charms, my spells, even my voice lacked strength when I made to summon the powers that would lead me over the last measure of earth into the land of the fleshless. You saw it, Iyaloja. You saw me struggle to retrieve my will from the power of the stranger whose shadow fell across the doorway and left me foundering and blundering in a maze I had never before encountered. (67–68)

The "colonial factor" is not a *cause* so much as a phantasm in the metaphysical crisis of transition. Elesin's bewilderment is the tragic awareness that he had become lost in the abyss of transition prior even to Pilkings's intervention.

"Transition" is the crucial paradigm in Soyinka's dramatic theory and practice. He agrees that ritual and theater can integrate players and audiences into a transforming experience, in which one apprehends oneself in community and in nature—an effect of theater with political implications.[14] He nominates theater as "perhaps the most revolutionising art form," revolutionary not because it subsumes individuals into processes of social change, but because it locates and connects the strong individual in community and among "chthonic" powers of creativity and destruction. These powers are evident in African, Greek, and Shakespearean drama and even, he observes, in such a ritual of American domestic neurosis as Edward Albee's *Who's Afraid of Virginia Woolf?*[15] Soyinka believes theater can dislodge compartmentalized and alienating versions of reality precisely by realizing communal and metaphysical connections through ritual-like dynamics. This view of theater owes something to Nietzsche, Brecht, and to his mentor at the University of Leeds, the Shakespeare scholar G. Wilson Knight.

But Soyinka's work claims principal provenance in the universe of Yoruba traditions, of which he develops a distinctive interpretation. While this worldview is historically particular, he offers its ontology as a claim on all. In "The Fourth Stage"—an essay he managed to prepare for a festschrift for Knight before becoming a political prisoner in Nigeria in 1967—he describes a region that surrounds three separate but contemporaneous realms of the living, the ancestral dead, and the unborn. The fourth, the metaregion, is one of chaos and nondifferentiation, an abyss that is alien yet near at hand. It is the ontological, existential, and social reality of *transition* that Soyinka finds implicit in Yoruba myth and cosmos.

Of the Yoruba *orisa* (god or gods) that interest Soyinka, it is Obatala and most especially Ogun who define the implications of transition.[16] Obatala is a creator god, whom Soyinka calls the serene *orisa* of "plastic healing" and "patient suffering," whose function is to create the outward forms of human beings, into which the supreme *orisa*, Olorun, breathes life. Ogun is a god of war, hunting, of iron and tool craft, even a maker of roads.[17] Soyinka regards various *oriki,* or praise-chants, as suggestive of how Ogun can be more profoundly understood as the god of creative essence, or the unity of creative and destructive impulses. The *orisa* can serve as paradigms for both divine and human action, because many of them crossed the gulf of transition. Ogun was a great warrior, Obatala an artist, Sango a legendary Oyo king, and many myths and ritual dramas tell of events associated with their apotheoses.

Soyinka calls Ogun the "first actor." In Prometheus-like *hubris,* he challenged the transitional void, was torn asunder and survived by the assertion of his will, to reemerge, "incorporating within himself so many contradictory attributes [that he] represents the closest conception to the original oneness of Orisa-nla."[18] Ogun's passage recapitulates the cosmogonic act when a first *orisa* was fragmented, and others collected the scattered pieces and ordered the world, albeit imperfectly. Ogun is the paradigm of "the actor in ritual drama. . . . [who] prepares mentally and physically for his disintegration and re-assembly within the universal womb of origin, [and] experiences the transitional yet inchoate matrix of death and being."[19] Characters embodying his spirit confront stagnation or oppression, in a *tradition* that exalts in *revolutionary* challenges.[20]

When Soyinka compares Obatala and Ogun with Apollo and Dionysus, as understood by Nietzsche, the differences are as important as the parallels. Soyinka is at pains to emphasize the essential realism of both Yoruba deities. Obatala is not well understood as

> Nietzsche's Apollonian "mirror of enchantment" but as a statement of world resolution. The mutual tempering of illusion and will, necessary to an understanding of the Hellenic spirit, may mislead us, when we are faced with Yoruba art, for much of it has a similarity in its aesthetic serenity to the plastic arts of the Hellenic. Yoruba traditional art is not ideational however, but "essential". . . .
>
> Ogun, for his part, is best understood in Hellenic values as a totality of the Dionysian, Apollonian and Promethean virtues. . . . Ogun stands for a transcendental, humane but rigidly restorative justice. . . . The first artist and technician of the forge, he evokes like Nietzsche's Apollonian spirit, a "massive impact of image, concept, ethical doctrine and sympathy." Obatala is the placid essence of creation; Ogun the creative urge and instinct, the essence of creativity.[21]

The insistence that Ogun and Obatala connote irreducible realities, means that Soyinka's hermeneutics is ontological or, as he says, metaphysical. He is thus liable to charges of essentialism or African logocentrism. But in his essays and imaginative works the abyss of transition appears indeterminate, the ultimate question as well as ultimate referent. Transition marks an intrinsically self-dispossessing moment in Soyinka's vision. For transition is realized in performative *praxis,* which in ritual, onstage, or in political life entails disintegration as well as transformation. Any reintegration, while possibly liberating, will likely be provisional. If the aim of Yoruba ethics is a harmony among the realms—living, dead, and unborn—such harmony is qualified by awareness of self's and community's possible dissolution as well as integration. What holds for self and community may also hold for acts of understanding.

DKH is also about the ambiguities of embodying the paradigms of Ogun and Obatala. Olunde, the medical student in England, would be a figure of Obatala, in that this *orisa* is a paradigm of healing and reconciling opposites. Obatala can be the patient saint, ransomed prisoner, patron of cripples and the malformed, of albinos—in part because he unwittingly caused their suffering. Once, drunk on palm wine, he slipped while he was molding the bodies of people (and so he forbade palm wine to his devotees thereafter). There is a sense in which, as Elesin desires to conceive a child at the intersection of the three realms, he forgets the paradigm of Ogun for that of Obatala. (This confusion of paradigms is no less suggestive when we know that Ogun too was a seeker of women and abuser of palm wine.)[22] Elesin's failure to conjoin the paradigms of Ogun and Obatala—as was perhaps the intent he claimed—is, then, what requires Olunde to assume prematurely the paradigm of Ogun.

As Elesin ventures toward the abyss, he does *properly* risk the disintegration of his being. But he also puts at risk his understanding, and later confesses to Iyaloja, "I need neither your pity nor the pity of the world. I need understanding. Even I need to understand" (69). At the edge of transition, he was defeated by an intruding, impossible notion: that in the white man's intervention there might be a divine reprieve.

> It is when the alien hand pollutes the source of will, when a stranger force of violence shatters the mind's calm resolution, this is when a man is made to commit the awful treachery of relief, commit in his thought the unspeakable blasphemy of seeing the hand of the gods in this alien rupture of the world. I know it was this thought that killed me, sapped my powers. . . . My will was squelched in the spittle of an alien race, and all because I had committed this blasphemy of thought—that there might be the hand of the gods in a stranger's intervention. (69)

Integrity, Alterity, and Understanding

We have now encountered alterity, or otherness, in two senses. We have met the one who performs cultural signs or ethical paradigms, with whom we might come to share a space of understanding, if in dialogue we put at risk or revise our claims to understand.[23] Soyinka is by no means despairing of dialogical alterity, but fears it may degenerate into "clash of cultures" talk, which can domesticate or demonize the other. Shortly I will look at another possible instance of culture clash in *DKH;* however, the play points to a more radical sense of alterity. What ultimately dislocates Elesin is not merely the speaker of other meanings (hermeneutical difference), nor the indeterminacy of signs (Derrida's *différance*), but an active abyss of transition that threatens performance in life even while providing possibilities for performance.

Does such alterity make integrity meaningless, an illusion masking how every soul is a muddle of scripts and performances with no whole, no center, no end, and threatened by the trickster *orisa*, Esu, or the mental clouding the Greeks called *atē*? Or if the integrity of wholeness and rightness is somehow real, will it nonetheless prove impossible to apprehend across cultural difference *and* metaphysical "transition"? Elesin represents the ontological side of the issue: integrity requires performance and others who cooperate in the performance, but his performance is interrupted. In the abyss he must cross, Simon is one danger; another is to confuse the paradigms of Ogun and Obatala. Jane and Olunde represent the epistemological side: to recognize the other's integrity entails *relinquishing as well as seeking* understanding.

1. For Elesin, integrity entails the give and take of performance. The *give,* obviously, is that his personal life is also a public mission. Being true to himself coincides with being true to the vocation of King's Horseman; had he successfully performed the dance of transition he would have been, in that dance, most completely himself. His community would have been complete as well, for its integrity and that of Elesin are mutually implicated in vocation and performance. Elesin's lively parody ("like a born raconteur, infecting his retinue with his humour and energy," 11) of those who flee death (the "Not-I bird") ends with a self-asserting expression of hubris: he boasts that unlike others in the song, he welcomes and has no fear of the Not-I bird. Such hubris is not always a fault in Soyinka's Yoruba world, but a dangerous yet necessary presumption authorized by the hubris of the *orisa* Ogun,[24] to which the people of Oyo give assent as he promises to perform his passage successfully:

ELESIN: . . . Not-I
  Flew happily away, you'll hear his voice
  No more in this lifetime—You all know
  What I am.

PRAISE-SINGER: That rock which turns its open lodes
    Into the path of lightning. A gay
    Thoroughbred whose stride disdains
    To falter though an adder reared
    Suddenly in its path.
ELESIN: My rein is loosened.
    I am master of my Fate. When the hour comes
    Watch me dance along the narrow path
    Glazed by the soles of my precursors.
    My soul is eager. I shall not turn aside. (14)

And so the *take:* Elesin's integrity depends on the performance of others, especially the elaborate praise chants that encourage him but further establish his character. Referring to Ladipo's *Oba Wàjà,* Robert Plant Armstrong considers praise names to be a "syndetic" or "additive" means of constituting character. "They represent an effective way . . . to bring a dramatic or a fictive character into existence."[25] In *DKH,* Iyaloja, the Praise-Singer, and the Women endow, through their praise, power to Elesin:

WOMEN: For a while we truly feared
    Our hands had wrenched the world adrift
    In emptiness.
IYALOJA: Richly, richly, robe him richly
    The cloth of honour is *alari*
    Sanyan is the band of friendship
    Boa-skin makes slippers of esteem
WOMEN: For a while we truly feared
    Our hands had wrenched the world adrift
    In emptiness.
PRAISE-SINGER: He who must, must voyage forth
    The world will not roll backwards
    It is he who must, with one
    Great gesture overtake the world. (17)

Much later, Iyaloja and the Praise-Singer confront the captured Elesin, and they present him with the body of Olunde, hidden in cloth, cloth which has been emblematic of enriched personality and power. Their words to Elesin enunciate his shame—yet urge him on to a last belated performance, to speak to Olunde, now on the way through the passage of transition.

ELESIN: . . . Take off the cloth. I shall speak my message from
heart to heart of silence.

IYALOJA (moves forward and removes the covering): . . . The son
has proven the father Elesin, and there is nothing left in your
mouth to gnash but infant gums.

PRAISE-SINGER: Elesin, we placed the reins of the world in your
hands yet you watched it plunge over the edge of the bitter
precipice. You sat with folded arms while evil strangers tilted
the world from its course and crashed it beyond the edge of
emptiness. . . . Your heir has taken the burden on himself. What
the end will be, we are not gods to tell. But this young shoot
has poured its sap into the parent stalk, and we know this is not
the way of life. Our world is tumbling in the void of strangers,
Elesin. (75)

Then Elesin, standing "rock-still," stares through the bars at Olunde's
body, a body with which he cannot now align. Elesin does not speak, but
garrotes himself with his looped iron chain.

If Elesin is lost in a confusion of paradigms—enamored of Obatala
when Ogun is required—then Olunde has picked up the pieces of his
father's shattered integrity by moving from the medicine of Obatala to
the venture of Ogun. Elesin had opposed his son's plans, disinheriting
him; and while nothing is said of it, that may be a reason for his desiring to conceive a child. Yet Olunde returns. What makes this reversal of
paradigms ironic is that improvising on tradition is part of the comic
genius of the Yoruba[26] (as when the Girls at the market in Scene 3 perfectly "play-act" the idiom of the English while humiliating Sgt. Amusa).
Iyaloja accuses Simon of interfering with an ultimate improvisation:

> you who play with strangers' lives, who even usurp the vestments of
> our dead, yet believe that the stain of death will not cling to you. The
> gods demanded only the old expired plantain but you cut down the
> sap-laden root to feed your pride. (76)

The alternative view, and finally Elesin's, is that Simon was *not* the cause
but merely a "ghostly one,"[27] an ephemeron in the abyss, another contingent obstacle Elesin failed to surmount as desire for the realm of the
living weakened him. When he strangles himself with iron, is he not still
seeking reintegration with Ogun?[28] If so it is late, and little would mitigate the impression that we have witnessed the dissolution of a world.

Little, unless it would be the play's last line, spoken as the Bride places earth on the eyes of Elesin, whose child she may carry. Iyaloja tells her, "Now forget the dead, forget even the living. Turn your mind only to the unborn" (76).

Have we been prepared to accept these deaths as acts straining after integrity? Or does the scene leave us the unwitting strangers we were when we arrived, unaware of the Yoruba paradigms? And if we translate the climax in terms of honor and shame, then are we trading in the anthropology of culture clash?

2. To be sure, Scene 4 invites this trade, and recapitulates the play's relation to its diverse audience. At the masked ball, the Pilkingses are in *egungun* costumes, entertaining the Prince. Simon leaves to investigate Amusa's report of a riot, and Jane immediately encounters Olunde, in Western dress, who has arrived to receive his father's body, assuming that Elesin has made his passage to the ancestors. Jane has admired Olunde for studying Western medicine; and while he thinks the English "have no respect for what [they] do not understand," he tells Jane that he has found her "somewhat more understanding" than Simon (50, 52). But now he accuses her of desecrating ancestral masks, and she is repelled to learn of his determination to participate fully in the traditions of his people—as if he was desecrating his tailored suit! Part of what repels her are his two intentions, to become a medical doctor *and* the next King's Horseman.

Their debate reaches a hysterical impasse—"You're just a savage like all the rest," she screams (55)—and is interrupted by an officer who would arrest Olunde. She stops him, and the interruption allows her to "recover herself." When the conversation resumes, Jane admits her incomprehension. There is a note of condescension here, but she begins to grasp her absence of understanding. "Your calm acceptance for instance, can you explain that? It was so unnatural. I don't understand that at all. I feel a need to understand all I can." Their dialogue swings between the words *understand* and *explain,* almost illustrating Ricoeur's dialectic: where understanding is the beginning and the aim of interpretation, while explanation critically enriches understanding.

> OLUNDE: But you explained it yourself. My medical training perhaps. I have seen death too often. And the soldiers who returned from the front, they died on our hands all the time.
> JANE: No. It has to be more than that. I feel it has to do with the many things we don't really grasp about your people. At least you can explain. (56)

And Olunde does explain. Despite having been apparently disowned by his father—"a man of tremendous will. Sometimes that's another way of saying stubborn"—Olunde, upon receiving news of the King's death, began mourning his father's. He immediately accepted Elesin's duty, his own, and that of the community. "Even if I had died before him I would still be buried like his eldest son" (57). Jane has no more than an ephemeral understanding, but she has at least that, and is beginning to relinquish self-possession. Earlier in their conversation, Olunde has confessed his own inability to fathom the West; he has been surprised by its capacities for sacrifice and survival.

> By all logical and natural laws this war should end with all the white races wiping out one another . . . and reverting to a state of primitivism the like of which has so far only existed in your imagination when you thought of us. I thought all that at the beginning. Then slowly I realised that your greatest art is the art of survival. But at least have the humility to let others survive in their own way. (53)

Jane and Olunde have both begun revising their visions. Her use of "understanding" and "your people" can be played as satire, but the seriousness of Olunde's replies gives both sides of their exchange a degree of seriousness, before we encounter the catastrophe of the last scene.

Moral and Ethical Improvisations

At the end of *Keely and Du,* long after the main action, Du has suffered a stroke, is on Prozac, and in prison. Keely visits, trying but still unable to forgive. She chatters at length about her life, and Du replies with a single word, "Why?" There is something right about this. The debate between life and choice, never adequately articulated, is set aside. What brings Keely to Du is acknowledgment of an odd and fragile relationship. But there is also something not right, if we feel the playwright has dispatched Du abruptly, withholding her narrative. Even so, we can at least debate what kind of ending this is. There is less debating *Guess Who's Coming to Dinner.* It was a good sermon, seeking to secure its audience in convictions that, by 1967, it should have already come to, even if it had not. Spencer Tracy isn't so much in a dilemma as he is being encouraged by Katharine Hepburn, his praise-singer, to stand by his convictions.

Death and the King's Horseman does open space for improvisation. In Ricoeur's terms, it juxtaposes British moral obligation with Yoruba ethical vision, but does so from a horizon that is neither Western nor even simply Yoruba, a horizon that unsettles explanations. It creates a demand for improvised understanding. Understanding, for Ricoeur, is implicitly an *ethical* dimension, in that it involves the dispossession of the narcissistic ego.[29] The *moral* is explanatory, because principles help validate and clarify the ethical, just as explanation "tests" understanding. But the ethical, involving the indeterminate concretions of the "good" in life, is not reducible to ideal principles. Ethical dimensions are witnessed, attested to, even explained but not explained away. Thus, a pattern of integrity could be thought of as an improvisation of the moral, and the ethical, with the personal. For the ethical life requires ensembles—other people, ideas, and paradigms—as we perform responsibilities and aspirations together.

When Elesin aspired to mix the paradigm of death with paradigms of marriage and birth, the Women of the market sensed the danger of this improvisation, but did not "understand" it. He replies in verse that his "seed," not needed in the ancestral realm, might yet "take root/In the earth of my choice, in this earth/I leave behind" (21). Iyaloja appears either to understand or acquiesce: "[I]t is good that your loins be drained into the earth we know; that last strength be ploughed back into the womb that gave you being" (22). Soon the Women will rue this "Esu-harassed day"—yet on another day it might have been that Elesin would succeed in his dance of birth-astride-death, all the way across the "fourth stage."

Realizing a pattern of integrity, on this account, is a matter of contingency and of discovery. It is to discover one's accountability to a dynamic nexus of relations: with histories and traditions; with religious and moral paradigms; with communities, economies, politics, and vocations; with other persons, nature, reason, circumstance; and with anticipations of possible futures. The body and brain give a material "center" to these relations, marking our being here or being there. But the body is a center subject to disintegration and change, pain and healing; later I will discuss how our bodies are strangers to ourselves. Integrity, then, would entail finding and losing ourselves in these relations, attempting to "integrate" them, even though they are fragmented and even though we always know too little and too late. These uncertain relations contribute to the very constitution of the self, but in a way that makes claims to sheer self-possession an illusion. Character, then, describes a self for whom "integration," "coherence," and "wholeness" are at once aims and problems, a self whose integrity is realized but partially and often only in the aspect of some future, in the realm of the "unborn."

As a partial realization of integrity, understanding has a moral dimension. It must improvise its obligations to "do justice" and "care about" and "not harm" the very meanings it would understand and those of the horizon from which it understands. Part of this obligation entails regard for inherent limits of understanding, and whether understanding meets such obligations will be as contingent as it is in *Death and the King's Horseman*.

As we watch aesthetically and critically, we may recognize that the colonial world has somehow intersected Elesin's world, with disastrous results. We may or may not recognize the paradigms of those worlds, or we may misidentify them. We may leave the theater impressed that we have seen and heard—even known—something astonishing and, as well, that we do not understand what we have known. And our responses may be more complicated than that. If, for us, *DKH* transcends culture clash we will resist fixation on cultural relativism. We will refrain from concluding only that "the British do not comprehend the Africans, or the Africans the British." We may also find we cannot fully account for the play's revelation by saying, "Because I have cultural paradigms, I can recognize that others have paradigms." Our deeper response may come as we intuit, first, that just as paradigms are "realized," "effected," or "instantiated"[30] in being performed, they are—as they are in Yoruba mythology—also "created" in performance. Then, to the extent we find ourselves implicated in this particular story and performance, we may also find ourselves acknowledging a claim made on ourselves. "These possibilities are possible for us." For the moment, the empty space of the theater is *realizing us* in its improvisations of integrity. Our bodies are juxtaposed with ethical paradigms appearing in theatrical space, inviting us to lend this space our embodied realities. We may accept or refuse this invitation to be recreated—because its personal and moral implications will need further examination.

Part II

Dramatis Personae and
the Eclipse of Personal Integrity

Give every man thy ear, but few thy voice;
Take each man's censure but reserve thy judgment.
Costly thy habit as thy purse can buy
But not expressed in fancy—rich, not gaudy;
For the apparel oft proclaims the man
And they in France of the best rank and station
Are of all most select and generous chief in that.
Neither a borrower nor a lender be,
For loan oft loses both itself and friend
And borrowing dulleth th'edge of husbandry.
This above all, to thine own self be true
And it must follow as the night the day
Thou canst not then be false to any man.

—POLONIUS TO LAERTES, *Hamlet* 1.3, 67–79

LET THE LINES ITALICIZED serve as a common maxim for *personal* as distinct from *moral* integrity: be, in all matters, true to oneself. Rather than aligning the body with an abstract or extrinsic principle, the paradigm of personal integrity would be *to align one's body with oneself,* apparently the inward self. Polonius, apart from other common "precepts" in his speech, implies a priority of inner before outer, of who we are behind our masks before who we are in front of them. One economic implication of this congruence is that integrity is inherently *relational*. A more worrisome economic implication is that integrity is something to *own* or even trade upon.

Polonius is blessing his son, Laertes, who is about to travel to another society. He wants him to fare honorably among the Parisians. So he advises that if Laertes can keep his inward and outward manifestations of selfhood congruent and constant, then he will not be false to anyone he is likely to meet. Like the liar's paradox, such categorical-yet-conditional statements concerning truth, self, and others are notoriously hard to parse. But let us suppose that instead of saying "Thou canst not then *be* false," Polonius had said, "you cannot then *prove* false." He would then be implying two reasons why integrity is valued. First, the *congruence* between inward thoughts and outward acts is expected to *communicate across personal and social differences*. If you align your body with your hidden depths, then those you meet will have fewer reasons to puzzle over what they see, even if you and they have opposing interests or habits of being. Integrity of this sort is valued for creating trust, especially when reliance on the mutual recognition of integrity is all there is to go on. Second, integrity would be *a guard or shield*.[1] If you are true to yourself, others will be unable to corrupt you. These two meanings are not irreconcilable, but they do create tensions. And the theatrical milieu in which Polonius and Shakespeare speak provided ways of exploring these tensions, ambiguities, and ambivalences.

Sincerity and Authenticity

Polonius, not without reason, is often portrayed as a vacuous hypocrite, and his maxim can sound hollow given the rest of his speech. Indeed, he later sends a man to spy on Laertes in Paris, just as he will spy on Hamlet; so we are not well disposed to trust his thoughts on true selves. Perhaps what his maxim really reflects is anxiety about *honor,* which in Polonius's era meant external *reputation*.[2] However, Lionel Trilling urges us to give Polonius his due. "To thine own self be true" seems to come upon him in a moment of self-transcending epiphany. Unexpectedly, the old apparatchik has articulated a value emerging in Renaissance consciousness, that of *sincerity*. In fact, Trilling thinks he also marks the beginning of a trajectory toward another value, *authenticity*. One question to be explored in part II is how sincerity and authenticity might be values that can *eclipse* the personal relationality that we hope to understand through paradigms of integrity. In any case, Trilling believes Polonius's maxim registers the new emergence of sincerity as "the congruence between avowal and actual feeling."[3]

Why this emergence? Many have noted how social mobility creates the possibility of re-tailoring identity.[4] Stephen Greenblatt, in *Will in the World,* imagines that Shakespeare—son of a failed, debt-ridden glove maker and local magistrate who yet died an affluent "gentleman"—had to undertake such "self-fashioning" and discovered in commercial theater a way to do it.[5] Trilling mentions another case of cultivated reticence to self-reveal. Elizabeth I—daughter of Anne Boleyn by Henry VIII, sister of the Catholic Queen Mary Tudor—had to watch from the Tower of London as Protestants and Catholics struggled for ascendancy. The princess could only keep her head if she kept her ecclesiastical preferences obscured by outward conformity. The theme of thwarted election in *Hamlet* might have brought Elizabeth to mind. In short, Trilling thinks that sincerity became valued in a milieu where one dreaded being fooled by social dissemblers. However, by the time of Romanticism, the climate had changed and another value emerged, authenticity: being an original, *not an imitation,* but one's own model. Among the literati, to uphold the social norm of sincerity could itself seem insincere, like an *actor playing a part.* In Rousseau, Hegel, Heidegger, and Sartre *authenticity* connotes the "sentiment of being" of the *poet*-genius, or the individual who creates selfhood uncomplicated by society's opinions, tastes, or mores.[6] Today, however, we may note another change. For Emmanuel Levinas, sincerity means ethical receptivity to exteriority, to others in suffering; sincerity is solicitude in life's ensembles where suffering calls us to play.[7] In any case, Trilling urges us not to discount Polonius. Yet Shakespeare is ambivalent. The maxim of sincerity is spoken by the "wretched, rash, intruding fool" Hamlet mistakenly kills. However, had Polonius been as concerned with truth as he was with honor, he might have put his finger on another sort of integrity. Yes, he seems to contradict himself: be sincere, but let not your sincerity show too much. Act so as *not* to disclose the congruence of your true feelings with your actions. But he might also have meant: your costume matters; you should attend to how you, *along with your fellow actors,* play your parts together. Had he meant something like that, then it would bear on the role- and other-relatedness of integrity. Hamlet also reflects these theatrical complexities. As he watches the affections of Gertrude and Claudius, he expresses condemnation by wearing apparel fitting for mourning, yet he cannot say what he most feels. "But I have that within which passes show,/These but the trappings and the suits of woe" (I.2.85–86). And then, "But break, my heart, for I must hold my tongue" (l. 159).

Integrity Eclipsed in the Mirror of Theater?

Shakespeare frequently does privilege interior over outer manifestations when he compares "true" life to life lived on the stage.[8] Acting can mark our lives as ephemeral. In the "All the world's a stage" speech of *As You Like It,* we exit our last scene "Sans teeth, sans eyes, sans taste, sans everything." But elsewhere he employs positive theatrical tropes, implying that in playing parts we may come to inhabit patterns of integrity. It is true that notions such as "art is at a third remove from reality," "hypocrisy as false show," and "*merely* wearing a mask" do not comport well with integrity. The idea that integrity emerges in theater-like modes of life is not one that arrives immediately. We generally lack, *but are not entirely without,* language that articulates how persons may come into themselves through embodying parts to play with others. The chapters in part II explore this ambivalence.

We have begun to see how integrity discourse is about holding together *being a person* with *being right or good.* We are uncomfortable speaking of "pirates with integrity." Pirates were and are economic "terrorists" or "gangsters." Yet pirates of yore had cultures, loyalties, codes, virtues, even standards of best practice, which seems horribly true of terrorist enterprises today. Pirate lore of Shakespeare's time suggests "a way of life," which Greenblatt likens to an improvisation of "legitimate" commerce and power.[9] This should caution us that accounts of integrated selves and societies based on forms of life and practice, cultural narratives, and even virtues such as courage cannot altogether satisfy our expectation that the wholeness of integrity should also be good. Typically, there are no "good pirates," and in exceptions such as Robin Hood norms get reshuffled. Robin robbed from the rich, gave to the poor, and did so with élan or joy.

Our desire to hold—and the difficulty of holding—"in a single vision,"[10] *the personal* and *the good* are why notions of integrity are important yet problematic. Rather than trying to synthesize the moral/ethical and the personal, we can think of these dimensions as "juxtaposed" in patterns of integrity. A person may "hold" the moral and personal in proximity. Or a person may "find" that, given some particular shaping of oneself, the personal and moral have both been in play. Such holding and finding *are* part of the pattern of one's ethos—at a given moment, or at many such moments, or over a lifetime of moments. The plays in part II help us explore such juxtaposing from the vantage of the personal. An advantage of drama is in how it realizes that inhabiting an ethos requires encounter and improvisation, even when the "part to play" or the principles to follow are well established. The Good Samaritan, I will later suggest, would have had to improvise his goodness the first time and to a different extent the umpteenth time he showed mercy. Drama helps us, along with other resources, reconceptualize integrity.

Still, our linguistic inheritance makes us cautious. *Improvisation* is a neutral term that suggests the question, who gets to improvise? Is improvisation only an avatar of will-to-power? That would be a good question for *Hamlet,* in chapter IV. Moreover, not only can theatricality be a trope for hypocrisy, but roles can be occasions of inauthenticity, as can be observed through the "naturalism" of many late-nineteenth-century dramas. In such plays, social roles, rather than fostering ludic or liminal aspects of persons-in-community, appeared to paralyze persons in their neuroses, classes, genders, households, et cetera. I will examine this in chapter V, reflecting on Strindberg, Ibsen, Chekhov, Stanislavski, and two theologians. Hans Urs von Balthasar thinks the self in realistic drama is ever unable to unite potentially alienating "roles" and self-transcending "missions." Tom F. Driver thinks the integrity of modern realism (which might begin with Hamlet's directions to the players) is eclipsed or comes to its "end" with Samuel Beckett, when theater in effect holds its mirror to itself and becomes lost in infinite self-reflection.

Sometimes, however, assessments of this eclipse seem wedded to what they are judging, namely a certain *reducing of imitation to objectification,* rather than envisioning imitation as a mutual participation with what is imitated—where both roles and selves may be transformed without utter loss of selves. Consider how Jean-Paul Sartre describes an awkwardly efficient waiter in a café, whose authentic selfhood is emptied into an imitation of being a waiter.

> He comes toward the patrons with a step a little too quick. He bends forward a little too eagerly; his voice, his eyes express an interest a little too solicitous for the order of the customer. Finally there he returns, trying to imitate in his walk the inflexible stiffness of some kind of automaton while carrying his tray with the recklessness of a tight-rope-walker by putting it in a perpetually unstable, perpetually broken equilibrium which he perpetually re-establishes by a light movement of the arm and hand. All his behavior seems to us a game.

Sartre's point is that the waiter, as he plays the game of being a waiter, is *objectified* both by the game—"his gestures and even his voice seem to be mechanisms; he gives himself the quickness and pitiless rapidity of things"[11]—and by a milieu that imprisons people in class or social roles.

Yet Sartre's description is almost *delightful*! Were actors such as Charlie Chaplin, Lucille Ball, Marcel Marceau, or Robin Williams to play Sartre's waiter, the result would certainly be delightful. Why delight? Why wouldn't we find them merely ludicrous? Because "The Waiter" can be played with such grace and wit as to elicit delight in the unexpected freedom and joy, as well as pathos, that such an actor might *bring to* and *discover in* the part of being a waiter. The delight we share with that actor or even with an actual waiter (working with a different spirit than Sartre imagined) may register an *intimation* of kenotic integrity. That is, in the aligning of oneself (i.e., the self one has been) with the part of being a "waiter" today (among other waiters, chefs, customers, maître d's, part-time actors, and café philosophers), there is, to be sure, a gap, a distance, a lack of fit. But the gap in the alignment may be thought of as "space" in which to await the arrival of future others, including *the arrival of oneself with others*. That theme will mostly have to wait until part IV. But this intimation of kenotic emptying into others receptively, along with our *reticence to name it integrity,* is examined in chapter VI, regarding integrity Bernard Shaw inadvertently discovered in the persona of Eliza Doolittle.

Chapter IV

"Who's There?"

Hamlet Between Dilemma and Delight

HAMLET: He that plays the King shall be welcome—his majesty shall
have tribute on me—the Adventurous Knight shall use his foil and
target, the Lover shall not sigh gratis, the Humorous Man shall end
his part in peace, the Clown shall make those laugh . . . , and the Lady
shall say her mind freely or the blank verse shall halt for't. What
players are they?
ROSENCRANTZ: Even those you were wont to take such delight in, the
tragedians of the city.

—Hamlet, II.2.285–92 WF

HAMLET: I'll observe his looks,
I'll tent him to the quick. If he but blench,
I know my course.

—II.2.531–33 WF

AN ORANGE SQUARE of carpet on a low thrust stage. The lucky ground-
lings in the front row sat on pillows, lap-level with the players. Props
included cushions and multicolored rugs. Bamboo sticks were swords
or shovels. Oil lamps lit space for "The Murder of Gonzago," the play-
within-the-play. There were plastic skulls for the graveyard scene. Upstage, under the proscenium arch, Toshi Tsuchitori played Japanese
instruments. Hamlet was Adrian Lester, a black man with dreadlocks.
Jeffrey Kissoon, a Jamaican, played both the Ghost of King Hamlet and
King Claudius. Ophelia (Shantala Shivalingpappa) and two multi-part
players (Naseerudin Shah and Rohan Siva) were Indian. The rest (Scott

Handy as Horatio, Bruce Myers as Polonius and the Gravedigger, Natasha Parry as Gertrude) were Anglo.

They were directed by Peter Brook,[1] whose book *The Empty Space* (1968) evokes the revelatory ephemerae of the stage, where persons are transformed through motion and language. In theater's expectant emptiness bodies and worlds appear, then disappear in potentially "rough and holy" spaces.[2] Brook has been a definer of late modern theater. Thus, it was with anticipation and trepidation that audiences greeted his transformation of *The Tragedy of Hamlet* in 2000–2001. After all, ideas of transformation or metamorphosis can have dreadful associations. To trans-form something can destroy its form. To undergo metamorphosis can be to lose oneself. While transformation in theater connotes something good (as it does in ethical and religious contexts), benign images of transformation are sometimes invoked as screens that obscure our complicity in power or violence. So knowing that this English play, an icon of both theater and violence, was being "adapted" by Peter Brook was to have one's expectations raised dizzily.

He drastically reduced it to what would perform uninterrupted in less than two hours. In the program he wrote, "Our task today is not one of finding new ways of staging an old play—there's hardly a device left that hasn't been squeezed dry. This adaptation seeks to prune away the inessential, for beneath the surface lies the myth. This is the mystery that we will attempt to explore." *Hamlet*'s mystery surely has to do with the protean nature of persons, which is arguably part of the good of being "infinite in faculties." If Brook succeeded, it was because he sought the play's essence less in its thematic possibilities (political, sexual, moral) and more in its evocation of the phenomenon of theater itself.

The plays-within-the-play ("Pyrrhus" and "Gonzago") were given centermost time and attention, complete with the problematic dumb show. Brook knows *Hamlet* to be a play about theater, and he framed it with a question about identity. Since he cut the sentinel scene with Bernardo and Francisco, things began with Horatio himself sensing a ghostly presence. He utters Bernardo's question, "Who's there?" And since the invasion of Fortinbras was also cut, a new closing speech was needed. After Hamlet's death, the dead onstage rose. Standing with Horatio they peered out into a future where we in the audience now dwell: "But look, the morn in russet mantle clad / Walks o'er the dew of yon high eastward hill. Who's there?"[3]

The rest of the script was also drastically cut, rearranged, and supplemented. Upon arriving in Elsinore the First Player answers Hamlet's request for the Pyrrhus speech in lines I assumed then were faux Greek,[4] with an incantatory emotion that arose from deep in the chest. When Hamlet tried the speech, the result was funny and indeed Brook found much comedy in this tragedy. Later the Gravedigger did an Irish jig, a spoof on Riverdance. Propped-up cushions indicated Ophelia's grave, behind which the Gravedigger could dig and disappear. As he joked, he cited scripture. Hamlet put Yorick's skull on a bamboo stick and chatted as with a Charlie McCarthy puppet. For Ophelia's burial, a length of bright red cloth served as her body. And Hamlet's first lines—moved to come after the Ghost appears to Horatio but before we meet Gertrude and Claudius—were from his first soliloquy: "O that this too too sallied flesh would melt, / Thaw and resolve itself into a dew" (I.2. 129–30).

To say this speech in advance of its motivation in the text (Hamlet's observing his uncle and mother's hasty bliss) was to make it a more universal comment on human mystery and misery. What was most distinctive about Brook's *Hamlet* was how it was at once a most bodily and a most thoughtful play. It was filled with movement, yet the soliloquies and asides invited us into the nuances of a nimble mind. Lester was gifted at thinking as if in conversation with those seated near him, then would skip back behind the fourth wall. I could not tell if he said "solid," "sullied," or "sallied," a famous textual conundrum. Is melting or transformed flesh a trope for theater? In its empty spaces and at its best, bodies and minds transform together.

Yet Hamlet and Shakespeare seem ambivalent about this "best." Locating the *good of theater* in *Hamlet* depends on respecting its many inconsistencies or gaps. But trying to distill the "essence" of *Hamlet* is to risk reducing these gaps to a disfiguring coherence. I will explore this risk by rehearsing the oft-told stories of Hamlet's personal-versus-moral dilemma, of Hamlet-on the cusp-of-modernity, and of Hamlet-as-maker-of-theater. The terms of his dilemma are in part medieval, in part modern, and are so intractable that Hamlet must invent his own ethical paradigm. Invention is an aspect of his modernity. The strategy he devises is at once sciencelike and theatrical and succeeds mainly by accident. Yet also available to him is another strategy from theater, presciently postmodern: *the transformation of the person through playing parts or roles with other persons, for other persons.* This I am calling a kenotic pattern. As a constitutive feature of being a person, its significance was long in eclipse, due in no small part to the enigmas of identity and representation we associate with *Hamlet*.

Gaps

Who's there? In reply to postmodern critiques of the substantial self, Paul Ricoeur and Calvin Schrag argue that the self should be conceptualized not as "what" but "Who?"[5] Who-questions are typically answered with names, that is, with identities, and postmodernity has transformed modern, existential questions of meaning and individual identity into questions of mixed communal identity. "With whom may we identify?" This is the question that appears (culturally, ideologically, religiously) most in need of anchorage. However, there is a sense in which Brook's *Hamlet* was a reversion to the older, modern question of meaning. In seeking the play's essence, he wagered that *Hamlet* can speak humanistically to all times and places. To this wager, Milan Kundera might object that such reveling in the oneness of humanity is a kind of kitsch—a totalitarian kitsch, be it communist, fascist, religious, or democratic.[6] Yet Peter Brook may be resisting a certain postmodern kitsch that revels in the *futility* of communication across the gaps between languages and communal identities. About the time Brook was adapting *Hamlet,* Harold Bloom, another late modernist, entitled a book *Shakespeare: The Invention of the Human* and meant its title to be taken literally.[7]

Most answers to "Who's there?" posit the integrity of identity. That is, to answer a query of identity with a person's name at least says, *she is herself, this one and not another.* So patterns of integrity may appear in response to the question, "Who?" However, I have also been suggesting that not only does integrity discourse connote the *wholeness of identity* but also *relationality among parts,* which introduces tensions between parts or fragments to notions of integrity. When we inquire after "Who's there?" we cannot simply assume the wholeness of an identity. Theater knows that no one is ever *only* or *wholly* all of oneself. With cues from Brook and Shakespeare, I think four problematic "integrities" are suggested by Horatio's question.

1. Brook's many liberties encourage us to ponder the *integrity of the script.* Shakespeare had his "sources."[8] There is a twelfth-century tale from Saxo Grammaticus and a 1576 version of it by François de Belleforest. Thomas Kyd's 1589 *Spanish Tragedy* has resemblances to *Hamlet,* and about the same time there are reports of a play by that title (c. 1589) probably not by Shakespeare. Of his *Hamlet,* there are three early versions: the First and Second Quartos (of 1603 and 1604/1605) and the First Folio (1623). Q2 and F—which are the play most of us know—seem far too long to have been staged without cutting. Q1, the much shorter

"bad quarto," has a more playable scene order, and its Hamlet is less reflective, less "delaying." But while no version springs unsullied from authorial intent, Q2 is often deemed the closest. All three are somehow "of Shakespeare," yet they reflect lost copies and the memories of actors, much as today's texts reflect decisions of generations of editors. Nor is it clear that Shakespeare was always consistent. Is Hamlet twenty or about thirty? Is Horatio a friend from Wittenberg unaware of Danish customs, or a familiar at the court of Elsinore who knows its history?

2. Of those countless indeterminacies, some might be solved by new evidence or inductions. But in a sense, these gaps are part of the art that is *Hamlet,* and they contribute to what we make of the *integrity of the prince.* Quite distinctive in Brook's production was how Lester played Hamlet as thinker and player: not melancholy or mad but intensely *in thought,* both when by himself and with the audience, who were there to give their minds to the mind of Hamlet and thus to help complete the pattern of the play.

3. Then there is *the integrity of the Ghost*—whom Brook's Horatio addresses, "Who's there?" A ghost is, much like a persona onstage, both there and not there—an uncanny other.[9] In the text(s), the identity of the apparition is so unclear that we are not sure if it is a "what" or a "who." The possible answers, which Hamlet ponders, bear on the personal, moral, and cosmological components of his complex, embodied self.

4. At the end Brook's adaptation, when Horatio gazes outward and repeats, "Who's there?" he speaks to the *integrities of the audience.* The part "others" play in the emergence of patterns of relational integrity is crucial to these chapters. In respect to *Hamlet,* we must not neglect the obvious: it was staged for people, who are invited to piece its parts together, for the sake of the play and for the sake of ourselves and others. *Hamlet* has, especially for modern viewers and readers, been a place to reflect upon integrity. Why integrity? Which integrity? Whose integrity? "That is the question"—or at least some of the questions.

I want to return briefly to the integrity of this, the longest Shakespeare script. It must have been written under the pressures of a company needing to keep many plays in repertory. The revising of "The Murder of Gonzago" may hint of the routine in which plays were written, so too the scenes of frantic composition in John Madden and Tom Stoppard's 1998 film, *Shakespeare in Love.* If, as Bloom thinks, the very plot of *Hamlet* is "revisionary," in that the prince is always revising himself, just as the playwright is always revising the text, then Hamlet's story reflects not only a solitary self but also the contingencies of making plays in ensemble.[10]

That it is a play of *gaps* borrows from Wolfgang Iser, among others,[11] who observes that areas of indeterminacy or opacity mark all narratives. Gaps, for Iser, make room for the reader's consciousness to enter and become engaged. Some works are gappier than others, owing to artistry, the conditions of composition, and the nature of the narrative or dramatic materials. Shakespeare, *Hamlet* especially, features many sorts of gaps; some are likely accidental or unconscious and some, as Stephen Greenblatt argues, are part of an authorial strategy of "opacity."[12] In any case, to stage or even to read *Hamlet* must be to *complete its composition*. While this quintessence of gaps may be completed in Brook's radical way, there is also much to be discovered by following each scene and line, as Kenneth Branagh attempts in his bravura 1996 film. I cannot do that. I can only touch some of the gaps,[13] to evoke the play's range of indeterminacy before seeking to define what patterns of integrity Hamlet may inhabit.

When he wishes his flesh would melt into dew, does "sallied" (First and Second Quartos) mean "assailed" or was it originally "sullied," suggesting that Hamlet feels defiled by his mother's sins; or is his flesh too "solid" (First Folio) as if he is frozen in his circumstances?

Are his circumstances, before he meets the Ghost, chiefly his mother's hasty remarriage; or did he also have expectations to attain the throne, which were thwarted in an "election" that implies a succession crisis?

Is the Ghost's call for revenge to be understood as a moral or sacred duty, or else a temptation that puts Hamlet's soul at risk?

After meeting the Ghost, does Hamlet delay or act in precipitous haste? By the end of his delays and actions, whose—if anyone's—justice has been served?

Is his madness feigned? Or if real, is it brought on by melancholy, by demonic powers, by sin, by Oedipal obsession, or by a cognitive crisis occasioned by personal and cultural disruption and by Hamlet's assuming unbearable responsibility?

Do his wild words to Ophelia come from knowing he is being overheard, by his falling out of love, by a spreading evil in society, or by a widening fault in his character that has interrupted his capacity to trust women or indeed anyone?

Are Rosencrantz and Guildenstern his dear good friends whom he murders, or factotums of the regime who get what they deserve? Are we to take Horatio's response—"Why, what a king is this!"—as irony or praise?

Does Fortinbras restore order providentially; or do we see a tyrant usurping the Danish throne and extending indefinitely a cycle of revenge?

Is *Hamlet* a late medieval morality play about a soul's dilemma in relation to kingdom and eternity; an early modern play about an ego empowered and possessed by his imagination; or a prophetically postmodern play about the improvised integrity of one who discovers that his relations with others, language, the world, and himself are always-already disrupted?

Ghostly Dilemmas

Imagine that among the *harms* persons or circumstances can impose on others are intractable dilemmas—of the kind the Ghost apparently imposes on Hamlet—which would threaten or destroy one's integrity, one's ability to live meaningfully and responsibly. Imagine as well that among the *goods* persons or circumstances might bring to others is relief from such dilemmas: lifting people out of them, or making the impasse pass by. And imagine further that not only could specters and persons bring about such harm or healing, *but so could theater itself.*

Such would be an implication of Greenblatt's thesis about ghosts on the Elizabethan stage. As belief in them shifted away from the provinces of church and society, ghosts (and the cultural and psychological baggage they carry) moved to the theater.[14] Ghosts became actors in costume, much as actors can assume a kind of uncanny presence, at once *there and not there.* If so, then can theater, like persons and ghosts, also *impose* tragic dilemmas on others? And can theater somehow *relieve* such dilemmas? If the ghost of old Hamlet can be a player, then can it also be a kind of playwright, stage manager, or one of the many "directors" in *Hamlet,*[15] who casts the prince in an impossible, dilemmatic role that may damn or redeem him? And does not the Ghost—without whom the plot of *Hamlet* would not get started—create a dilemma for its audience: how to interpret its import for ourselves?

The Ghost certainly intensifies the primary complication of Hamlet's "ground project," as Bernard Williams might put it. But what is the complication? Only that his uncle has just wed his mother? Or is Hamlet also a frustrated heir apparent? At court, Claudius would "let the world take note" that his nephew is "the most immediate to our throne" (I.2.108–9). Is Hamlet trapped in the loitering role of a crown prince? Ronald

Knowles thinks his later recourse to theatrics indicates how, in the end, his "selfhood recapitulates to the role."[16] René Girard and others think Hamlet cannot escape his imitative roles and emerge as an independent person. However, I think role entrapment is truer of others in the play than of Hamlet, for whom theater *almost, and in a certain way, frees* him—by Act V—from the dilemma defined by the Ghost. (The issue will concern, as we will see, Hamlet's different views of *playing.*)

The Ghost's demand for revenge is vexed by two conditions: "But howsomever thou pursues this act/Taint not thy mind" and "nor let thy soul contrive/Against thy mother." Hamlet is to have no evil intent in dealing with Claudius,[17] and is not to harm his mother: "leave her to heaven . . ." (I.5.84–86). So his mission is to avenge old Hamlet rightly, but without exposing Gertrude, which will constrain his range of action. But to say even this much is to poke into dim corners. The old Ghost debate bears on the integrity of the Ghost, on what sort of ethical paradigm Hamlet is obliged to inhabit, and on how he is going to play it. However, for all the time he takes investigating the Ghost's charges—of murder, treason, adultery—*these are never proven to anyone except the audience.* Only *we* hear Claudius's self-disclosure in the chapel scene, when Hamlet is out of hearing. And Hamlet's "grounds more relative" do not, after the Mousetrap scene, amount to public evidence but are compelling only to his mind and perhaps to a predisposed Horatio. Two critics of a generation ago, Fredson Bowers and Eleanor Prosser, took different positions on the dilemma created by the call for revenge. Their observations deserve a new look in light of recent reflections on the cultural and religious dynamics of power and vengeance. They also help us examine one of the mysterious gaps in *Hamlet.* What, if any, good is accomplished by the play's end?

Bowers

> For this same lord
> I do repent, but heaven hath pleased it so
> To punish me with this, and this with me,
> That I must be their scourge and minister.
> I will bestow him and will answer well
> The death I gave him. (III.4.170–75)

Both Bowers and Prosser begin with the fact that Christianity, Elizabethan or modern, prohibits personal revenge. Bowers, however, contends that *public revenge,* where just reasons for retribution are demonstrated, could have been justified in Shakespeare's day,[18] and therein would be Hamlet's dilemma—a *moral* dilemma for Bowers, both because of Hamlet's complicated moral status (he is a wronged prince guilty of killing Polonius, for which he expects heaven's punishment) and because of the political context of the Ghost's injunction to him.

In a moral dilemma, both options make pressing yet exclusive moral claims; opting for one incurs guilt for leaving the other, yet the choice is unavoidable. Bowers and recently Gene Fendt[19] (who reads *Hamlet* as an anthropologically and metaphysically Catholic play) believe the prince faces a succession crisis: "He that hath killed my King and whored my mother,/Popped in between th'election and my hopes . . ." (V.2.63–64). If Hamlet is as much wronged prince as aggrieved son—if his "election"[20] was thwarted by treason—then special responsibilities befall him to rectify injustice. Bowers contends that Hamlet is indeed bent on a private vendetta until he kills Polonius and contemplates the body. Then his mind and soul become clarified, and he interprets the Ghost's command in a new way: Hamlet is to become heaven's "scourge and minister." These terms may be more or less synonymous,[21] but Bowers would distinguish them.

Medieval and Renaissance Christians believed God may act through persons, who might be, on one hand, a "scourge" on behalf of heaven. A scourge would be a *corrupt* person whom God nonetheless uses to advance justice. A "minister of heaven," however, would be a *just* person whose necessary acts of violence would be like those of a just warrior.[22] Hamlet would be both scourge and minister because though guilty, he discovers a public duty to bring Claudius to justice. Fendt, like Bowers, observes that as a prince, Hamlet's "task . . . is more difficult than the unvalued person's is. He must do justice justly. On this depends our whole earthly state."[23] The dilemma: assuming that the uncanny "Specter"[24] has been allowed to visit Hamlet from purgatory and enjoins him to right an injustice justly, then Hamlet would be right to avenge treason, *provided it is revealed openly with evidence.*[25] But in doing so, Hamlet must not expose his mother to shame, *so it appears he must act secretly.* Thus, if he acts openly as minister, he will be guilty of harming her; if he acts secretly as scourge, he damns himself.

Many puzzles are illuminated by how the Ghost bequeaths *a part to improvise,* a role whose ethical dangers Hamlet accepts to his own endangerment. Many of his self-reflections—"The time is out of joint; O cursed spite/That ever I was born to set it right!" (I.5.186–87); "To

be, or not to be" (III.1.55); "How all occasions do inform against me"
(IV.4.31)—reveal the ethical and existential impasse he must navigate.
Goethe interpreted him in terms of the *subjective* weakness of "a fine,
pure, noble and highly moral person" who "goes to pieces beneath a
burden [he] can neither support nor cast off."[26] But the burden is *objectively* there. His part is so morally, culturally, and personally convoluted
that to improvise it is nearly impossible. Yet Hamlet returns to Denmark calm, not vengeful, not torn by conflicted duties—almost as if a
new character. Bowers's reading is that providence has lifted him out
of the dilemma, leaving him willing for things to unfold as they will.
And indeed, the switched swords of circumstance ("no precise plan")
punish Claudius and bring Hamlet to a grace-filled death. "From the
Elizabethan point of view, divine providence works out the catastrophe
with justice."[27] But is this a satisfying reading of a revenge play about the
violent uses of theater?

Prosser

> The spirit that I have seen
> May be a de'il, and the de'il hath power
> T'assume a pleasing shape. Yea, and perhaps
> Out of my weakness and my melancholy,
> As he is very potent with such spirits,
> Abuses me to damn me! I'll have grounds
> More relative than this. . . . (II.2.533–39)

Prosser's startling answer is that *Hamlet* is not a revenge play at all.
She disputes Bowers's parsing between private and public vengeance.
While revenge may win our sympathy, it should not win our approval,
and Elizabethans would not have coat-checked their morals at the theater
door.[28] The dilemma, then, would be not moral but *personal,* wherein
at least one of the choices is merely preferential. Hamlet may risk damnation by satisfying vengeance (preferential) or wait patiently for circumstances to unfold (moral). His change occurs not at the death of
Polonius but offstage between Acts IV and V, upon his return from England.[29] However, to see the issues in this way means deciding against
the Ghost when he claims, "I am thy father's spirit,/Doomed for a certain term to walk the night/And for the day confined to fast in fires/Till
the foul crimes done in my days of nature/Are burnt and purged away"
(I.5.9–13). A visitor from purgatory—whose denizens are on their way

to heaven—would never enjoin vengeance. So as to whether the Ghost is "a spirit of health or goblin damned" (I.4.40), Prosser insists the answer was even clearer to the Elizabethans than it is to us moderns. The Ghost must be a devil.[30]

Actually, the implications of the personal version of the dilemma do not require adjudicating the Ghost or knowing whether it is Protestant or Catholic. Prosser aligns Shakespeare with the Protestants, thus ruling out purgatory, a doctrine condemned in England for nearly fifty years. Greenblatt places him more or less with the papists, noting how his father was likely a recusant Catholic.[31] He also demonstrates in *Hamlet in Purgatory* that medieval and renaissance Catholics would imagine the flames of purgation to be just as horrible as those of damnation.[32] Nonetheless, the personal dilemma remains. How can Hamlet navigate between desire and restraint? And surely—when he is persuaded to "couple hell" (I.5.93) and "drink hot blood" (III.2.380)—the Elizabethan playgoers would have feared for his soul. But if so, can we accept Horatio's shining judgment, "Now cracks a noble heart. Goodnight, sweet Prince,/And flights of angels sing thee to thy rest" (V.2.343–44)? Yes, because vengeance has not happened.

In this respect, Prosser's answer is similar to Bowers's. Between England and Elsinore, Hamlet has "checked his own descent into Hell. It is not a barbaric young revenger, consumed by rage and confirmed in murderous thoughts, who appears in the graveyard, but a mature man of poise and serenity" who has "come to terms with himself."[33] Inexplicably, his "fury is spent." He is angry over Ophelia's grave, but repents to Laertes for slaying Polonius. His thoughts are on mortality, "providence," and "readiness." "Let be," he says. Prosser thinks the gap between the acts has been filled by grace, and Hamlet can calmly wait. As it happens, when Laertes exposes Claudius as the slayer of Hamlet and Gertrude (but not of old Hamlet), Hamlet responds—not in premeditated vengeance but justified self-defense. Yet Prosser's reading can be infuriating.[34] Could there not have been a *plurality* of attitudes about vengeance in the Globe theater? How much would doctrine influence reactions? Might some have simply accepted the Ghost as a heretical hybrid, an *unrepentant* spirit from purgatory, frozen in rage against his brother, compassion for his wife, and fear of being forgotten? Greenblatt suggests as much, yet does not think these conjectures moot Prosser's issues, because the text itself raises them.[35] Nonetheless, all the homicides may lead us to shout: By heaven! The play *is* driven by revenge!

As Hamlet watches Fortinbras march to Poland he is frustrated by a "craven scruple" when "all occasions do inform against me/And spur my dull revenge" (IV.4.39, 31–32). Girard thinks Hamlet is searching for *a pattern to imitate.* Scrupulous morality has dulled his urgency to vengeance,[36] so he needs a new model to follow and finds it in *theatricality* and *violence:* in the players, in Fortinbras, and in Laertes. "[S]how me what thou'lt do," Hamlet shouts at him over Ophelia's grave, "I'll rant as well as thou" (V.1.263, 273). Girard theorizes that imitating vengeance and ritual violence (e.g., in sacrifice, scapegoating, and even judicial process) is the hidden basis of all culture; he also thinks Shakespeare comments on this reality by knowingly employing the revenge genre without explicitly acknowledging the prohibition against revenge. "In *Hamlet,* the very absence of a case against revenge becomes a powerful intimation of what the modern world is really about."[37] When Fortinbras claims "rights of memory," he—whose father Old Hamlet defeated—would exemplify how structures of reciprocal violence are screened behind the language of jurisprudence.

However, in the gap between the acts, Hamlet has somehow been cast into a revised script, whether it is one of mimetic, state-sanctioned retribution (Girard) or of providence and grace (Bowers and Prosser). Either way, a transformation is improvised. Bloom notes how Hamlet "has aged a decade in a brief return from the sea, and if his self-consciousness is still theatrical, it ensues in a different kind of theater, eerily transcendental and sublime, one in which the abyss between *playing* someone and *being* someone has been bridged."[38] In the crux where Hamlet finds himself (and before providence and fortuitous pirates rescue him), he has no clear ethical paradigm to follow, so he must fashion his own. He begins by making theater.

Players and Playing

In the frantic scene after meeting the Ghost (I.5.149–88), a wild and whirling Hamlet decides to put on an "antic disposition." How this theatrical strategy is to work is not clear. Is it to distract others from his secret purpose by affecting melancholy? Is it to provoke Claudius into open conflict, where Hamlet could be seen to do justice? Is it to buy time, to determine whom he can trust?[39] The strategy of performing madness may further attenuate his sanity, already tested by the dilemma itself. But it may also prompt him to employ other uses of "theater."[40]

Shakespeare's attitude toward the trope of playing a part in life as an actor onstage ranges from suspicion to celebration. Before learning of the Ghost, Hamlet's first theatrical metaphor (I.2.76–86) about "seeming" and "the suits of woe" is suspicious yet complex. His newly wedded mother and uncle complain about his funereal attire, but he says his costume is appropriate to his inmost reality. And yet he also says his dejected sighs and solemn clothes—"Together with all forms, moods, shapes of grief"—cannot by themselves "denote me truly. . . . For they are the actions that a man might play." Outwardly he wears "inky black," yet he privileges what is "within," as if even *honest displays* of sincerity are inevitably insincere.[41] Later Hamlet will again link insincerity with "playing." But after the Ghost commissions him, he must devise or divine a role that can touch the public and personal sides of the conflict.

Whatever madness hovers near Hamlet's mind (evident to Prosser in the infernal oath he insists that Horatio, Marcellus, and Bernardo swear) is in part comprised of the dilemma that has almost "o'erthrown" his complex identity as prince and person. It has harmed the integral pattern of his intelligence and nobility, which Ophelia—after he recommends her to a nunnery—describes as having been once a thing of beauty:

The courtier's, soldier's, scholar's eye, tongue, sword,
Th'expectation and rose of the fair state,
The glass of fashion and the mould of form,
Th'observed of all observers. . . .
. . . that noble and most sovereign reason . . . (III.1.150–53, 156)

Moreover, to imitate personal fragmentation—to put on formlessness—is to risk disintegration of form. But such imitation can also hint of mode of reintegration, a new way of being, after the ground-of-being-Hamlet has been displaced. Above the cellarage, as Ghost and cosmos become strange, Hamlet elects to become strange precisely *to be* in such a cosmos.[42] It is as if he finds *a space* between the horns of his dilemma, wherein to become the auteur of his own morality play. Jan H. Blits writes, "While he rejects the actions that a man might play, Hamlet plays the actions that a moral life might contain. His moral life becomes a self-dramatization. This inversion goes to the heart of the play."[43] In other words, he begins to improvise the modern, autonomous imagination.[44] Yet his need to improvise also anticipates the contingent, postmodern nonself. For it is with a company of traveling players—vagabonds seeking royal patronage, and who in turn might add aura to the royal pa-tron[45]—that Hamlet begins to refine this theatrical strategy.

A fresh breeze blows through Elsinore when the "tragedians" arrive. Hamlet's real-and-feigned melancholy lifts. He loves the theater, he de-lights in it. After welcoming them, he attempts the Pyrrhus speech himself and then is moved when the First Player does it justice. His appreciation should be seen in the foreground of Shakespeare's many discouraged musings on theater as a metaphor for life. For he recognizes how there is in stage playing a certain good, one that may elicit naive or witting delight. What delight or *good* is this? In *Hamlet* we may distinguish—no doubt artificially—two aspects of an implicit phenomenology of dra-matic performance, which involves both mirroring and improvisation, a kind of participation.[46]

Mimesis as Objectifying

We see the more troubling of these aspects when Hamlet instructs the tragedians (III.2.1–43) on the "purpose of playing." They are to hold "as 'twere the mirror up to Nature" and thereby effect a temperate and smooth congruence of passion, speech, and bodily expression ("do not saw the air too much"). This has been long thought excellent advice, reflective of Shakespeare's own practice. It aims to reveal what is essen-tial and invisible, "to show Virtue her feature, Scorn her own image, and [to show] the very age and body of the time his form and pressure." Just as theatrical *mimesis* may delight the audience, it may also examine humanity critically.

But Hamlet deems this mirror so powerful as to prompt individuals to reveal their secret faults. Those hostile to art as mimesis (because it passes off the pretence of objectifying observation as truth) could find their casus belli in this strategy. To "catch the conscience" would be to objectify the soul in order to decode its essence in a slice of time. Even if naturalistic drama can do this—and it is not clear that it can, if persons exist only *in the flow* of time[47]—a play is not expected to spur "guilty creatures" to reveal for all to see their "malefactions" (II.24–27). As a student once commented, Hamlet is inventing the polygraph machine. He is asking a play to detect the interiority of Claudius. However, what the scientism implicit in his invention actually reveals is Hamlet's own ethos, urgent for justice or vengeance. This urge now defines Hamlet in terms of his gaining access to the state's retributive and coercive pow-ers. The prince begins to look like a modern artist becoming a modern tyrant; Greenblatt and others notice how the economies of power in theatrical and political improvisation mirrored, indeed embraced one another in Elizabeth's England.[48]

The fact that the King does blench, as if proving the Ghost honest, does not make this a sound forensic method, despite the theatrical lore Hamlet knows.[49] Critics have worried that Claudius might be reacting not to the occulted accusation but to Hamlet's insulting behavior, or to the implied threat to himself, for Gonzago is murdered by his nephew, and Hamlet is his nephew. What really establishes Claudius's guilt is not "Mousetrap," but our hearing him attempt to pray. "A brother's murder. Pray I cannot" (III.3.38). These and other interior thoughts are spoken before Hamlet approaches and after Hamlet withdraws.

Mimesis as "Delight"

There is, however, another aspect to Hamlet's phenomenology of performance. Just before the players arrive (II.2.261–76), Hamlet says he has "of late . . . lost all my mirth" and "Man delights not me," after he knows Rosencrantz and Guildenstern have been sent to observe him. In losing delight in the earth and the "brave o'erhanging firmament," and in human beings ("the beauty of the world; the paragon of animals") Hamlet implies what *would be* normatively delightful. Whether he alludes to a Renaissance or a medieval vision of reality, or both,[50] what delights him in happier seasons are *embodied form, freedom in motion,* and *humanity's intelligent embrace of possibilities*—"how noble in reason; how infinite in faculties"—all qualities enjoyed under the "majestical roof" of the theater of the world. The speech implies an interplay between humanity and cosmos, presupposed by theater's imitative functions.[51] Hamlet's delight is reawakened when told the players are arriving. He suddenly and warmly anticipates their performances: the "majesty" of the King, the "Adventurous Knight," the Lover, the Clown, and the boy who convincingly plays the female parts. These players, Rosencrantz reminds him, are the people "you were wont to take such delight in, the tragedians of the city" (ll. 291–92).

What may well delight Hamlet is how these actors—probably persecuted as vagrants and accustomed to stock parts—may enjoy a freedom from fixed social roles, which threatens Polonius but which Hamlet desires.[52] If so, then he is vicariously enjoying the capacities of selves and identities to be transformed. This delight in protean humanity suggests another way that theater might engage nature, not by capturing it as in a mirror but by participating in the entrance of persons into other parts and stories.[53] While the purposes of such participation would make it seem morally neutral (it can liberate or tyrannize, be a diversion or subversion, arouse compassion or cruelty), it nonetheless has ethical import for community and human well-being (or *eudaimonia*). It can enable self-transcendence, congruent with the good of being drawn from the confines of one's station toward those of other lives. Another hint of this delight comes as Hamlet greets the players. To one young "old friend," he notices a new growth of beard "since I saw thee last" (II.2.361). He teases the boy who takes ladies' parts, hoping that his voice hasn't cracked. And he rounds on Polonius for hesitating to bestow good accommodations on these guests: "let them be well used, for they are the abstract and brief chronicles of the time. . . ."

> POLONIUS: My lord, I will use them according to their desert.
> HAMLET: God's bodkin, man, much better! Use every man after his desert and who shall scape whipping? Use them after your own honour and dignity—the less they deserve, the more merit is in your bounty. Take them in. (ll. 461–70)

Hamlet asks them for "a passionate speech," and much may be made of how the First Player's body affects such grief and resolution as Hamlet wishes he could sustain, and of how the long Pyrrhus speech (ll. 406–56) is boring to Polonius—but not to Hamlet. As the player recites Hecuba's horror to see her husband Priam killed by Pyrrhus (another name for Achilles' son Neoptolemus, extremely violent in the *Aeneid* during the sack of Troy), the uncanny transformations of grief put Hamlet in awe[54] and disturb Polonius: "Look where he has not turned his colour and has tears in's eyes.—Prithee no more!" (ll. 457–58).

Hamlet as Ambivalent Player Transformed by Play

These aspects of a theatrical aesthetics, one aiming to represent realities and the other to participate imaginatively in realities, interact ambivalently.[55] Hamlet's soliloquy, "O, what a rogue and peasant slave am I!" (II.2.485–540), speaks of the falseness of performance;[56] but his scorn is directed less to dramatic artistry than to himself. In his stasis and isolation, he may misinterpret the significance of the actor's transformation. He credits it less to the *part being recited* than to the objectifying will of the player, who

> But in a fiction, in a dream of passion,
> Could force his soul so to his own conceit
> That from her working all the visage wanned
> —Tears in his eyes, distraction in his aspect,
> A broken voice, and his whole function suiting
> With forms to his conceit—and all for nothing—
> For Hecuba?

Hamlet is aware of the part but does not consider that *participating in the part of Hecuba* is what *frees* this actor to become a "brief chronicle of the time." Hamlet's focus on the player's will betrays a false assumption if taken literally, namely that if one had the actual motive of one's part, one would act better.[57] If the First Player really had Pyrrhus's or Hecuba's or Hamlet's "motive and the cue for passion" (l. 496 wF), he might cease being an actor or at least a good actor who can empty momentarily into a part not his own. He might merely "drown the stage with tears" or bellow "with horrid speech" as to "Make mad the guilty and appal the free," but this is precisely *not* the kind of advice Hamlet later gives the players. If his thinking about performance is here at odds with itself, perhaps it is because his own conscience has been "caught" by the Pyrrhus speech. Unlike the First Player, Hamlet is trapped in a role that is hardly effective. He is a prince without a realm and an actor without a stage, in a part he cannot trust. But now he gains the insight that the players themselves might release him from his stasis—but only, he thinks, if he interposes into their play his own entrapped self: "some dozen or sixteen lines" (536) to insert into "The Murder of Gonzago."

If his Mousetrap strategy nearly fails, is it because Hamlet is thinking only of the *mirror* of the stage and not of its unpredictable effects. Of all the reasons suggested for why Claudius does not flinch at the prefatory dumb show, the most obvious is that audiences rarely respond *like that*. They will not usually leap up to proclaim their malefactions but will either enjoy the play or tolerate it.[58] As Hamlet impatiently watches the player dither about poisoning ("Begin, murderer: leave thy damnable faces and begin," III.2.246) does it dawn on him his trap may fail? Having revised the text, directed the cast, and coached the audience, Hamlet improvises the crucial lines himself: "He poisons him i' th'garden for his estate. His name's Gonzago. The story is extant and written in very choice Italian. You shall see anon how the murderer gets the love of Gonzago's wife" (ll. 254–57 wF). Even here he obscures the issue of murder by alluding to a hasty *remarriage*. Is *that* why the King reacts—be it angrily, guiltily, inscrutably? Hamlet sees no more than he imagined he would see, even though what he imagined happens to be true.

Thereafter, Hamlet plays the part of an autonomous secret agent, and his hasty performances are mostly unfortunate. He misreads Claudius at prayer. He holds a mirror to his mother's soul and nearly throttles her, whose outcry prompts Polonius's fatal outcry, which may drive Ophelia to her death. Hamlet envies the will-to-power of Fortinbras, whose ambition may doom the independence of Denmark. In consigning his "excellent good friends" to the block, he attains the self-sufficiency of a tyrant. But by now Hamlet may have warmed to the tyrant's part, for he has sealed their deaths with his father's signet ring, which just happened to be in his purse, "heaven ordinant" (V.2.48). When Horatio, absent for so many scenes, now hears of this from Hamlet he exclaims, "So Guildenstern and Rosencrantz go to't. . . . Why, what a king is this!" (ll. 56, 62). The royal antecedent could be Claudius or Hamlet. If the latter, is Horatio judging Hamlet or admiring him? Hamlet calmly says that he acted in "perfect conscience" (l. 66).

How do we account for this transformation when Hamlet returns from England, in command of himself and seemingly older, as if to a different part in a different play? Prosser speculates that somewhere between England and Elsinore he encounters providential grace. "There's a divinity that shapes our ends,/Rough-hew them how we will" (V.2.10–11). While the transformation is not depicted, it is recapitulated in the Gravedigger dialogue, where Hamlet and Horatio are at ease with mortality. And there is among the bones another player, who Bloom thinks provided paternal nurture to the boy prince, Yorick the clown, "A fellow of infinite jest, of most excellent fancy," who "bore me on his back a thousand times" (V.1.175–6).[59] Yorick not only signifies the stench of the grave, the passing of innocence, and a fatherly attention Hamlet might otherwise have lacked, but he also *models theatrical skills of jest and imagination,* as Hamlet entertains Horatio with good lines about the dust of Alexander and Caesar.

Somewhat in contrast to a providential reading, in a classic ritual interpretation of theater, Francis Fergusson sees Hamlet presiding over maimed and improvised rites that seek to restore a poisoned community. He heals by becoming at once prophet, exorcist, clown, and sacrificial scapegoat.[60] We could take the ritual account further. When Hamlet returns to Elsinore he is outward bound from a rite of passage over dark waters, with "My sea-gown scarfed about me" (V.2.13). He has been an ephebe, a young soldier whose self is secured by appropriating knowledge of death. Following Girard's theory of mimetic sacrifice, we could say still more about this rite. Upon reading Claudius's fatal letter, Hamlet finds the model he has sought, one of royal initiative and effective sacrifice. In double dealing Rosencrantz and Guildenstern with his father's ring, he has exorcized the Ghost and become at ease in his own royal (and deadly) identity. Pirates-with-integrity rescue him, as if they too were divinely (or demonically) sent. These readings would not be altogether contradictory, were we to grant that providence might use ritual, improvisation, and violence as scourges to its ends, as well as patience.

The Eclipse of Hamlet's Kenotic Integrity

Let us leave aside the *moral* evaluation of the pattern of integrity that emerges between the acts. To credit its *religious* design is to acknowledge the design is not Hamlet's alone. He is improvising a scenario no longer of his composing, yet now he speaks as if free. "There is special providence in the fall of a sparrow. If it be now, 'tis not to come. If it be not to come, it will be now. If it be not now, yet it will come. The readiness is all. . . . Let be" (V.2.197–201 wF). Knowles and others note Elizabethan interest in Stoic passivity here,[61] but its syncretism with Christian lore need not be "fatalistic." The pattern of readiness into which Hamlet empties is like a player improvising with providence; and providence itself could be likened to divine improvisation. Even to so anti-theatrical a visionary as Augustine—whose view of time and eternity in *The Confessions* can seem to moderns deterministic—God had intervened in his life primarily by *using his free will,* luring it toward the good; freedom and selfhood are hedged by the irrationality of sin, not of fate.[62] Moreover, Augustine attempted to learn from what persons and ideas providence sent his way. The conjunction of providence and freedom suggests something of the *mutuality* of theatrical improvisation, which is part of the "delight" Hamlet had lost in the "I have of late . . . lost all my mirth" speech.

Hamlet's sense of improvising is aware both of sin and chance when asking forgiveness from Laertes (V.2.211–22). He both disavows *and* avows responsibility, appealing to his "madness" (which appears now to have been in some way real, part of the unreason of revenge), to his being and not-being himself ("If Hamlet from himself be ta'en way,/And when he's not himself does wrong Laertes,/Then Hamlet does it not"), and to an archery metaphor ("I have shot my arrow o'er the house,/And hurt my brother"). The archery word, *hamartia* or "missing the mark," which Aristotle uses in the *Poetics* for a tragic deed, is translated in scripture as "sin," and in Greek epic and tragedy could mean both unintended error and culpable fault.[63] As Hamlet acknowledges he is both agent and victim, and as he tells Horatio he belongs as much to divinity and unfolding events as to himself, his awareness begins to approximate a self-emptying or kenotic paradigm of integrity, especially with Bowers's and Prosser's views of his death.[64]

Yet this paradigm is finally eclipsed. Yes, Hamlet may die administering rough-hewn justice, as if a martyr to the realm. Yes, Horatio witnesses his provident integrity, "Now cracks a noble heart." Yes, "Tell my story" is Hamlet's dying request, which gives the momentarily suicidal Horatio a reason to live. But Hamlet apparently endorses the "election" of Fortinbras, who has seized Elsinore; and Horatio can seem Machiavellian as he becomes a collaborator in the making of state theater. As he promises to recite for Fortinbras and the English ambassadors the whole tragedy of accident and culpability—omitting reference to the Ghost and other things unknown to his philosophy—he is attaching himself to the new regime: "give order that these bodies/High on the stage be placed to the view" (V.2.361–62). Horatio is gathering up the dead, which could be seen to validate a new order of authorized vengeance.[65]

At this same moment, Fortinbras also uses theater to attach his rule to the old regime. "Remember me," the Ghost had once commanded Hamlet. Now Fortinbras, whose father Old Hamlet defeated, asserts, "I have some rights ["Rites," F] of memory in this kingdom" (l. 373). With his first decree in Elsinore, Fortinbras becomes the last director-player in *Hamlet,* and he aligns himself with the aura of Hamlet's "most royal" body, borne "like a soldier to the stage."

> And for his passage
> The soldiers' music and the rite of war
> Speak loudly for him.
> Take up the bodies. Such a sight as this
> Becomes the field but here shows much amiss.
> Go, bid the soldiers shoot. (ll. 380–87)

He commands the prince to be exalted as soldier and king but not as paragon of infinite faculty, noble reason, excellent fancy, nor as a minister of heaven. Of course, we could locate this new, Norwegian King of Denmark in the providential design of Act V.[66] However, most productions now, if they keep Fortinbras at all, treat him as another episode in a cycle of usurpation hidden in a cosmic order Shakespeare never quite reinstates in his tragedies. These alternatives—providence or vengeance—need not be mutually exclusive. If Fortinbras were a *scourge* on Denmark, then divinity might be using revenge to further hidden ends. But if we combine this metaphor with Fortinbras as impresario, will we be happy with the implication that theater remains only a scourge? What of ministry? What of the delight in mutable persons transformed through the improvised play of the stage? Does Shakespeare let us lose sight of that as *good*?

Coda: Prospero's Spirits

In the comedies—such as *A Midsummer Night's Dream,* which I will in the last chapter juxtapose with *King Lear*—the misprision of private playing can be corrected by public playing, wherein the tragic is transposed toward romance. Romance, of course, can be a very shallow stream, and Greenblatt warns that most marriages in Shakespeare are worrisome or not altogether promising.[67] Other than romance, however, we have few paradigms for readily grasping the good of human mutability and the transformations that can happen in playing parts. Among the dangers of correlating romance with this good is entrapment in habits of gender and hierarchy. So we will later have to ask, Are such connubial endings more about pandering to patriarchs and consumers than deliverance from social and personal bondage?

Then there are the "problem plays." If in *Hamlet* the possible good of kenotic transformation is eclipsed by the theater of Fortinbras, Jeffrey Knapp alerts us to a moment in *The Tempest* when kenotic theater eclipses reciprocal violence.[68] Prospero was the weak Duke of Milan whose realm has been reduced to an island; there he is an expressive artist and bored conjurer, a frail actor-impresario in a costume that at once fits and ill befits him. We see him staging a magical masque to celebrate his daughter Miranda's betrothal to the shipwrecked Ferdinand, and Ferdinand is amazed by the strange and charming players he beholds: "May I be bold / To think these spirits?"

> PROSPERO: Spirits, which by mine art
> I have from their confines called to enact
> My present fancies. (IV.1.118–22)[69]

Prospero's ghostly players are indeed so marvelous as to make him momentarily forget the "foul conspiracy" of Caliban. He tells Ferdinand and Miranda not to worry and then famously defines the protean marvels and meanings they have enjoyed.

> These our actors,
> As I foretold you, were all spirits and
> Are melted into air, into thin air;
> And—like the baseless fabric of this vision—
> The cloud-capped towers, the gorgeous palaces,
> The solemn temples, the great globe itself,
> Yea, all which it inherit, shall dissolve,
> And like this insubstantial pageant faded,
> Leave not a rack behind. We are such stuff
> As dreams are made on, and our little life
> Is rounded with a sleep. (ll. 148–58)

Greenblatt thinks the most apposite way to interpret the ghosts, fairies, and spirits in Shakespeare is as figures of stage acting. If so, this figuration is ambivalent, for it registers both the spirituality of theatrical play and also its emptiness. But perhaps the good of theater is in both its transforming spirits *and* its emptiness: its thin air, its very baselessness, which might be said *to create by making room* for possibilities we can see and, indeed, for other possibilities we cannot.

Shakespeare was self-critically ambivalent about gorgeous pageants. They would be, on one hand, *something that is nothing*. Prospero promises to burn his books—his theatrical magic, which he had attempted to use vengefully against his Milanese usurpers—and return to his former, dull life as Duke of Milan, where "Every third thought shall be my grave" (V.1.312). The umbra of doubt, eclipsing the moonbeams of theatrical delight, is often noticeable in microscopic scenes such as this and in the larger vistas of Shakespearean drama. However, our receptivity to the spirits suggests they are *not merely nothing*.[70] The theatrical intimation of relational, performative integrity seems least eclipsed when the audience's imaginative responsibilities are elicited, as in the Epilogue, when a weary Prospero requests the grace of applause to release him from his wizardry. "As you from crimes would pardoned be / Let your indulgence set me free." Later, we shall consider how seriously Shakespeare means us to be adopted into the mutual play of this priestly penitent role.

Chapter V

"Why Do You Always Wear Black?"

Truth and Naturalism, Chekhov and Others

Yes, Torvald, I've changed my dress.
—NORA, IN HENRIK IBSEN, *A Doll House*

ARKADINA: (*To her son*) Dear boy, *when* are we going to start?
KONSTANTIN: In just a minute. Please be patient.
ARKADINA: (*Recites from* Hamlet):
"Oh, Hamlet, speak no more!
Thou turn'st my eyes into my very soul,
and there I see such black and grained spots
as will not leave their tinct."
KONSTANTIN: "Nay, but to live
in the rank sweat of an enseamed bed,
stewed in corruption, honeying and making love
over the nasty sty—"
(*From behind the stage, the sound of a horn.*)
Ladies and gentlemen, your attention please! We are about to start!
—ANTON CHEKHOV, *The Seagull*

A PLAY (within a play) is about to begin. Konstantin Treplev is the author. Irena Arkadina is his mother. Shortly she will join a small audience by the lakeside of the country estate of her older brother, Pyotr Sorin. A celebrated actress, Arkadina is forty-three and sorry to be away from the city. She thinks her son's artistic efforts are decadent and he knows this. Yet he also wishes to impress her with his genius, and accuses her of jealousy for not being in the cast. So when mother and son quote lines at each other, from Hamlet and Gertrude's closet scene, their banter is witty, venomous, and more despairing than either realizes. She is saying: You think my acting is passé while your art has integrity, but this is all rather silly. He is saying: Yes mother and what's more, you are the mistress of Trigorin, that petty novelist who also has no integrity. Unwittingly, their allusion to *Hamlet* reveals the futility of reflecting interiority or integrity, or their absence, in the mirror of detached realism.[1] Many dramatists in the late nineteenth and early twentieth centuries were posing the question Gertrude had asked Hamlet, and with which *The Seagull* (1895) begins.

> MEDVEDENKO: Why do you always wear black?
> MASHA: Because I'm in mourning for my life. I'm not happy. (111)

This metatheatrical question can mean: Do your costumes and habits of speech and gesture reveal your soul from within or determine it from without?

Naturalism's answer was that an accurate exterior should assist in revealing human interiority. Strindberg, Ibsen, and Chekhov worked through and then beyond naturalism, while the impressionists and symbolists (of whom Konstantin's play may be part parody and part homage) opposed it. Stanislavski, who was associated with naturalism and directed *The Seagull* with ambiguous results, explored the capacity of actors to transcend the fatalism of genetic inheritance, history, social roles, and psychological limits—even while staging plays by writers who found it difficult to portray human existence as anything but a trap.

This chapter will juxtapose moments from Strindberg and Ibsen, and then return to Chekhov. For these dramatists, a kind of authenticity—being true to oneself and to the world as one finds it—was the implicit norm for their portrayals of characters, many of whom destroy themselves. Like Stanislavski, they looked for means beyond naturalism, as do two later interpreters of theater and religion, Hans Urs von Balthasar and Tom F. Driver. In their different ways, they think that art can be realistic in respect to persons, without self-contradiction, only by transformative participation, a phenomenon that theater is especially suited to explore.

Mirrors, Dreams, Houses

We saw how Hamlet had two accounts of theatrical drama. In one, the human being is the highest creaturely realization of cosmic order, open to motion, intelligence, and freedom, capacities especially exemplified in a player's transfigurations onstage. Yet Hamlet also had another account of theater. When he urged the players to hold a "mirror" up to human nature, the implications could imply observational detachment. While he intended such detachment to ferret out injustice, it also interrupted a sense of "delight" in theatrical participation. To be sure, watching actors performing "true to" nature can be a delight, but a delight that may devolve into curiosity, voyeurism, indifference, even vague despair.

Hamlet's purpose was to x-ray the King's conscience. Yet such objective knowledge of interiority is impossible, and by the time of Chekhov it had become clear as to why. For Søren Kierkegaard, any particular subjectivity is inherently lived in time; thus, no person's life can be mimetically objectified, or lifted out of time for dissection. A human life *is* only as it acts, interacts, and discerns itself in temporal passage. One cannot, then, hold a mirror to a person's nature and fix it in an instant. If theatrical space is to represent human lives at all, it must do so indirectly (Kierkegaard's way of "indirect communication," and perhaps Chekhov's) or through some kind of nonobjectifying participation with the other's story, as in rituals. But how is a modern dramatist or actor to portray lives that are *not* commonly viewed as co-participants in a sacred cosmos? The question is not just about drama in the secular city. It is also about how drama can avoid destroying what it would mirror by the very act of mirroring it; that is, can theater avoid reducing a character's life to what Stanislavski called a "stencil" or abstract form?

Naturalism and Dream Plays

In imitating positivist science, naturalism could intend the stage to be an experimental laboratory (though as obsessed as it could be with real props and noises, this was more an ideal than a fully realized practice). We find one of its maxims not in a play but in a preface to a play, where Emile Zola reports why he dramatized his novel *Therese Raquin* (1891). "Given a strong man and an unsatisfied woman," he wished "to seek in them the beast, to see nothing but the beast, to throw them into a violent drama and note scrupulously the sensations and acts of these creatures . . . I have simply done in two living bodies the work which surgeons do on corpses."[2]

This image of theater-as-dissection makes the problem of objectification quite literal, so literal that it might seem too obvious to charge naturalism with leaving suicide the sole option for so many characters. But these plays do show how nature, history, psychology, and society can be imprisoning. And naturalism can also implicitly imprison players and audiences—because its transparent "fourth wall" *pretends* to suppress metatheatricality, that is, the play's self-awareness that it is a performance. If a play does not acknowledge, albeit subtly and indirectly, that *persons* are enacting it and that *other persons* are watching and trying to grasp it, then the patterns of integrity that may be manifested in theatrical relationships are elided. As it happens, however, the metatheatrical impulse persists in naturalism and is what often gives us insight into how these plays *do* make significant inquiries into problems of recognizing integrity in selves and others.

August Strindberg, in prefacing *Miss Julie* (1888), likens the dramatist to a "lay preacher peddling the ideas of his time in popular form."[3] He comments on the sociopsychological factors bearing on Julie, a woman raised by her father, the Count; on Jean, the valet with aristocratic airs; and on Kristen, the unwittingly hypocritical cook. Strindberg also enumerates what dramatists should strive to avoid: scene breaks, musicians visible in the pit, inappropriate music, too complicated sets, footlights, and excessive make-up. He calls for "a *small* stage and a *small* house" (73), with the audience seated in darkness. Again, it can sound as if he is imagining a laboratory, in which to analyze the "circumstances" leading to Miss Julie's fate:

> the mother's character, the father's mistaken upbringing of the girl, her own nature, and the influence of her fiancé on a weak, degenerate mind. . . . the festive mood of Midsummer Eve, her father's absence, her monthly indisposition, her pre-occupation with animals, the excitement of dancing, the magic of dusk, the strong aphrodisiac influence of flowers, and finally the chance that drives the couple into a room alone—to which must be added the urgency of the excited man. (63)

Miss Julie has been recently jilted, and is "crazy again to-night," the play's first line; she is distracted with despair and desire. After their tryst, Jean proposes that they go to Switzerland to run a hotel. He kills her pet finch to facilitate their travel plans and briefly thinks they can pull off this elopement—until it becomes clear they have no funds, that Jean cannot escape his psychology of subservience to Jean's father, and that Julie can never accept the shame of being a mistress. Jean now loathes her, she loathes herself, and both tremble in fear of the Count. So Julie asks Jean to save her by performing an act of hypnotism. He does, and hands her a razor.

Midsummer's Eve and dancing to cover sexuality anticipate the expressionism of Strindberg's later plays. And while devising psycho-circumstances with no escape, he professed to resist reductionism: "My treatment . . . is neither exclusively physiological nor psychological." He thought "character" in popular theater had become nothing more than "fixed and finished" types, and that it was "the Naturalists who know the richness of the soul-complex and realise that vice has a reverse side very much like virtue." He regarded his characters as "conglomerations of past and present stages of civilization, bits from books and newspapers, scraps of humanity, rags and tatters of fine clothing, patched together as is the human soul. And I have added a little evolutionary history by making the weaker steal and repeat the words of the stronger, and by making the characters borrow ideas or 'suggestions' from one another" (64, 65).

If one regards persons as "conglomerations" of such traits, then integrity may have to do with how they manage to hold the traits together or to seek truth despite their chaotic conflicts—comparable to integrity as envisioned by Raymond Gaita.[4] Strindberg entertained some hope Jean might finally elevate himself, but he had none for the ill-bred Julie. Nonetheless, the chance that a person's "scraps of humanity" might indeed be reconfigured is a sign of incipient expressionism. Dreams are another sign. Jean dreams of literally climbing out of his station in life, and cannot; Julie is dizzy with a dream of falling from hers, and does. Dreams, with their expressive power, are a realistic part of life. But if in naturalism *there are dreams in the play,* in expressionism the dream expands to encompass the play—*so there are plays in the dream.*

In *A Dream Play* (1902), an Officer waits in unrequited love for an Actress to emerge from a stage door. The surreal alignments of time, space, and character—reflecting Strindberg's own tormented memories—imitate the odd logic of dreams. "[O]n a slight groundwork of reality, imagination spins and weaves new patterns made up of memories, experiences, unfettered fancies. . . . The characters are split, double and multiply; they evaporate, crystallize, scatter and converge. But a single consciousness holds sway over them all—that of the dreamer. For him there are no secrets, no incongruities, no scruples and no law."[5] Yet it is never clear precisely who this dreamer is. People are in the dream, not dreams in the people. So the two plays illustrate the emergence of expressionism *out of* and even *as* a mode of realism: the dream presses upon the dramatic form from within,[6] giving the play the protean shape of a dream.

The dream of *Dream Play* is framed by a myth that depicts a mission. The Daughter of the god Indra has descended from the heavens to live as a human being, in order to discover the extent of human suffering. The Hindu motif is perhaps used to defamiliarize Christ's kenosis, that is, his becoming incarnate, motivated by divine compassion.

> DAUGHTER [OF INDRA]: Do you know who lives in the castle?
> GLAZIER: I used to know, but I've forgotten.
> DAUGHTER: I believe there is a prisoner inside, waiting for me to
>   set him free. (199)

In his Author's Note, Strindberg wrote, "however agonizing real life may be, at this moment, compared with the tormenting dream, it is a joy." This may sound like a rather masochistic "joy," but Strindberg was affecting not cynicism but a "compassion for all living things." Other joys we might take from the play are its transformations of places and persons and its lyricism. But will the audience discern this joy as Indra's Daughter journeys through painful episodes, repeating the refrain, "Human beings are to be pitied"? If we do, it will probably be because the theatrical dream form is being transformed in behalf of a vision of compassion.[7]

Brand, Hedda, Nora

Before becoming a master of naturalism, Henrik Ibsen mounted huge verse dramas on national and spiritual themes, with heroes such as the Norwegian Faust, *Peer Gynt* (1867, performed in 1876), and *Brand* (1865, 1885), who is an uncompromising, post-Christian Savonarola (a comparison Strindberg made). Shaw announced that Ibsen was an advocate of "reality" and an opponent of "the ideal." By the ideal, he meant both the project of commonplace morality (bad, insofar as it screens off the social and biological facts of reality) and the monomaniacal programs of geniuses such as Reverend Brand. But the very title of Shaw's *The Quintessence of Ibsenism* suggests that "the ideal" can be opposed only in the name of some sort of idea, which Shaw took to be his own version of socialism. Even so, it is hard to sort out why Ibsen buries Brand under an avalanche as the play ends, yet thought that "Brand is myself in my best moments."[8]

Others view Ibsen through Kierkegaard's three stages of existence: the aesthetic, ethical, and religious. Ibsen was aware of Kierkegaard,[9] at least insofar as he frequently denied the Dane influenced him, and there are resemblances. Brand echoes SK's critique of "Christendom," of Christianity as a form of national culture rather than a faith that poses sharp choices. "The God of our country, the people's God [is]/A feeble dotard in his second childhood" (61). Brand's own God is the hard Voice who commanded the sacrifice of Isaac; however, in the play this God may be nothing but Brand's uncompromising ego. "Ibsen had a Calvinist conscience without Calvin's respect for law," writes Driver. "He had a Lutheran intensity without Luther's belief in Grace. He was caught up in the romantic quest for the Absolute, which he turned inward toward the will and the conscience of the solitary individual."[10] To Brand, being "wholly what you are, not half and half" (60) is the integrity of the uncompromising will. But if he *and* Ibsen *both* are seeking the Absolute, then what do we make of the play's judgment on Brand?

Brand rejects all who reject his austere calling, but Agnes chooses to marry him in a bleak parish in a cold mountain valley. To all who will listen he proclaims, "I know but one law for all mankind./I cannot discriminate" (96). He refuses to absolve his dying mother's sins unless she bequeaths her fortune to charity, and she won't, until she leaves it to him. When told his son Ulf will die unless they escape the climate, he refuses—the rumor is out that he wants to leave the high valley only to enjoy his inheritance. So they stay, and Ulf dies. Brand then tells Agnes to give Ulf's precious clothes to the poor; she does, and later dies of grief. Meanwhile, he has needed a bigger church and with his mother's wealth has built one. Agnes's death prompts him to think he has compromised his ideals. So he takes his flock to the mountains to worship in whatever wild and freezing spaces nature will provide. "After a brief practical experience of this arrangement," Shaw comments, "they stone him."[11]

So Brand flees even higher into the mountains, where the ghost of Agnes appears, telling him to abandon his stance of All or Nothing so life can return to normal, as it was before this horrible "dream." He knows she is an illusion and now approaches the Ice Church, presided over by Gerd, a gypsy associated with trolls; it was she who spread the rumors that led to the deaths of Ulf and Agnes. Hunting a hawk of some symbolic significance, she greets Brand as the "Saviour Man," a title he rejects. And, after what in 1885 were more than six hours of performance, Brand begins to weep. Gerd worries that his tears will melt the Ice Church. The strange hawk distracts her. So she shoots it, and then is horrified to see that it is as white as a dove. Before the reverberations of her rifle shot bring down an avalanche on top of Brand, he prays a final question:

Answer me, God, in the moment of death!
If not by Will, how can Man be redeemed?
The avalanche buries him, filling the whole valley.
A VOICE, *cries through the thunder.* He is the God of Love. (157)

Shaw does not mention these, the play's last lines; Driver and Balthasar are as uncertain as others as to how to interpret this benediction.[12] Brand is bound to an ideal of his own imagining, and his purist, isolated authenticity takes him far beyond the point where the pattern of his life can be sustained in relationship with anyone. Balthasar thinks such self-sufficient idealism is the pattern of Ibsen's earlier epic and verse plays; when Ibsen turns to realism, that pattern is put in doubt; characters either lapse into moral isolation (e.g., Stockman in *Enemy of the People*) or come to violent deaths or suicides. *Hedda Gabler* (1890) possesses a "Dionysian" personality searching for beauty and autonomy but finds ugliness and bondage; she "unlocks everything that has been carefully kept within limits and thereby destroys it,"[13] and then destroys herself.

To play Hedda, you must choose. If she is very strong, "the only woman in Scandinavia with a sense of humor"[14] (as Kate Burton played her in New York in 2001), it will be hard to accept the inevitability of her gunshot. But to play her with ragged, unsettled mental boundaries may undercut the integrity of her resistance (as in Martha Plimpton's intelligent performance at the Steppenwolf Theatre in Chicago, also in 2001). One advantage to Burton's charming yet willfully aware Hedda is to raise questions that, were it not for the play's melodramatic plot set in its patriarchal period, would be obvious. Why doesn't she simply walk away from the males in her life? How could someone so shrewd be trapped in sexual blackmail? Could she not turn her obstacles to her advantage? Or could she not succeed by improvising, by being theatrical? In regard to these questions, *A Doll House* (1878) is an exception, in that one similarly entrapped escapes. This play came earlier than *Hedda* and implicitly referred to itself as melodramatic.

> NORA; Just let me loose. You're not going to suffer for my sake.
>   You're not going to take on my guilt.
> HELMER: No more playacting. (105) ["We won't have any melodrama" (Watts), no "melodramatic airs" (Archer)]

Most of such metatheatrical references receive an anti-theatrical slant, as when she performs the Tarantella less modestly than her husband Torvald Helmer has taught her. She is hoping to delay his finding a blackmail letter (proving she forged her dead father's signature on a note, to finance Helmer's health-saving sojourn in Italy). The dance alludes to a spider's bite and to the cure of sweating out its poison—as if in a purgation ritual. But it fails to avert her exposure, and thereafter her transformation from childish adult to a paragon of independence can seem too rapid. Moreover, the feminist echoes of her slamming shut the household door have been so strong that the play's other utopian implications may be lost, namely, that she has no place to go.[15]

There are, however, metatheatrical moments when Nora *is* transformed by entering into a new part. Before considering these, it would be good to recall elements of her long, modernist manifesto of integrity-as-authenticity. She declares she must *educate herself*. She will have to do it *standing alone* "if I'm ever going to discover myself and the world out there" (110). Against Torvald's claim she has a sacred duty to her husband and children, she affirms "other duties equally sacred. . . . Duties to myself." These duties cannot be discovered through books or "religion"—"When I get free of my life here and on my own, I'll go into that problem too. I'll see if what the minister said was right, or, in any case, if it's right for me." Utterly exasperated and beside himself, Torvald then asks her about "conscience."

> You do have some moral feeling. Or, tell me—has that gone too?
> NORA: It's not easy to answer that Torvald. I simply don't know. I'm all confused about these things. I just know I see them differently from you. (111)

Nora will rely not on "tricks" or "doll wife" performances but on her ability to think. She will rely not on traditional education, religion, common morality, or gendered roles. Aspects of her declaration reach back into distant antecedents of modernity. Like Antigone, she must associate her body with sacred duties; but to live in the same *room* or *house* (extensions of the body) with her husband would violate her emerging pattern of integrity, in that conjugal relations would have to be tolerated or resisted. So she must move her body, from the house to the principle.

> NORA (*putting on her coat*): I can't spend the night in a strange man's room.
> HELMER: But couldn't we live here like brother and sister—
> NORA (*ties her hat on*): You know very well how long that would last. (113)

To critics of modernity, of course, her self-sufficiency has no moral or personal substance and cannot be sustained. She herself acknowledges, "I haven't the least idea what'll become of me." But are her declarations and gestures really so isolated or isolating?

"Metatheater," we recall, is not just theatrical self-awareness but also how a play's *story* makes us aware of the realities of performance in life. Nora, now an advocate of authenticity, opposes the hypocrisy of play-acting. Yet she describes what she is doing (after Torvald "forgives" her) as changing out of her party "costume" (107), "fancy-dress" (Watts), or "doll's dress" (Archer). She changes—screened from his sight, not necessarily from the audience's—as he prattles to his "little songbird." When she reappears, she has donned traveling clothes, which are probably stark and to Torvald very frightening. Were it not for the famous "slam" or "reverberation" (Archer) of the front door[16]—which can also be viewed as a piece of Nora's theater—her reappearance in a new costume might be remembered as the finale's most visceral moment. She is now *clothed* as one who stands alone and educates herself as a "human being."

One metatheatrical point here is that authenticity is itself a role or part to play. By putting on this part—a new costume, a voice no longer showy but unperturbed—Nora discovers herself *in this part*. She has always been a performer. A "doll house" is itself a toy stage.[17] She has identified herself as a puppet for others, who in turn are identified by her as puppets to manipulate. Her transformation, then, is realistic to herself in that she is still performing, but now performing a significantly better part that breaks her slide toward self-destruction. Another metatheatrical point, however, is that when a part like authenticity is defined as not-a-part (not-a-role, not-a-mask), it may lack definition and move in no particular direction. With Kierkegaard one could ask whether Nora, having leapt from the aesthetic toward the ethical, also discloses the limits of the ethical, and faces beyond the house a void—yet one that is numinous, something religious.[18]

Were Torvald's moral voice not so desperate, he might have made some solid points, especially about the children, whom Nora will not see before she leaves.[19] The play, however, is as much about the futility of *his* aesthetic stage in a doll house as hers. Yet before the great door closes, Torvald's integrity emerges as an unexamined glimmer. Nora says, "You and I both would have to transform ourselves to the point that— . . . our living together could be a true marriage" (114). This would require, she tells him, "the greatest miracle of all"—but she says she no longer believes in miracles. Torvald now wants to *believe,* as he looks about the room. "Empty. She's gone. (*A sudden hope leaps in him.*) The greatest miracle—?" If we could treat this last *question* as the shape of a new pattern of *his* integrity, then it would arise not in himself alone but within an empty space, a gap in his life, where he begins to recognize *Nora's* emerging integrity. But the door shuts on such mutuality, so briefly imagined.

Nina, Konstantin, Chekhov

Metatheater in *The Seagull* also exposes the limits of naturalism as an imitation of temporal life. As the characters arrive at Konstantin's outdoor stage—the schoolmaster Medvedenko and snuff-taking Masha (whom he loves, but who yearns for Konstantin), Sorin and Trigorin (who is having an affair with Arkadina while his eye is on Nina, whom Konstantin would love), Paulina and the physician Dr. Dorn, and at last Arkadina and Shamrayev (the estate's manager, Paulina's husband and Masha's father)—they, as an audience, serve to mirror our own situations as we gather in a theater to see a play by Chekhov.

Again, Metatheater in Naturalism

The Seagull can first be viewed through naturalism's lens. Konstantin is oedipally obsessed and knows that becoming free of his maternal prison is likely impossible. His dominant mood is flippant despair punctuated by histrionic rage. After his first attempt on his life, Sorin suggests to Arkadina that she give him some money. (She prudently if selfishly declines—an actress always needs more costumes.) Sorin sees that Konstantin is a smart young man without money, social role, decent clothes, job prospects, or pride. "He has nothing to do. He's ashamed, afraid of what will happen to him if he keeps on doing nothing" (138). And Konstantin has himself confirmed this, when describing Arkadina's parties: "I'm the only one there who isn't famous, and they only tolerate me because I'm her son. And who am I? I left the university after my third year, I'm not talented, I haven't a cent to my name. . . ." He says he counts as "middle class" only because his father "just happened to be a famous actor!" (114).

This picture of a social misfit receives still even more shading when we hear that his writing lacks "ordinary people" or a "central idea," and when we learn of the other characters. Trigorin (after Konstantin presents Nina with a seagull he has shot) tells Nina he will write a story about the illusions of freedom: "The shore of a lake, and a young girl who's spent her whole life beside it, a girl like you . . . [as] happy and free as a seagull. Then a man comes along, sees her, and ruins her life because he has nothing better to do. Destroys her like this seagull here" (135). Trigorin becomes that man to Nina, though she manages to survive complete destruction.

Two years after the first three acts, and against all expectations, Nina seems to have resisted shame, loss, abandonment, and artistic failure. She has turned fate into something else—although whether it is enough to overcome harm remains doubtful, for she still thinks she loves Trigorin and wonders whether she is to become the fated seagull of his story or a "real" actress. Konstantin also seems changed, having been published—although he has been poorly reviewed and has not, Trigorin says, found his authorial voice. "He writes very strange stories, you know, very vague; sometimes it sounds like raving" (154). Arkadina has never found time to read them, but Dr. Dorn admires their impressionism. When Nina at last tells Konstantin she has found her vocation as an actress, he finds the implications of her news devastating.

> NINA: . . . You don't know what that's like, to realize you're a
> terrible actor. I'm the seagull. ... No that's not it. . . . I'm not
> like that any more. I'm a real actress now, I enjoy acting, I'm
> proud of it, the stage intoxicates me. When I'm up there I feel
> beautiful. . . . I know, Kóstya, I understand, finally, that in our
> business—acting, writing, it makes no difference—the main
> thing isn't being famous, it's not the sound of applause, it's not
> what I dreamed it was. All it is is the strength to keep going,
> no matter what happens. You have to go on believing. I be-
> lieve, and it helps. And now when I think about my vocation,
> I'm not afraid of life.
> KONSTANTIN: I *don't* believe, and I don't know what my voca-
> tion is. You've found your way in life, you know where you're
> heading, but I just go on drifting through a chaos of images
> and dreams, I don't know what my work is good for, or who
> needs it. (159)

Depending on how these lines are played, one may ask who is the more self-deluded. Just how beautiful and strong is Nina's faith in acting, and how much is it the meaningless endurance of Sisyphus? And how poor are Konstantin's stories? The comedy and irony of *The Seagull* invites us to evaluate and then reevaluate whether it is necessary that these people be so confined in their natures, societies, and unrequited loves. The play keeps asking, "It is so, but must it be so?"

The Play Within the Play

Tom Stoppard thinks the problem of staging Konstantin's play—Nina's monologue in Act I—is that it must be boring, yet interesting.[20] The imperative about "new forms" echoes Chekhov, whose style in *The Seagull* began a departure from what might be called melodramatic naturalism. "What we need are new forms," Konstantin says, "and if we can't have them, then we're better off with no theater at all" (114). Yet the forms he has in mind are abstract, disembodied, and not themselves Chekhovian.[21] As if presiding at a cosmic ritual, he awaits the full moon to rise over the lake. Only then can the curtain open upon a primordial vista. Nina, who lives on a neighboring estate, has escaped her tyrannous father just in time to perform; in white, she nervously sits on a large rock as the "universal soul." Behind the rock is Yakov, the stagehand who will work glowing red eyes and release sulfuric vapor heralding a Demon, "the eternal father of eternal matter," whom the universal soul must challenge. Nina says she contains all souls from the centuries past, now that life on earth has been extinguished. Konstantin is attempting to create a symbolic form to overcome the stasis of the theater. But his mother thinks this is decadence; later, in a *Hamlet*-like closet scene, she calls him a "Symbolist" (141). As his play begins, this insult is anticipated:

> KONSTANTIN: . . . Oh you ancient shadows, that float at night
>   above this lake, wind us in your magic spell, make us sleep,
>   and make us dream of what this place will be two hundred
>   thousand years from now!
> SORIN: In two hundred thousand years there'll be nothing left.
>   Nothing!
> KONSTANTIN: Then let them show us that nothing.
> ARKADINA: Let them, please! The magic spell is making us sleepy.
>   (118)

Now Nina speaks, and how far should her words be open to ridicule? I once saw her played enveloped in a nylon bag, moving a bit like an amoeba. That risks our not noticing what she actually says. So too if she hams it up, which is tempting for a speech that invokes "Human beings, lions, eagles, quail … you horned deer, you wild geese, you spiders, and

you wordless fish who swim beneath the wave . . . all, all, all . . . all living
things have ended their allotted rounds . . ." Her monologue, however,
ends abruptly:

> Yet I know that victory will at last be mine . . . and then matter
>   and soul will join in beautiful harmony. But that moment will
>   come slowly, after a long procession of centuries, when the
>   moon, the bright star Sirius, the earth itself, have all returned
>   to dust. And until that moment all is horror, horror....
> (*Pause. From the lake come two burning red eyes.*)
> See! He approaches! My mighty enemy, the Demon! I see his ter-
>   rible crimson eyes! I—
> ARKADINA: Something smells. Is that part of the effect?
> KONSTANTIN: Yes.
> ARKADINA: (*Laughs*) I can always recognize an effect. (119)

Moments later, his mother's and other interruptions cause Konstantin
angrily to stop the play.

Trigorin later says Nina was "wonderful," which if not a charming or
lustful lie implies a modicum of talent. The Hindu, Gnostic, and eschatological pastiche she recites must sound portentous if it is to provoke
Arkadina's taunts; and yet there must be enough in the speech for Medvedenko and Trigorin to criticize seriously and for Dorn to appreciate.
Trigorin claims not to understand it, Medvedenko objects to its dualism.
"There's no scientific basis for separating soul from matter; I mean, the
soul itself may be nothing but a collection of atoms" (121). Nina complains the play lacks love interests, action, or "ordinary people," which
prompts Konstantin's retort that he must "show life not the way it is, or
the way it should be, but the way it is in dreams!" (116).[22] But Dorn tells
Konstantin he admires the play and the impression it made.

> You have to keep on writing! . . . But you must deal only with serious,
> eternal topics. You know, I've led a … varied life, lived it with taste, I
> like to think, and I've enjoyed it. But if I could experience, just for a mo-
> ment, the excitement that must come with artistic creation … (123, 24)

As Dorn projects his own life into the play, Konstantin is at first gratified
and amazed—"You really think I should keep on writing?"—but then
he becomes distracted and does not hear the doctor's note of constructive criticism:

DORN: Everything you write has to have a clear, concise, central
idea. You have to be aware of what you're writing, otherwise
you'll … you'll lose your way, and your talent will destroy you.
KONSTANTIN: (*Impatiently*) Where's Nina? (124)

Years later, after Konstantin's more conventional stories have found a
readership, Dorn's literary diagnosis is unchanged: He believes in Konstantin and is moved by his images and stories. "The problem is, though,
they don't have any clear-cut point" (155). Did anything in the monologue
warrant Dorn's measured praise?[23] The dullness of a doctor's life might
have made him susceptible to the promise of victory over the "material
impulses." Perhaps he resonated with the universal soul's suffering: "I am
like a prisoner thrown into a deep empty well," Nina recites, "I have no
sense of where I am or what awaits me" (119); for Dorn, escaping from
prisons is the possibility everyone around him lacks. So Konstantin did
have something to say, though in an abstract form that was not a good
alternative to Arkadina's mix of melodrama, naturalism, and romance. "I
used to talk all the time about new forms," he says, "but now everything
I write seems like a cliché" (156). As Nina tells him of her success onstage
and nostalgically repeats his invocation to "Human beings, lions, eagles,
quail" (159), he is observing his failure as artist and lover in his own symbolist mirror of nature.[24] Afterward, when he destroys his manuscripts
and shoots himself, we are not told whether he did so successfully.

The Play Outside the Play

When Konstantin's play fell out of his control, he stopped it. Yet it
evoked different and meaningful responses as Dorn and Nina remembered it. Konstantin thought his loss of artistic control had invalidated
him, and it was almost so with Chekhov. He read *The Seagull* aloud to
friends, one of whom recalled that their reaction to Chekhov's play was
comparable to Arkadina's to Konstantin's: "Something decadent."[25] And
when Chekhov later heard the boos and catcalls on opening night, he
fled the theater and wandered the dark streets of Saint Petersburg.

As biographer Ronald Hingley tells the story, that first production
in October 1896 was doomed from the start. It was hastily staged and
underrehearsed for a benefit honoring Elizabeth Levkeyev, a "fine old
character actress." She was not in the cast, which meant her fans would
arrive at a gala, to see a diva who would not appear in this "comedy,"
whose main action occurs offstage, which ends in apparent suicide, by a

playwright few of them knew. Nina's monologue "evoked jeers and derisive guffaws."[26] Chekhov vowed never to write another play and was
not mollified by news that, despite hostile reviews, the subsequent seven
performances actually went well. Apparently there were Dorns as well as
Arkadinas in the audience, implying that *The Seagull* had unexpectedly
transcended its theatrical circumstances, as it would again.

In December 1898, The Moscow Art Theater had existed for but four
months, and after initial success it was nearly bankrupt. Its founders,
Constantin Stanislavski and Vladamir Nemirovich-Danchenko, knew its
future depended on a hit, and Danchenko was determined to do *The
Seagull,* despite the Petersburg fiasco. But Chekhov, fighting tuberculo-
sis in the Crimea, doubted he could survive another failure, as did his
sister, Maria; but Danchenko prevailed upon Chekhov and Stanislavski
(who neither understood the play nor much liked its author), so another
catastrophe was likely. This time, however, the cast rehearsed for twelve
weeks. Stanislavski played Trigorin and also directed; Arkadina was
played by Olga Knipper, who later married Chekhov; the future theater
experimentalist, Vsevolod Meyerhold, was Konstantin.

This was in a period in Stanislavski's self-education when what later,
in America, came to be called the "method" was gestating. Even though
he was beginning to realize a new form of acting—in which players locate aspects of their parts in their own lives and emotions—he was himself a character actor who relied on "stencils," especially when he did
not understand the part. And he did not grasp Trigorin, especially his
lightness, irony, and attractive obliviousness to social expectations. So
Stanislavski, a rather serious man, directed *The Seagull* as if it were an
Ibsen-like tragedy. Chekhov was in Yalta, unable to intervene. The director told the players, with their company's future and Chekhov's life
at stake, that success was not enough, it must be a "triumph." Hingley
describes the overwrought actors backstage at the opening.

> Everyone had taken valerian drops, the tranquillizer of the period;
> Stanislavsky, as Trigorin, found it hard to control a twitching of his
> leg. As Act One proceeded audience reactions were hard to gauge, and
> when the curtain came down the house seemed frozen into immobil-
> ity. Standing on the curtained stage, Olga Knipper fought to control
> hysterical sobs amid the silence of the tomb. . . .

Stanislavski says she fainted,[27] as others went to their dressing rooms in
Konstantin-like despair,

until, at last, when it seemed that not a single clap would reward so carefully nurtured a production, a delayed action fuse seemed to have been detonated. . . . Members of the audience rushed the stage amid tears of joy and kissing so general as to recall the Orthodox custom of mass ritual osculation at Easter. People were "rolling around in hysterics," says Stanislavsky, who himself celebrated by dancing a jig. After the remaining three acts had been greeted with comparable enthusiasm, Nemirovich-Dancheko sent an ecstatic telegram to Chekhov in Yalta. . . . Chekhov had been restored to the theatre.[28]

But was it Chekhov's theater? At a later, private performance, he was irritated by interpretations of Nina as a weepy hysteric rather than a struggling actress, and of Trigorin as a weakling no woman would find attractive.[29] Chekhov gnomically told Stanislavski that as Trigorin he should wear checkered pants and broken shoes, not the neat white suit he did wear—an insult lost on Stanislavski, who for years tried to fathom it.[30] If there is a moral to all this, it must be that no single vision controlled *The Seagull:* the first production was likely better than its first audience or Chekhov thought; the second was evidently an effective *mis*interpretation; both were ahead of the wave, but not so far ahead as Chekhov; nor could *The Seagull* be confined by Chekhov's imagination. The intentions of script, author, players, and audiences had all been transcended, possibly by the play's complex metatheatrical relations, in which they all participated.

Stanislavski, Balthasar, Driver

To correlate theater with a view of life (be it sociological, philosophical, or theological) one must decide what to make of two perennial traits: the impersonation of dramatic action and our fascination or enjoyment of such impersonation. So I turn to Stanislavski's pessimism about inherited theater practice, which has been recapitulated by two theological interpreters of drama: the Swiss Catholic, Hans Urs von Balthasar, and the American Protestant, Tom F. Driver.

Stanislavski

Stanislavski benefited from the "more" of *The Seagull,* which he could not fully grasp. He was, like most dramatists of the day, enamored of a kind of authorial or directorial control that the theater both requires yet inherently resists. This control is, of course, a matter of power and self-authorization, and it is resisted in at least two paradoxical ways.

The first way is the more obvious. Stanislavski knew that stage acting is an extremely artificial form of behavior. When persons are viewed as inhabiting roles or wearing societal masks—more or less for the good, as in Calderón's *The Phantom Lady,* or for ill, as in Moliere's *Tartuffe*—then there is a plausible fit between stage and life.[31] But when theater probes "beneath" the persona or mask, to what persons supposedly truly are, then the "artificiality" of acting would *seem* to contradict the "natural" dynamics of living. The second paradox of control may be subtler. An actor must have command of body and mind, both to achieve spontaneity and to preserve that spontaneity over the run of a production. Yet to do this, an actor must give control over to the dynamics of the play and the ensemble. This is also true of authors and directors; even though some control is needed, they are tempted to overassert it. So by fits and starts, Stanislavski came to the view that directors should not dictate to actors, and that actors should not merely *observe and imitate* their characters but must find ways to *participate* in them.

In effect, Stanislavski turned the trope of theater-as-hypocrisy upon itself. If theater was assumed to use human pretence as its medium, no wonder it was unsatisfying. Instead, theater should try to unite the two accounts of "delight" we found in *Hamlet:* delight in seeing a mirror held up to nature and delight in persons becoming transformed in play-within-nature. If the contradiction of theater was between pretending and being—which Hamlet recognized is a problem in life—then Stanislavski's remedy was that *the integrity of the person who plays* is the medium *through which this player can represent another person.* Driver writes, "He integrated the actor into the total instrumentality of the theater without reducing him to a puppet."[32]

Stanislavski describes perfecting his portrayal of the idealistic reformer, Dr. Stockman, in Ibsen's *An Enemy of the People.* He intuitively found an organic fusion of himself with "inner" and "outer images" of Stockman's rather naive character: "the childlike and youthful manner of movement, the friendly relations with his children and family, . . . the forward stoop of the body, the quick step, the eyes that looked trustfully into the soul of the man. . . ." He realized that these "habits" had come to him unbidden ("quite apart from myself") from other plays or people he had met (e.g., a scholar from a sanatorium, a music critic). As years passed, he had only

> to assume the manners and habits of Stockman, on the stage or off, and *in my soul there were born* the feelings and perceptions that had given them birth. In this manner, intuition not only created the image, but its passions also. *They became my own organically,* or, to be more true, *my own passions became* Stockman's. And during this process I felt the greatest joy an artist can feel, the right to speak on the stage the thoughts of another, to surrender myself to the passions of another, to perform another's actions, as if they were my own.[33]

"To be more true," actually, Stockman and Stanislavski were recreating each other in relations of continuity and novelty; in no performance would they be exactly who they were before.

There have been persistent criticisms of "method acting." To begin with, there is nothing inevitably *in*authentic about external technique (as Stanislavski himself implies). The path from inner to outer goes both ways, and both modes produce great actors. If the danger of "technique" is falsified mannerisms, a danger of empathy is stereotyped emotions (as in parodies of Marlon Brando). Another risk of the method is to neglect dramatic literature in theater practice and education.[34] Stanislavski was more interested in characters than in a play's meanings or depth structures; he would reduce it to its "ruling idea" or the emotional "through line" of its roles. The actor may further reduce these to simple images and motives—"What is my motivation?" I also find that while Stanislavski eschewed individualism (the star system), he often valorized the actor's self-contained "will" and had difficulty finding consistent language for what his vision implies, namely, the mutual implication of selves and others.[35] Another common criticism concerns the naïveté of trying to become a fictional *other* by correlating one's emotional memories with emotions implied by the part: to "become Ophelia" is to court madness. Yet Stanislavski was not a philosopher, and Driver distinguishes his aim from his inadequate terms.

> What Stanislavski was really after was a dialectical movement generated between "sincerity" of emotion on the one hand and method on the other, which is the actor's equivalent of the dialectic between realism and theatricality in all stage presentations. This dialectic . . . had the aim of all great acting, which was to pass beyond mere repetition, however convincing, into a creativity transcending technique and unpredictable in effect. Thus, the goal of the method was not the *production* of emotion but the *control* and *release* of it under such conditions as might result in creativity.[36]

When Stanislavski reviewed what he had seen both of poor and truly effective acting,[37] he observed how when actors walk onstage they are usually self-conscious and terrified. The conventions of acting, then, are a bag of tricks for hiding this terror and for pleasing the spectators. But, like fear itself, the tricks severely hamper creative spontaneity. So his earliest insights concerned relaxation, breath control, and abandoning external imitation. His internal approach is analogous to a hermeneutical theory associated with an early-nineteenth-century Protestant theologian, Friedrich Schleiermacher, whose insights were later adapted by philosopher Wilhelm Dilthey. I doubt Stanislavski had heard of either of them, but they may clarify his aims.

Much as Stanislavski tried to sort out the grab bag of acting techniques, Schleiermacher sought to give an orderly account of the art of understanding (*verstehen*). Understanding grasps the meaning or the thought someone intends to express through language. It is true that understanding puts into play knowledge of language, history, culture, or biography; but such knowledge is not in itself understanding. The methods of understanding involve comparison and intuition (or "divination"). We start by guessing the meaning; there is no other way to begin. We do this by comparing the parts and the whole of a text, reaching for the author's thought. Comparison narrows the possibilities of meaning, yet intuition is always required. This dialectic of comparison and divination is not just for interpreting hard cases but for everything, from gossip to Shakespeare—because, as Schleiermacher observed, *misunderstanding is not the exception but the rule.* His hermeneutics, however, was not usually concerned with gossip but with great innovators of thought and language, analogous to poetic geniuses. Their texts are interesting because they increase the possibilities of human expression. But the elitist tinge to this romanticist theme is balanced by its egalitarianism: we divine of the other's thought as we compare the meanings with ourselves. Within each of us is a bit of everyone else; we each have "a receptivity to the uniqueness" of others. On this basis, Schleiermacher held that the aim of interpretation is "to understand the text at first as well as and then even better than its author." One must "put oneself objectively and subjectively in the position of the author."[38]

Stanislavski struggled to know how best to arouse an actor's receptivity to the uniqueness of a character. "One must get under the skin of a character so thoroughly that, for instance, Anna Karenina should cease to exist merely as a part that has to be presented on the stage, but instead should become a certain woman-actress who shares the same thoughts and ideas as Anna Karenina."[39] This requires the actor to develop both a sense of herself as individual—otherwise there is no basis for comparison—and a capacity to receive and relinquish herself to the part.

Now while Schleiermacher was here concerned with *meanings* (as opposed to the *Gefühl* of his theory of religion), Stanislavski usually spoke of *emotions*, even when he had meanings or ideas in mind. This is where Schleiermacher's successor, Dilthey, is clarifying. Dilthey concluded that we cannot view understanding simply as the reproduction in ourselves of the author's *thought*. Rather, meaning is conveyed when a whole field of *lived experience* (related to the author's life and times) is somehow *relived* by the interpreter. Also, meaning for Dilthey is temporal, experienced in time. Thus, meaning can be understood only *when experienced in time, anew*. This view also has its problems, but it approximates what Stanislavski was seeking. Emotion for Stanislavski is similar to what Dilthey means by meaning and experience. Stanislavski does speak as if the actor's process of relinquishing oneself to the part can be willed or controlled by training. But he also says that training can only develop a heightened *receptivity* to this creative encounter. Grace, as well as will, is required. "The creative mood," without which actors cannot attain the truth of their parts, "is not given them to control it with their own will. They receive it together with inspiration in the form of a heavenly gift."[40] Balthasar notes, "There is something sacramental about Stanislavsky's method."[41]

Balthasar

Balthasar's interpretation of theater begins in the first of a five-volume analysis of God acting on the world stage in behalf of persons, in the drama of Christ's death and resurrection. Christ is the actor whose *role is one with his mission,* where "mission" enables the realization of the individual, through "world-embracing" self-transcendence.[42] To undertake such a massive theological project in the midst of postmodernity is to confront a quixotic dilemma: On one hand, no one in the academy or the pulpit can employ classical theological distinctions (e.g., between nature and the supernatural) as if unaffected by modern epistemologies, views of language, or natural science. But neither can one do what Schleiermacher is alleged to have done: translate faith into anthropological or philosophical terms that make religious doctrines mean something else.[43] Not only might such transmutations obliterate faith testimony, they would likely rely on styles of thought that have themselves come into postmodern disrepute.

Ever since World War I, one solution has been to keep searching for better ways to translate faith via philosophy or the sciences.[44] Another (not necessarily exclusive) solution is to *rehearse* the witnesses of scripture and tradition to *divine love* (arguably the basic substance of the Abrahamic faiths) *without* giving it a modernist gloss. For this strategy there are various tactics. One is to shift from substance to form and view the witness of faith as being expressed in mythical, symbolic, metaphorical, midrashic, or otherwise unusual language.[45] Thus, faith language shapes and conveys meaning differently than ordinary language. Another tactic, closer to Balthasar's, is to recognize that the traditional witnesses arrive for the most part *as narratives,* which, because they are about events *in time,* cannot be translated into static concepts. But they can be *redescribed and renarrated,* just as stories can be retold.[46] Theology thus *describes*—albeit with new insights and sometimes in voluminous detail—the narrative's plot, characters, themes, and logic of love. Some find that to so interpret faith is like describing ethnographically a culture with its particular lingo and grammar.[47] Others emphasize that to re-describe narratives of divine love is inseparable from reenacting their claims upon those who hear them.[48]

Balthasar takes up an early Christian tradition in which the narrative of divine redemption is viewed as a drama. The triune God is author, fellow actor/player, and also participatory audience, in a theater of the world wherein human beings also enact their "search for self-realization."[49] So Balthasar thinks it is fitting that elements of drama can contribute to a better framework for understanding aspects of faith than do a number of recent theological organizing motifs: *event, history, orthopraxy* (right action, ethics), *dialogue, politics, futurism* (concerning hope), *function or structure, role,* and the *free choice of good and evil.* Each motif by itself misses implications of God acting *toward* (i.e., for, in behalf of, among, with, as) persons; and that the genuine insights of each motif would make greater sense if we could put them together in a "dramatics" of God acting in the "theater of the world" (the title of a play by Calderón). Thus, Balthasar is reconstructing an old analogy, in which the theater and drama of God's love enlarges the stage (or the playing space) for finite freedom,[50] a space where *mission* breaks open the paralysis of human existence and identity as entrapped by *social roles.*[51]

One of the motifs Balthasar examines is the sociological view that persons are roles or bundles of roles. On one hand, he grants its insight is that roles *are* ways in which persons find identities, relations with others, and directions in life; its limitation is that if persons are merely roles, their uniqueness is destroyed and with it any possibility of "mission," which must be freely offered and freely chosen. Balthasar thinks the history of drama has been all about the tension between role and identity, and for the most part modern realistic drama has never disclosed the transition "from role to mission." We have already seen instances of what he might mean:

> Mission is not even a possibility in *Miss Julie*. Agnes in *A Dream Play* has a role-with-a-mission, but the mission is mythological, outside the play's dream; inside the dream her mission appears futile. There is, however, the chance that those of us in Strindberg's audience may find ourselves in the play's emancipatory mission of arousing others to compassion.
>
> Ibsen's Brand is on a mission whose idealism turns out to be destructive and self-destructive; Nora's new mission-without-role is barely a mission at all, in that it has yet to find its content and self-transcending aim.
>
> Chekhov's Nina claims a calling as an actor. The play may regard her as self-deceived, yet some of her words resonate with mission as viewed by Stanislavski. Chekhov, like Ibsen, wanted audiences to examine themselves in ways for which compassion appears to be the norm.

The example of Nina exposes problems, however, with both Balthasar and Chekhov. We in fact *do know of missions that coincide with roles,* and not just in ecclesial life. What Alasadair MacIntyre calls *practices,* in vocations such as medicine and education, entail roles and identities whose goods are "internal to the practice."[52] As soon as a doctor or teacher gauges her work by her retirement plan, the work has likely ceased to be meaningful; but doctors and teachers readily testify that the reward is inseparable from the practice. Theater can be another such profession. But missing in Nina's confession are the *ensembles* in which she worked. Acting, even one-person shows, is not sustainable alone—another feature common to practices. Medicine is an extreme example: the burden of others' suffering is infinite, and cannot be borne alone; so doctors rely on other medicos.[53] Even solitary practitioners like Albert Schweitzer had their staffed clinics; he also had the pipe organ. But Balthasar's critique of the role/mission split seems to think mainly of individuals in their roles and missions, even though the context is ecclesial.

"Mission" has at best ambivalent attraction in late modernity, from public relations mission statements, to missions "impossible," to John Belushi and Dan Aykroyd's refrain in John Landis's 1980 film *The Blues*

Brothers, "we're on a mission from God!" Mission can be but a glossy term for "strong male role"—except when it passes through the emptying-out of the cultural-religious self, as in Shusaku Endo's novel *Silence* (1966) or Caryl Churchill's *Light Shining in Buckinghamshire* (1976). The plays Balthasar treats most hopefully are horizon-expansive works by Thornton Wilder and Bertolt Brecht. However, those dramatists would not so emphatically endorse Balthasar's relatively strong individual, for whom a transcendent mission secures identity and freedom.[54] Although the drama of Christ and the drama of discipleship are kenotic for Balthasar, he lacks an extensively kenotic account of theater. His identity-seeking, existential individual seems unlikely to embrace the mutable, soft-edgy self that is made receptive to kenotic integrity, which theatrical drama can help us recognize.

Driver

Drama comes to an end, Tom Driver concludes, because modernity does; drama, in form and substance, culminates as an expression of modernity. Driver was a student of Paul Tillich, one of the last monumental figures in a line of theologians who self-consciously translated biblical faith via forms of modern thought, in his case romantic, existentialist, and ontological. With others, Tillich recognized that the distinction between nature and the supernatural had given way to that between objectivity and subjectivity, between the world and the self apprehending itself in the world.[55] Religion, here, is primarily a response to the situations we implicitly share: we are anxious in the world and have a receptive "feeling" of absolute dependence (Schleiermacher) or of "being grasped by an ultimate concern" (Tillich). If for Balthasar, the meaning of God is revealed in narratives and dramas of identity and faith, then for Tillich and Driver such meaning appears in questions of ultimate concern, concern for what would answer and transform the anxiety over contingency and nonbeing.

For Tillich, a religious interpretation of a work of art traces how its generic form and particular style disclose apprehensions of ultimate concern. He was especially interested in what he deemed expressionist styles. In an "expressionist" work, apprehensions of ultimacy are disclosed through alterations in its form, as if the vitality of and anxiety of existence were shaping the form from within, as in *Dream Play.* In respect to Tillich, Driver's diagnosis of modern drama is that it has exhausted its expressionist impulse. In European drama of the eighteenth century, he

notes three early traits of modernity: *historicism* as the method of understanding; a transition in which the *quest for* reality became the *question
of* whether anything is real; and *romantic irony* in regard to how "fickle
truth" changes with changing experience. He finds the last trait captured
in these lines from Heinrich von Kleist's *The Prince of Homburg* (1811),
which also express issues of role, identity, and authenticity in matters
of integrity. A young woman, "caught between her uncle, the sovereign,
and the prince, her suitor," protests:

> The rules of war and the soldier's life
> Must be obeyed, I know. How much more
> The rules of real, human love must be obeyed!
> The heart has its rules and reasons too.[56]

But does the heart have its rules? The title of Driver's *Romantic Quest
and Modern Query: A History of the Modern Theatre* sums up the modern answer. Because irony puts every method of approaching the real in
doubt—including the way of subjectivity—then the *quest for reality* in
Romanticism arrives at modernity as a *question*. Romanticism at least
had confidence in the expressive search, if not always in the goal; but for
modernity, the search for reality itself was in question and on a trajectory toward meaninglessness.

The sort of historicism known as logical positivism affected modern theater in ways Driver has helped us see in naturalism and in Stanislavski's response to it. Driver locates another of historicism's effects in
French avant-gardist Antonin Artaud's plea for "total theater" or what
Driver calls "theatrical positivism."[57] This, in the first place, is a denial of
the expressive naturalism of Stanislavski, where roles and meanings still
have dramatic consequences. For Artaud, *language* in theater should not
be primarily a communication of meaning but another *body* in the spectacle; to this extent, Driver thinks Artaud was radically incarnational,
even when he attacked Christianity. However, Driver also finds that in
theatrical positivism, theater regards itself as the *only* thing, the only
body, the only reality. In dramatists such as Samuel Beckett, it is as if
the mirror of theater were held up to itself. Reality disappears in infinite
self-reflection. "The search for reality has turned in upon itself, not now
toward the interior subjectivity of the person . . . but inward to the form
of the work of art, which is an island of structure in a sea of chaos."
It is true that the mirror of such art, so transparent to chaos, can, he
says, elicit something like a mystical intuition of emptiness. Nonetheless,

with Beckett, realism appears to reach its closure. "The quest for reality, turned into a query, has no further to go."[58]

This outlook would not be refuted by the fact that the long dying of theater still creeps and creeps in its petty pace—and will continue, if only to provide "talent" for screen and video. Driver would argue that as long as theater keeps producing *drama* by staging *plays*, it is at worst spinning its wheels and is at best serving as an archive.[59] To overcome this diagnosis would require showing that modern theater has often misunderstood certain theatrical aspects of itself that nonetheless remain alive. For instance, when defining theatrical positivism, Driver writes that theater has "*embraced* its own alienation, in a perhaps *desperate* effort to *absorb* the world into its own mode of being."[60] Embrace, yes. But absorb in despair? Curiously, for Driver, Hamlet's mirror would be indicative more of the play and less of *the players;* yet the players are the ones who, along with playwrights, *embrace, hold, and play with the mirrors.*

Is there no way to imagine that what is delightful about theater is the *mutual mutability of the embrace,* which even when moving toward self-obsession can also involve motions of self-emptying and receptivity? Driver is looking for this, when turning attention from drama to myth and ritual.[61] Their renewal would probably preclude "drama" in the sense of plays, plots, characters, and stages. But suppose the "histrionic impulse" he thought was lacking by 1970 remained alive, both as inquiry and as play? Suppose it lived not only in performing but in the interplay of performance and dramatic representation (i.e., in plays)— alive in participatory mimesis that both delights in and criticizes the performative lives of persons and communities. Theatrical drama might then provide space and time for reconsidering assumptions about identity, and for becoming newly attentive to guises of integrity among selves and other persons.

Chapter VI

"Where the Devil Are My Slippers?"

The Eclipse of Integrity in Pygmalion, Educating Rita, *and* Six Degrees of Separation

I have forgotten my own language, and can speak nothing but yours.
—ELIZA DOOLITTLE, IN BERNARD SHAW, *Pygmalion*

FRANK: I'm going to have to change you.
RITA: But don't you realize, I want to change!
—WILLY RUSSELL, *Educating Rita*

You let me use all the parts of myself that night— . . . I'll tell you my name. . . . It's Paul Poitier-Kittredge. It's a hyphenated name.
—PAUL, IN JOHN GUARE, *Six Degrees of Separation*

MANY OF US past a certain age have a distinct impression of a bit of dialogue that echoes in English-speaking memory: "The rain in Spain falls mainly in the plain." "I think she's got it. . . . By George, she's got it."[1] As Professor Henry Higgins pronounces favor on Eliza Doolittle's pronunciation, some of us do not merely read these words but hear them in the mind's ear and see them in the mind's eye. And I suspect that a good many of us, while *hearing* the voice of Julie Andrews, are *seeing* the face of Audrey Hepburn. How Eliza Doolittle came to be impressed upon the mid-twentieth-century cortex as a composite persona—Julie's voice from the stereo and Audrey's face on the screen—is an accident of theater history that can serve as a reference point for how integrity might be conceived as emerging in performance with others.

The premises of *My Fair Lady* (1956) and its source, Bernard Shaw's *Pygmalion: A Romance in Five Acts* (1912), are well known. A linguist boasts he can teach a cockney flower girl to pronounce English so well as to pass in high society. He wins his wager, then she turns on him in rage. The casting of Andrews recapitulated the story. When rehearsals began, she was but twenty and not yet the global celebrity. The director of *MFL* was Moss Hart. His wife, Kitty Carlyle Hart, recalls how at first Andrews had trouble inhabiting the part of Eliza; so Hart put rehearsals on hold and coached her privately. For two weeks Kitty could hear the voice of Moss in Julie's delivery, but thereafter "she had made the part her own."[2] However, in 1964 Andrews's fans were dismayed when the film role went to Audrey Hepburn, while the songs were dubbed by Marni Nixon. The producers knew Hepburn would need no transformation into the box office glamour she already exuded, no matter she was not a strong singer. Do we value this composite persona as something "good"? Does Andrews/Hepburn/Nixon enhance or diminish the discovery that Eliza, a fiction, is something like a person? Or does it accentuate how theater is a place where persons are exchanged willy-nilly for fleeting pleasures and economic gains?

My "positive" answer is that emergent patterns of integrity in stories and characters created for live performance can arouse a sense of moral and ethical discovery: as when Antigone and Thomas Becket align themselves with principles or causes that claim others, or when Jane Pilkings witnesses an alienating moral alignment in Olunde. These patterns can also arouse a sense of delight or awe, when aesthetic appreciation is mutually implicated with ethical discovery. Such patterns occur when someone "makes the part one's own," which may also be the part making or transforming the person. In the plays I will discuss with *Pygmalion*—Willy Russell's *Educating Rita* (1980) and John Guare's *Six Degrees of Separation* (1990)—persons enter new patterns of integrity, in part through taking up others' voices, roles, stories, and tasks.

My "negative" answer continues the theme, introduced with *Hamlet* but as old as drama, of theater as a trope for falseness. *Pygmalion, Educating Rita,* and *Six Degrees of Separation* are ambivalent about the emergent patterns of selfhood they explore. They revert to norms of individualism and authenticity that may eclipse the performative patterns of integrity they celebrate. Eliza, somewhat like Ibsen's Nora, thinks of suicide before she goes alone into the world. Why the ambivalence of these plays? Is it only because "playing a part" is a favorite trope for lack of integrity? It may also be because in the ordinary discourses of morality there are few paradigms for valuing how persons emerge or change through other voices, roles, and narratives—even though the phenomenon in life and in art can be as delightful as it is troubling.

Educating Rita

There is a paradigm for the protean self we do embrace, *education,* which is how Higgins justifies his work on Eliza. Education's bundle of values authorizes us to deliver our children to forces that would transform them. Classrooms and professorial offices are places where liminal selfhood seems valued as such, especially if what happens there helps one find one's authentic self! Not surprisingly, institutions of education become suspect in times of cultural anxiety over identity. In the two plays that frame *Pygmalion* here, education is celebrated but cannot fully account for what the plays explore: patterns of integrity that emerge as one performs as another.

Rita's post-Eliza persona is already remarkable the moment she manages to open the stuck door of the office of her Pygmalion—"It's that stupid bleedin' handle. . . . You wanna get it fixed!" Frank is a failed poet and alcoholic professor of English literature, who tutors in an Open University in northern England, to cover his bar tab. Rita is twenty-six. She has observed the hopelessness of her working-class associates, including her husband, from whom she keeps her birth control pills a secret. She knows that "to change y' have to do it from the inside" (11) and has taken the name "Rita" after Rita Mae Brown, whose *Rubyfruit Jungle* initiated her into the nourishments of literature. Frank thinks he is too jaded to teach such untrained integrity, and tries to foist her onto someone else. But Rita recognizes that this "geriatric hippy" is indeed the tutor for her and recalls him to his vocation. So a reversal of the Pygmalion story is under way. Not that she reforms Frank, although the film version plays up that possibility.[3] The reversal is more in his knowing that the kind of education he can offer will likely stifle her expressive voice.

The scenes all take place in Frank's office. Early on he says that her essay on *Rubyfruit Jungle,* while not "crap," is merely "an appreciation." She must learn that criticism must be "purely objective," almost a science, "supported by reference to established literary critique. . . . In criticism, sentiment has no place" (18). Rita makes progress with an essay defending her proposal to stage *Peer Gynt* on the radio, because it is "a play for voices." She is thrilled to see a performance of *Macbeth* and submits a paper on it. "It's not rubbish," Frank tells her, but "a totally honest, passionate account of your reaction to a play. It's an unashamedly emotional statement about a certain experience" (47). He warns that if she is going to pass her exams she is "going to have to change"—but he is convinced her own voice is valuable as it is.

> RITA: Valuable? What's valuable? The only thing I value is here,
>   comin' here once a week.
> FRANK: But, don't you see, . . . you're going to have to suppress,
>   perhaps even abandon your uniqueness. I'm going to have to
>   change you.
> RITA: But don't you realize, I want to change! (48)

She has been reading E. M. Forster's *Howard's End,* where she discovers literary irony. Just because no character connects with anyone else, that does not invalidate its maxim, "only connect." Rita already has made a connection between "the prose and the passion," as Forster put it, and Frank fears she will lose it. Her last essays, while on a par with those of his best students, are trendy, and they overcomplicate poems that he values for their simplicity. Her Blake essay is academically acceptable, "but there is nothing of you in there." She replies,

> Or maybe Frank, y' mean there's nothing of your views in there. . . .
> [W]hen I first came to you, Frank, . . . you told me not to have a view.
> You told me to be objective, to consult recognized authorities. Well
> that's what I've done; I've talked to other people, read other books
> an' after consultin' a wide variety of opinion I came up with those
> conclusions. (62)

She drops the name "Rita" and with it her admiration for *Rubyfruit Jungle,* which Frank by now appreciates. Jealous, boozy, and disappointed he tricks her into criticizing his own pretentious poems. She likes them, making him think he has created a Frankenstein's monster. Actually, she sounds more like Shaw's Eliza: "I know what clothes to wear, what wine to buy, what plays to see, what papers and books to read. I can do without you" (68). However, she discovers her fellow students live lives as despairing as those in the working class. So—and it is not really clear why, given her disillusionment, except that it is there to be done—she sits for her exams, passes with an essay on *Peer Gynt,* and returns to thank Frank for his help. She doesn't know what she will do or where she'll go next, but at least it will be her choice: "I'll choose."

Rita's education occurs not in a classroom, but in an office, and until the very last instant there hovers the temptation of a student-professor affair. It ends with gifts. His for her is a new dress. Hers for him is a good haircut, "It's gonna take years off you" (73). Her gift says, at least: whatever else I'll be, I'll be proud to be a hairdresser, thanks to you. She begins to cut and nicks his ear, as if to seal her gift in blood, so the last word is his, "Ouch." In effect, Russell echoes Rousseau, dislocating the bundle of norms codified as *education*. What is praised is another value, *choice*, which Rita pretty much has to begin with. The play does not effectively portray the antecedent sources of her already rich voice, though there is a hint of that when she tells how at a pub her mother confided to her, "we could sing better songs than those" (46).[4] *Educating Rita*, in endorsing the value of an established self's authentic choosing, turns away from what it nonetheless dramatizes, how a self comes to inhabit a pattern of personal integrity by receiving, entering, and revising another's form of life.

Pygmalion, by Shaw et alia

In celebrating, yet resisting what it celebrates, *Educating Rita* recapitulates an aspect of *Pygmalion* in which discomfiture with protean selfhood and liminality of performance are alleviated by more acceptable paradigms of education and romance. Moreover, a number of theatrical and personal affairs associated with the casting, performing, revising, and filming of the play bear upon whether there is implied (at the finale) a romantic conciliation between Higgins and Eliza. This question, in turn, reflects ethical contexts in which the play and its audiences have understood Eliza's transformation.

The Emerging Integrity of Eliza Doolittle

Shaw helped rehearse the first English production of *Pygmalion* in 1914.[5] Like Moss Hart, he had to coach his West End star, Mrs. Patrick Campbell ("Mrs. Pat"), both because at forty-nine she was rather old for the part and she had to learn to speak cockney without affectation. It had been Campbell's voice, beauty, and excellent acting that inspired Shaw to create Eliza many years before; but her surprise marriage a week before the opening exasperated him, sealing the end of their intermittent (and probably chaste) affair. Shaw had almost as difficult a time with Higgins, played by the impresario Sir Herbert Beerbohm Tree, who agreed to direct as well as star.[6] Tree desired there should be, somehow, a hint of romance between Higgins and Eliza at the final curtain, even though she has for two scenes berated him and vowed (albeit ambiguously) never to see him again. Higgins, as Shaw originally wrote him, is proud of his achievement after Eliza finally exits. He kisses his mother, chuckles while rattling change in his pocket, "*and disports himself in a highly self-satisfied manner*" (209). Tree thought this ending would be unbearable, and wanted Higgins to toss flowers to Eliza as she exited. Shaw refused, insisting that Eliza was destined to marry the haplessly sincere Freddy Eynsford Hill. But after Shaw was safely out of the way, Tree added all sorts of comic business, including the flowers.

The 1912 text does leave some room to imagine a Higgins/Eliza liaison, but even though it is subtitled a "romance," Shaw wanted to scotch the issue. He published a narrative epilogue showing how Eliza married Freddy and opened a flower shop; yet that had little effect on the reception history of *Pygmalion*. In 1938 he had written most of the screenplay for Gabriel Pascal's production of the film, but could not prevent the final scene where Eliza (Wendy Hiller) returns to the laboratory of Professor Higgins (Leslie Howard), who is listening to recordings of her voice. Behind him she says, "Washed my face and hands before I came, I did." Without turning around, he smiles roguishly: "Where the devil are my slippers?" The 1956 musical ends similarly and even more romantically, and neither finale would be what Shaw intended. He lobbied for a last scene in Eliza and Freddy's flower shop, but Pascal wanted Eliza attached to Henry, and by the final cut it was a fait accompli. So Shaw published a longer version of *Pygmalion,* incorporating his film scenes and adding yet another ending. Mrs. Higgins, upon seeing Eliza depart the stage, tells her son she is hopeful Eliza might be fond of Colonel Pickering. "Pickering! Nonsense: She's going to marry Freddy. Ha ha! Freddy! Freddy!! Ha ha ha ha ha!!!!! (*He roars* with laughter . . .)."[7] The laughter, derisive of Eliza, has prompted speculation that it was really Shaw's long-nursed jealous rage at Mrs. Pat.[8]

Later, I will return to what the paradigm of romance has meant for the reception of *Pygmalion*, that is, for the audience's desire that the new Eliza be normatively comprehensible. But for now, these stories—not unlike those associated with Treplev, Chekhov, Stanislavski, and *The Seagull*—illustrate how Eliza's attempt to inhabit a proffered part to play is recapitulated by the theatrical medium. The story and the performance of the story reconstitute one another, as we perceive them. Our recognition of an actor performing the part of Eliza mingles with the story of Eliza performing a part, and this particular mixing of story and performance may shed some light on how patterns of integrity can be constituted and recognized. At this point, however, two related objections must be acknowledged. One is that Eliza's integrity is best seen in her *resistance* to the part Higgins has given her, in their debates in Acts IV and V. This antagonism issues especially from moral contexts within and surrounding the play, a matter to which I will return. The second objection is that if anything, *Pygmalion* shows what is wrong about the whole notion of playing a part external to oneself.

By Act V, Eliza thinks she has no viable identity or future. "What have you left me fit for? Where am I to go? What am I to do? Whats to become of me?" (180). Mrs. Higgins reports she is near despair and has spent "the night partly walking about in a rage, partly trying to throw herself into the river and being afraid to" (192). The experiment now seems monstrous, more like Frankenstein's than Pygmalion's.[9] Higgins is turning Eliza's voice into a diminished dialect of correct sounds and absent meanings.

> LIZA: . . . Last night, when I was wondering about, a girl spoke
> to me; and I tried to get back into the old way with her; but
> it was no use. You told me, you know, that when a child is
> brought to a foreign country, it picks up the language in a few
> weeks, and forgets its own. Well, I am a child in your country.
> I have forgotten my own language, and can speak nothing but
> yours. (197)

As Higgins teaches her to enunciate the rain in Spain[10] and the manners that go with proper speech, he would be threatening to efface her own "Lisson Grove lingo." We might say he is "colonizing" her. However, we might ask, *has* she really lost her lingo?

Jacques Derrida considers the distinction between one's native tongue and that of the colonizing other to be unstable and dichotomous. He elaborates on a paradox. While he (a francophone born in French Algeria) has no other language than "his own," his own (French) is "another's" language.[11] All language is, in a sense, imposed, with all the ambiguities for justice and authenticity such imposition may entail. In applying Derrida's insight to *Pygmalion,* two conclusions might occur. First, that Higgins, in imposing Standard English, is reducing Eliza's voice to that of a child. And second, as Eliza has begun to realize, there is really no alternative. Whether she speaks cockney or Received Pronunciation, she is trapped with no voice of her own, and any imagined alternative is an illusion. However, Derrida's essay takes an unexpected turn. As he reviews how his own life transpired with the French language (which is and is not his own) he comes to express gratitude for it, especially French literature. Why gratitude? He now suggests that a gift *has* been given. So then, does *Pygmalion* disclose the emergence of a person, an amalgam of self and other, who might come to esteem herself in gratitude, not resentment?[12]

Many of us remember the Cinderella moment where Eliza enters a lavish embassy ball and another linguist proclaims her to be a Hungarian princess passing as British, because her English is too perfect. This scene is reported but not staged in the 1912 play; Shaw thought such a display would be merely a fashion show. And that lovely show (in the film, the revised play, the musical, and the musical film) is where Eliza puts on a new persona she momentarily enjoys. But there is in the play and in all later versions another dramatization of Eliza's emergence, which is *not* entirely under Higgins' control.

In Act III, Higgins has arranged for a phonetically reformed Eliza to meet his mother, forgetting that Mrs. Higgins is to receive guests, namely Freddy, Clara, and Mrs. Eynsford Hill.[13] So he is resigned to them being Eliza's first audience. She arrives distinguished and beautiful. She performs her "aitches" impeccably, if hesitantly. Higgins has warned her "to keep to two subjects: the weather and everybody's health" (159), and to his horror, she does. After Freddy is charmed by her stately weather report—"The shallow depression in the west of these islands is likely to move slowly in an easterly direction"—Eliza warms to her part, as the conversation turns to the flu. She tells a dark suspicion, "My aunt died of influenza: so they said. . . . But it's my belief they done the old woman in" (165). And so begins a narrative, in which while speaking in her Lisson Grove cadences, she pronounces perfectly. This speech is hilarious, and all the more so when whoever plays Eliza allows it to shape her own interpretive tones.

MRS. HIGGINS (*puzzled*): Done her in?
LIZA: Y-e-e-e-es, Lord love you! Why should she die of influenza? She come through diphtheria right enough the year before. I saw her with my own eyes. Fairly blue with it, she was. They all thought she was dead; but my father he kept ladling gin

> down her throat til she came to so sudden that she bit the
> bowl off the spoon.
> MRS. EYNSFORD HILL (*startled*): Dear me!
> LIZA (*piling up the indictment*): What call would a woman with
> that strength in her have to die of influenza? What become of
> her new straw hat that should have come to me? Somebody
> pinched it; and what I say is, them as pinched it done her in
> (165–66)

What we have seen of Eliza has until now been somewhat unimpressive.
She appeared first as the aggrieved victim, whining about her "rights"
and "reputation," as Higgins transcribed her speech. "I'm a respectable
girl. . . . They'll take away my character. . . . I'm a good girl, I am" (118–
19, 121). There, in Covent Garden, what distinctive character she has is
the amusing way her assertiveness clashes with stereotype—which might
be perceived as Shaw patronizing the "common flower girl." In Act II, to
her credit, she approaches Higgins on her own initiative. But again, more
noticeable will be the audacity of Higgins's wager, her fear of bathtubs,
and the arrival of that emissary of the "undeserving poor," Mr. Doolittle,
looking to extort a price for his daughter. Eliza is illegitimate and her
narrative seems to have little connection with his. "I aint got no parents.
. . . I aint got no mother. Her that turned me out was my sixth step-
mother. But I done without them. And I'm a good girl, I am" (136–37).

Yet in Mrs. Higgins's drawing room she has entered an unfamiliar
space, a stage to perform on but not exactly before the audience Higgins
intended. If she emerges here as a more fully expressive person, it is less
because of who she "is" or "has been" (although now her mother and father do figure in her story) than because the part given her to play turns
out to be richer than Higgins knows. Genteel pronunciation, cockney
idiom, plus a vague script about "the weather and everybody's health"
make for a chance to recover and reconfigure fragments of her past in an
expansion of expressive possibilities. To be sure, part of what is funny
about her disquisition is the way two lingoes clash on the same tongue.
But she implicitly treats of the existential verities of embodied life and
death, of love and despair, of happiness and the guilt-ridden conscience,
and she weaves wisdom out of particular experiences.

> When [my father] was out of work, my mother used to give him
> fourpence and tell him to go out and not come back until he'd drunk
> himself cheerful and loving-like. Theres lots of women has to make

their husbands drunk to make them fit to live with. (*Now quite at her ease*) You see, it's like this. If a man has a bit of conscience, it always takes him when he's sober; and then it makes him low-spirited. A drop of booze just takes that off and makes him happy. (166)

Rather than Eliza's voice being colonized, she is, as Max Harris would put it, finding a voice in another's speech, and indeed is subverting a moral hierarchy. Exemplified here is what Mikhail Bakhtin calls "heteroglossia," a concept of discourse that denies there are in practice pure speech types but considers all speaking to be inhabited by the speech forms and social strata of others.[14] The implication would be that in providing Eliza with putatively pristine speech, Higgins has really set in play dynamics he neither anticipates nor controls.

These dynamics are also comprehended through ritual theory. Not only is Eliza betwixt and between being cockney and something whose status is not yet clear. More to the point is Victor Turner's contention that many cultural paradigms might or might not engage such a person in transit. How an individual grabs or is grabbed by symbols in a rite of passage or social drama is more or less indeterminate.[15] Thus, to perform a new practice or theatrical part is no singular thing, for roles (like heteroglossia) are intersected and compounded by other social strata and cultural forms.[16] Eliza is both constructing and being renewed by an unpredictable pattern of relationality, as she improvises on Higgins's supposedly innocuous script. Her improvisation includes interactions with the Eynsford Hills, the two Higginses, and Colonel Pickering. They in turn mediate the audience's relations with the emerging integrity of Eliza Doolittle.

Her last bit of performance is to refuse Freddy's offer to walk her home. "Walk! Not bloody likely. (*Sensation*). I am going in a taxi" (167). I take it we delight in the way she spoofs polite society, and in how her hybrid lingo (what Higgins passes off as "the new small talk") begins to contaminate the younger Eynsford Hills. Clara also utters the "b" word, the "sensation" that in 1914 thrilled West End audiences and scandalized moralizing critics. As her lingo rubs off, she is passing on the gift— extending to others the very lines of relationality that are now allowing Eliza *to be*. To say we delight in these matters is to say we intuit something good in her emergence into a new pattern of integrity. But to say *why* these delights are good is not easy, and the script swerves away from Eliza's emerging integrity to other issues.

MRS. EYNSFORD HILL: I daresay I am very old-fashioned; but I
do hope you wont begin using that expression, Clara. I have
got accustomed to hear you talking about men as rotters,
and calling everything filthy and beastly; though I do think it
horrible and unlady-like. But this last is really too much. Dont
you think so Colonel Pickering?

PICKERING: Dont ask me. Ive been away in India for several
years; and manners have changed so much that I sometimes
don't know whether I'm at a respectable dinner table or in a
ship's forecastle.

CLARA: It's all a matter of habit. Theres no right or wrong in it.
Nobody means anything by it. And it's so quaint, and gives
such a smart emphasis to things that are not in themselves
very witty. I find the new small talk delightful and quite innocent. (167–68)

This cultural commentary from Pickering and Clara diverts our attention from Eliza to the fun of Shaw's lampooning of manners and mores.
Eliza, just as soon as she emerges as an interesting person, begins to be
eclipsed by a muddle of moralities.

Romance and "Middle Class Morality"

There is a veritable cornucopia of moral discourses in *Pygmalion* that
eclipse or "pass over" Eliza as a person, because they cannot cherish
her in particular and tend to impose a leveling impartiality. Shaw's play
seems at once to expose this problem and perpetuate it. What Higgins
later lacks after the embassy garden party triumph—when he literally
overlooks Eliza while searching for his slippers—is *language* for attending to what, at some level, he does sense, namely the integrity of the person who emerged in Act III. He is amazed that she thinks he has harmed
her. He cannot express his attachment to her, nor can he recognize her
performance as the gift that it is. What she did for him "was not for the
dresses and the taxis; I did it because we were pleasant together and I
come—came—to care for you . . ." (205). This caring he does not comprehend. And when he is finally amazed by the force of her resistance
(she threatens to hang out her own shingle as a speech teacher and put
him out of business), he redefines her in terms that he does understand,
the sheer will to power:

HIGGINS: (*wondering at her*) You damned impudent slut, you! . . .
By George Eliza, I said I'd make a woman out of you; and I
have. I like you like this. . . . Five minutes ago you were like a
millstone around my neck. Now youre a tower of strength: a
consort battleship. You and I and Pickering will be three old
bachelors together instead of only two men and a silly girl.
(208)

Higgins's dullness toward Eliza as a person is not just the habit of a
confirmed old bachelor. It also follows from the mix of principles surrounding him and most of the other characters. When her father, Alfred
Doolittle, calls this mix "middle class morality," it sounds like a critique
of the status quo. As a man pleased to be of the "undeserving poor," Mr.
Doolittle regrets having to sacrifice his ad hoc happiness to the ordinary
respectability that comes with sudden wealth. "I have to live for others
and not for myself: thats middle class morality" (190). "Middle class
morality" is really a grab bag of ethical outlooks. It entails a concern for
the common good, and the virtue of having (or being known to have) a
"good character," about which Eliza is quite concerned and which Higgins assures Perkins he has in respect to his female students (142–43). It
also includes an impartial, Kantian respect for persons, which Mrs. Higgins, Colonel Pickering, and the cleaning lady Mrs. Pearce express when
they upbraid Higgins for bullying Eliza. Mrs. Higgins comes nearest to
recognizing what is crucial about Eliza's story: "she did this wonderful
thing for you . . . ," she tells her son (192). But even Eliza appeals to
impartial respect when she protests, "Hes no right to take away my character. My character is the same to me as any lady's" (122).

The cornucopia of moralities must also include Shaw's utilitarian incli-
nations, reflected in the play albeit with comic irony at Higgins's expense.
Consistent with his Fabian socialism,[17] Shaw believed that commonality
in speech would help dissolve human inequities. "I care for life, for humanity," Higgins tells Eliza, "and you are a part of it that has come my
way and been built into my house. What more can you or anyone ask?"
(202). What she asks for is her independence, prompting his bracing reply, "Independence? That's middle class blasphemy. We are all dependent
on one another, every soul of us on earth!" (207). This last sentence, by itself, is exhilarating. But Higgins's general concern for humanity obscures
Eliza the individual who, as far as he can tell, will be of no great use to
humanity's advancement. Shaw's own philosophy of "creative evolution"
and the "Life Force" (the latter associated with "female" strength) would

really appreciate Eliza more as an allegory than as a person. Against her bitter protestations, Higgins defends himself as one who treats everyone exactly "the same."

> The great secret, Eliza, is not having bad manners or good manners or any other particular sort of manners, but having the same manner for all human souls: in short, behaving as if you were in Heaven, where there are no third class carriages, and one soul is as good as another. . . . The question is not whether I treat you rudely, but whether you ever heard me treat anyone else better.
> LIZA (*with sudden sincerity*): I dont care how you treat me. . . .
> But (*standing up and facing him*) I wont be passed over. (201)

So between Mrs. Higgins's ethic of impartial respect and Professor Higgins's vision of social reform, there is a gap in the play's self-understanding. And it is within this gap that Eliza Doolittle appears as a "sincere" and delightful force. But what is missing in the 1912 play is any ethical paradigm by which to grasp or value how Eliza emerges through her performance of Higgins's script. Thus, to keep her from being "passed over," audiences have been invited to read a "feeling heart" into Higgins's head. The play itself invokes the paradigm of romance, in spite of Shaw probably intending the subtitle to be ironic. But beneath his socialism, Shaw arguably was something of a romantic.[18] While he did believe there are no isolated voices, that no one is all of oneself, he also thought that the spiritual destiny of humanity depends on individuals of practical creative genius. However, both his rhetoric of equality and his rhetoric of romantic creativity can eclipse Eliza as a distinctive person. As Higgins harshly tells her in Covent Garden (Act I),

> A woman who utters such depressing and disgusting sounds has no right to be anywhere—no right to live. Remember you are a human being with a soul and a divine gift of articulate speech: that your native language is the language of Shakespear and Milton and The Bible; and dont sit there crooning like a bilious pigeon. (124)

Higgins and Shaw dreamt of a common language by which to rescue flower girls from the gutter, but their dream eluded particular flower girls. Indeed, after World War I, Shaw, thoroughly disillusioned with liberal democracy and unwilling to recognize the demonries erupting in

Europe, gave voice (and not a clearly ironic or satiric voice) to notions of "exterminating," without "cruelty," the inferior multitudes who could only retard creative evolution.[19] Such hyperbolic remarks may be consistent with his vision of a distant future, where creative evolution will have produced disembodied beings of pure intellect.[20] Thus, strong, creative, idiosyncratic characters—often powerful women working through reliably clever men—are justified in Shaw's ethics, in that they are useful to transforming society toward socioeconomic equality. But the equality he had in mind was not altogether one in which the integrities of ordinary blokes—that is, Eliza's and Alfred's—could be valued.

We saw how Bernard Williams thinks the impartial, overriding logic of obligation in modern moral philosophies cannot grasp the distinctive projects, desires, and fidelities that make a particular life seem to itself worth living, that give it integrity.[21] His critique is interesting in confirming how difficult it can be to hold together, in a single thought, universal moral forms and the integrity of a particular person. I have agreed that when Williams, Martha Nussbaum, Charles Taylor, and Paul Ricoeur view *moral obligation* as but an aspect of *the ethical* (defined by the broader question, "how should one live?" and inclusive of cultural *paideia*, tradition, lore, etc.), they begin to recover the breadth of "moral philosophy." I have also agreed with Ricoeur that moral principles are rooted in the ethical and as such contribute to the shaping of persons, but within the ethical, questions about moral and personal aspects of integrity remain.[22]

As we ponder such questions, Williams would want us to recognize that integrity entails contingencies, circumstances, and what he and several others call "moral luck,"[23] as exemplified by Gauguin. The French painter came to a pass where his vocation led him to abandon his family for the landscape, people, and isolation of Tahiti. His departure would appear to break with some obvious norms of "middle class morality." Yet Williams thinks we can ethically assess such choices only retrospectively. We have to wait and see how they turn out. Had Gauguin's "ground project" failed, that is, if he had not painted in Tahiti so effectively—something none can rationally know in advance—then a utilitarian might assess his life differently, as if only great art could justify such a choice.[24] Or if Gauguin was as a person in artistic crisis, then judging him deontologically by his familial obligations would eclipse his grounding reasons for living, reasons that may become justifiable only after the fact. From both perspectives, Williams's point is not that "moral luck" calls into question moral obligation per se, but rather its *primacy* in a thick description of human well-being.

The Gauguin-in-Tahiti example is rather exotic, but two points seem realistic. First, it is hard to hold together in commensurate terms the good of creative expression and the good of, say, social justice.[25] Second, over time the paradigms by which we order our lives undergo reconfiguration; the flow of circumstance—the matter of luck—does have a bearing. This is obviously true of vocational paradigms: versions of "being a mother," "being an artist," or even "being a pirate." This is also, if less obviously, true of the moral norms that have a bearing on our lives. On one hand, moral norms are so in the background of our identities as to work on us, unwittingly. On the other hand, as circumstances bring them to light, we may weigh and specify them differently, or discover conflicts among them, or else encounter the norms anew. I may have thought I should treat persons impartially, until I became a father and discovered all sorts of relations of partiality that are ethically compelling. These particular relations, a MacIntyre or Clifford Geertz would say, may well be cultural as well as personal.

What Williams might have articulated is that since abstracted moral imperatives are culturally rooted and embedded, they too are forms of culture and discourse, which a person inhabits over the changing courses of life. As cultural forms, principles and their frameworks (e.g., versions of the categorical imperative, the utilitarian demand to maximize welfare, the Golden Rule, the Love Command, the Eightfold Path) are part of the milieus in which selves and communities find shape. This much is so, whether we view principles as fragments uprooted from traditions, or grounded apart from tradition in reason or nature. They are in any case *signs*, matters to recognize, remember, and revise. Aided by them, thinks Ricoeur, we clarify obligations and criticize actions. To the extent they are *culturally* mediated and relative, such principles have to figure in considerations of personal integrity. But they also have a logical form and context-transcending force sometimes incommensurate with other cultural matters.

This worries Williams, the lack of fit between lives and principles. But we could say this much, that in the persisting-yet-changing patterns of relation in which we find ourselves, we *juxtapose and find juxtaposed* moral principles alongside other personal, vocational, and cultural concerns and paradigms: justice with motherhood, for instance, or obedience to God, and sometimes to the rules of origami. We try to *hold* them in spatial proximity. To add time to the metaphor, we *juggle* them or improvise them with other players. Thus, Eliza Doolittle, the flower girl, speaks in Covent Garden of her moral "right" to equal regard as a "lady." Her declaration of this principle is as much a part of her as is her dream of a flower shop. Her declaration and dream are not easily sewn into whole cloth in the time she has at hand. To acknowledge such contingent juxtapositions of principles and projects in the patterns of persons is to recognize that while we cannot fuse different aspects of integrity, we yet have *a desire not to separate them*. We try to speak as though moral and personal integrity were integrated in what Ricoeur calls "aiming for the good life." The juxtaposition of norms and projects in a living relationship, however, is never settled. It has its gaps and flux. And we may lack paradigms for saying how this moral and personal flux is, on occasion, good.

Six Degrees of Separation

Recall that for Lionel Trilling, sincerity—of the sort Polonius recommends—became a late medieval virtue in reaction to nascent social mobility, where dissembling about identity and status might win one entrée to privileged social orders, or else might promote one's survival in such orders. (Indeed, at the turn of the twentieth century, Higgins says he can make a very fine living teaching upwardly wealthy "upstarts" to lose their accents.) However, the worry about being made a victim of a confidence game has a counterpoint: namely, that in such playacting, contact is made with other lives, and with this contact there may also arise relationships of responsibility, even charity. The danger of playing a part to win one's own advantage implies the reverse possibility of playing a part for another's joy or suffering, an aspect of kenotic integrity. These dangers and possibilities are the subtext for John Guare's Pygmalion story, which is more explicitly ambivalent than *Educating Rita* about the theatrical paradigm for emergent integrity.

The three families whose lives intersect in *Six Degrees of Separation* are apparently linked only by their college-dispersed children who attended the same New York City high school, and this happenstance connection provides the database for a confidence game. The Eliza/Galatea figure is a young African American male, who has an envious fascination for the wealthy in their flats adjacent to Central Park. Before becoming "Paul Poitier," he has been an anonymous hood, a stereotype of urban fear, with no apparent identity of his own. He is also gay, and is taught refined manners and pronunciation in exchange for sexual favors by his white Pygmalion, Trent Conway, "the Henry Higgins of our time" (81).

TRENT: This is the way you must speak. Hear my accent. Hear
my voice. Never say you are going horse-back riding. You say
you are going riding. And don't say couch. Say sofa. And you
say *bodd*-ill. It's bottle. Say bottle of beer.
PAUL: Bodd-ill a bee-ya.
TRENT: Bottle of beer. (76)

Trent shows Paul his address book and provides details about the
wealthy parents he knew from high school, including the art dealers,
Flanders and Louisa Kittredge. In their sector of Manhattan society, ties
of moral community are virtually unknown. Their children despise them,
their friends are merely economic opportunities, and what few traditions
they share are popular icons. One of the play's sources of comedy is the
marvelous gullibility to which they are susceptible in this rarified air.
Hungry for connective "experiences," the Kittredges are ready to believe any plausible story. They do, however, put to us serious questions.
If there is no secure, substantial self, then how do we manage to "only
connect," as Forster and Rita say? If the self is a theater-like construction—an illusion not essentially *there*—then do we have an infinite burden of responsibility to all selves, from whom we are separated by but
six degrees of otherness?

Saying he's been mugged, Paul shows up bleeding a bit at the Kittredge's Fifth Avenue apartment, where Flan and Ouisa are strategically
entertaining. They are desperate to secure two million dollars from a
white South African friend, Geoffrey, so they can leverage a Cézanne to
sell discretely to Japanese buyers. Liberal guilt is in the air as the wounded
stranger performs his well-considered opening lines, offering Flan and
Ouisa an opportunity to be Good Samaritans. "I'm sorry to bother you,
but I've been hurt and I've lost everything and I didn't know where
to go. Your children—I'm a friend of—" and he names their children
now at Harvard (14–15). South African wealth, a black graduate student
dripping blood in their doorway, and admiration for their kids cannot be
ignored. Even more amazing, this articulate young man admits to being
the son of a matinee idol they hold dear, Sidney Poitier! So they allow
Paul to cook and spend the night, and then give him fifty dollars to be
safely on his way the next morning.

Paul flatters the Kittredges. He performs a lecture on what is missing in their lives: the integrity of "imagination," as that which connects
every individual to everyone else. This, he explains, is the theme of his
master's thesis. "The imagination has been so debased"—it is no longer

the "personal link" between "our inner lives and the world . . . we share."
It is now merely a synonym for "style," not for the "most uniquely us."
The imagination should be "the passport we create to take us into the
real word," "God's gift to make the act of self-examination bearable"
(33–34). Later we learn Paul has lifted this manifesto from a commence-
ment address, just as he has inserted his life into Sidney Poitier's biography. At the moment, however, his thesis strikes Geoffrey, Flan, and
Ouisa as something to believe in. And their will-to-believe in that which
connects the "uniquely us" to everyone in the world is probably shared
by much of the audience. Why should the fact that he plagiarized it make
any difference?

It turns out that the imagination *is* in effect something outside of Paul;
it is a script he finds, memorizes, and inhabits with a good deal of creative skill. But such a view of imagination may seem to him too close
for comfort to stealing, so he appeals to *authentic inwardness* and even
alters subtly Salinger's text. *The Catcher in the Rye,* narrated by a boy
who berates phoniness, heralds what Paul calls the "death of the imagination." He quotes Holden Caulfield, "I'd rather push a guy out of the
window or chop off his head with an ax than sock him in the jaw. I
hate fist fights ... what scares me most is the other guy's face ..." (32).
Paul then interpolates: "*most of the time the faces we face are not the
other guys' but our own faces. And it's the worst kind of yellowness
to be so scared of yourself you put blindfolds on rather than deal with
yourself*" (34).[26] This change is a shift away from "the face of the other,"
as Levinas would put it, to a matter of interior identity. Paul is, at best,
confused whether the imagination is a mode of interpersonal connection or narcissistic self-reflection. But the result of his performance is
as compelling, for a while, as Eliza Doolittle's. But if he fascinates us at
first, he soon appalls us—when the next morning Ouisa finds him in bed
with a naked male hustler, or when weeks later he insinuates himself into
two other households, or months later, after the suicide of Rick, a young
actor from Utah. Paul had persuaded Rick to loan him his meager bank-
roll, then seduces him after a night of dancing at the Rainbow Room.
"I came here to have experience" (91), Rick says before jumping to his
death.

The tale has become very dark. As Guare explores the contingency of
the self and its being pliable as clay, he plays to fear of such contingency
and to the commonplace that gays and actors have insecure selves. Paul
says, "My father, being an actor, has no real identity" (30). However,
what invalidates Paul's performance as counterfeit (besides its being lar-

ceny) is that until he is caught, his only witting audience, as such, is himself. He does not give to others on his stage room to share the stage knowingly; they rightly regard themselves as violated, unless they reflect on this one who came their way.

The play, in this respect, is less about Paul's desire for a pattern of integrity than Ouisa's, and perhaps Guare's. Paul does emerge, to Ouisa, as more significant than an anonymous cipher. He awakens her to a sense of participatory responsibility, as she responds to his pursuit of an identity that intersects lives like hers. Before disappearing, he tells her she has allowed him to use "all the parts of myself," as if arranging pieces in a collage (107). His name, he says is "Paul Poitier-Kittredge. It's a hyphenated name" (109). Ouisa cannot let go of the discovery of "such promise." She never learns his real name and can do nothing, after arranging for his arrest, to keep him from vanishing into the oblivion. Cringing at the dinner party conversations she imagines his story will inspire, she vows, "I will not turn him into an anecdote" (117). Yet the play is an anecdote, based on accounts of David Hampton, an African American teenager, who in the early eighties charmed New York celebrities into believing he was Poitier's son; he later unsuccessfully sued for Guare's profits, having "felt used" by *Six Degrees*."[27] And he continued his con artistry for two decades, until dying, alone, of AIDS in 2003.

"It was an experience," Ouisa concludes. "How do we *keep* the experience?" (118). She is asking two questions, one more articulate than the other. Articulately, the play is framed by references to Cézanne and Kandinsky. Flan says that Cézanne left "blank spaces in his canvasses if he couldn't account for the brush stroke, give a reason for the color." Kandinsky's abstract expressionist works were sometimes controlled and geometrical and sometimes bursting with color; Guare has imagined a double-sided painting suspended in the flat. One side is "somber" and ordered, the other "wild and vivid" (3). Ouisa says she can account for the color in her life, but not the structure. "I am a collage of unaccounted-for brush strokes. I am all random" (118). She seeks a structure that does not invalidate the color—color being for Kandinsky what discloses spiritual depth.[28] Less articulately but more significantly, Ouisa is asking whether the structure she desires is one of responsibility, of mutuality and caring. The no more than six degrees between every person on earth are

> A) tremendously comforting that we're so close and B) like Chinese water torture that we're so close. Because you have to find the right six people to make the connection. It's not just big names. It's *anyone.*

A native in a rain forest. A Tierra del Fuegan. An Eskimo. I am bound
to everyone on this planet by a trail of six people. It's a profound
thought. How Paul found us. How to find the man whose son he pretends to be. . . . How every person is a new door, opening up into other
worlds. (81)

Revolving over the stage is the idea of an artist who reached into depths
where "the harmony of form must be decided only by a correspond-
ing vibration in the human soul" (19). In respect to Kandinsky, Guare
discloses no inward pattern for "Paul Portier." Paul can only insinuate
himself into blank spaces in the lives of others. But in another respect,
Guare succeeds showing how we *do* empty ourselves toward such empty
persons (as they may empty into us); and we, for better and worse, are
discovered to be such persons, ourselves.

• • •

These versions of Pygmalion transform the myth of the artist, who
carves a person out of ivory, into the myth of the player who receives a
pattern of integrity through the medium of other voices. They explore
a mode of selfhood not well secured by past narratives but emergent in
performance with others. Each play, however, remains ambivalent about
this transformation. Each is hesitant to embrace what is disclosed and is
unable to avoid the discourses of individualism and inward authenticity that authorize modern selves. But each is seeking ethical paradigms
through which to reassess and valorize the emergence of persons in
performance.

One paradigm was *romance,* another was *education.* Each play is
vaguely aware of the paradigm of *the gift.* But gifts can also be dis-
trusted, be they styles of speech, great literature, or the fancy pots of jam
Paul sends to those whose unwitting hospitality he has enjoyed. Each
play admires the transforming and connective powers disclosed in *enacting a part.* But the ancient wariness about the actor's pretence is still
at large. Yet another paradigm of emergent integrity is that of the Good
Samaritan or suffering servant. Paul is eliciting a Samaritan response,
which of course shows how the paradigm can be manipulated. Yet "the
quality of mercy" hangs over the play and becomes the crucial issue
when Ouisa attempts to articulate the nature of responsibility across the
degrees of separation and connection.

The paradigm of *kenosis*—emptying receptively into the forms of others—has affinity with that of enacting a part, our concern in part IV. But the kenotic paradigm also depends upon the actor being embodied in flesh as well as personality. Do our bodies secure our otherwise ephemeral patterns of integrity? Or is the body inevitably a site of objectification that would disconfirm notions of integrity, leaving them at best consoling illusions? Would not theater be the ultimate purveyor and exposé of such illusions? It is to such questions that we now turn.

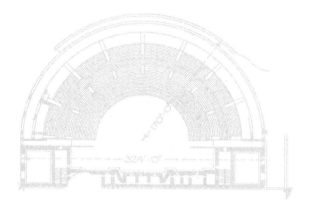

Part III

Integrity and Embodiment

ESTRAGON: Don't touch me! Don't question me! Don't speak to me! Stay with me!
VLADIMIR: Did I ever leave you?
ESTRAGON: You let me go.
VLADIMIR: Look at me. (*Estragon does not raise his head. Violently.*) Will you look at me!
Estragon raises his head. They look long at each other, then suddenly embrace, clapping each other on the back. End of the embrace. Estragon, no longer supported, almost falls.
ESTRAGON: What a day!

—SAMUEL BECKETT, *Waiting for Godot*

Dua thinned. She thinned more than Tritt had ever seen a person thin. She thinned more than Tritt would ever have thought possible. She became a kind of colored smoke that filled the room and dazzled him. He moved without knowing he was moving. He immersed himself in the air that was Dua.

—ISAAC ASIMOV, *The Gods Themselves*

IS EMBODIMENT THE GROUND of personal integrity? And does the body secure the relations of wholeness and rightness that appear in patterns of integrity? We have already seen reasons for being hopeful and doubtful about these questions, given the tensions in the personal and moral aspects of integrity discourse. Perhaps we should say the body is the "site" of such tensions. If so, theatrical drama, with its complications of story and performance, might provide both a phenomenological description and critique of integrity as embodiment. Theater explores the connectivity of patterns of integrity and the limits of this connectivity, as when the

171

body becomes objectified in debility, by wounding, and in the harming (or helping) gazes of others.

But any alignment of *my cause* with *my body,* which can lend personal commitments or moral principles verisimilitude in integrity dramas such as Hamlet's or Becket's, is subject to deconstruction. That is, the overt body makes the cause compelling, when reasons alone are not as compelling; yet such alignments of body with cause typically do not acknowledge their arbitrariness. Deconstructions (not rejections) of these tropes of alignment make room for other tropes of kenosis, which may claim less coherence or stability—although this remains to be seen. Here Samuel Beckett's *Waiting for Godot* can introduce the theatrical description and critique of integrity and embodiment, which the chapters of part III will examine further.

Didi and Gogo as Embodied Patterns of Integrity

First-timers are often pained by the almost palpable sense of waiting, which practically defines the heaviness of static time and emptiness of space as absolute void.[1] Yet on subsequent encounters, *Godot* can be delightful, even lightening. I missed the humor the first time; perhaps I was too earnest, or the production too solemn. (I do remember a viscous, green drool issuing from Lucky's mouth as Pozzo led him in on a rope.) What strikes me about productions since then is the laughter. *Godot* is funny, and its humor is not only about cruelty or brutality.

The time scale is compressed, as if all humanity passes through the interval of a day (or two), and attenuated, as if the interval stretched out forever. It has been compared to the time of God's absence, between crucifixion and resurrection: Holy Saturday becomes a day that repeats forever.[2] Godot (or Meaning, or The Holy, The Future, Death, a character named Godeau from Balzac, or a tardy bicycle racer) is neither really present nor definitively absent, and the tramps play out this indeterminacy with absurd business and dialogue that provokes sympathy. But is the sympathy invalidated by cruelty? Pozzo and Lucky are cruel in Act I; in Act II Vladimir and Estragon ignore the now blind Pozzo's cries of "help!" while pleased with their good luck to be in a position to help someone, which might give their lives an aura of purpose.[3]

> VLADIMIR: Let us not waste our time in idle discourse!
> (*Pause. Vehemently.*) Let us do something, while we have the
> chance! It is not everyday that we are needed. Not indeed that

we personally are needed. Not indeed! Others would meet the case equally well, if not better. To all mankind they were addressed, those cries for help still ringing in our ears! But at this place, at this moment in time, all mankind is us, whether we like it or not. Let us make the most of it, before it is too late! . . . (51a)

This riff ebbs and flows for some five or six pages, reaching the overwhelming insight, "We have kept our appointment"—all the while punctuated by Pozzo's cries, until:

VLADIMIR: He wants us to help him get up.
ESTRAGON: Then why don't we? What are we waiting for?
They help Pozzo to his feet, let him go. He falls.
VLADIMIR: We must hold him.
(*They get him up again. Pozzo sags between them, his arms around their necks.*)
    Feeling better?
POZZO: Who are you?
VLADIMIR: Do you not recognize us?
POZZO: I am blind.
Silence.
ESTRAGON: Perhaps he can see into the future. (54b)

How has the cruelty become humane comedy?
First, throughout the play Didi and Gogo appear as patterns of integrity inasmuch as they undergo, comment upon, and respond to their own and others' bodily suffering. To be sure, they are not much as patterns go: their biographies are slight, and they cannot remember the recent past or what day it is, but they are distinct persons. Estragon, who has been frequently beaten, is the wearier. He is impatient with blathering and complains of hunger and ill-fitting boots. Vladimir suffers from urinary or prostate pain, but is given to flights of speculation and oratory. He has to be reminded to button his fly. Their physical complaints would themselves confirm Maurice Merleau-Ponty's views that the body is the "intertwining" of self and world, that this sense of mutual "porosity" is more primordial than Cartesian doubt.[4] However reduced may be their context in life, Didi and Gogo regard their bodies as their own; they belong to the world through their bodies; so too do they express themselves, and they constantly speak to this principal, bodily capability and liability.[5] "There's man all over for you, blaming on his boots the

faults of his feet" (8a). And in their spats, in the manner of music hall or
vaudeville comedians, they desire and fear relations with other bodies.
It is as if they are in a parable. First they are suffering in a ditch, but no
Samaritan comes; then they are ambivalent Samaritans to Pozzo and
Lucky; soon they again will be alone beside the ditch.

Second, we see actors lending their bodies to these parts. This is what
the experienced audience may more readily notice. However alienating
the circumstances of *Waiting for Godot,* its performance styles elicit
our validating attention (alluded to as "bloody ignorant apes" below),
through physical humor and metatheatrical irony.

> ESTRAGON: We always find something, eh Didi, to give us the
>   impression we exist?
> VLADIMIR: (*impatiently*). Yes yes, we're magicians. (44a)

In the first few minutes, Vladimir performs business with his hat, Estragon with his boots, and these routines flow into a meditation on the four
Gospels ("One of the thieves was saved"), which Didi plays like a comic
to Gogo's straight man.

> VLADIMIR: And yet ... (*pause*) ... how is it—this is not boring you
>   I hope—how is it that of the four Evangelists only one speaks
>   of a thief being saved. The four of them were there—or there-
>   abouts—and only one speaks of a thief being saved. (*Pause.*)
>   Come on, Gogo, return the ball, can't you, once in a way.
> ESTRAGON: (*with exaggerated enthusiasm*) I find this really most
>   extraordinarily interesting.
> VLADIMIR: But all four were there. And only one speaks of a thief
>   being saved. Why believe him rather than the others?
> ESTRAGON: Who believes him?
> VLADIMIR: Everybody. It's the only version they know.
> ESTRAGON: People are bloody ignorant apes. (9a–b)

*Third, the tramps/actors are waiting to receive a pattern of integrity
that we, their audience, may help impart.* Today, most of us know what
magic to expect en attendant Godot. It is not the waiting or the absur-
dity that draws us but the expectation of a theatrical revelation. Again,
awareness of physical embodiment establishes a field of reference between us and the players that transcends the stasis of waiting. While Godot never arrives, we do—lending ourselves to the patterns of Vladimir

and Estragon. That they remain so minimal as persons might reveal how their sheer embodiment provides a field in which to recognize integrity and its threats, marked by bad shoes, blows fallen or fended, attention given or withheld. We are invited to grant the tramps a certain dignity in reference to their fragile embodiment, to that of the players, and to our own. In life, by gestures between bodies we are open to meanings across times and spaces and, momentarily but significantly, transcend some of our differences. We can even communicate with animals, to degrees, on bases of embodiment. Is embodiment, then, the ground of integrity? In the metonymic logic of Godot, however, the bodies of Didi and Gogo lend verisimilitude neither to their inward lives (which remain obscure) nor their hope (which never comes) nor even their despair: they may hang themselves tomorrow but cannot move today. Their integrity is that of bodies aligned with bodies, but is there integrity in that?

Bodies Hard and Soft

Actors lend their bodies and persons to the motions and stories of other persons. We may find that possibilities of kenotic integrity are owed in part to the porous and protean aspects of persons, selves, and identities. These qualities correspond to how we overlap one another's lives, being transformed by emptying into other parts, roles, and lives. Our protean qualities are both a condition without which we would not be (as we emerge from other bodies) and a condition by which we confront various constraints in existence, and so is a condition for capable freedom.

There is, obviously, another side to this protean view. The physical body has a numerically unique location in space and time, and a person is oriented to the world from this embodied "location," moving spatially and temporally.[6] There are countless aspects of a person's uniqueness—the genetic, psychological, social, cultural, and historical strands that intersect each personal nexus. Such myriad, mostly changing relations texture our uniqueness, and also make us pliable and open to transformation; they constitute the "smeared-out" boundaries of selves and others. What is, however, impossible to smear out is the animate body. Except for organ and blood donation, Siamese twins, and perhaps other limit cases, we cannot share bodies with other persons in the same space and moment. Intimate relations are those of touch, friction, enfolding, but not of fusion. Another implication of embodiment is that the self (i.e., who we are _to ourselves_) and identity (i.e., who we are as _particular, named_ persons) are not like digital programs that can be copied from one computer to another. Neither the body nor self-and-identity can be copied, and in that sense persons are nonsubstitutable and nonreplaceable.

And yet, there are contexts, some commonsensical and some exotic, in which we can imagine this condition to be otherwise. The biblical phrase "to become one flesh" is a locution for sexual intercourse, not an image of the flesh melting together like wax or soft clay. Yet in the lore and imagery of sexuality are suggestions both of the ecstatic desire to be lost in the other—John Donne invokes the sense of sexual "dying" in his sonnet "The Canonization"—and of loneliness, solitude, and alienation. The body is both open and opaque in such imagining. In the novel *The Gods Themselves,* Isaac Asimov imagines a parallel universe where the "strong" nuclear force, which holds atomic nuclei together, is much stronger than in our universe. As a result, atoms take up less space and matter is more attenuated. Among the beings in the parallel universe are Hard Ones and Soft Ones, and the Soft Ones can willingly thin and "melt" together. If Soft Ones were to shake hands, their hands could thin and pass through each other as easily as smoke. Asimov imagines thinning and melting to be pleasurable. Procreative sex among the Soft Ones involves the melting of not two but three gendered bodies—one "rational," one "emotional," and one "parental" (whose body incubates the offspring). Yet as the epigraph implies, however much Dua thinned, Tritt still recognized her as Dua and not another.

Other science fiction scenarios have received more attention. The "transporters" of Gene Roddenberry's *Star Trek* TV and movie series in effect *do* treat persons as programs, or software, which might run on different hardware. Since transporters reduce matter to electromagnetic patterns and beam them to other locations, such devices imply the possibility not only of moving but also of *duplicating* the patterns of individual persons. Although allowing this to happen is regarded as taboo on *Star Trek,* multiple copies of persons have been replicated, who then meet and interact—although they at least have physical bodies. Not necessarily so, however, in the far, far distant future, when physical conditions in the universe will no longer support the carbon-based biology that makes our relatively hard bodies pleasantly soft. Physicists John Barrow and Frank Tipler speculate that only artificial intelligence will be able to continue the adventure of human experience.[7] "Experiences," here, are patterns of information that are quite separable from the bodies or machines that run them. A kind of cybernetic immortality can thus be imagined. This scenario still involves physicality, of a digital sort, but no longer the integral and temporal relationship of a particular-body-as-a-particular-person.

The *Star Trek* examples are popular counterparts to discussions in analytical philosophy about the requirements of personal identity over time. Does identity reside principally in *bodily continuity,* or in the *continuity of a chain of experiences and memories,* or in *something irreducible to the body and the stream of experience,* such as the Cartesian ego or a transcendent soul? Regarding irreducible identity as an illusion (though an intuitively very strong illusion), Derek Parfit argues that neither my body nor my chain of memories and experiences—when tested by hypothetical scenarios of teleportation, replication, or neurosurgery—yield a strong enough sense of identity to satisfy our intuitive desires. The chain of experiences proves to be an insufficient criterion of unique identity over time. And even bodily singularity and continuity (which Bernard Williams regards as the necessary though insufficient condition of identity) cannot withstand thought experiments involving brain division and transplantation.

What Parfit proposes is to view the person as a "Relation" of continuities, one that frankly admits of many discontinuities, and which satisfies some but not all of our intuitive desires. His aphorism is, "Our identity is not what matters." What matters is "the Relation." Would Parfit himself enter a teleporter to be painlessly annihilated and replicated on Mars? He admits that while his reasoning says Yes—after all, his Relation will continue, albeit with some interruption—his intuition cannot suppress the impulse to say No. But that nagging doubt is but the vestige of an illusion he thinks human reason should overcome.[8] Ricoeur, however, proposes that this nagging doubt means Parfit's identity seems to matter to him after all!

Much of Ricoeur's account of the self in *Oneself as Another* is implicitly a reply to Parfit, who he thinks exposes the "crisis within selfhood."[9] Ricoeur regards the odd sci-fi scenarios as being concerned with "what" I am, rather than "who" I am. That is, they are about identity as sameness (*idem*), not as self-relatedness (*ipse*). To be a person involves complex dialectics of sameness-and-difference and self-and-other-relatedness. These are played out amid life's continuities and discontinuities and among other persons who recognize us for who we are, not just what we are. Ricoeur does not mean to postulate an essential, Cartesian, self-substance. Rather, he thinks Parfit's scenarios simply do not touch upon aspects of self and identity that involve my sense of owning my body or having experiences in relation to persons who call me into account. Following Merleau-Ponty and others, Ricoeur notices that the first word of the phrase "Our identity is not what matters" betrays a sense of "mineness."[10] Mineness, however, is a quality meaningless apart from others.

The sense of narrative identity Ricoeur proposes is radically dialogical: there are no selves apart from others. So he agrees there is a sense in which identity (if regarded by itself) is not what matters. Yet the self's dispossession, which Parfit and Ricoeur both value, requires an identifiable self to dis-pose.[11]

Asimov's and Roddenberry's ideas may be most interesting to the extent they are impossible. Replication technology—if it had to accurately record body-states down to the quantum level—would violate the uncertainty principle, which forbids knowing location and motion simultaneously. This impossibility suggests that *both* the soft, protean aspects of persons *and* our being hard and un-duplicable are rooted in the fabric of space and time. Thus, the Star Trek or Barrow-Tipler scenarios would contradict the kind of integral, embodied, temporal phenomena we are. Yet if we treat these tales as hypothetical limit cases that "prove the rule," then again we should ask, Is the integrity of persons grounded in the singular, physical body?

For Ricoeur, the answer cannot quite be "yes." To be sure, in his *ipse* ethical universe, multiple copies of *Star Trek*'s Commander Riker would be regarded not as the same (*idem*) but as *new*, singular persons. They would be like twins or clones, albeit created by odd means; their self-identities would quickly diverge as time passed. (Perhaps the ethical question here is not one of duplicating persons, but whether reducing them to energy patterns, to be reconstituted elsewhere, involves homicide, which Parfit intuitively dreads.) For Ricoeur, there is no *ipse* identity without significant *idem* continuity, hence bodily integrity. And yet, are not coma and general anesthesia—if not sleep, or tissue replacement over time—analogs to the transporter, in that they involve material discontinuity? The question is whether the *wholeness* of self-continuity is so inherently interrupted by discontinuity as to seem paradoxically *not whole*.

Gaps "In" and "Between" Bodies and Persons

A particular body may be a *sign* of a pattern of identity and integral wholeness and a *symbol* of it. As Paul Tillich used these terms,[12] the body as sign means it can point to something absent or other, as when an actor's body onstage signifies Hamlet. The body as symbol also *participates in, without being identical to,* what it signifies, as when the actor inhabits and instantiates qualities of the persona of Hamlet, and we respond to these qualities in the presence of the actor. Through the persistence of the body, in its thereness and in its actions, we can participate in and recognize patterns of integrity. Yet there are reasons why the body cannot secure or ground such participation.

All the ways we relate to others—in our most intimate and most transient meetings; in life projects and aesthetic preferences; through cultural, ethical, and religious forms that "clothe" us or whose cloth we shed; through our histories and the histories of others; through the futures we imagine, fear for, or hope for, with others and in solitude—all these contribute to the distinct nexus of relations that is each person. These ways would also "embody" our integrity. Thus, the physical body's contribution to patterns of personal and moral integrity is but an incomplete or partial contribution. Moreover, the body is never altogether the whole it seems to be. The body develops, and hence is *not yet what it will be*. The body ages, and hence is *not what it was*. The body is damaged, and hence is a *fragile or broken wholeness*. And the body can be objectified by others and by oneself, and hence is *not entirely coincident* with the person or the self. In the tradition of Gabriel Marcel, Sartre, and Merleau-Ponty, Richard Zaner writes,

> I am my body; but in another sense I am *not* my body, or not simply that. This otherness is so profound that we inevitably feel forced to qualify the "am": it is not identity, equality, or inclusion. It is "mine," but this means that the person is in a way distanced from it, for otherwise there would be no sense to "belonging"; it would not be characterizable in any sense as "mine."[13]

We do and do not identify ourselves by our bodies; others do and do not identify our bodies with us. There are gaps between the "is" and "is not" of embodied integrity. These may be imagined as sometimes-widening and sometimes-narrowing gaps: in space and over time, within bodies and within persons, between the body and the person, between embodied persons. There are indeed gaps betwixt and between all the relational aspects of persons. Our relations of identity with ourselves and our bodies are also relations of nonidentity, which would be a way of understanding "natural evil"—our vulnerability to contingencies of no one's making. But that we are not seamless wholes is, viewed from one angle, simply an aspect of our finitude. And if Augustine allows us to say that finitude is part of the created good, then "gappiness" must be part of the possibilities of happiness. It contributes to the pliability that

Hamlet thought made bodies paragons of delight. Our finite gappiness is, as well, a way of thinking about how we juxtapose bodies with others and with causes or principles. Gaps make room for attachment, emptying, and reception—spaces to exist and enter.

Viewed from another angle, the disjunctions between body and self, and the finite voids in our nexus of relations, become places of enjambment with other sorts of "gaps," characterized by suffering and fault: by the harm we suffer and the harm we inflict. The nonidentity of body and person leaves us pliable to manipulation and violation, to being a property or commodity or datum—as in *Venus, The Elephant Man,* and *Wit.* We are indentured, trampled, blown away, torn apart, marketed, tortured, made to be precise war weapons or else "cannon fodder," the site of projected fantasies, gazes, hatreds, and ruminations of self- and other-loathing: all things that *Philoctetes* and *The Bacchae* and their like may "truly deliver." So dramatists confront our bodies and their own as a *medium,* with consumptive and objectifying motives mixed with motives of critique and delight. These ways in which embodiment becomes problematic mean that, like social roles and economic conditions, the body can contribute to a person becoming a prison unto oneself. *The desire to escape the body/person,* as in Mary Zimmerman's *Metamorphoses,* does not contradict so much as *follows from* our embodied condition.

Chapter VII

Who Has the Body?

The Contingency of Integrity in Philoctetes and The Cure at Troy

For one brief shameless portion of a day
give me yourself. . . .

—SOPHOCLES, *Philoctetes*

You've turned yourself into a Trojan, lad . . .

—SEAMUS HEANEY, *The Cure at Troy*

AS WE HAVE SEEN, *metatheater* refers to how performed drama makes meaning by enacting stories in the presence of others, and to how drama refers to its own theatricality and to theater-like dimensions of life. Sophocles' *Philoctetes* is an early study of how the stage recapitulates these performative dimensions, and it also explores how the human body—particularly the "body in pain"—can both occasion one person's assent to another's integrity, yet also be a site of contested and interrupted integrity. In this instance, a young soldier-ruler, Neoptolemus, must play a part scripted by Odysseus in order to deceive an isolated, suffering man; but in so playing this deceptive part he changes course, in a self-critical moment of self-and-other recognition.

However, Neoptolemus's transformed integrity is insufficient to persuade Philoctetes to relax his refusal and return to the Trojan War, which by tradition he did. So Sophocles employs a deus ex machina: the god Heracles appears and appeals to a shared history of bodily suffering to change the mind of Philoctetes. In the second part of this chapter, I will consider how Seamus Heaney transforms this theophany in *The Cure at Troy.* He enlarges upon Sophocles' implication of the contingency of transformation, and helps us see how an expansive pattern of integrity can arrive as an unexpected, contingent gift. To enter some new pattern of integrity may require "moral luck" as Bernard Williams terms it, or else some providential arrangement, just as great misfortune may destroy such a pattern. To be sure, the conversions of Neoptolemus and Philoctetes are contiguous with certain moments in their pasts. Yet we cannot account for what is ethically and personally required of them only in terms of narrative coherence, for their prior narratives are being reconfigured in these dramatic and metatheatrical encounters.

Philoctetes

Sophocles was nearly ninety when he mounted this, his next-to-last tragedy, in 409 B.C.E. during the Peloponnesian war.[1] Aeschylus and Euripides had already written versions of the story, and Sophocles introduced the innovations of making Neoptolemus Odysseus's go-between, removing the island's inhabitants from the scene, and making the wounded hero a focus of pity, apart from his utility to the Greeks.[2] On his way to Troy, Philoctetes wandered into a sacred place and was bitten by a magic snake. His poisoned foot would not heal, and when his incessant cries disrupted the routines and rites of the other warriors, Odysseus abandoned him on the island of Lemnos. Alone for nine years, in constant pain, he scrounges out a marginal existence, hunting birds with his divine bow that never misses. Meanwhile, a captured Trojan seer, Helenus, has revealed that without Philoctetes and his weapon, Troy cannot be conquered. The play begins with the arrival of Odysseus and young Neoptolemus, son of Achilles. Odysseus cannot approach Philoctetes safely, but the innocent youth can. "Ensnare the soul of Philoctetes with your words," Odysseus says; in effect, he takes command of Neoptolemus's integrity or "nature."

> I know, young man, it is not your natural bent
> to say such things nor to contrive such mischief.
> But the prize of victory is pleasant to win.
> Bear up: another time we shall prove honest.
> For one brief shameless portion of a day
> give me yourself, and then for all the rest
> you may be called most scrupulous of men. (ll. 79–85)

Sophocles thus introduces elements of metatheatricality into a story of contingent integrity. Prior to the deus ex machina, these elements bear on how Philoctetes will be persuaded to go to Troy, and bear on what we believe about his suffering and refusal. Metatheater is evident in (1) Neoptolemus enacting a false "script" authored by Odysseus;[3] (2) the display of a body in pain, which is by turns seen, abhorred, and respected by Neoptolemus and his sailors (the Chorus); (3) the tableaus in which the bow and arrows are given, returned, or aimed between contesting parties; and (4) the transformations of Philoctetes and Neoptolemus on account of these performances.[4]

Playing the Script

As Odysseus introduces Neoptolemos to Philoctetes' haunts on Lemnos—and thus describes what the audience is to "see"—he recites the history that has brought them to the island, and the plan of complex deception. The bow must be taken by guile, since neither persuasion nor force will work against Philoctetes' rage and magic arrows. So Odysseus composes a script of lies, truths, and half-truths for Neoptolemus to perform.[5] He should pretend to be furious that Odysseus has robbed him of his inheritance, the armor of the slain Achilles. "Say what you will/against me; do not spare me anything./Nothing of this will hurt me" (ll. 64–66). When Neoptolemus objects to such trickery, Odysseus says that when young, he too preferred forthright action to words. But now he sees "that everywhere among the race of men/it is the tongue that wins and not the deed" (98–99)—sophistry to persuade an honest lad to lie. As we have observed, an old intuition about theater and integrity is that the former denies the latter; accordingly, Neoptolemus plays a role and disgusts himself. But a counterintuition, I have urged, is that one may discover one's integrity through the performance of the role. What is unclear here is just how much of Neoptolemus's performance is entirely a lie: that he has been robbed of his father's armor? That he is embittered? If, as he performs before Philoctetes (ll. 343–90), he warms to his part, it may be because the part is at least implicitly true.[6]

It has some truth because Odysseus—who seems the utilitarian—has taken from him, if not his father's armor, then his virtuous, even deontological convictions.[7] For the boy identifies with an Achilles he never knew and believes his nature was to prefer honest deeds to deceitful words. It might seem, then, that his character, far from being contingent, is fixed. *Phusis* or related words frequently describe the boy's relation to

Achilles, as if the father's nature had passed to the son.[8] Yet all he knows of Achilles he has been taught, and teachings are vulnerable to other teachings. "I have a natural antipathy," he says, "to get my ends by tricks and stratagems./So, too, they say, my father was. . . . I would prefer even to fail with honor/than win by cheating" (ll. 87–88, 94–95). Odysseus's reply is droll, "You are a good man's son. [But] I was young, too, once." In persuading him to set aside Achilles' *phusis,* Odysseus orphans him again. "Give me yourself [*dos moi seauton*]"(l. 84), he says. As Neoptolemus recites his concocted tale, Philoctetes identifies with the claim of betrayal (ll. 403–9). And as the youth sees the older man softened by the promise of a voyage home, he also begins to identify with him, like a son to a father. So it is hard to know when Neoptolemus is disingenuous as he slanders Odysseus, and when he half-believes what he says.

The performance Odysseus designs also includes the False Trader's deception (ll. 542–627). He arranges to send, if the boy takes too long, a sailor disguised as a merchant. "Whatever clever story he give you, then/fall in with it and use it as you need" (ll. 130–31). And so the Trader arrives to say that Phoenix, Agamemnon, and Menelaus are chasing Neoptolemus while Odysseus is hot after Philoctetes. The scene has several functions. Philoctetes' solidarity with Neoptolemus increases, further showing that persuasion is unlikely.[9] The Trader's report of the prophecy also establishes that the issue is persuasion; guile and force are ruled out. Up to this point, after Neoptolemus has won Philoctetes' trust and assuming he can finesse control of the bow, an impasse remains: What use is a magic bow if an angry Philoctetes aims it at Greeks instead of at Trojans? Odysseus ignores this problem; in fact, if we think of him as the author of the Trader's script, then he thus reveals how from the beginning he has been oblivious to the import of the prophecy. According to the Trader, when Odysseus heard the seer Helenus say that Philoctetes must be persuaded, Odysseus

> promised at once to bring the man before them,
> for all to see—he thought, as a willing prisoner,
> but, if not that, against his will. (ll. 615–17)

So we learn, albeit in a moment of deception, that Philoctetes must be persuaded and that Odysseus has never really grasped the meaning of persuasion.

More subtly still, the False Trader, in effect, reminds Neoptolemus he is enacting a part: "Apparently you do not know/much of your own affairs" (l. 553), "Well, watch what you are doing. . . . I put the whole responsibility/squarely upon yourself" (ll. 589, 90). But once the Trader departs, the sense of pretense actually lessens. Neoptolemus expresses friendship, and Philoctetes beckons him into his cave. The dialogue becomes more intimate as the old man prepares to pack his few belongings and invites the boy to hold his bow. "The sickness in me," he says, "seeks to have you beside me" (ll. 674–75). But then the pain in his foot intensifies, as does Neoptolemus's moral distress. "I have been in sorrow for your pain" (l. 806), he says. And later, when Philoctetes asks why he hesitates ("Is it disgust at my sickness?"), Neoptolemus is distraught and in a state of liminality. "All is disgust when one leaves his own nature/and does things that misfit it" (ll. 900–3). Has the boy's anti-theatrical conscience been "caught" by the theatricality Odysseus has put on him?

Recognizing Pain

When we, the audience, first "see" Philoctetes, he is absent. As Odysseus and Neoptolemus scout the island and his cave, they describe his pathetic contrivances: leaves for a bed, a hollowed-out block for a cup, oozing rags drying in the sun. He is described as living on the boundary between person and beast. But as a boundary figure, he is no mere blurring of monster and man; his human ethos is neither fulsome nor absent but is a wounded ethos—now eloquent, now inarticulate. He has maintained threads of continuity with himself, and his first spoken desire is for language: "May I hear your voice?" (l. 225), he pleads when first approaching Neoptolemus.

Hegel thought the central issue was not pain but the moral opposition between Neoptolemus and Odysseus. "The malady of Philoctetes, the loathsome ulcer on his foot, his ejaculations and outcries, are as little likely to awaken the genuine interest of a modern audience as the arrows of Hercules."[10] But since Hegel, his affliction and exile have become emblematic of the suffering of artists, of veteran soldiers, the isolation of the ill, and of relations between pain, integrity, and compassion.[11] Philoctetes' pain is comparable to that of the severely burned, who may consider themselves dead though still lucid among the living, and who may at different moments desire to be understood or left alone, touched or not touched, saved or killed. Their personalities, after excruciating treatment, may be altered to the point of discontinuity with their pasts.[12] Elaine Scarry suggests that because the feeling of pain is so interior, it cannot be communicated directly. If so, pain raises questions of integrity intrinsically: for the one suffering, expressions of pain carry conviction yet can be doubted, Scarry thinks, by others who cannot "see" the pain itself. I can show you my burn, but not my burning, my head but not my ache, and my telling may remain inarticulate. Philoctetes "utters a cascade of *changing* cries and shrieks that in the original Greek are accompanied by an array of formal words (some of them twelve syllables long). . . ."[13] *Philoctetes* stages a fearsome phenomenology of pain, and shows its bearing on character and integrity.

Neoptolemus, moreover, suffers ethical pain as he observes Philoctetes' pain and anguish. That the man and boy come to believe in one another, and we in them, turns on perceptions of mutual suffering. Although Aristotle criticized the play for its imperfect ending, it is a perfect instance of tragic learning through the arousal of compassion and fear. The pain would have been staged mimetically. In the iconography of Greek vase painting and relief sculpture, Philoctetes' foot is prominently bandaged. When Neoptolemus first sees the oozing rags, he utters, "*iou, iou*" (l. 38), a reaction of disgust and pain. Lessing observed how Philoctetes' harsh screams would have been prolonged onstage as a principal means for presenting pain in this spectacle.[14] So also would be the testimony of suffering that constitutes the education of Neoptolemus.

In retrospect, he is one who could touch, as if from inborn sympathy, a wretched stranger. But he is young, and the play may allude to a ritual by which one becomes a soldier upon swearing an oath; Neoptolemus would be an *ephebe* in passage between childhood and vocation.[15] Upon arriving at Lemnos, it is not he but the Chorus of mature sailors (though subordinate to him) who first demonstrate sympathy. They note how they are strangers on the island and ask about his plan. Neoptolemus's answers can seem presumptuous.[16] "Take your cues from me. Help me when you can" (ll. 148–49). The Chorus then teaches him more about the pathos they and we are about to witness:

Perhaps this man is as well born as any,
second to no son of an ancient house.
Yet now his life lacks everything,
and he makes his bed without neighbors
or with spotted shaggy beasts for neighbors.
His thoughts are set continually on pain and hunger. . . .
NEOPTOLEMUS: I am not surprised by any of this:
this is a God's doing, if I have any understanding. (ll. 180–85, 191–92)

As Neoptolemus spins an explanation, a theodicy ("This, too, no doubt is part of the God's plan" [l. 196]), the Chorus seems impatient—"Hush. . . . No more now, my son" (ll. 201, 210)—as Philoctetes approaches. Later, the pedagogical relationship will be reversed, and Neoptolemus will teach the Chorus a deeper discernment of Philoctetes. But for now, a metatheatrical effect of its teaching is to implicitly offer him an alternative script to play, which may also elicit the audience's virtual participation in the training of Neoptolemus.

As the Chorus hears Philoctetes coming, he sounds to them like a babbling infant or wounded beast. He explains his suffering in long, fierce speeches, but it is when words fail that his pain is most apparent. He begs for amputation, begs not to be touched, but also not to be abandoned. And yet Neoptolemus is amazed that even in agony Philoctetes can pity the death of Achilles (ll. 339–40). In these ways the mutuality of compassion becomes visible. Marcia Day Childress has noticed that his questions about Philoctetes' pain (ll. 733–61) make Neoptolemus vulnerable to answers that are painful to hear.[17] And when the pain overcomes him, he hands over the bow (ll. 762–78) in an action ritual-like and visually intense—then falls temporarily into soothing sleep (ll. 821–32). So Neoptolemus's compassion aligns with Philoctetes at the very moment he can capture him.

While Odysseus has been fixated on stealing the bow, the boy now realizes that Philoctetes himself will be needed at Troy. "I see we have hunted in vain," he tells the Chorus, "if we sail without him. His is the crown of victory, him the God said we must bring" (ll. 839–41). Written in hexameters, the lines suggest that Neoptolemus has achieved insight into the prophecy of Helenus. Does he also understand that Philoctetes must be persuaded, must come willingly? He may, but he must also see that persuasion is still unlikely and trickery remains necessary, which contributes to the self-loathing that overcomes him. Philoctetes awakens, delighted not to have been abandoned, and we see another powerful tableau. He asks to be lifted to his feet. As the two stand in physical contact, the boy questions himself, "Now is the moment. What shall we do from now on?" (l. 895). At this stunning moment of one's self-critical integrity, the other senses betrayal. "Give me back my bow" (l. 924), Philoctetes screams and delivers a fabulous speech of anger and terror (ll. 927–62). The young man listens, mesmerized, and comes to a second recognition of self and other: a wondrous or "terrible [*deinos*] compassion" comes upon Neoptolemus. "I have felt for him all the time" (ll. 965–66).

The Bow and the Wound

Alfred Hitchcock would call the bow a "Maguffin," something everyone wants that drives the plot along. It is a weapon and a gift, it wounds and saves. Without it Philoctetes will not survive on Lemnos nor the war be won at Troy. Its presence onstage is powerful, for whoever holds it would be invulnerable—it never misses. It instantiates friendship; in seeing it exchanged we see trust established, something like a promise made. The bow is given twice, first from Philoctetes' hand to Neoptolemus, then from Neoptolemus back to Philoctetes. Neoptolemus tells Odysseus, "I go to undo the wrong that I have done" (l. 1224) and vows to sail the wounded man home if he will not be reconciled with the Greeks. Odysseus twice interrupts the return of the bow. There is a frozen image when, holding it, Neoptolemus stands silent between Odysseus and Philoctetes, who rage against each other, each powerless to act (ll. 974–1080) because neither holds the bow. After Neoptolemus returns it, Odysseus again threatens (l. 1293) and Philoctetes aims his arrow. But Neoptolemus steps between them, and Philoctetes' trust must be established yet again.

As a visible object of danger and desire, the bow communicates by itself. We may or may not also know that in it is concentrated much that Philoctetes was, has become, and is now becoming. Such gift-objects, in Greek literature, often gather up hidden threads of a character's destiny. From other sources we learn that Philoctetes' bow was a gift from the mortal Heracles in gratitude for what amounts to an act of euthanasia. Heracles' wife, Deianira, unwittingly tainted his coat with a magic poison, which continued to burn flesh; in agony, he persuaded Philoctetes to light the fire that occasioned his apotheosis upon Mt. Oeta. The bow, then, is a hierophantic as well as personal object.[18] We are reminded of all this as Philoctetes now begs for death:

> Boy, my good boy, take up this body of mine
> and burn it on what they call the Lemnian fire.
> I had the resolution once to do this for another,
> the son of Zeus, and so obtained the arms
> that you now hold. What do you say?
> What do you say? Nothing? Where are you, boy?
> NEOPTOLEMUS: I have been in pain for you; I have been
> in sorrow for your pain. (ll. 799–806)

When we see the transferals of the bow, we see not only a sign of character and transformations of character; we see the embodied nexus of

relations, values, and prospects—what there is of a person to be integrated—transformed before our eyes.

Narrowing Horizons and the Chance of Transformation

But character is fragile, and in Philoctetes we see how suffering can con-
strict the personal and moral nexus, in spite of transformation. He now
identifies with his wound, his island, and his humiliation, and so he resists the cooperative alternatives Neoptolemus offers. While he projects
"the integrity of refusal,"[19] his is a much attenuated pattern of integrity,
the prospects of which are nil. Once their friendship has been established,
Neoptolemus faces him and utters a concise critique (ll. 1314–47): You
cling to suffering, your anger has made you savage, you reject the words
of friends, you suffer a "sickness of God's sending." You will not heal until you see the physicians at Troy and take that city "that has cost infinity
of tears." Philoctetes then speaks incredulously to his own body:

> Eyes of mine, that have seen all, can you endure
> to see me living with my murderers,
> the sons of Atreus? With cursed Odysseus?
> It is not the sting of wrongs past
> but what I must look for in wrongs to come. . . .
> No, boy, no; take me home as you promised. (ll. 1353–59, 1367–68)

After more futile exchanges, Neoptolemus resigns to keep his promise
and sail Philoctetes home. "Come now; kiss this ground farewell," he
tells him (l. 1408). Philoctetes, in turn, promises to protect him with his
bow. They recognize themselves to be configured in one another's pattern
of integrity. "I am bound/To you, and bound to take you,"[20] Heaney's
Neoptolemus says earlier. But they are turning away from wider obligations and social horizons, which bear upon the Trojan War.

The Cure at Troy

Contemporary audiences are probably bothered no less than Aristotle
by gods from machines, yet Seamus Heaney uses the deus ex machina to
frame *The Cure at Troy*. Even in Grene's Sophocles, Heracles seems of
uncertain bodily status: "I am the voice of Heracles in your ears;/I am
the shape of Heracles before you" (ll. 1411–12). In Heaney, Hercules

speaks from volcanic fire through the voice of a Chorus, in a prologue and at the end, in parts assigned to three women. Sometimes these also represent Neoptolemus's crew; sometimes they are a collective muse; sometimes they are the god. In specifying the Chorus as female, Heaney may recall a tradition that Lemnos was inhabited by women who slew their husbands.[21] However, his Chorus is irenic and speaks to humanity at large. After the crater flames, Hercules via the Chorus Leader ritually chants:

> Go, Philoctetes, with this boy,
> Go and be cured and capture Troy.
> Asclepius will make you whole,
> Relieve your body and your soul. (79)

"Win by fair combat," "shun/Reprisal killings," "take just spoils," and "sail at last/Out of the bad dream of your past." Philoctetes replies, perhaps with laconic laughter, "Something told me this was going to happen," that "the channels were going to open" (80). To be able to say so is to be healed.

One could interpret Sophocles' deus as tragically ironic: that after a sacred serpent instigates Philoctetes' suffering, a god demands he renounce his integrity of resistance. This reading has validity, and is part of the distant provenance of *Venus*, *The Elephant Man*, and *Wit*. By such a reading, Heracles would accomplish what Odysseus and Neoptolemus cannot, he would *possess* Philoctetes.[22] Heracles would realign the wounded man's body *and his mind* with the paradigm and cause of the Trojan War—much as field psychiatrists helped return shell-shocked GIs to battle in World War II. But Heaney's irony is comic, not tragic; the "cure" is gracious, not manipulative. Yet it remains contingent. It has roots in Celtic lore and Christian humanism as well as in Sophocles' plot. Heaney does not turn the story into forgiveness, but he does envision motives that transcend vengeance.[23] Philoctetes at the play's end is already a transformed body—in effect, already healed by the physicians at Troy—and it has been aligned with a different cause.

To ask why Philoctetes is not persuaded until a god speaks is yet another way to frame our queries into theater and integrity. Can we believe in sudden transformations: in which harming one's foes becomes less urgent than being healed, in which a past is not denied but redescribed, and in which integrity receives a new pattern of embodiment? Do such possibilities of conversion reside in the ranges of experience and language to which a dramatist is presumably accountable? Heaney and Sophocles are exploring a pattern in which minds can change—yet change contingently, in unexpected encounters. Neoptolemus becomes self-critical and revises his loyalties; Philoctetes' hold on a narrative of unjust suffering is relaxed. This pattern first appears when strangers become friends, and again when their horizons widen under the aspect of Hercules. But are we compelled by this pattern? Why should we believe that intractable anger is relieved and new directions open?

Heaney retains Sophocles' metatheatrical elements: playing a false part, the ritual-like transfers of the bow, the spectacle of a wounded and isolated body. The dialogue only occasionally departs far from Sophocles' denotative sense; but it frequently sharpens expressions of implication, as when Neoptolemus sees the import of the oracle only after witnessing the man's suffering: "I see it all now. Without him the cause will be shamed and our victory hollow" (46). And as when Philoctetes' prior link with Heracles is made more explicit: "What I did for Hercules / You should do for me" (43), that is, accept the bow in return for the gift of euthanasia in volcanic fire. Heaney also extends on many of Sophocles' thematic values. Hospitality to strangers becomes a global "economy of kindness" (37). He imitates and subverts the idiom of violence in Northern Ireland,[24] so Philoctetes as betrayed could be an angry Republican or a Unionist, and we may hear allusions to other narratives of conflict as well. In Sophocles, the conflict involves the claims of the Greek tribe set against an abused individual. In Heaney, justice for the individual is linked to humanity apart from tribal identity.[25] Odysseus taunts Neoptolemus about his loyalty to justice, which "isn't only Greek." Odysseus replies, "You've turned yourself into a Trojan, lad . . ." (67).

While the dialogue usually elaborates Sophocles' sense, the choral odes invite us to project more expansive visions upon the island seascapes of Eyre and Lemnos. Over his career, Heaney has widened the geography of his poetic sources from Ireland to the rest of Europe, and *The Cure at Troy* is part of this motion.[26] He began it in 1989 as Eastern Europe was opening. "For once, I felt, the historical record was giving a glimmer of justification of optimism."[27] So the Chorus articulates a rhetoric of self-critical hope. In the prologue, the Leader sounds a mythic roll call—"Philoctetes / Hercules / Odysseus"—and asserts a version of tragic history in which gods, heroes, and victims are

> All throwing shapes, every one of them
> Convinced he's in the right, all of them glad

To repeat themselves and their every last mistake,
No matter what.
                                        People so deep into
Their own self-pity, self-pity buoys them up.
People so staunch and true, they're fixated,
Shining with self-regard like polished stones. (1)

The Chorus accepts this judgment upon itself and upon us. They hate the nurturing of old wounds—and yet, "I am/A part of it myself.//And a part of you . . ." (2).

The Chorus says its voice marks the border between subject and object ("The you and the me and the it of it") and between divine and human perspectives. It makes a cautious mediation between the "I," the "Thou," and what Gadamer calls the subject matter (*die Sache*) of a dialogue. Between hope and reality, the Chorus also identifies with "poetry." It was poetry that "Allowed the god to speak," and remains the boundary between desire and reality. Poetry was also "the voice/Of reality and justice" (2). The women of the Chorus explain that each time the volcano erupts, Philoctetes will remember the funeral pyre that consumed Hercules' body. "The god's mind lights up his mind every time" (2). And near the end of the play, as Philoctetes and Neoptolemus bid farewell to Lemnos—but before the final theophany—the women again return us to a more contemporary awareness. They declaim a stirring ode ("Human beings suffer . . . ," 77)—now famous for its political and ceremonial uses—which reminds us of how bodies of the jailed innocent and of the tortured, wounded, and bereaved have so often been aligned with memories of bitterness.

So within the frame the theophany provides we have witnessed an encounter, in which one person's pattern of integrity, however attenuated, is received by another as a binding claim. Odysseus, by contrast, had been no less confronted by Neoptolemus's integrity than the boy was confronted by Philoctetes' claim. But Odysseus is one who is deft at turning aside such claims, without being transformed by them. Onstage, these encounters have been made visible in actions of begging, gift giving, assisting, abiding, delaying, departing, and returning—and have been realized in the voicing of pain and in the revulsion and compassion that pain can elicit. Thus, personal integrity is made visible by referrals to bodily wholeness and disintegration.

These realizations also involve shared, yet fragmentary narratives. The framing theophany is contingent but not arbitrary; it gathers up a narrative continuity between Philoctetes and Hercules. Philoctetes can be persuaded by the god (and not by the youth) *in part* because Hercules suffered similarly and received deliverance from Philoctetes. So in carrying the bow, Philoctetes has all along carried a reason for letting his anger go. Hercules reminds him, "Burn spoils to me./Shoot arrows in my memory" (79). But Hercules also signals the discontinuities of history and of healing, be it of one's body or one's soul. His entrance comes unexpectedly, or expected only in retrospect: "Something told me this was going to happen" (89), Philoctetes says. The theophany is a "miracle," an encounter that opens horizons in which all at once we see more. Though unaccounted for by historical explanation, such transformations, it seems, do happen. Thus it is that the Chorus's aforementioned ode instructs us,

> History says, Don't hope
> On this side of the grave.
> But then, once in a lifetime
> The longed-for tidal wave
> Of justice can rise up,
> And hope and history rhyme.
> So hope for a great sea-change
> On the far side of revenge.
> Believe that a further shore
> Is reachable from here.
> Believe in miracles
> And cures and healing wells. (77)

Moments later Philoctetes, upon hearing the god through this voice, discovers that the range encompassed by his embodied nexus of social and moral relations is vastly extended.

In Sophocles, this expansion is signaled by the farewell to Lemnos, in which Philoctetes acknowledges the island as a home and friend, and he prays for its blessing as he goes to meet his "great destiny." "I am leaving you. . . . I had never hoped for this" (1461–63). In Heaney, Philoctetes does not speak to the island; however, in wonderment he reflects on what future awaits him: "But I can't believe I'm going" (80). He knows himself to be ever a convalescent, and knows that the circles of place and language are there for the sake of spinning outward at a tangent, from a local center and a particular past toward another horizon.

> My head's light at the thought of a different ground and a different
> sky. I'll never get over Lemnos; this island's going to be the keel under
> me and the ballast inside me. I'm like a fossil that's being carried away,

I'm nothing but cave stones and damp walls and an old mush of dead
leaves. The sound of waves in draughty passages. A cliff that's wet with
spray on a winter's morning. I feel like the sixth sense of the world. I
feel I'm a part of what was always meant to happen, and is happening
now at last. Come on, my friends. (80)

These things happen, but not always and not often. Heaney's treatment
of the theophany as miracle draws from Sophocles an implication of the
contingency of integrity. Like healing and reversals from tragic courses,
integrity can require something such as luck, or gifts of chance that allow
us to leave our former selves behind ourselves. The widening pattern of
Philoctetes' integrity is made of fragments of his past; yet it expands in
an encounter that, while fitting, cannot finally be accounted for in terms
of plotted probabilities or smooth theatrical coherence. The last lines of
The Cure at Troy, again spoken by the Chorus, express an imperative of
gratitude, directed both to poets—"Suspect too much sweet talk"—and
audiences—"But never close your mind." One is invited to be grateful
for a moral and sacred achievement that was chancy.

> It was a fortunate wind
> That blew me here. I leave
> Half-ready to believe
> That a crippled trust might walk
> And the half-true rhyme is love. (81)

The Cure at Troy broaches upon substantive meanings of integrity.
One such meaning is that the "good" of patterns of integrity is realized
when a person's achievements of partial wholeness become configured
with ethical paradigms such as hospitality, justice, and in particular compassion. But another meaning is that integrity is marked less by constancy
and consistency with a prior narrative than by one's being opened to the
risks, gifts, and possibilities that impinge upon and interrupt narratives.
The body is both solid and ephemeral; like memory, it persists, changes,
and passes away. It signifies how a person's self-continuity does not persist apart from impingements of nature and history and encounters with
others; these, of course, can enhance or wound the nexus of the body
and its relationships, and allow its transformation. As one inhabits such
a transformed and transforming pattern of integrity, one might reflect
that the pattern has come as a gift, and perhaps a chance gift configured
with loss. Such integrity would be, then, "half-true."

It may well be that the embodied character of patterns of integrity—that is, their impression of definite presence with another's body in space and time—is a reason why they can appear as claims, which we feel impelled to embrace or resist. As in Soyinka's play, the manifestation of another's integrity, especially one whom we are inclined to oppose, may attract or repel us, like a wound, precisely because it makes a claim upon our ways of perceiving, knowing, and being in proximity to others. Such a claim puts our own integrity at risk, which can be why we often resist integrity in others. But to say that another's integrity puts our own at risk is to say that we are *offered* a risk, a risk to what we are now or may have been, a risk that can only be resolved by an enacted response to the other's offering.

Chapter VIII

What Do You See in My Body?

*Anatomies, Norms, and Desires of Integrity
in* Venus, The Elephant Man, *and* Wit

Turn uhway. Don't look. Cover her face. Cover yr eyes.

—SUZAN-LORI PARKS, *Venus*

See Mother Nature uncorseted and in malignant rage! Tuppance.

—BERNARD POMERANCE, *The Elephant Man*

If I were writing this scene, it would last a full fifteen minutes. I would lie here, and you would sit there.

—MARGARET EDSON, *Wit*

THE *GAZE*—the word makes us ambivalent when we contemplate theater and embodiment. It can mean the objectifying "look," which Sartre thought threatened the integrity of the human subject. It can denote the "male gaze" upon the body as sexual object. But without the gaze, even with its threat (also noticed in animals when they avoid another's eyes) there could be no theater. Theater relies on a desire to perceive, to hear and see compelling or grotesque voices or bodies in motion, speech, song, interaction, and intellection—even when this desire threatens the very medium of theater, embodied persons. We can also construe the gaze as the gaze of delight, the invited gaze, the look of acknowledgment, the attentions of interest, love, gratitude, or accountability before another, the return of joy before another's countenance and living body. In the theater, the impulse to perceive may give us back to ourselves even as we risk ourselves, and in two ambivalent senses: we can lose ourselves in the lives of others, and we can lose ourselves when our gaze bodes harm to them. The plays in this chapter explore the valences of the body and the gaze and further the examination of the embodied limits of relations of integrity.

By its freak show form and culling of reports from nineteenth-century anatomical science, Suzan-Lori Parks's *Venus* (1996) alludes to Bernard Pomerance's *Elephant Man* (1979). That play is based on British surgeon Sir Frederick Treves's account of a patient he examined, presented, and later arranged to live at the London Hospital from 1886–90. The man was probably stricken with Proteus syndrome, a rare genetic disorder affecting bones and skin.[1] Both plays hold up the extraordinary or deformed body as an artlike mirror of nature and culture, into which we peer voyeuristically even if critically. However, these plays move along different trajectories. *The Elephant Man* is more easily in the company of *Philoctetes,* for unlike Saartjie or Sara Baartman in *Venus*—whose large buttocks (steatopygia) is common among the Khoisan of southern Africa—John Merrick (historically Joseph Merrick) was disfigured by a disorder, a "freak" of nature as well as history. Ross, the carnival impresario, barks out his Step Right Up.

> This side of the grave, John Merrick has no hope or expectation of relief. In every sense his situation is desperate. His physical agony is exceeded only by his mental anguish, a despised creature without consolation. Tuppence only, step in and see! To live with his physical hideousness, incapacitating deformities and unrelenting pain is trial enough, but to be exposed to the cruelly lacerating expressions of horror and disgust by all who behold him—is even more difficult to bear. Tuppence only, step in and see. (3)

In terms of form, both plays employ techniques from the "epic" or "dialectical" theater of Bertolt Brecht. The crux of such theater is to find strategies for resisting a show's being a mere commodity to be consumed. Rather, it should be an occasion for education and criticism, as well as entertainment, employing distancing effects (*Verfremdungseffekte*) to keep us aware of its illusions. Like Brecht, Parks and Pomerance employ parable-like episodes, narrators, historical notations, and carnivalesque singers and choruses, who sometimes announce provocative scene titles and give away how the play will end—for in epic theater, *suspense* should never distract us from *thinking.* Another axiom is that actors should not "identify" with their characters (à la Stanislavski), lest the audience become enthralled by the illusion of real people onstage. This axiom has always been troubling. Brecht wanted to treat his ostensibly heroic characters so ironically that we, rather than admire their virtues, will notice the effects of economic structures on their motives and actions. We are to be suspicious of the good, while dispassionate about the despised. But it is hard not to admire someone called *Mother Courage,* and few directors take Brecht's theory completely at its word, for his plays are full of remarkable people. They play better if we do feel for them as persons—as we do, of course, for Baartman and Merrick.

The source of a play's normative vision is a Brechtian issue as well. Insofar as Marx informed him, Brecht sought to locate in the present or the past signs of a future classless society. A hypothetical, regulative community provides the perspective from which history may be judged (Brecht's theatrical parables are thus analogs to biblical prophecy and eschatology).[2] Such a hoped-for community is sometimes dramatized, as in the framing scenes of *The Caucasian Chalk Circle.* But most of Brecht's works signal such a community indirectly, through ironies that comment on the story as it is performed. The audience is implicitly asked to become critical voices, observing and thinking from the vantage point of a future in which bodies will not be alienated from their material needs or from the meaning of their labor. *The future integrity of the social body becomes the basis for respecting the body's integrity today.*

Margaret Edson owes less to Brecht than to the metatheater of Thornton Wilder. The community that judges the demise of cancer patient and English professor Vivian Bearing is realized more in the play's present than its future. Perhaps the least original aspect of *Wit* is its critique of medicine's reducing Vivian not to a freak show curiosity but an object of research; but the play has other insights as well. Edson places Vivian in a tragedy, a morality play, and finally in a redemptive epiphany. Bald in her hospital gown, she wants to set the terms of her confinement in the theater of medicine, and cannot, and so we admire her and are outraged for her. Yet we also see how she has slammed her views of John Donne into her students with as much dispassion as her doctors pump chemicals into her. By ironizing her readings of Donne on death, Edson moves Vivian into a religious horizon that Parks and Pomerance only cautiously acknowledge. Yet does this intimation of immortality finally spiritualize Vivian into an epiphany of disembodied light? What implications does this vision bode for the body in patterns of integrity?

For the Love of Venus

The normative horizon of *Venus* may be hard to discern behind the play's horrific foreground. A nineteenth-century French anatomist purchases an African woman with a rather large bottom from an English carnival; he makes her his mistress, may even love her, and then (to save his personal and professional reputation) allows her to die of exposure so he can dissect and macerate her (chemically remove her flesh) in order to publish articles on Hottentot anatomy faster than his "scientific" peers can. On the dry bones of this fictionalized plot is hung a multi-aspect play of signs that distances us from the history Parks freely adapts—and for such departures she has been criticized. In 2002, the remains of Sara Baartman (d. 1815) were repatriated from museum storage in France for burial in South Africa, in a public act that symbolized a people's restoration after apartheid and which further encouraged the growing interest in Baartman's biography. But Parks was adapting and endowing her with a degree—only a degree—of "complicity," precisely to invite us to reflect on our participation in both the humanity of Saartjie and the horror of her exploitation. *Venus* consciously signals its own theatrical complicity through the narrator-like Negro Resurrectionist. He has renounced his vocation of disinterring black corpses to sell to doctors, but is blackmailed into delivering the body of Saartjie Baartman, "the Hottentot Venus," the only persona in the play with a name.

Perhaps anyone who digs into the record of enslaved or exploited African individuals inevitably becomes, after a fashion, a Negro Resurrectionist. Parks knowingly exposes our curiosities, which have been shaped by the history she is exposing. After all, you can hardly criticize freak shows without exhibiting freaks yourself, nor watch them in a play without some complicity, nor write about them in pure disinterest. We are made to be quasi-voyeurs: first of Baartman and her story. It is historically fascinating, just as it fascinated The Baron Docteur, the playwright Parks, the naturalist Stephen Jay Gould, and others who have written insightfully about it.[3] We will also be voyeurs when gazing upon the players who risk placing themselves in this story and becoming complicit in it, even in their critique of it. The form of the script elicits at least the complicity of participation. The stage directions are minimal, including a convention of Parks's own: short "rests" and longer "spells" indicate when characters interact without speaking, leaving "directors [to] fill this moment as they best see fit." Finally, the pastiche of medical terms in the dissection reports (recited during intermission and in several scenes and defined in an appendix) must be received as a warning to scholars who would gaze on this story for our own fine reasons.

The text implies but does not insist that whoever plays Venus be at times naked, which forces players to decide how to do this—a decision about exposure that also recapitulates something of the nineteenth-century exhibitions. Some productions have opted for exaggerated, stylized padding for the buttocks and breasts with no attempt at realism, which probably heightens the satire; others have used realistic body stockings. In 2001, I saw a very effective performance by the Live Arts Theater in Charlottesville, Virginia, in which only prosthetic hips were used, after the actor playing Saartjie became completely undressed for bathing. Then while we watched she put on the prosthesis, apparently just before the stage direction reads, "She is now the Venus Hottentot." This display of the actor's naked body and her assumption of an artificial naked body part were followed by the words of the Mother-Showman:

> With yr appreciative permission
> for a separate admission
> we've got a new girl: # 9
> "The Venus Hottentot."
> She bottoms out at the bottom of the ladder
> yr not a man—until you've hadder.
> But truly, folks, before she showd up our little show was in the red
> but her big bottoms friendsll surely put us safely in the black! (35)

The moment was extremely uncomfortable, which raised the question of how *Venus* was to be "enjoyed." The indictment of historical exploitation was perfectly clear. To "turn uhway" (and some did) seemed false; why else did we come, but to *see* this exhibition of an exhibition? The African American playing Saartjie, Teresa Dowell-Vest, was, with director John Gibson, instrumental in persuading Live Arts to produce *Venus,* as she explained in the program. So our permission to be voyeurs was complex: we were being asked to recognize our places in a history of complicity (with many of us named in the program as contributors to Live Arts). And yet the scene of exposure had a beauty and poignancy that pseudo-nakedness would not have created.

Any ambivalence we felt now took on further significance as we discovered Parks's other metatheatrical schemes, which investigate the body as a mirror of *desires*—desires aroused by cultural imposition (e.g., Girard's view that our desires imitate the desires of others' desires . . . , etc.) and perhaps also by gestures toward *love*. In what amounts to a farce-within-a-scene-within-a-play, Saartjie periodically watches the Baron Docteur sitting alone, as if before a TV, watching a show entitled, "For the Love of the Venus." (Only after seeing some of these scenes does he purchase Saartjie from the Mother-Showman.) In the farce, a Young Man is about to reject his Bride-To-Be.[4] Why? Because, having been encouraged by his Uncle to travel in the "wild" unknown, to seek his "place in the Great Chain of Being" (28), the Young Man decides he fancies a Hottentot. Oh, how terrible for the Bride-To-Be! But her Mother tells her she can win back her Young Man by disguising herself as a Hottentot. She does; he eyes his Bride's delectable false bottom; she reveals her disguise; and now the sweet European couple can eat chocolates, fantasizing happily forever after about each others' "other" bodies.

These farce scenes suggest certain ambiguities of mastery, desire, and making, which *Venus* as a whole iterates. First there is the instability of mastery created by the *mutual* gaze. The Young Man wishes to be empowered—to realize his "I"—by mastering the Unknown by gazing on it. But as this requires him to gaze into the "eye" of the Unknown, the eye of the Unknown must also gaze on him. In objectifying the other, he is also objectified, weakened, mastered; thus, the Young Man goes native in desiring the Hottentot. Then there is the ambiguity of making and being made. The none-too-bright Bride-To-Be voices how she cherishes a "poem" the Young Man has sent her. "My love for you is artificial/Fabricated much like this epistle" (a couplet the Baron Docteur also repeats to Saartjie). Ostensibly, the irony is anti-theatrical. But "fabricated" love is "made" love, and what is love if not made? In master-slave instabilities, and in the performative possibility of making-real by making-as-if, love somehow insinuates itself, *which makes love's destruction all the more horrifying and grievous*. Something of the good is at stake in the farce's mirror of colonial, racial, and sexual desire.

The first act of *Venus* is a game of surfaces, with none portrayed in any depth. The freak show gives way to trial scenes, wherein the show is almost shut down for violating the new British antislave law; but the judge rules that since Saartjie has freely allowed herself to be exhibited, she is no slave. So for little pay she continues to work, a "Human Wonder" whose ugliness "God hisself dont wanna look at" (32), yet also advertised as the Hottentot ideal of beauty. If the Victorian bustle is any indication (though still in the "future" of these events), her large posterior is likely to register erotically also on the European cortex. As the Baron Docteur watches the farce scenes, he is gazing into his own unaccountable desires.

In the second act we do get to know Saartjie and the Baron Docteur more as individuals. When not showing her off at the Academy (where the Chorus of 8 Anatomists measure her and marvel at her fluency in French, shades of Henry Higgins), the Docteur and Saartjie share a bed, their bodies, and chocolates—consuming some that are molded in the shape of African children. A "Glossary of Chocolates" is provided in the text, and Saartjie declaims a "Brief History of Chocolate" which, she says, "is primarily today a great source of fat,/and, of course, pleasure" (156). As they talk and touch in the dark, their hermetic enclave creates an impression of intimacy, of how they each fill, yet fail to fill, one another's emptiness. The Docteur is childless by his wife, so Saatjie gives him an aphrodisiacal feather: "It might help." In bed with Saartjie he turns his back to masturbate. When he does impregnate her, he persuades her to be aborted.

If these bedroom scenes are enacted with tenderness and trouble, then a chance of love will be evident. But what together the Docteur and Saatjie can become, and what patterns of integrity might emerge, would depend upon their interactions with others, as in all relationships. They would need to be witnessed as a relationship in order to be realized in relationship. But the Docteur cannot in fact connect his own emptiness-as-filled-by-Saartjie with his emptiness-as-filled-by-fellow-Anatomists, who are the ones that secure his vocational role. They validate him-alone; they invalidate him-with-her. He confesses his fantasy, envy, and inadequacy.

> You were just yrself and crowds came running.
> I was fascinated and a little envious but just a little.
> A doctor cant just be himself
> no onerll pay a cent for that.
> Imagine me just being me. (103)

But as he confesses, and as she invites his love, there occurs to him a "specific circle" of thought that will soon encompass her death:

> Most great minds discover something.
> I've had ideas for things but.
> My ideas r—
> (You wouldn't understand em anyway.)

THE VENUS:
> Touch me
> down here

THE BARON DOCTEUR:
> In you, Sweetheart, Ive met my opposite-exact.
> Now if I could only match you.

VENUS:
> That feels good.
> Now touch me here.

THE BARON DOCTEUR:
> Crowds of people screamed yr name!
> "Venus Hottentot!!"
> You were a sensation! I wouldn't mind a bit of that.
> Known. Like you!
> Only, of course, in my specific circle. (104)

Of course, crowds of people did not actually scream her *name*. Even so, Saartjie has emerged in the play as a particular and interesting personality. This has to be the case if the horror that follows is to affect us, when the School-Chum warns the Docteur that the Hottentot is tolerable only as an object of science, never as an object of love. But by the last scene, she is not merely a fetish to be sacrificed but someone who has been loved and desires love. Farfetched? Not in Virginia, where Thomas Jefferson and Sally Hemings were not far from our minds.[5]

That the body is both a mirror and construction of desire is also explored in the interplay of costuming and measuring. Measuring purports to establish objective reality, and Gould comments on the extent to which scientists used anatomical measurements (e.g., determining how much BB shot would fill the cavities of African skulls) to validate racialist premises. What the dissection reports and the scenes wherein the Venus is poked and measured by customers and anatomists really show is how her body, even as a naked corpse, remains clothed in projections and constructions. (Her painted death cast was on display in Paris until 1976.)[6] The body as a "thing in itself" is nearly invisible; and there is a sense in which the body's retention of traces of acculturation is a good thing, if that resists the naturalistic pretension to *objectify* persons. If we could easily view a body apart from cultural clothing, there would be lost the sense of *reality-emerging-in-participation* that makes a person a personality.

But cultural clothing can obviously be a vector of harm. And how our projections of meanings may assist in creative and destructive relations with others is what Saartjie imagines in her longest speech, in a scene that will end with her asking about the meaning of "maceration." Her speech can be read as an *allusion* to Hegel's master-slave reversal, or else as her *illusion* that mastery will be available to her if she can share the Baron Docteur's social status. But her words are also an articulate *improvisation,* which may elicit both our admiration and chagrin as Saartjie imagines being at once the Docteur's master and mistress.

> He is not thuh most thrilling lay Ive had
> but his gold makes up thuh difference and hhhh
> I love him.
> He will leave that wife for good and we'll get married
> (we better or I'll make a scene) oh, we'll get married.
> And we will lie in bed and make love all day long.
> Hahahaha.
> We'll set tongues wagging for the rest of the century.
> The Docteur will introduce me to Napoléan himself: Oh,
> yes yr Royal Highness the Negro question does keep me
> awake all night oh yes it does.
> . . . .
> Every afternoon I'll take a 3 hour bath. In hot rosewater.
> After my bath theyll pat me down.
> Theyll rub my body with the most expensive oils
> perfume my big buttocks and sprinkle them with gold dust!
> *The Baron Docteur enters and watches her. She does not see him.* (135)

The projections of signs on the bodies of Saartjie and the Docteur are finally destructive. But before leaving *Venus* we should ask what normative vision, virtue, or principle is implied in this critique of the commerce of embodiment. In an afterword, Parks says her "angle" in retelling Baartman's story was, "*History, Memory, Dis-memory, Remembering, Dismembering, Love, Distance, Time, a Show*" (166). Of these, the play seems to shout a plea for love. It also shouts for justice; but the category "injustice" hardly does justice to the extreme harm depicted here, and the trial scenes are a bitter critique of distracted or distorted powers of instituted "justice." Are other principles evident? The Baron is a "Docteur," but has not come to cure or palliate. As an anatomist, the medical maxim "first do no harm" is not compelling in his "circle." So is it the Kantian principle of respect for personal autonomy that the play most desires, or is it "human dignity," or is it something else? These are the last lines:

THE NEGRO RESURRECTIONIST:
    A Scene of Love:
THE VENUS:
    Kiss me *Kiss* me *Kiss* me *Kiss* (162)

These lines may be glossed by the dedication page, thanking those contributing to the realization of *Venus*. The list does not say, "with love to," but "with Love from." It concludes, "with Love from Saartjie Baartman." So where is Saartjie? From whence her love? From what ancestral or celestial place may it find us? Whatever love means in *Venus*—traditionally a goddess of love—it may be from some future "scene of love" that her critical forces flow, toward our own bodies.

The Mirror and Art of John Merrick

In *The Elephant Man*, the prophetic community of judgment, if not of love, is signaled by the Pinheads, part of the freak show from which Merrick was abandoned. The Pinheads know more about the economics of exploitation than their conical brains would seem to contain:

We are the Queens of the Congo,
The Beautiful Belgium Empire
Our niggers are bigger
Our miners are finer
Empire, Empire, Congo and power
Civilizuzu's finest hour
Admire, perspire, desire, acquire
Or we'll set you on fire! (10)

When much later Merrick dies, the Pinheads are the divine fates. They arrange his body into a "normal sleeping position," which kills him (for he is strangulated by the drop of his inordinately heavy head), and in effect they receive him as they sing:

We are the Queens of the Cosmos
Beautiful darkness' empire
Darkness darkness, light's true flower,
Here is eternity's finest hour
Sleep like others you learn to admire
Be like your mother, be like your sire. (67–68)

The Pinheads frame a play that opens onto horizons of nature and spirit somewhat more metaphysical than in Parks or Brecht. While both Pomerance and Parks are confident we will be appalled by how bodies could be viewed by nineteenth-century scientists and citizens, Parks attributes such views to structures of self-interest and self-deception that might be repaired. The Venus was a freak not of nature but of inhumanity, and Parks assumes her audience will recognize its complicities in history, transcend them, and affirm that evils can be overcome. Yes, one could argue that the "cultural" structures of distortion (e.g., a physiognomy that reflects hidden Western desires and so must be expelled) are so pervasive as to be "natural." Even so, Parks's play gazes back upon us with greater hope than Pomerance's. For the unmasking of ideology in *The Elephant Man* is counterpointed by the view that historical injustice is tragically entangled with nature. To overcome this entanglement would require divine transcendence, a theme modeled by St. Phillip's church, which John completes just before he dies. But the anatomist, Dr. Treves, looks upon possibilities of transcendence with doubt and despair.

That nature is part of the tangle of contingency and fault is signaled by Merrick's disorder, to be realized by the actor who plays Merrick. He is not to wear a makeup artist's creation, as in David Lynch's 1980 film (not based on the play). Pomerance notes, paraphrasing Treves, that "Merrick's face was so deformed he could not express any emotion at all" (v). Rather, when Merrick is medically displayed we see an athletic and lithe actor, who contorts his nearly nude body "to approximate the projected slides of the historical Merrick" shown on or behind the actor's body. As the actor alters his posture and voice, he signifies personal transcendence expressionistically; the ability to achieve and relax contortions is another instance of the performative and protean nature of the embodied person. Expressionism is also implied when Merrick tells the actress, Mrs. Kendal, about his head, "so big because it is full of dreams."

> MERRICK: . . . Do you know what happens when the dreams cannot get out?
> MRS. KENDAL: Why, no.
> MERRICK: I don't know either. Something must. (32)

Merrick imagines himself distorted from within, by the pressures of dreams, which he channels into his own work of art, the model of St. Phillip's church. His expressionism is also platonic, as when he discovers the principle of art as "a third removed from reality."

MERRICK: . . . St. Phillips really . . . is an imitation of grace flying
up and up from the mud. So I make my imitation of an imitation. But even in that is heaven to me. . . .
TREVES: That thought's got a good line, John. (38)

The body of the one who plays Merrick recapitulates this line: the actor in effect reveals the eternal *eidos* of Merrick, as he distorts his fine
body to show both beautiful form and hideous surface at once. Thus,
we would see an image of Merrick's soul or spiritual body, so to speak,
which his acquaintances only rarely saw. What nature provided would
be the distortion; what the actor shows of his own body would be Merrick's essential physiognomy.

However, Pomerance prefaces this juxtaposition of the embodied and
the ideal with a medical warning label: "No one with a history of back
trouble should attempt the part of Merrick as contorted" (ix). Perhaps
this warning is another sign of ambivalence about theater, art, and the
meaning of the body. Treves complains about the unnecessary ailments
he treats in women who wear corsets, and Merrick's body, Ross says,
is "Nature uncorseted." The role of art would be to corset nature, and
everyone seems in the business of turning Merrick's body into one sort
of objet d'art or another, which would then become a source of consolation, like religion. As Treves displays Merrick to his fellow physicians, he
lingers over one of his arms, as if a fragment in a collage. The arm "was
not only normal, but was moreover a delicately shaped limb covered
with a fine skin and provided with a beautiful hand which any woman
might have envied" (6). His oddly gendered description is reminiscent of
Michelangelo's unfinished *Rondinini Pieta,* where only one awkwardly
detached arm of Christ has been polished out of the rough-hewn marble;
and it introduces the theme of seeing in art and in the broken body
whatever we desire. In their first meeting, Merrick astonishes Mrs. Kendal with his appraisal of *Romeo and Juliet* (a moment he confuses with
the mirror used at the end of *King Lear*) when Romeo finds Juliet in the
tomb and, thinking she is dead, kills himself.

MERRICK: Does he take her pulse? Does he get a doctor? Does
he make sure? No. He kills himself. The illusion fools him
because he does not care for her. He only cares about himself.
If I had been Romeo, we would have got away.
MRS. KENDAL: But then there would be no play, Mr. Merrick.
MERRICK: If he did not love her, why should there be a play?
Looking in the mirror and seeing nothing. That is not love.

It was all an illusion. When the illusion ended he had to kill
himself. (33)

Treves arranges for Merrick to be visited by members of high society,
and once they get used to his appearance, they see him as a mirror of
their own ideals, as does Mrs. Kendal. Treves thinks an actress might
succeed in *pretending* to see Merrick as a human being, but in pretending so, she does so. She tells Merrick she stands before him not as a stage
illusion but as "myself" (32). Later she considers that Merrick's interest
in fancy toiletries has only to do with "props" he can use "[t]o make
himself. As I make me. . . . He is gentle, almost feminine." Again, she is
seeing herself in him—"Cheerful, honest within limits, a serious artist in
his way. He is almost like me" (39). When Treves first shows her pictures
of Merrick, she notices both his splendid hand and perfectly formed
genitalia; she now suspects Treves of avoiding the fact that Merrick is
a sexual being. Treves cruelly banishes her after she briefly shows her
breasts to Merrick and undoes her hair.[7] "I saw photographs of you," she
says (49). Merrick looks and sees her as the ideal, feminine form of art,
which, he has told her, he has longed to find.

MRS. KENDAL: My dear she doesn't exist.
MERRICK: That is probably why I never saw her.

Mrs. Kendal then explains to John how there happen to be women who

are lucky to look well, that is all. It is a rather arbitrary gift;
it has no really good use, though it has its uses, I will say
that. Anyway it does not signify very much.
MERRICK: To me it does. (48)

Mrs. Kendal regards beauty as arbitrary, and indeed the question,
"Chancey?" is the last word spoken by Merrick (67). The play leaves us
with a different sort of perplexity than *Venus*. Treves dreams of Merrick
lecturing on Treves's body and on Victorian attitudes, and thus registers anguish about the meaning of "normality." He later confesses that
the people involved with Merrick "have polished him like a mirror"
(64), creating the illusion of commonality. "I am in despair," he tells
the Bishop. "Science, observation, practice, deduction, having led me to
these conclusions, can no longer serve as consolation. I apparently see
things others don't." He hastens to add, "I am sure we were not born
for mere consolation" (65), and goes on in this vein until he falls into

a fit of weeping; the Bishop then *"consoles him"* (66). In the last scene, after being asked if there is anything to add to Merrick's obituary, Treves belatedly thinks "of one small thing," but whatever it is turns out to be too late to publish.

Juxtaposed with Treves and the Bishop is the moment Merrick affixes the last piece to his model of St. Phillip's and says, echoing Christ in John's Gospel, "It is done" (66). Merrick falls asleep with his large, heavy head in a fatal, prone position and is received by the Pinheads. In a 2002 New York revival directed by Sean Mathias, this moment was marked in a number of ways, including its juxtaposition with Treves's (Rupert Graves) despair. The Pinheads (among them Kate Burton, who also played Mrs. Kendal) did not arrange Merrick's body into its final position until the one playing Merrick (Billy Crudup) relaxed his contorted posture, as if released from his body. They then covered him with a sheer cloth. The effect, as they sang "We are the Queens of the Cosmos," was to receive him into eternity or oblivion.

The Body and Wit of Vivian Bearing

Wit is also concerned with how the integrity of the personal body *depends on* and is *vulnerable to* the reception of others. Margaret Edson takes advantage of our familiarity with the lingo and postures of the "doctor show" genre. More than ovarian cancer, it is the physician-researchers who interrupt Vivian Bearing's pattern of integrity. This impression is maintained almost until the last moment, when a code team leaps upon her with defibrillator paddles, ignoring a Do Not Resuscitate (DNR) order. Their automatic reduction of Vivian from person to patient, then from patient to datum, is no less urgent a tale for being common. Yet the portrayal of medicine is not the strongest aspect of *Wit*: the doctors are too stereotypically insensitive and nurse Susie is too cozy, at least until their roles are filled by idiosyncrasies of particular actors.

That caveat aside, it should be noticed how Edson overlays the medical business of *Wit* with themes that are not stereotypical. The irritated and irritating research fellow, Jason Posner, has crucial insights. And the attending, Dr. Kelekian, is honest when he informs Vivian that his motive for having her go eight rounds of experimental chemotherapy is to gather data. While it is true that the clash of his professional jargon with hers demonstrates her helplessness (she cannot really hear what he tells her), it also indicates their symmetry, for they are both people whose visions are focused by professional lenses. "Professional integrity," the dominant pattern of their lives, mostly blinds them from others and from themselves and cannot promote the discernment of humane matters. Yet at the same time, their professional integrity enables them to see amazing things—especially, as Donne would say, under "emergent" conditions.[8]

Medicine as Trope for Religion

Young Dr. Posner—clinical fellow in oncology, interested only in research, and who is an A– alumnus of Professor Bearing's give-no-quarter course in seventeenth-century poetry—is doing a pelvic exam to assess the tumor on her ovary. Her pain and humiliation are obvious, and she recites Donne's "Death be not proud" sonnet to keep herself distracted. And although Jason probably has not (as Edson probably has) heard of Rudolf Otto's "idea of the holy" (where the holy is experienced as at once awful and fascinating, the *mysterium tremendum et fascinans*),[9] Jason experiences his discovery quasi-religiously. "(*He feels the mass and does a double take.*) Jesus! (*Tense silence. He is amazed and fascinated*)" (31).

To Jason, cancerous cell growth is every bit as fascinating and indeterminate as the ironies of the Holy Sonnets. "Why cancer?" Vivian means, why did you not go into cardiology or dermatology? He can't find the right word at first, but then agrees that the never-ending cell division in cancer is "awesome." Cancer cells resist death. This is where he first speaks of the object of his research being something like an ancient text, to be read and appreciated in abundant detail but not finally deciphered. He speaks of "intercellular regulatory mechanisms—especially for proliferation and differentiation," the functions that give normal cells their destiny and particular integrity, one might say. But they are absent in cancer:

> You grow normal cells in tissue culture in the lab, and they replicate just enough to make a nice, confluent monolayer. They divide twenty times, or fifty times, but eventually conk out. You grow cancer cells, and they never stop. No contact inhibition whatsoever. They just pile up, just keep replicating forever.

This phenomenon has "a funny name," he tells her, "immortality in culture."

> It's an error in judgment, in a molecular way. But *why*? Even on the
> protistic level the normal cell-cell interactions are so subtle they'll
> take your breath away. Golden-brown algae, for instance, the lowest
> multicellular life form on earth—they're *idiots*—and it's incredible. It's
> perfect. So what's up with the cancer cells? Smartest guys in the world,
> with the best labs, funding—they don't know what to make of it.

Jason though, if he can "survive" his clinical fellowship (the irrelevant
part of his training where he is forced to interact with patients), says he
has "a couple of ideas" (56–57).

Medical stories like *Wit* are appealing in how they seem to locate
common values and beliefs in secular society, such as the healer's principle, "first do no harm." Medicine—in both its "normal" and "alternative" varieties—can stand in for the integrative work of religion, and
biomedical phenomena become tropes for the verities and vagaries of
human existence.[10] So when Vivian is interviewed, x-rayed, scoped, and
prodded, there is the pretension of science to look "within" the person.
That it *is* a pretension is signaled in Jason's interview with Vivian, "Well,
that about does it for your life history" (24). As for cancer's "immortality in culture," the phrase signals the entanglement of death *as curse* and
as gift, for it is the cell's immortality that threatens the biological whole,
as we would threaten the social whole if we did not die.

Wit Resisting Tragedy and Theodicy

Vivian describes herself as an actor and "impresario" in a sometimes
comic, finally tragic drama—as when she introduces the theater of Grand
Rounds:

> You cannot imagine how time ... can be ... so still.
> It hangs. It weighs. And yet there is so little of it.
> It goes so slowly, and yet it is so scarce.
> If I were writing this scene, it would last a full fifteen minutes.
> I would lie here, and you would sit there.
> (*She looks at the audience, daring them.*)
> Not to worry. Brevity is the soul of wit.
> But if you think eight months of cancer treatment is tedious
> for the *audience,* consider how it feels to play my part. (35)

In Greek tragedy, religion is a sphere of misfortune and fortune, which
oracles express and seers interpret. Dramas such as *Wit* can approximate

tragedy in that Nature is like a god that establishes life and functions as a sacred horizon; yet the patient suffers *both* because of Nature (like tragic *até*) *and* because the blows of Nature may be compounded by human errors and dispositions (*hamartia* and *hubris*). Jason, who erroneously calls a code for dying Vivian, has his own tragic recognition (85), horrified to realize he forgot or missed the DNR order.

But Jason is also the one who most clearly voices to one of the meanings that John Donne gives to the whole picture of Vivian. He tells Suzie about the course he took from Vivian Bearing in metaphysical poetry. Donne's Holy Sonnets "were mostly about Salvation Anxiety."

> [Y]ou know you're a sinner. And there's this promise of salvation, the whole religious thing. But you just can't deal with it. . . . It just doesn't stand scrutiny. But you can't face life without it either. So you write these screwed up sonnets. Everything is brilliantly convoluted. (75–76)

Like research in cell biology, the point of this poetry, as Jason learned, was not to solve the puzzle but "to quantify the complications of the puzzle" (77). Similarly, Greek tragic realism resists the consolations of theodicy, that is, the solutions to how there can be a just, merciful, and powerful divinity despite the realities of evil and suffering. Even so, while Aeschylus, Sophocles, and Euripides resisted consolation, they did so in behalf of religious and ethical visions. *Mere* dissent from justifying God or the gods runs the risk, paradoxically, of ignoring the very insight that occasions theodicy in the first place, that suffering is a perplexing mix of human causes with other realities not reducible to human causes.[11]

However, in a good deal of postmodern thought, the refusal to engage the questions of theodicy is approximated in "irony," that is, a knowing reticence to express ultimate values in tones of conviction.[12] Vivian is a scholar of irony who, at all cost, will not be caught in any mode of belief in or sensibility toward "absolute dependence" (as Friedrich Schleiermacher defined religion early in the nineteenth century). Wit has been, since her days in graduate school, a screen against what Jason calls "*meaning-of-life* garbage" (77). By emulating what she takes to be Donne's wit, she avoids tracing the threads of contingent suffering and culpable malice mixed in the life around her—at least until the play's last scene.

Wit as Morality Play

Much as we are to feel Vivian's predicament and enjoy her wit, we are not altogether to *like* her. Her cancer is not only an occasion of self-scrutiny, but also of judgment, which culminates in what amounts to a deathbed redemption. However, when at last she stands "naked, and beautiful, reaching for the light" (85), the question is for what theodicy does the play reach. Does she rise into a new "spiritual body" (1 Corinthians 15:44), which would have continuity with her old body? Or, is it a cliché of pop spirituality, the near-death "tunnel of light"—thus diverting us from how there is only "More a little, and then dumb" (6)? Or is the last stage direction, "then, lights out," the last metaphysical word the play says about Vivian?

On the way to her epiphany, she is witty and habitually cruel. She was cruel to herself as a graduate student, forsaking sunshine for the library cubicle where she became a literary "force," never to be caught by the delusion of determinate meanings. She was contemptuous of her students in the usual ways (allowing hesitant insights to degenerate into inarticulacy, not accepting "my grandmother died" excuses, being offended by witty jokes about her lectures). Even near the end, as she realizes that "kindness" may now be in order, she cannot censor her tongue about Susie ("my brain is dulling, and Susie's was never very sharp to begin with," 69). And she is a little cruel in the ingratiating, condescending way she addresses us, who are sitting, in effect, in her seminar room. (Here Edson faces the dilemma of teaching us just enough Donne that we may enjoy how Vivian condescends to us and perhaps outwits herself, just as Donne may or may not knowingly have tried to outwit his readers.)

I take it that the meaning of the final epiphany—reaching for the light—is to be found in a reading of Donne that Vivian has made a career of rejecting. In flashback, her mentor, Professor Evelyn Ashford (alluding to Donne scholar Helen Gardner), once upbraided her for using a bad edition of "Death be not proud," one with "hysterical punctuation." "And Death—*capital D*—shall be no more—*semi-colon!*/Death—*capital D*—comma—thou shalt die—*exclamation point!*" In the "Gardner edition," the sonnet ends quietly, explains Ashford, with neither semi-colon nor exclamation point: "Nothing but a breath—a comma—separates life from life everlasting. It is very simple really" (14). But the seed of Vivian's forced insight germinates at this instant of seeing through Donne's theodicy: "It's a metaphysical conceit. It's wit! I'll go back to the library and rewrite the paper." But Ashford pronounces: "It is *not wit*, Miss Bearing, it is truth. . . . Do not go to the library. Go out. Enjoy yourself with your friends" (15). By the end of these ninety minutes of *Wit*, Vivian recognizes the consequences of her choices.

Her great moment, her *coup de théâtre,* is her lecture on Holy Sonnet 5, "If poysonous minerals," where she demonstrates how her teaching could be perplexing yet "so powerful." As the text is projected on a screen, she wields a pointer to analyze it; and if her lecture is done well we will follow its gist, if not its nuances. The speaker of Sonnet 5 passes from "aggressive intellect" to "pious melodrama" to "a final, fearful point" (i.e., while some feel grateful that God remembers them with their sins, it would be more merciful if God would "forget"). And Vivian takes this to mean, "if thou wilt forget . . ." *me.* The speaker wants to be forgotten, "so he crawls under a rock to *hide*" (49), "to *disappear*" (50). But we may assume that one of Vivian's own fears is that she, the scholar, will be forgotten—though, at the peak of her pain, humiliation, and isolation in the hospital, she might indeed want to hide.

Her point about wit is much as Jason explains: Donne wrote of endlessly ramifying spiritual conundrums, where nothing less than salvation was at stake, salvation about which Vivian thinks Donne was incredulous. Wit (were she correct) would be his way of deflecting attention away from the poem's serious subject matter and toward the nimble facility of the poet's (and critic's) intellect. In the case of Sonnet 5, Vivian with an assist from an actual Donne scholar, Richard Strier, points out that normally, a true believer would pray to be *remembered* by God.[13] The poem's speaker, however, wants to be *forgotten,* which might mean the believing reader is to recognize, against the speaker, the readiness of God's grace, which the speaker cannot believe. "It is that simple. Suspiciously simple." Why does Vivian say suspiciously?

> We want to correct the speaker, to remind him of the assurance of salvation. But it is too late. The poetic encounter is over. We are left to our own consciences. Have we outwitted Donne? Or have we been outwitted? (50)

It is hard to grasp exactly what she finds "suspicious"—but we are not allowed to think immediately about it, because Susie interrupts with the nonnegotiable demand that Vivian must go for another ultrasound test. (The frustration is devastating, she is losing her reason to be.) It is hard to follow Vivian, unless we are to assume that *Donne,* and not just the *speaker* of Sonnet 5, is burdened by a salvation anxiety overwhelming his belief, and that we have now figured this out (i.e., we have outwitted Donne's puzzle). But this is the very assumption Ashford had earlier contradicted; so is Vivian letting slip that it is she ("we") who is outwitted?[14]

Vivian has fashioned a career of resisting a straightforward reading of Donne; she is burdened not by salvation anxiety but by what Harold Bloom calls "the anxiety of influence."

Who Receives the Body?

The deus ex machina really begins not when she reaches into the light, but earlier when Ashford, now eighty, visits and gets into her hospital bed and reads not Donne but Margaret Wise Brown's *Runaway Bunny.* Ashford has bought the book for her great-grandchild and calls it "a little allegory of the soul" (80), about a rabbit who learns it cannot escape the love of its mother, who can disguise herself in all sorts of ways. When she finishes, Vivian is asleep, so she quotes Horatio's blessing on Hamlet ("And flights of angels sing thee to thy rest")—and this must be when Vivian expires. She has received her morphine, so it remains uncertain whether Ashford has visited objectively or in a dream. But it is real onstage, and in Evelyn Ashford the personae of mentor, academic precursor, parent-substitute, and even God have come together.

What may not come together is the meaning of the last epiphany, Vivian standing alone and reaching out. It may be finally a denial of human embodiment, if she is seen as a light-going-into-the-light. Or an affirmation of embodiment, because the naked, fifties-something woman playing Vivian is the last thing we gaze on. Or it could support a Pauline interpretation, that Vivian rises as a spiritual body.[15] Her physical body, which has been its own indefeasible antagonist, has been an occasion for both the constriction of her integrity and now, with another's intervention (Ashford, somewhat like Heracles in *Philoctetes*), an occasion for her pattern to be enlarged. Edson has taken us on a passage through judgment and redemption, giving it the form of a medical story about an interesting patient, the designs of her doctors, and cancer, which for many in the audience is the most feared form of illness.

However, insofar as her passage has a scriptural and communal pattern, an ambiguity remains, for the play's last image is of one person standing *alone*. It is *we* who are assigned to be the community that receives her into the light, we who have been her students and fellow patients. This issue of how the audience is to "receive" Vivian probably cannot be resolved by acting or staging; it is an ambiguity intrinsic to the play, and one which endangers it, pressing it to the edge of sentimentality. Nonetheless, a production I saw at Chicago's Goodman Theatre in 2001, with Carmen Roman as Vivian and directed by Steve Scott, came close to realizing the *question* of what the audience's metatheatrical role in seeing and receiving the ill will be.[16] Where the script calls for the actor to be naked and beautiful for only an "instant," the Goodman production allowed this instant to last long enough to prompt thought as well as amazement. Even so, I think we are likely to "forget" these questions about Vivian's passage, and enthusiastically applaud the courage of the particular actor who gives it life.

What then of the body's integrity? All three playwrights display the body as a trope of integrity-realized and of integrity-attacked, and all three—including Parks as interpreted by John Gibson at Live Arts—risk displaying the actor's body as both a verification of integrity and a temptation to objectification. If we in the audience recognize the danger *we pose* by our gaze, then we may also verify the actor's own fragile integrity. If we recognize how our gaze *threatens the gift* of integrity being offered us, namely, the living bodies performing personae, then we may be impressed with the *gift's reality*. On the other hand, the danger we pose to the other is so real that these plays may give us reason to doubt that the body connects with integrity at all. Again, Mrs. Kendal: "Some women are lucky to look well, that is all. It is a rather arbitrary gift. . . . Anyway, it does not signify very much." "To me it does," replies Merrick. The body needs others' bodies, yet bodies threaten it. So much as to make us desire to escape the body, when it imprisons our patterns of integrity.

Chapter IX

Do We Desire to Escape the Body?

Anticipating Kenosis in Schechner's Euripides and Zimmerman's Ovid

CADMUS: Look directly at it. Just a quick glance.
AGAVE: What is it? What am I holding in my hands?
CADMUS: Look more closely still. Study it carefully.
—EURIPIDES, *The Bacchae*

Your body is not your "instrument"; your body is you.
—RICHARD SCHECHNER

Make me something else; transform me entirely;
let me step out of my own heart.
—OVID, DAVID R. SLAVITT, MARY ZIMMERMAN, *Metamorphoses*

THE BODY SPECIFIES and locates each person as a nexus—a node of intersecting and changing relations in space and time—neither duplicated nor repeated. We have noticed how theater celebrates and explores critically the solid persistence and the mutability of this nexus, with its realizations of self and character. We have also seen how the body is as much a social construct as a natural phenomenon, which can be exploited and celebrated. The body does not secure or ground integrity but provides a site for concretizing patterns and dramas of integrity. Bodies, social and biological, are also like roles that may emancipate or imprison us.

Thus, modes of embodiment may prompt the desire to escape the body. This desire takes numerous forms and can be both creative and destructive. It may also enter patterns of integrity, as when persons seek to transcend suffering or physical destiny, or seek to surpass their bounds in place and time. These possibilities are explored in Richard Schechner's historic 1968 version of Euripides, *Dionysus in 69,* and a recent, popular appropriation of experimental theater, Mary Zimmerman's *Metamorphoses,* from Ovid and other sources. The first is a disclosure and critique of the social body, and continues the critique of theater we are tracing through part III. The second is an elegy to our desires to transcend forms of the body.

The Body Eclipsing Character: *Bacchae* et alia

In the *Birth of Tragedy* (1872), Friedrich Nietzsche considered Euripides to have betrayed the tragic chorus, whose dithyrambic music revealed the form-breaking eruption of the Dionysian spirit; he thought *The Bacchae* repressed the Dionysian experience it should have privileged. In this his first book, Nietzsche was something of a romantic, for whom art taps into depths of nature and culture. What made this idea avant-garde, in respect to theater, was its subordination of plot, character, and speech to the revelatory power of music and spectacle. The pursuit of a quasi-sacred *experience* became a desideratum of avant-garde theater.

As to our interest in integrity, this emphasis on experience, especially primary, unitary experience, is at the beginning of a trajectory from modern to postmodern, which Elinor Fuchs calls the "death of character."[1] By character, she primarily means the second element of drama in Aristotle's *Poetics,* which he regarded as subordinate to plotted action. But with Shakespeare and on into Romanticism character became of first concern to dramatists and audiences, a quest for experience that continued in different ways in Stanislavski, in Brook's vision of theatrical space, and even in Brecht. For in "alienating" actors from the personality of the part, Brecht turned his characters into political allegories. To make them come alive, many actors find they must invest them with "character" after all. However, the quest for primordial experience eclipsed not only traditional dramatic forms but also the individuality of character itself. We saw this in the parody of symbolist theater at the beginning of *The Seagull.*

While the ascendancy of experience continued in experimental theater, another mode of eclipse became evident, thinks Fuchs, in the problem of the sign.[2] Experience is usually taken to be a *referent,* something real, to which signs point. Even structuralism implies a kind of referent, in the oppositions underlying mind and culture. But when signs are regarded as gesturing only to other signs—and everything in theater, from ushers to actors, to dust on the props are "signifiers of signifiers"—then theater would be less about "real" experience and more a game of signs and surfaces. The French dramatist Antonin Artaud (1896–1948), articulated the axioms for what Tom Driver calls "theatrical positivism."[3] Although Artaud is associated with the abolition of the authoritative, representational script in behalf of a vision of total theater (in which a disclosure of "metaphysical," Dionysian-like "cruelty" is sought), his plans for bodily and vocal movement were semiotic or hieroglyphic.[4] They would be a spectacle of signs with little reference beyond performance. Performance, observes Fuchs, now is "about" the reality of performance,[5] and we would be far from Aristotle's "character."

For instance, in Elizabeth LeCompte's 2002 *To You, the Birdie! (Phèdre)* (with badminton duals, video monitors, and enema bags indicating just how love*sick* Racine's Queen really is), the lines were sometimes spoken by players other than those performing a character's movements. One delightful bit, as I recall it, occurred when Willem Dafoe entered as Theseus, his lines momentarily intoned by Scott Shepherd, imitating the voice of Dafoe. Not only were we alienated from the characters but from the "stars" as well.

Our studies are somewhat limited by the fact that *haut avant-garde théâtre* has generally been a high-urban phenomenon. Local community theaters might but are not likely to produce *Birdie*. This limitation leaves many of us in the awkward position of relying on discursive texts such as Fuchs's to appreciate performances that inherently resist discursive language. As it happens, LeCompte has been artistic director of the Wooster Group, descended from Richard Schechner's Performance Group, which in 1968 began work in a high-ceilinged garage on Wooster Street in Lower Manhattan. One afternoon in 2002 I went to Brooklyn to see *Birdie,* in part out of piety for a work I can never "see," *Dionysus in 69.*

Birdie reminds us that besides *experience* and *sign,* the *body* is usually the basis of "presence" in live theater (even in puppetry the persons moving the puppets are of interest and are sometimes visible). So when LeCompte covered naked body parts with video screens showing the same naked parts doing the same-or-not-quite-the-same things, we were confronting the body mainly as signifier that questioned its significance. But such questioning does not abolish the body's excess of presence,[6] although it may distance us from the excess. The Wooster Group was exploring the reduction of experience to the coarse thing-ness of bodies, much as Schechner and Beckett had. While LeCompte placed the body in a high-tech game (although the badminton was real, not virtual), Schechner in 1968 used low-tech platforms, mats, few props, and lines from William Arrowsmith's translation of *The Bacchae* to realize the loss of structural and social boundaries that overcomes Euripides' Pentheus. Before *Dionysus in 69* began each ticket holder was individually "initiated" into the performance space; some joined the players in dances and rituals (with or sometimes without their clothes), and at the end all could follow Dionysus and the cast out into Wooster Street. The title played on a political slogan. If "Nixon in '68," why not "Dionysus in '69"? Dionysus was revealed as the demigod of demagogues, and the audience was to realize it was being co-opted by the tyrant. If embodiment is the medium of theater and the condition for being a person, both Euripides and Schechner were experimenting with the limits of both.

The intent of *The Bacchae,* in which the sacrifice of a god is replaced by that of a man, is a conundrum. Was Euripides proto-feminist? The attention he gives to women's suffering can suggest so, but the frequency with which his women are harmed gives some credence to Aristophanes' charge of misogyny.[7] Was he celebrating Dionysus? The god's fierce judgment on the impiety of Thebes makes this plausible, were it not for the horrible delusion put upon Agave or Euripides' alleged religious skepticism. Would, then, *The Bacchae* be an attack on the "god of mob action"?[8] That question recalls Nietzsche's complaint about the betrayal of the Dionysian impulse. Must it be either-or? Arrowsmith cautions against reducing this play, "so moved by profoundly religious feeling," to Euripides' "hostility to received religion."[9] It has even been argued that rather than reflecting Dionysian religious practice in the fifth century, the chorus of Asian bacchants may have provided an innovative model for its later developments.[10] Those unfamiliar with the play must remember that the Chorus is composed entirely of Dionysus's Asian followers, who are quite sane; we never see the inflamed Theban women except for Agave. (Both groups were represented by the players in *Dionysus in 69.*)

The Bacchae begins with the god telling us he is disguised in the form (*morphēn*) of a man. Were the play part of the distant Hellenistic background of the *kenosis* hymn (Philippians 2:6–11), where a preexisting Christ empties into the form of a human slave, the precedent would still be one of contrast. Dionysus has come not to serve others or obey Zeus but to punish slander. The sisters of Dionysus's late mortal mother, Semele (sisters who include young King Pentheus's mother, Agave), have claimed Dionysus did not spring from the seed and "womb" of Zeus, who sewed the fetus into his thigh, but from Semele's fornication with a mortal. So Dionysus has put the women of Thebes into a state of frenzy. Like Odysseus in *Philoctetes,* he is orchestrating a performance, to demonstrate that he is indeed the son of Zeus.[11]

After Dionysus and his Chorus recount the migration of his rites from Persia to Greece, two old geezers enter, blind Teiresias and decrepit Cadmus (retired king of Thebes), dressed in bacchants' fawn skins and ivy. They say they feel young again, young enough to dance their way into the hills, seemingly to worship the new god. Cadmus asks, "Are we the only men/who will dance for Bacchus?" Teiresias replies, "They are all blind./Only we can see. . . ."

> We do not trifle with divinity.
> No, we are the heirs of customs and traditions
> hallowed by age and handed down to us
> by our fathers. No quibbling logic can topple *them,*
> whatever subtleties this clever age invents.
> People may say: "Aren't you ashamed? At your age,
> going dancing, wreathing your head with ivy?"
> Well, I am *not* ashamed. Did the god declare
> that just the young or just the old should dance
> No, he desires his honor from all mankind.
> He wants no one excluded from his worship. (200–209)

These lines, as rendered by Arrowsmith, can be read as either parodic or sincere.[12] They may also cause a shudder, for Pentheus opposes the converts among the Thebans, including his mother, Agave. He also wants to arrest a foreigner, "one of those charlatan magicians," he says, "with long yellow curls smelling of perfumes" (234–35). The stranger, Dionysus, is captured but miraculously escapes and, still disguised, puts Pentheus in a trance and suggests he put on female clothing to spy on the Theban women. Pentheus hesitates, averse to shame, but cannot resist his desire to see what he condemns. Dionysus then betrays him, making Agave and the women perceive him as a lion, which they rip limb from limb. A report of this horror prompts the Asian bacchants to "dance to the glory of Dionysus/We dance to the death of Pentheus" (1154–55). The tone changes when Cadmus, having gathered up fragments of Pentheus's corpse, approaches Agave and carefully leads her to see the head she is holding is not a lion's but her son's.

This intersection of pathos with religious innovation may have been experimental in its day[13] and has long inspired experimentation. The Performance Group's descriptions of exercises in "environmental theater," inspired by Polish director Jerzy Grotowski and from which *Dionysus in 69* emerged, recapitulate something of Pentheus's unsettling fascination with psychic and social boundaries. The Group helps us to reflect upon three common terms—representation, participation, and embodiment—that have become fluid in theater and in ethical reflection.

Is a Theatrical Drama a Representation or an Event?

Schechner maintained a certain fidelity to Euripides; about half of Arrowsmith's lines were used.[14] So *Dionysus in 69* was a representation of the ancient story. Any performance is an event, but to intensify the openendedness of this event and thereby resist static mimesis, the Group introduced elements of ritual and games. Ritual was to create participation, of which I will say more. Games were to create uncertainty about how the "game" would turn out.

Early in its run, the performance would pause until the actor playing Pentheus actually felt abused by the taunts of other cast members. They knew one another enough to be genuinely hurtful, and only when he really felt hurt would he say, "This is mortifying," signaling the show could go on. But in time it became harder to mortify him. At one performance, William Shephard as Pentheus allowed the mortification to go on for more than an hour, infuriating cast and audience, and thereafter this element was changed.[15] A more crucial instance was Pentheus's search for a woman in the audience who would agree to have sex with him. This was simultaneously a game in which Shephard invested his desires and insecurities, and also a game with a fix, in that he was to deflect any volunteers. But one day it happened. Shephard left the Performance Garage with a woman who had attended several performances and now persuaded him to call the play's bluff. They merely walked around the block, but the anger of the cast underscored how *Dionysus in 69* had to remain more of an honest play than an honest game.[16]

Does Participation Dissolve the Aesthetic Boundary Between Performers and Audience?

Much like a game, a ritual is a transactional, rule-governed activity that includes performer and community.[17] Before—or, rather, "as"—the performance began, a member of the Group led the audience, individually, from a sidewalk queue into the Garage, and encouraged them to select a place to sit, perhaps near the center of the space or else at a "safe" distance away. From this moment of initiation, each was challenged to be more a player, less a spectator, that is, to make a choice between active and passive attending. One of those who played Dionysus, William Finley, articulated the choice in the idioms of stand-up comedy and the New Left.

> Now for those of you who believe what I just told you, that I am a god, you are going to have a terrific evening. The rest of you are in trouble. It's going to be an hour and a half of being up against the wall. Those of you who do believe can join us in what we do next. It's a celebration, a ritual, an ordeal, an ecstasy. An ordeal is something you go through. An ecstasy is what happens when you get there. (PG)

Ritual elicits participation but usually of an authorized kind, a fact that occasioned more ironies. Performers encouraged the audience to join in the "ecstasy dance" and "total caress." That strangers were being invited to join in a degree of physical intimacy could be exciting or threatening, but as the run continued people came to the show knowing its "rules" in advance. Some knowingly vied for control, and the cast began to feel seriously abused by the very sort of chaos they were creating. So the dance and caress, which featured sensuous touching and eventually unwanted groping, were after a time replaced by elements that kept the audience more at bay. Did this assertion of power and boundaries make the play any less a ritual? Perhaps it became more so, in that now there were *Dionysus in 69* cognoscenti: the ritual makers and their community were negotiating how to *be* within the ritual's special precincts.[18]

Among the play's startling images was a birth ritual, adapted from the Asmat people of New Guinea. Performers playing Dionysus and Pentheus were pushed and pulled through a writhing prism or birth canal created by the backs of male players lying on their stomachs and the legs of female players standing astride the males. Another arresting moment transformed Dionysus's demand that Pentheus cross-dress into a demand for oral sex, fraught with homo- or hetero-erotic tension depending upon whether a male or female was playing Dionysus (the players exchanged parts in the course of the run).

They kiss.
PENTHEUS: I can't do it here.

> DIONYSUS: Who said you had to do it here? We can go upstairs,
>   or in the toilet, or behind the dimmer board, or down in the
>   pit. . . . No one will see us there. It will be very private. . . .
> PENTHEUS: Either I'll do what you want or I'll tear you limb from
>   limb. (PG)

Pentheus now plays out the sacrificial passage Dionysus has scripted, entering the blood-smeared choreography of hunting, chasing, and being slain. When, in a reversal of the birth ritual, he enters the birth canal to be "dismembered," a petit tyrant is supplanted by a divine/social tyranny. There was, to be sure, something like a happy reintegration of play space and city space as everyone emptied into Wooster Street. But the parade was bitter fun. Dionysus was Nixon, signifying the *sparagmos* being performed in the venues of Vietnam and Cambodia.

Dionysus in 69 was an inherently ambiguous experiment with boundaries. Audience responses ranged from the impulse to join the players, to anxious withdrawal, to voyeurism. In the photographs published by the Group, one finds properly dressed students with neckties, neat skirts, and horn-rimmed glasses sitting very still—almost as if at a play! Some in the audience have become participants, but most appear more curious than enraptured. Others seem disoriented, as if straddling a shifting border. In Brian DePalma's film of the performance, many do dance, caress, and undress enthusiastically; however, Shephard reports that a picked audience was invited for the second of two filming sessions.[19] Occasionally, members of the Group expressed hostility at the audience, which were outsiders to the Group's insiders. Vicki May Strang, whose job as stage manager included seating those waiting impatiently outside, confessed "to a perverse pleasure in teasing the people in line. Many will come up and ask anxiously, 'Has it already begun?' 'Well,' I say, 'it begins before we let anybody in, but it begins when everybody is in, and it really begins when you go in'" (PG). Interaction of this kind did not abolish the boundary between players and spectators so much as reassert it in a different way.

Are Bodies Particular and Irreplaceable in Theater, or Substitutable?

In Euripides, eroticism plays no part in the revels of the Theban women or the rites of the Bacchants; it is only Pentheus who imagines they must be lewd.[20] But Schechner sought to realize "spiritual nakedness"[21] by challenging performers to risk the divestiture of their cultural trappings:

the suits of status and personal narrative as well as clothes. A naked player can be a "sign" or "presence" that breaks the frame between art and environment, at least until the frame is reestablished. In 1968, naked performing was hardly conventional, and Schechner wanted to see how far identity could be reduced to behaviors and emotions inherited more from biology than culture.[22] The performers' and audience's bodies would be the site of this reduction, as the Group attempted to become *nothing other than* the physical medium of ritual and play.

The players adapted their parts in accord with their personalities, but their personalities were also meant to blend with their personae, and their bodies at crucial moments were to be indistinguishable. This was especially so after Pentheus's sacrifice. Photographs show the male players in a heap with limbs akimbo, signifying sundered body parts; the women are ecstatically dismembering the collective Pentheus. This blurring of minds and bodies was ambivalent. In confronting personal inhibitions and in transgressing bourgeois authority and sexual-social taboos, the revelation of an all-in-all oneness was being celebrated. Combined with Schechner's interest in the biological roots of ritual, the play was affirming the commonality of natural environment with theatrical environment. Yet this hypothetical good is contradicted by the gist of the story, in which a group-mind-and-body is created by Dionysos Tyrannos.

At the end, as the cast recovered their clothes and mopped up the stage blood, Dionysus (here played by William Finley) pronounced "doom" on each player—as when he curses the two who originally performed Agave as a dual part.

> Upon you, Agave, Ceil [Smith] and Joan [MacIntosh], I pronounce this doom. In some ways you took peace and solitude away from Bill Shephard. You tried to mortify him and hardly touched me at all. You both shall leave this garage in expiation for the murder you have done. You shall wear out your wretched lives never knowing which of you played Agave. (PG)

Humor, yes. But why should this never knowing *which you* was *which who* be a doom? In a show that protested tyranny in the name of freedom, and cautioned against mob rule in the name of *communitas*, it was a hard riddle to answer—which was why the riddle was so compelling. As the audience cheered in fun, following Dionysus into the street, did it desire to join or escape the social body? *Dionysus in 69* tended to confirm a Euripidian suspicion that the body divested of individuation would be less an emblem of peace than an occasion of corporate violence.[23]

There is, however, another scene of the body in Euripides (and Schechner). Agave enters triumphantly with her son's head on a thyrsus or wand. "Men of Thebes," she says, "behold the trophy of your women's / hunting." What would the Greek player actually be holding? A prop? A mask?[24] Would the prop signify beyond itself, from being a sign of brutal death to being a sign of more radical displacement, namely, that we both *are* and *never are, our* bodies? Or would the mask Agave might hold signify persona without person, part/role without a body? Would this be the objectifying meaning of death: that the mask loses the body and the body loses the mask? Here, the mask/head is held by another masked body, the actor playing Agave, a persona whose mind is displaced. And what would this prop suggest of theater and life? Would we recall how the play began with an actor wearing the mask of a god disguised as a man? Now Agave's father, Cadmus, enters, holding other pieces of the body:

> This was Pentheus
> whose body, after long and weary searchings
> I painfully assembled from Cithaeron's glens
> where it lay, scattered in shreds, dismembered
> throughout the forest, no two pieces
> in a single place. (1217–21)

Cadmus has gathered the fragments of Pentheus, but can do so only incompletely, until he quietly poses a series of devastating, therapeutic[25] questions

> CADMUS: Do you still feel
>   the same flurry inside you?
> AGAVE: The same—flurry?
>   No, I feel—somehow—calmer. I feel as though—
>   my mind were somehow—changing. (1268–71)

He slowly turns her eyes away from the head or mask and restores her spirit to sight; then together they try to restore a modicum of integrity to Pentheus. Agave will soon be doomed to exile, but Arrowsmith has her say: "We must restore his head / to this unhappy boy. As best we can, we shall make / him whole again."[26] These are extreme images and laments, which history enacts again and again after battles, atrocities, and accidental carnage. Yet the scene does indicate in death something required in life. Being more or less displaced fragments ourselves, we await the arrival of others to place the fragments into patterns of integrity. The gaps in our bodies and selves, it would seem, are portals through which persons might be given and received.

Metamorphosis and the Body in Ovid and Zimmerman

The transformation of the self—who does not need to be transformed into a better self, or the same self but with richer relationships, more flourishing circumstances, or with keener intelligence, memory, and sensibility, or with deeper feelings and self-knowledge?

The transformation of the body—a more ambivalent phrase, akin to the negative connotations of *metamorphosis*. We can speak positively of makeovers or bodybuilding exercises. But, except when illness or poor health has been overcome, there is something awkward about paying compliment to someone's bodily improvement. The enhanced body is something to gaze upon and objectify, as in the "before and after" photographs in supermarket tabloids. In these corporeal improvements, we may sense the silent intention to compensate for another kind of bodily transformation, toward decrepitude and death.

Mary Zimmerman explores such permutations in *Metamorphoses,* based mostly on tales from David Slavitt's translation of Ovid. She has renewed the idea of story theater,[27] having adapted the *Odyssey, Arabian Nights,* the seventeenth-century Chinese novel *The Journey to the West, The Notebooks of Leonardo Da Vinci,* the story of *Galileo Galilei* (for a Philip Glass opera), and other works. In 2001, I was prompted to see *Metamorphoses* by pictures of actors floating in water and the headline, "How Ovid Helps Deal with Loss and Suffering,"[28] shortly after the *sparagmos* of the World Trade Center. Ovid is typically associated with horrible transformations and cautionary morals, so I wondered about the water and the promise of "helping."

The water was a large rectangular pool, knee to ankle deep, framed by a deck in splashing distance of the audience (the first row in New York was hospitably provided with towels).[29] Above the pool, a crystal chandelier. Upstage, steps led to a heavily framed door, which seemed floating in an impression of night. There was suspended a pale blue screen with fluffy clouds, hiding a platform where players as gods could stand. The surface of the pool was at once restful and restless to contemplate. We took our seats and wondered what shapes or phantoms would appear in it or be reflected on it. As we waited, our attention was drawn to an armchair in the water, soon to become Midas's throne.

Anticipating Kenosis

Metamorphoses exemplifies how popular theater may incorporate experimental performance practices. Yet the result is a *play*, with a published script that others can produce creditably, provided they come up with the pool (similar to the impluvium in Peter Greenaway's 1991 film, *Prospero's Books*). Such an intersection between avant-garde and popular theater inevitably prompts anxiety about "popularity." Was *Metamorphoses* successful because it was so accessible in language, imagery, and emotion? Or because its ideas—which cite Freud, Jung, Joseph Campbell, and James Hilman and which prompted an approving television interview with Zimmerman by Bill Moyers—appealed to a kind of self-help, pan-traditional hopefulness? Or was it because the part of the theater audience that desires something other than musical revivals and naturalistic realism is actually quite large?

It struck me that what touched many, emotionally and intellectually, was to be found in the performance of a text about the ambiguities of embodiment. Zimmerman was not, with Schechner, trying to dissolve psychological and sociospatial boundaries; nor was she mixing bodily and electronic surfaces, as did LeCompte, but was striving for a kind of distance-with-intimacy that can come with the telling and showing of stories. The result was a space and mood that was contemplative. Aside from being splashed, we were not bodily invited to cross the boundary of performance space. But the telling and performing did create a participatory presence, insofar as the rhythms of emotion and acknowledgment were exchanged in this space. The potential for nostalgia was high, but the myths and the players' commentary on them provoked critique as well as delight, for the myths concerned the dissolving of bodies and how such dissolution might be desired as well as feared.

The imagery of transformation, of course, can be worse than merely ambivalent. It can be emblematic of monstrosity, as in *The Elephant Man*, Kafka's *Metamorphosis*, and "morphing" in fantasy and science fiction. The morphing body conjures up terrors, frequently of lost identity. Only rarely in such tales (as when frogs or other beasts become princes) is identity *recovered* via bodily transformation. And when it is, as in the raising of dry bones in Ezekiel or the shrouded Lazarus by

Jesus, there may remain something alarming or grotesque. My colleague Frank Burch Brown cautions that images of metamorphosis can be a dangerous implication of happier images of erotic love, transformation, and kenosis.[30]

To see this ambivalence, we might note how Paul Tillich defines love, including eros, as "the urge toward the reunion of the separated."[31] In that we are all existentially separated from the "ground of being," then our thirst for knowledge as well as for each other would be eros. Reunion, however, does not entail the abolition of difference. When two become "one flesh" or "one mind," they remain two bodies and two minds. Eros can involve friction but not fusion of selves. It may be different with kenosis, but later we will see how early Christian interpreters went to great pains to clarify that self-emptying need not mean utter loss of continuity with what was before.[32] Today kenotic self-emptying can be regarded as relinquishing the priority of one's claims—even one's life—for others' suffering. An objection to such kenosis is that it can seem to define one as a "slave" to the other, a metaphor that can rationalize subservience. Retrieving the figure of kenosis will require determining whether this paradigm entails only subordination, or whether kenosis can embrace mutuality, and be *a reception of self from others* as well as giving of self to others. Even so, worries about identity loss hover over the image. Would "bad kenosis" be some sort of eros-without-edges (as in the joining of two spirits in one body in S. Ansky's 1920 masterpiece of Yiddish theater, *The Dybbuk*)?

Images of bad kenosis are what Brown alerted me to in the twenty-fifth canto of Dante's *Inferno*. Here, a number of robbers undergo transformations into lizardlike creatures that grasp, bite, and penetrate each other and, indeed, exchange bodies, as if robbing one another's identities. If the integrity of body and soul is our most profound "possession," then here the punishment of "identity theft" would certainly fit the crime.

> "Alas! Alas! Agnello, how you change!
> Already you are neither two nor one!"
> The two heads had already blurred and blended;
> now two semblances appeared and faded,
> one face where neither face began nor ended.[33]

For Dante, the literal emptying of one damned soul into the form of another is motivated by greed and also punishes greed. So Brown's caution about kenotic emptying can be understood in a number of ways.

Augustinian anthropology would regard episodes of bad kenosis as *distorted* loving, hence sin. The thieves, who robbed others of possessions in life, are now robbed of self-possession in eternity. Augustinians would understand that it is not kenosis that can be "bad" but rather its distortions, which can be understood through paradigms of agape love and justice.[34]

Another way to account for the dangers of the paradigm of kenosis, and not exclusive of the first way, is to consider how language and understanding is finite and indeterminate. It may be that *no principle or paradigm, including that of kenosis, is by itself adequate for conceiving a "fit" between personal and moral integrity*. Without being part of constellations of many norms and tradition-embedded narratives (e.g., concerning justice or respect for persons as well as Hebrew *hesed* or Greek *agape*), the trope of kenotic emptying can be inadequate and at times harmful. No sign or paradigm will be adequate, nor any "system" of signs or paradigms.

Yet there is another possible objection, which would not be settled either by agreeing that kenosis is but a finite idea, or that it may be distorted by sin. Perhaps kenotic transformation (our capacity to receive others into our selves and lose ourselves in others) *inherently* means loss of identity—which could be the worst contingency we can imagine, if our identities are all we really possess. I hasten to say that this objection is not one that Frank Brown would likely propound, given his conviction that metaphoric "transfiguration" can be analogous to grace.[35] But the concern that heedless self-giving or profligate self-fashioning inherently threatens the self will need consideration. We might begin by noticing how, paradoxically, utter self-loss in metamorphosis is not really a possibility for Dante; and that in some of the Ovid and Zimmerman's tales, were it possible, it would be less a danger than a blessing.

Near the end of Canto 25 of *Inferno*, one of the thieves, Agnello, remarks, "It is Buoso's turn to go/crawling along the road as I have done" (137–38). This suggests Agnello has not lost touch with his former self. Exchanging bodies, indeed *faces*, with one another does not imply, for Dante, dissolution of identity. In fact, the justice of his entire penal scheme depends on the shades of the damned and the redeemed retaining their identities. Although those in the circles of Hell, Purgatory, and Paradise are organized by the moral *genres* of their earthly lives, they do not lose continuity with the *individuals* they were before. The whole problem in Hell is that there is no way out of the prison one has made of oneself. Identity is frozen. In Purgatory, however, there is progress toward Paradise, where in turn there will be transfiguration and even a softening of individuation. In short, in Dante the most grotesque kenosis-as-metamorphosis does not dissolve the self. Actual embodiment does not secure the self's continuity, though it is a sign of it. It is hinted that the self's integrity is established as a creation, not a possession.[36]

"Transform me entirely"

But loss of identity through metamorphosis, were it possible, might come as a blessing. In Ovid, moods and thoughts alternate among amusement, sadness, hope, and horror. What follows is a paraphrase of Zimmerman's scenes, hinting of possibilities they contemplate.

King Midas He is a modern, corporate mogul who can't be bothered by his noisy little girl. But drunken Silenus visits, falls into the pool, and Midas makes sure he is rescued from drowning. Bacchus, then, rewards Midas for his hospitality, which occasions his famous wish—deemed by Bacchus to be "a really, really bad idea" (17). Midas's daughter suddenly leaps into his arms and is objectified by his golden touch. An actor lifts her from the water and carries her away, frozen in the pose of her embrace.

Comedy has changed instantly to grief and guilt. Bacchus sends Midas on a journey, to wash in a sacred pool, where his gift might be returned and his daughter restored.

Alcyone and Cyex King Cyex, sailing to consult an oracle, is lost in a storm sent by Poseidon. Before drowning, he prays that his devoted Alcyone will find his body—and for a long time she waits on the shore, in despair. Morpheus, taking the form of Cyex, comes in a dream to tell her of his death. Soon the body is washed up by the waves, and she reaches down to kiss it. The gods witness her grief with compassion, and change the two of them into sea birds, flying together over the ocean, "in the days we call the halcyon days" (35).

Does this scene of primal separation end in hope, or resignation? Are we invited to imagine how such a transformation pertains to us?

Erysichthon He is a man like Midas, only interested in "useful things." Erysichthon cuts down a sacred tree, and as punishment will forever suffer an insatiable appetite. The nymph Hunger "breathes her spirit into his spirit" (36, Slavitt) and rides upon his back, tormenting him. The more he eats the more he craves. He even sells his mother to raise funds for more food. At last he places his foot on a silver platter and takes up knife and fork—to objectify and consume himself.

Pandora's Box   Pandora opens a small chest and incense suffuses to us from the stage. This is a division point in the play which, along with Narcissus, frames the central Orpheus scene.

Orpheus and Eurydice   At their wedding, she dies from a snakebite. Inconsolable, he follows her to the underworld. There, Hades is moved to allow Orpheus to rescue Eurydice, if he forswears looking at her as he leads her away. But he looks, and their moment of loss—they reach closer, almost touch, then Hermes lifts her away from him—is repeated. With each repetition, the interpretation of sorrow deepens.

Ovid's and then Rilke's[37] versions of the myth are quietly recited from music stands. Questions are asked. Whose loss is this? Is it a loss of creativity that befalls the self-conscious artist? Or a lover's loss, whose gaze objectifies the beloved? (If you look you lose—but you love, so how can you not look?) Or is it the unraveling thread of memory? When Rilke's Eurydice hears that Orpheus is following her, she wonders (47), "Who?"

Narcissus   A visual joke: he stares at his reflection in the pool. He cannot escape himself. So an actor carries Narcissus off—stuck in his pose of self-contemplation—and another actor replaces him with a narcissus in a flowerpot (48).

Pomona and Vertumnus   The manly Vertumnus, shy god of spring, dons disguises (farmhand, fisherman, then a soldier) to woo Pomona, a nymph who skips along the deck with flowers. Finally, disguising himself as an old woman, "he" recommends the virtues of Vertumnus. And warns her not to offend Aphrodite, by telling her of the fate of Myrrha—but to no avail, Pomona won't have him. Finally, she insists that he get rid of his silly dress and wig. Vertumnus does, and although he is embarrassed to be revealed as the shy god he is, she happily loves him, "much to his surprise" (62).

This tale of love frames a tale less of grief than of compassion mixed with horror.

Myrrha   Having seen her spurn many suitors, angry Aphrodite causes young Myrrha to lust after her father, Cinyrax. Myrrha's maid pities her and arranges to shield her father's eyes, so that Myrrha can come to him. For three nights she dances and tumbles with him in the water. When his terrible desire prompts Cinyrax to rip off the blindfold, he is overcome by shame and rage and he heaves sheets of water, spraying the audience, and tries to drown Myrrha. She escapes, praying, "Make me something else; transform me entirely" (60, Slavitt), and it seems to us that she dissolves into the pool.

Phaeton   Phaeton, in swim trunks and sunglasses, floats on an air mattress and whines to his analyst about his father, Apollo, the Sun—in terms from Freud, Jung, James Hillman, and Joseph Campbell. Phaeton has borrowed the keys and wrecked Dad's chariot. "It was chaos, okay? Out of control, as if no one was driving. You know, my knees were weak, I was blind from all the light. I set the earth on fire. And I fell. And it just destroyed me." All the while, Apollo intones detached, paternal exhortations. The therapist says, "The myth is a public dream, dreams are private myths. Unfortunately, we give our mythic side scant attention these days. As a result, a great deal escapes us" (67).

Do we construct these archetypes, or do they precede us? If we are moved by an illusion we know to be an illusion, does our emotion witness to the pressure of the real? Do we console ourselves, or are we consoled by some real illusion?

Eros and Psyche   Eros is blindfolded, naked, with white wings and a gold arrow. Psyche wears a sleeveless gown and holds a candelabrum. She is his wife but—punished by his jealous mother, Aphrodite—she has never seen Eros and has been told he is a monster. Two players, Q and A, discuss the myth as it unfolds, as if chatting across a fire. "Q: Why is he naked? A: To make us transparent. . . . Transparent in our love. Foolish to others. Exposed" (69). It so happens that Psyche (Soul) sees sleeping Eros (Love) and awakens him with a drop of candle wax. His flesh is burned, they are separated, and Psyche must undergo travail. Eventually, however, they reunite, and kiss lingeringly on a raft.

Q and A tell the story by interrogating it. The myth[38] is the complement to Orpheus and Eurydice; touching and seeing now unite bodies rather than separate them.

Baucis and Philemon   An elderly couple shows hospitality to Zeus and Hermes, disguised as beggars. Offered one wish as their reward, Baucis and Philemon desire never to outlive one another. So as they embrace, they are changed into trees, whose branches mingle. And as if setting a table around them, the other players light tiny candles in floating shells and whisper, "Let me die the moment my love dies. . . . Let me not outlive my own capacity to love. . . . Let me die loving and so never die" (83). Midas now enters to wash in the pool. His daughter appears, she hesitates . . . then they touch gently as the candles are extinguished.

The myths are Hellenistic, but if the play ends in hope it might be that of the Song of Songs 8:6, where "love is strong as death." What could have been a sequence too fraught with sentiment was to Ben Brantley, the *Times* reviewer, a cathartic "fugue" of sorrow. He commented on the tears of tough New York theatergoers, and he compared the repetitions of Orpheus and Eurydice's separation to replays of the falling Twin Towers, which seemed to have paralyzed all our minds that autumn. "Those images from television stay the same; metamorphosis occurs in the human imagination. There can be artistry and solace in remembering." *Metamorphoses* opened up spaces, Brantley suggested, in which memory and emotion could coalesce with what we can hardly speak—but so much desire in grief—the presence of absent others.

So what is the "great deal that escapes us"? Not only how we live within archetypes; it is also how seemingly opposed emotions and meanings mix on the same occasions: despair with joy, blessing with curse, punishment with release, transparency with opacity. The beat of the play wants to come down in translucent blessing. When Eros and Psyche kiss, after surmounting their obstacles, the Questioner is amazed.

Q: So it has a happy ending?
A: It has a very happy ending.
Q: Almost none of these stories have completely happy endings.
A: This one is different.

Is this "different" and "complete" ending only an abstract idea? "The soul wanders in the dark, until it finds love. And so, wherever our love goes, there we find our soul." Zimmerman does not allow us to forget that this idea of Eros is realized only in contingencies of chance and character, but perhaps she is too quick here to explain the point:

Q: It always happens?
A: If we're lucky. And if we let ourselves be blind.
Q: Instead of watching out?
A: Instead of watching out. (76–77)

Didactic, yet these lines remind us of Orpheus turning, "watching out," and losing Eurydice. If this is the saddest moment, it is in part because Zimmerman, through Rilke, suggests that their separation is due not only to Orpheus's gaze. Eurydice has other things on her mind, "She was deep within herself, like a woman heavy/with child" (46, Rilke). Or else she was like a person bereft of memories, even of loved ones. She simply asks, "Who?" when told Orpheus had come. Here, there is no continuity in the discontinuity of her metamorphosis. Elsewhere in *Metamorphoses* there is continuity. But we might be led to wonder, how much does continuity matter? Need the seabirds remember they were once Alcyone and Cyex, or the mingled trees that they were Baucis and Philemon? Need we remember details of a good day long ago, or even yesterday, for that day to be blessed? Does anticipation outlive memory?

By reading Ovid in these ways, with the water implying the pool of memory, our spirits are to be transformed and not yet lost. That is hopeful; what is more hopeful in *Metamorphoses,* in its troubled depths and pleasing surfaces, is that these are *bodies* we see and contemplate:

> Bodies, I have in mind, and how they can change to assume new shapes—I ask the help of the gods who know the trick: change me, and let me glimpse the secret and speak, better than I know, of the world's birthing. . . . (5, Slavitt)

Each performer remained recognizable but seemed to transform from fable to fable, much as in Ovid the metamorphosis of one tale flows into the next. Doug Hara changed from Silenus to Narcissus to Phaeton to Eros, among other personae; Anjali Bhumani was Midas's Daughter, then Hunger, then Myrrha, and joined the laundresses in narrating from the deck. The water—which made the costumes sometimes heavy and opaque, sometimes streaming and translucent—was suggestive of bodily shape-shifting, as was the choreography, as the players lifted one another in and out of the pool. Sometimes the water seemed to flow upward into human forms.

• • •

There is a kenosis in acting, in the pouring of body and mind into the forms of other bodies and minds, usually with others in an ensemble. This can be something wonderful, a sign that we can be ourselves without being prisoners of ourselves. This can also be worrying, as when actors speak of coming near to losing themselves or even passing that invisible, shifting limit. Euripides and Ovid provide images of both possibilities. Schechner and Zimmerman are witnesses to why we should not wish our protean selves to be entirely otherwise; to lose the capacity to be transformed would be to lose a mode of continuity with other lives and even with ourselves. We would be static, frozen in objectification, without possibilities of kenosis.

Euripides and Ovid, together with the arts of drama and performance, also suggest limits to the imagery of kenosis. We do not really know how two or more *minds* can touch and penetrate. There is a hard-headed style of philosophy that says they cannot; there are spooky ways of saying they can; there are experiences of intimacy and insight that say our spirits are permeable and receptive to the gifts as well as invasions of other personalities. But two living *bodies* cannot occupy the same space and time. Violations of the body by other bodies are among the oldest taboos. If body and mind make a dialectical whole, then the body contributes a good deal to the singularity of the whole. Our *memories are knitted by tissues* that cannot be duplicated by any way we know. They somehow communicate from life to life, and change over time, and are as ephemeral as water and dust—yet they carry our continuity across time.

If we could exchange our bodies, we would be entirely different sorts of creatures. Still, when we suffer to great extreme, we may with Myrrha desire other streams than our embodied condition. Or, with Orpheus in one way and Agave in another, the presence and the loss of another can leave us longing to flow into others, or to piece them together, or to be emptied of ourselves, for them. The plays in part IV look for a kenotic return, a receptive emptiness, some other integrity than the integrity of secure self-possession.

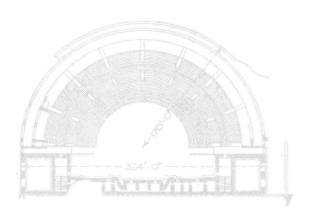

Part IV

The Empty Forms of Kenotic Integrity

[He] emptied himself,
taking the form of a slave,
being born in human likeness.

—PHILIPPIANS 2:7

Just as there were many who were astonished at him
—so marred was his appearance, beyond human resemblance,
and his form beyond that of mortals. . . .

—ISAIAH 52:14

FREQUENTLY, I HAVE SUGGESTED that integrity is not a *fusion* but a *juxtaposition* of personal wholeness with moral rightness, reflecting tensions in life not easily resolved in discursive language. But I have also suggested that integrity language is heuristic, relying on metaphors and other tropes that *search for* rather than establish what they would mean. We cannot pin down integral patterns of persons—who live in persisting and changing relations over time—with concepts unaffected by time and by the flourishing and suffering we mean to comprehend. This is, in part, why narrative and theater are appropriate for re*describing* forms of integrity. The question now is whether theater can inform the *good* of integrity.

We have seen two clues, the first mostly negative: the figure of the player-actor has long carried normative weight when used to attack hypocrisy. The second clue is in how theater invites us to reconsider what happens as persons and players perform parts, especially in ensemble and especially when the audience is viewed as part of the pattern. Hamlet delights in theater; yet, given all the bad theater ranging from dull and pandering to persecuting, how could this delight indicate the *good* of integrity? The pattern to be explored now places theatrical play beside the idea of *kenosis,* that is, emptying into the forms of others, for others. In scripture, this idea is observed in the figure of Israel-as-a-servant who "poured out himself to death and was numbered among the transgressors" (Isaiah 53:12) and in what was likely a song used in Philippians 2.[1] These verses summarize a dramatic narrative, which Paul introduces by exhorting, "Let the same mind be in you that was in Christ Jesus," then apparently quotes a hymn in which an actor, so to speak, forgoes one part to become lost in another part:

> 6 who though he was in the form of God did not regard equality with God as something to be exploited, 7 but emptied himself [*heauton ekenōsen*], taking the form of a slave, being born in human likeness. And being found in human form 8 he humbled himself and became obedient to the point of death—even death on a cross. 9 Therefore God also highly exalted him and gave him the name that is above every name, 10 so that at the name of Jesus every knee should bend, in heaven and on earth and under the earth, 11 and every tongue should confess that Jesus Christ is Lord to the glory of God the Father.

The kenosis paradigm has analogs in other traditions, as in Buddhism, where the Bodhisattva delays entering Nirvana for the sake of others' enlightenment. I am asking how the Isaiah and Philippians instances, juxtaposed with theatrical emptying, bear on how integrity involves personal encounter and ethical improvisation. Can kenosis conjoin delight and responsibility? This question intersects culture, ethics, and religion.

Whence Kenosis? Cultural and Religious Encounters

Isaiah's suffering servant is a cultural *and* a scriptural paradigm. Culturally, it is language that signals a human possibility. Religiously, it would signal something of the divine or sacred. Even for believers, these signs can be in tension. Culturally speaking, religious traditions are finite forms of expression and social authority (i.e., "cults" are also "cultures"). Theologically, religious traditions *are also concerned with* the infinite, transcendent, or deeply immanent reality (i.e., other than *only* of nature and culture). This tension, between religion as culture and as faith, also speaks to how a sense of fragmentation characterizes late modern relationships with most sources of authority. When we try to identify intellectual and ethical authorities, we often find we are moving *between fragments,* finding insights in the lights and shadows among them, seeking connections. We may even regard such moving-and-seeking as being itself a religious orientation. And when we encounter the illuminating pressure of revelation, it likely comes *among and in-between* fragments of scripture and tradition, cultural forms and expressions, and experiences of selves and others.

So in this attempt to reenvision integrity, I come to another moment of juxtaposition—finding cultural paradigms set side by side with religious paradigms—in hopes of mutual illumination. But this juxtaposition offers to us a choice, namely, whether to regard this reenvisioning as *only a cultural/ethical* assessment of patterns of integrity, or to interpret it *theologically* as well. Why do I say this choice is *offered,* but not demanded? Could it be postponed? Yes, in part because there is some overlap between the alternatives. They are not as either-or as they might seem were we to adhere strictly to Clifford Geertz's well-known anthropological definition of religion.[2]

For Geertz, a religious symbol or sign system (a type of cultural system) creates meanings with an "aura of factuality" outsiders usually find opaque. In the Abrahamic faiths, this factual/counterfactual aura includes the conviction that the destiny of individuals and communities has everything to do with God's love, justice, and ends for creation. There is also the conviction that certain communities, persons, or communications disclose connections between God and creaturely life. When this connection is neglected or opposed, suffering enters creation, for which there are remedies. In Judaism, it is a divine law or way, received by a certain community (Torah, given to the People of Israel); in Christianity it is a certain person (Christ); in Islam, it is a final reception of divine revelation (Qur'an). These are provisions for revealing truth and for overcoming sin, death, and meaninglessness. Ethical implications that follow hold that no person is self-sufficiently oneself apart from God, others, and creation. Cultures *within* the religious cultures of Judaism, Christianity, and Islam interpret these implications differently; and Geertz implies that their "auras of factuality" will likely remain unintelligible to outsiders, like foreign languages.

Yet that is not really his intent. Geertz wants us to be able to learn other cultural-religious lingoes as anthropological participant observers. He finds religious and cultural boundaries to be *permeable* in ad hoc ways. Different sacred convictions *can sometimes* be understood across their distances, and culture and religion can sometimes give entrée to each other. Much of what it is like to live as, say, a Roman Catholic is cultural, even from Catholic perspectives. And sometimes outsiders may overhear, so to speak, Tibetan Buddhist teachings and find them compelling, even life-altering. To be sure, this very example may owe itself to historical circumstances that have made Tibet a "strange attractor" to the West.[3] Be that as it may, outsiders frequently hear and become persuaded by aspects of Catholicism or Buddhism, without becoming converts. Some do become converts. And some may "overhear" and become newly prompted by set-aside fragments of traditions, which may have once shaped their lives.

So it is that we can overhear things about kenosis that may revise our descriptions of integrity and theater, and which may help us normatively to assess theater and integrity. From one perspective, it may appear I am simply employing "emptying" as an interesting way of *describing* theater and integrity. From another, my *assessments* of integrity are informed by religious ideas. Again, these two tacks are better thought of as being heuristically juxtaposed rather than conjoined or disjoined. Let us continue a bit longer along the cultural tack.

Self-described secular moral discourse is historically specifiable, rooted in cultural and religious traditions, though it often gets by without reference to its roots.[4] In biomedical ethics it is now common to employ principles that could, in effect, be ethnographically read off of common life in pluralistic societies. Norms are recognized, such as (1) autonomy, or respect for individual persons; (2) nonmaleficence, or "at least do no harm"; (3) beneficence, or actively offering care; and (4) justice, treating persons fairly and equitably. (Other ethicists define or enumerate basic moral principles differently.) An advantage of "principlism" is in how different norms or goods can be "weighed and balanced" in hard situations without one's being committed to the traditions in which the principles are historically rooted (an "advantage" that is often criticized).[5] My interest here, however, is with implications that follow from *regarding principles as linguistic expressions, not unlike other cultural signs and expressions.*

Insofar as principles are instances of language, they are *encountered and interpreted.* Like all forms of mind or spirit, they can *address* us, as Martin Buber says.[6] These encounters may have components of active remembering, as when a doctor thinks, "First, do no harm," or of passive memory, when "Do no harm" is heard again as an unbidden voice.[7] Or the encounter may come when a patient says, "Please help me." If the physician is focused on research just then, this *principle of care* might pull her up short, prompting her to reassess what is going on. She also might reassess the principle of care. What is the imperative of care saying *now*? Am I now to care, or to cure? Who is asking me, the patient or the family? What medical resources are available? Who else needs them? Where do we each hail from, my patient and I, culturally? In other words, principles are encountered and interpreted anew. They are both abstractions we think with, but are also voices we hear anew, from occasion to occasion.

To the extent kenosis is a cultural paradigm, it is also encountered and interpreted. In communities for which it is a religious paradigm, it is encountered as something like a divine voice or a window transparent to its ultimate source. Seen from certain angles in either context, kenosis provides clues to how the integrity of performing parts in ensemble may be "good" in the broader senses of "the ethical." If kenosis can be imagined as the emptying and, as well, the receiving of life and lives into the "space" between the personal and the moral—and thereby, in a "weak" sense, *connecting* them—then perhaps we can speak of *kenotic patterns of integrity*. Let us look further into this kind of discourse.

Encountering the Paradigm of Kenosis

The Greek verb *kenoō* has practically no positive connotations.[8] To "make empty" is to make void or of no account. Predicated of a person, it almost always connotes subordination, powerlessness, and suffering. However, as a conceptual metaphor, kenosis can convey the rather liquid image of form flowing into no particular form (as onto the ground) or into another form (perhaps a vessel), and it plays on senses of ideality and mutability latent in the notion of form.

Perhaps it would be easier to imagine a pattern or rhythm emptying into another pattern or rhythm. As when a flower girl empties into the form of a duchess; or a hairdresser into an English major; or an actor into a part written by Shaw; or when a playwright's imagination empties into the myth of Pygmalion. We can think of troubling examples as well. An unhappy hustler imagines himself the son of a movie star; an adolescent finds himself in the story of Holden Caulfield; a youngster in Europe awakens to a sense of identity among neo-Nazis. Inasmuch as personal integrity can be a neutral category ascribable to pirates or tyrants, I keep asking if kenosis is only another neutral cultural category. To have normative meaning, will it require other paradigms or principles, such as love or justice? What is inherently good about emptying into another social or personal form?

Kenosis prompts still other questions. It may have conceptual dangers if it valorizes *total* emptiness, in which particular relations and singular events dissolve into insignificance.[9] It may have ethical dangers if imperatives of self-abnegation were to rationalize the situations of those who can *least* afford to become weak; or were to privilege those who already can *most* afford to become weak.[10] Both Nietzsche and, among others, many feminist thinkers have criticized traditional Christian ethics for making a virtue of weakness, which can rationalize social marginality or oppression. Yet in postmodern circles, the "weakening" of thought and the egoistic self is why some, like Italian philosopher Gianni Vattimo, have found the idea of kenosis attractive.[11] Emmanuel Levinas in effect endorses a kenotic ethic, and is criticized for creating and inverting a host-hostage opposition. That is, if I am to regard myself as "hostage" to the others' suffering, have I not unwittingly defined the other as a hostage taker? Instead of undoing forms of thought that inscribe violence, as I intended, has my metaphor and possibly my argument simply rewritten violence in a different way? With Levinas, the challenge is whether altruism and mutual desire for others can cohere, and whether his thought meets that challenge.[12]

In short, kenosis can seem to mean the opposite of what it is supposed to mean. For Harold Bloom, it names a strategy whereby a strong poet, anxious about her originality, makes room for herself by making it appear that her precursor poets have emptied their power into her work, thus leaving them empty and her full.[13] Gestures of indebtedness can disguise self-enlargement—a strategy we might imagine Bloom attributing to Paul in respect to Jesus.[14] Bloom's "ratio" of kenosis also complements Thomas Altizer's elaboration of Hegel's view of "the death of God," in that on the cross Christ emptied into a strong, universal humanity.[15]

To address these doubts about the paradigm of kenosis, one could say that insofar as it takes cultural forms of life and meaning, kenosis can become a distorted form of loving (can become sin, in Augustinian terms). Insofar as kenosis approximates altruism, it can be regarded as an image or paradigm behind principles like beneficence or care, which must be weighed and specified with other principles and circumstances.[16] Insofar as it figures in an eschatological ethic, kenosis involves a critique and transvaluation of the values of autonomy and self-sufficiency. These alternatives would begin to address the ethical objections. In some religious thought, kenosis implies ever-expanding and inclusive movements

of relationality that overcome *the idolatry of identity,* that is, the attempt
to identify and protect the interests of self or tribe as a matter of infinite
concern. Certain meanings of kenosis in scripture, philosophy, and dramatic performance can be mutually illuminating. They help us envision
integrity in terms of kenotic patterns of selves with others, and of life
and cosmos pouring into one another.[17]

Paul's Kenosis Drama

A number of early interpretations of Pauline kenosis developed in response to the Arians, for whom the Philippians hymn would have sub-
ordinated the Son to the Father. In reply to this heresy, various orthodox
voices (in holding that Christ was both human and divine) read the
"hymn" as a drama in which the Son or Logos of God was veiled or
clothed in flesh and took the "form" of a servant or slave.[18] The motif
was not without problems, for *veiling* or *clothing* can sound like an actor
wearing a disguise, which in turn might imply that Christ was not truly
human, or that God wears a sequence of "masks" (as Father, Son, then
Spirit) and so is not simultaneously three-in-one. While refuting heresy
is not the point here, it is my view that the analogy between kenosis and
theater has less to do with disguise and more with *players realizing their
whole being by giving their being to a part.* In the Philippians drama,
there is a prologue ("Let the same mind be in you that was in Christ
Jesus") that can sound like "motivation" in acting. The kenosis of incarnation (emptying into the form of a human being and slave) entails the
kenosis of obedience unto death. Christ is then exalted by God and by
the audience, in that creatures witness, applaud, and participate ("every
knee should bend") in the drama of kenosis.

But for centuries, theologians have not agreed on even the surface
meaning of the song, one of the oldest strands of Christian discourse.
Perhaps we should be content that its verses are radically polysemic, with
meanings pouring out in numerous directions, inviting us to bring other
meanings into proximity with their form. It is not necessary to decide
finally on any of the numerous permutations of kenotic interpretation
to notice their dramatic and ethical possibilities. With Martin Luther,
the humanity of Christ came into greater focus. German kenosis theologians of the nineteenth century, such as Gottfried Thomasius, seemed to
founder on the difficulty of explaining literally how the Son could be at
once *here* and *there,* the baby in the barn and the ruler in heaven.[19] How
could the Son's *total* loss of divinity or for that matter God's total loss be

avoided? (Indeed, Altizer would say that the death of God *is* the whole point of kenosis.) Or, can kenosis be viewed as something *more* of God or humanity, rather than less?[20]

Again, the figure of veiling in flesh suggests something of a player assuming a part through costume, mask, action, memory, habit, mind, emotion, and speech. Insofar as the Logos empties into "human form," the form is a *representation* of human life. But insofar as the *form is flesh,* there is also mutual *participation* of Logos and life. These connotations of God as protagonist, player, and audience-with-humanity upon the world's stage are reflected in Hans Urs von Balthasar's elaboration of the theater analogy. He may not give as much emphasis as I do to the ethical kenosis of persons emptying into others, for others.[21] But his basic point—that the logic of divine love involves the mutual emptying of the divine persons into one another and into creation—implies that divine self-emptying into and receptivity of flesh is a mutual drawing of God toward flesh and flesh toward God, in time and eternity.[22]

Attempts to read the passage independently of developing doctrine often hypothesize that the "hymn" predated Paul and was recognized by his readers.[23] Did it refer to a Hellenistic "divine man" myth or Jewish "second Adam," descending in human form and thereafter receiving a new heavenly status?[24] Again, such a scenario is a drama. Terms for *form* in the hymn (*morphē, homoiomati, schemati*) would not have the precise meanings they had in Plato or Aristotle (i.e., eternal or underlying form), but could have referred more loosely to a physical form or external stamp of appearance.[25] Their valences lead Ralph Martin to translate the hymn in a way that, if anything, overdetermines the sense in which the preexistent Christ exchanges one social role or rank for another.[26] A minority of interpreters find no evidence for a preexisting Christ as early as Paul, but hear the hymn celebrating how Christ's obedience, as "the last Adam," overcomes the old Adam's disobedience.[27]

Others, who do find the verses to be an eschatological redeemer drama, read "form of God" (*morphē theou*) as a "field of force" or "realm in which one stands" (Käsemann) or as Lucien Richard puts it, "the field of reference in which the encounter between God and Christ took place." He concludes that the redeemer's emptying meant "that the divine realm is not in opposition to the human."[28] Here it would seem that the dramatic implications of "form" have more to do with *performance space* than with the player's appearance. In the field of encounter, Christ takes the part of God precisely by accepting the conditions of humanity and suffering. Self-emptying, then, is also *receptive.* God receives forms of human life; humanity is to be receptive to God's entrance into life. Self-emptying includes dispossession (on the cross) and exaltation. The latter (God's elevating or enthroning Christ) may refer to resurrection, but also means God and humanity witnessing the whole pattern of the drama. The drama, then, is of *emptying, receptivity, and witness.* It is completed as others empty into it with their bodies and spirits, theirs being a kenotic response to kenosis, a pattern in which there are different aspects of emptying and receptivity on all sides.

Some insist that with the hymn Paul had salvation in mind, not ethics. However, interpreters such as Martin or Käsemann may construe ethics in the narrower sense of moral obligation. Paul's context suggests his readers were to share, enjoy, and suffer *in the pattern* of Christ's sharing, enjoying, and suffering. In the broader senses, the ethical and eschatological are mutually inclusive. Richard Hays thinks Paul asks his readers to "imitate" (3:17) the "pattern" or "paradigm" of the hymn. "Just as he humbled himself (*etapeinōsen*, 2:8) and took the form of a slave, so the Philippians should in humility (*tapeinophrosynē*, 2:3) become servants of the interests of others."[29] There is another place where Paul employs a theater-like trope to defend his pragmatic ethics of service across the divisions of cultural, religious, and personal status:

> For though I am free with respect to all, I have made myself a slave to all, so that I might win more of them. To the Jews I became as a Jew, in order to win Jews. . . . To those outside the law I became as one outside the law . . . so that I might win those outside the law. To the weak I became weak, so that I might win the weak. I have become all things to all people, so that I might by all means save some. (1 Corinthians 9:19–22)

Against the Protestant charge that theater was hypocrisy, Renaissance defenders of theater found Paul's thoughts on *playing as others for others* to be especially relevant.[30]

Kenosis, Encounter, and the Space of Atonement

Paul Ricoeur holds that ethical life with others must involve irreducible mutuality, if it is not to devolve into hostage-holding or master-slave diversions. As far into ourselves as introspection takes us, what gives us confidence in reality—and answers skeptical doubt that we even exist— is not self-authorizing certainty but voices of others *already there,* as it were. We *attest*[31] or bear witness to dialogues that precede us. Kenosis has mutuality when it includes both emptying into others and receptivity to others pouring into us. But this reciprocation is not given necessarily in a zero-sum game; the return is contingent. A kenotic gift is like water poured into soil or seed dispersed in the wind: any return must await particular encounters with others.

What also prompts me to speak of the contingent mutuality of kenosis is the paradox of *emptying* and *filling* a form.[32] Abstract forms seem inherently empty, and so lack for what may fill them. However, whatever might fill a form (be it nature, culture, or persons), will itself be an ensemble of forms, which is in turn a playing out of relations and differences. Forms entail, then, emptiness. And yet in life we also experience forms as fulsome, in that the world overflows with forms, and in that forms are spaces and times to be filled. We desire forms. We fill them, and they us. The incessant play of matter-and-form beckons and delights us in trivial or significant ways. And in Genesis 1, forms of life created in the midst of chaos or nothingness are pronounced "good" and delight God. Yet if we imagine them as retaining their inviting emptiness, then what can fill them and fill us are also variations on emptiness-in-form.

Kenosis, then, implies a relatively negative theology, where forms and relations are sought in an emptiness that, by "hosting" them, participates in their birth and death. Why do I say, "relatively negative"? Positively speaking, one can juxtapose the analogy of God's hospitable emptiness with traditional divine attributes—for example, creator, sustainer, redeemer—and with other cultural expressions and religious traditions. Negatively, one doubts that anything "positive" can be *univocally* predicated of God (the *via negativa* tradition in theology). To identify "being"—or even "emptiness"!—with God will never grasp adequately the odd primacy of divine love[33] or the particularities of nature, time, sin, and suffering.

Emptiness, whether of finite form or of the ultimate horizons of reality, can give rise to dizzying anxiety. For Kierkegaard, anxiety before infinity can prompt idolatrous denials of our finitude and freedom.[34] We may sin either by pretending to be infinite or by retreating from responsibilities and opportunities. The gracious opposite of such idolatry would be *both* to acknowledge the hollows in ourselves *and* to discover room, in our hollows, to receive the forms of other selves and beings. In this regard, one interpretation of kenosis has been that God withdraws or *contracts* to make room for created forms.[35] Yet the metaphor of contraction is not required if the emptiness of form creates an "inside" larger than the "outside." Can we imagine, borrowing an image from Robert Jenson, that the emptiness of divine and creaturely kenosis is "roominess"?[36] And that if God's many rooms provide space and time for encounters, then the space and time of the rooms is oddly enlarged with each encounter? It would be as if a number were not an abstraction only but also a unique instance, so that each addition of 1 and 1 would result in at least 3: the original 1s would remain (= 2), but now also in a relationship (= 3), and each one of the 1s would relate to the relationship differently (= 4, 5, . . .).[37]

It is not only persons who meet, but also cultural and ideal objects. They meet us as if speaking, perhaps as voices of conscience or principles of hospitality: "love God and neighbor and even your enemy," "enjoy life compassionately," "welcome friends and strangers," "serve justly the common good and rectify injustice," "do no harm," "do unto others as . . . ," et cetera. While we usually think of such words as abstractions or universals, we encounter them anew, and we may hear them as asking us critical questions: "Who are our neighbors, now?" "What principles are at hand, here?" Although any answer we gave *last time* may serve us again, we cannot know until we hear the query *this time*. The space and time wherein we receive these maxims and questions, in all their awkward specificity, may be likened, again, to a divine emptiness wherein room is made to become *atoned* with, to become "all in all" with, or all "at-one"[38] with ourselves, others, and the questions we are offered by one another. However, temporal realizations of atonement, of *being-at-one-with,* are matters of juxtaposition, proximity, and contingency. We wait. When we do meet in emptiness, our horizons touch but do not merge. In our intimacies and relative proximities, there are distances, gaps, and separations old or new.

Why do I persist in calling such moments of receptivity "encounters"? Every moment has a dimension of contingency, in which we "bump into" the form, as it were. Second, moral and other sorts of principles are not merely hardwired in us but are lively signs and expressions. They are cultivated forms of expression and discernment that may speak to us and then be reconsidered and applied—much as we meet and think about persons. Or we can think of such forms as markers of some particular "moral space" we are entering.[39] Third, they may become reconfigured, newly embodied, or undergo critique in the encounter. The import of Jesus' performance of the Good Samaritan parable would have confounded the moral habits of Jews forbidden to deal with Samaritans and possibly vice versa.[40] To follow the voice of the parable would be to risk a transformation of values. The hearer's religious and existential world—hence one's sense of integrity—might be threatened or transfigured *in* the parable's very performance.[41]

To bring this line of thought back into the theater, I suggest now that if there is ethical good inherent in the paradigm of theatrical performance, it may be this: *in the practices of enacting parts with others—albeit practices liable to distortion—there are chances to enjoy the forms of others and space to attend caringly to the suffering of others.* In theater, the empty-yet-eliciting forms of others are provided by: performers with their bodies and voices, audiences with their desires and fears, scripts, production histories, other plays, the social contexts of this particular new performance, and what principles may be appearing and speaking in these contexts. The mutuality of the emptying self and the reception of other selves can be aesthetically delightful and ethically imperative. And it would prompt our search for kenotic patterns of integrity, arriving more in the forms of contingent gifts, less as secure possessions.

Traits of Kenotic Integrity

It may seem odd to speak of "traits" of kenotic integrity, given my emphases on encounter, emptiness, pouring and filling, and the good of performed and transformed identities. Traits may seem too settled, too much like axioms. Perhaps *motifs* would capture the fugue- and jazzlike improvisations of kenotic integrity. But while *axiom* is too heavy, *trait* has a commonsense conceptual value, and it is the job of concepts to clarify complex realities. Kenotic integrity is a concept meant to clarify persons and performances—descriptively, normatively, and critically. Yet the traits enumerated here still have a heuristic purpose, to promote discovery. They are all exemplified by the film-of-the-story-of-a-play-being-performed, Denys Arcand's *Jesus of Montreal,* in chapter X. Subsequent chapters give some traits special illumination, with chapter XI (on Noel Coward and T. S. Eliot) exploring mostly the first three traits, chapter XII (on Caryl Churchill and Tony Kushner) the fourth and fifth, and chapter XIII (on *King Lear, A Midsummer Night's Dream,* and other works) the sixth.

1. Kenotic integrity emerges through our capacities to *perform parts*— in life as in art—which we receive from others and do not completely make by ourselves.

2. We recognize kenotic patterns of integrity in *transformations of, yet in continuity with, prior narratives of identity.* Such transformations of personal narrative may bring risk as well as enrichment, though not necessarily the risks of violent antagonism.

3. Patterns of kenotic integrity have a contingent gift-character and may be engendered or completed by others, be they strangers, friends, ensembles, or forms of expression that arrive unlooked-for.

4. Kenotic patterns of integrity include relations with moral norms and principles, which may be reconfigured and reinterpreted, critically and self-critically.

5. Kenotic integrity is ethically receptive of other persons and other creatures, and is directed toward the interplay of persons with society and nature, *polis* and *cosmos.*

6. Insofar as we "find ourselves" in patterns of kenotic integrity, we may also find we are "losing ourselves," *moving into expansive relations of continuity and discontinuity* between who we have been and are yet to be. We meet the ultimate horizons of integrity in moments when we find ourselves "at-one" among historical and personal entanglements of joy and suffering, when we are emptied toward others, receptively.

Chapter X

Who Is Playing Jesus?

Traits of Kenotic Integrity in Jesus of Montreal

HAITIAN LADY: Jesus, I am yours! I belong to you! Forgive me Jesus, forgive me, I have sinned. Speak to me Jesus, speak to me, Jesus, my sweet Jesus ...

CHALIFOUX [*a policeman*]: Lady, please. Don't disturb the actors!

—DENYS ARCAND, *Jesus of Montreal*

WHEN STUDENTS READ but one medieval play, it is likely to be the widely anthologized Second Shepherds' pageant from the Towneley cycle of plays of Wakefield, England.[1] If they never read such a play, the chance remains of discovering something of the genre in venues such as Mel Gibson's *The Passion of the Christ* (2004) or Denys Arcand's *Jésus de Montréal* (1989). Both films, otherwise utterly incomparable, attempt to verify or substantiate materially the significance of their subjects.[2] Gibson does so with blood. The more we see the tortured Jesus profuse blood (the supply is infinite!) the more we are to attach our vicarious sense of pain to the film's spiritual ideas. Arcand also uses a fair amount of stage blood, but here material verification has another source, a handful of actors creating an avant-garde passion play in contemporary Montreal. To see how their metatheatrical labors connect with traits of kenotic integrity requires a glance back at the theatrical innovations of pageant or "mystery" plays.

In a Multicultural Mélange

The Second Shepherds' Play is interesting in seeming to parody the birth of Jesus. It is also, Sarah Beckwith notices, a nod to the ambiguities of acting.³ Mak has stolen a sheep and has brought it home to Gill. The poor shepherds he stole it from—who sound like they live in cold climes of England, not the environs of Bethlehem—are hot on his tail. So Gill wraps up the sheep and lays it in a cradle, to be passed off as a babe with a sadly deformed nose. She even coaches Mak, who warms to his paternal part when the suspicious shepherds arrive. The play is also a metatheatrical celebration, for after the Angel sings *Gloria in excelsis,* the shepherds, back in their fields, review the singing (not a note out of place, one remarks) and sing the song themselves. They then go to enact the angelic script, which takes them to Bethlehem with gifts for Jesus. Scholars have observed how the play did not force a choice between piety and parody but mingled them; and to call this theatrical mix "realistic" refers to its commentary on the harsh lives of English peasants and on how Bethlehem was regarded in proximity to those lives.⁴

Beckwith regrets that today we have little grasp of the integrative, "sacramental theater" realized in Wakefield, York, and elsewhere. Most modern revivals of the Corpus Christi festival are exercises of nostalgia, of *not* participating in the temporality and sociality of the plays, in which the various political and economic strata of the late-medieval towns were made to intersect on days the cycles were performed.⁵ Or else modern revivals do not grasp how the semantics of Corpus Christi were sacramental, how several actors would translate Christ's body on a circuit through the town, by way of their own performing bodies. If we cannot easily grasp the "real presence" of these plays, it is not only because of our secularism, she argues, but also because the Protestant reformers effectively changed how we habitually think about theater. When they accused the "papists" of turning the mass into mere *show*—where the priest was alleged to magically conjure up Christ, "hocus pocus"—then *theater itself* was associated with that slander, and came to regard itself more in the business of illusions not realities. There are exceptions today, however, when avant-garde dramatists do manage to approximate the social dynamics of the Corpus Christi performances, which in their time were multisocial, so to speak. Arcand's *Jésus de Montréal* is among the exceptions Beckwith notices.⁶

It portrays an itinerate actor commissioned to revise a pageant, "The Passion on the Mountain," performed outdoors around St. Joseph's Oratory on Mount Royal, from which we see neon vistas of Montreal. These shots punctuate the film's diachronic structure of *casting, performing, resisting, dying,* and *harvesting.* But while the shrine may be the pinnacle of Montreal spatially, it is not so culturally. Arcand depicts it as a loft above

a city that was once thoroughly Catholic but is now self-consciously multicultural. Yet it is misleading to call it simply a "secular city." If we imagine the culture of a medieval city as a circle with a church spire in the
middle among the other institutions; and if we imagine secular culture
as a similar circle, but with the spire off to the side, along with the logos
of Standard Oil and the BBC, with perhaps Science or the Market in the
center; then a pluralistic society would be an unbounded field of many
circles, some with religious logos but most without, some overlapping,
and a few circles in apparent isolation. Such a mélange would be, in part,
the Montreal of Arcand's film.

I say "in part" to avoid the impression that history doesn't count here.
It is not just that many in Montreal are Catholic. It is that fragments of
biblical language and lore rearrange themselves with trivia and icons
of other traditions; these fragments inhabit memory and discourse and
may be rediscovered; indeed, a source of humor is how the Quebecois
critics and artists come to regard Jesus as avant-garde. Arcand speaks of
the lure of certain scriptures: "Where your treasure is, there your heart is
also," or "If you love those who love you, what merit do you have?" He
says that "across the thick mists of the past there echoes a deeply troubling voice" (8). This echo, in turn, competes with all sorts of noises and
images: in supermarket aisles one can find "the novels of Dostoevski,
cologne, the Bible, pornographic videos, the works of Shakespeare, pictures of the Earth taken from the Moon, astrological predictions, and
posters of actors or Jesus, and all the while loud speakers and TV screens
endlessly blare their buzzing background of Pergolesi, rock and roll, or
the voices of Bulgarians."[7]

With plays and films such as *JM,* which relocate Jesus beyond the pe-
ripheries of tradition, we can anticipate fairly predictable reactions. Critics tended to say that it was: profoundly serious—or profoundly trivial;
an interesting reflection on faith in a godless world—or a satire on Christianity; subtle in its use of the Jesus story—or full of obvious clichés;
morally inquisitive—or sophomoric; sharply critical of the church—or
ignorant. Many see the film as basically about hypocrisy. But that view
does not interpret it but states its *premise;* like countless fictions, it depicts
Father Leclerc as another exhausted cleric who would impose a faith and
discipline he no longer shares. The theatrical, medical, and legal institutions are also skewered. Yet *JM* is really much better if the hypocrisy motif
is seen as a premise that does not limit the film's range of significance.

What does define its range is the *uncoupling* of hypocrisy from playacting and the *coupling* of acting with patterns of kenotic integrity. In his

Preface, Arcand remembers meeting an actor playing in a Stations of the Cross pageant. Each evening he would declaim, "Whoever would gain his life must lose it," then the next morning might "audition for an erotic film or beer commercial" (7). In *JM*, Daniel Coloumb (Lothaire Bluteau) accepts the part of Jesus. He pours himself into the part and persuades four other actors to join him. They lose themselves to find themselves. Not only does *JM* explore kenotic integrity, it takes a scriptural story, vaguely remembered among the literati of Quebec, and makes it illuminate other fragments in the cultural mélange.

Not only does Coulomb's ensemble empty into their parts, but the film realizes kenotic patterns on several synchronic, or overlapping narrative levels.[8] Most immediate is the story of *the actors performing the Jesus text*. Father Leclerc (Gilles Pelletier) approaches Coulomb to revise the dated pageant. Coulomb recruits other actors, creates a controversial spectacle, is touted as a Montreal celebrity, and defends rather violently fellow actor Mireille (Catherine Wilkening) from humiliation at a beer commercial audition. This results in his arrest for assault and vandalism. But he is declared quite sane by a court psychiatrist, is released on his own recognizance, refuses Leclerc's order to close the show, and dies of an untreated head injury—after his cross is accidentally toppled by a spectator defending the play against a hapless cop, who has arrived to stop the performance. This level is naturalistic, but is intersected by the other narrative dimensions.

So there is, second, *Coulomb's interpretation of the Jesus text*. He learns provocative things about Jesus from a scholar who thinks that as an actor, he is free to say what a Catholic professor cannot. This research is incorporated into the performance, when Mireille and Constance (Johanne-Marie Tremblay) play as archeologists, lecturing with trenching tools and laptop computers. Coulomb's research emphasizes what secular scholarship might know of the "historical Jesus" (even calling the Evangelists "liars" for editing and inventing things) which, paradoxically, increases the Montreal audience's projection of an aura around Jesus. They are incorporated in the play inadvertently, when a Haitian woman rushes up to Coulomb as if he really were Jesus, and intentionally, when he distributes bread to the crowd and intones Arcand's favorite sayings of Jesus.

Third, *Coulomb's actions seem to be affected by the Jesus text*. We notice this first when a spooky librarian tells him that Jesus "will find you." It becomes more explicit when he stops Leclerc from censoring the play, and it nearly passes beyond aesthetic control when, in defense

of Mireille, he smashes camera equipment and strikes a female producer with a cord—all too much like Jesus driving moneychangers from
the temple. After his brain injury, he descends into a metro station and
preaches an apocalyptic sermon based on Mark 13.[9] Even so, his relation to Christ is mainly by association, for Coulomb through it all is just
another, serious actor. The association is mostly made by the audience
and by the camera eye of the film itself.

Thus, fourth, *the film's own seeing is affected by the Jesus text.* At a
performance of *The Brothers Karamazov,* Pascal Berger (Cédric Noël)—
who plays the suicide, Smerdiakov—is associated with John the Baptist,
when a stylish publicist "wants his head" for her advertising campaign.
When Berger sees Coulomb after the play, he exclaims, *"there* is a real
[*bon*] actor" (20) and rushes to greet him. This allusion to Jesus reflects
neither Coulomb's nor any character's awareness, but is entirely the
film's, or Arcand's awareness. But by the last scenes of *Jesus of Montreal,*
these levels have emptied into each other and provide a context in which
to see Coulomb and his ensemble in terms of what I am calling certain
"traits" in patterns of kenotic integrity.

Traits in the Patterns of Kenosis

*Kenotic integrity emerges through our capacities to perform parts—in
life as in art—which we receive from others and do not completely make
by ourselves.*

There are a number of instances in *Jesus of Montreal* of the theatrical
critique of theater. Indeed, our Jesus calls his players out of unfulfilling
acting jobs. Constance works in a church soup kitchen, but we first see
her in a video of the earlier, pious version of "The Passion on the Mountain." Martin (Rémy Girard) dubs dialogue for porno movies, and we
meet René (Robert Lepage) recording narration for a science documentary on the Big Bang. He, in turn, directs Coulomb to the Parisian ingénue, Mireille, who cannot bear to speak or be seen without makeup, and
is being filmed in a perfume commercial directed by her smarmy lover;
he tells her that her talent is "in her ass." Leclerc has also been an actor.
He is secretly shacking up with Constance but, at age sixty, is afraid to
leave the security of the priesthood. Yet it is Leclerc who hires Coulomb
and early on signals the good of transformation through performance:
he says he entered the priesthood to escape poverty when his real love
was theater, and has wistful memories of wanting to do Brecht's *Galileo*

in seminary. Coulomb is doing what Leclerc has not done for a long while, finding himself anew in a part larger than himself.

That theatrical performance can occasion the self's emergence or renewal may seem contradicted by the cult of celebrity. But acting is not about stardom, and the performance-as-integrity paradigm must include how theatrical play occurs in ensembles, with writers, directors, managers, as well as actors. Thus, when they all seem resigned to the play being stopped, Mireille protests. She says that before joining them, her "idea of paradise was a beach on Bora Bora," and believed every man she met wanted to have her. It is not just Coulomb whom she credits with her recovery but the ensemble. "What we have is precious; it must go on" (159).

We recognize kenotic patterns of integrity in transformations of, yet in continuity with, prior narratives of identity. Such transformations of personal narrative may bring risk as well as enrichment, though not necessarily the risks of violent antagonism.

Little is revealed of Coulomb's prior narrative. He trained in the same acting school as Constance and traveled to India and Nepal. The court psychiatrist is impressed that he has no resentment for not being born in a better theater city such as New York or Los Angeles. We glimpse other histories as well. Constance has a five-year-old daughter, Rosalie; the other actors play with her, as if to underline the significance of this unexplored strand of her past. Constance is at peace working in a soup kitchen, yet is pleased when a local TV star notices her acting.

If part of the good of acting is revealed in how human beings can transcend themselves and resist entrapment in prior narratives, then part of the "bad" of acting can be forms of typecasting, as with Leclerc and Mireille. René hesitates to join the company unless he can examine the script, protecting the actor he imagines himself to be. When Coulomb explains the text will be composed collectively, René hesitates—until they agree to include Hamlet's "To be or not to be" soliloquy (it might be his "only chance," he explains). The ensemble does need a text to perform; they take responsibility for it, and are not fenced in by its apparent boundaries.

Patterns of kenotic integrity have a contingent gift-character and may be engendered or completed by others, be they strangers, friends, ensembles, or forms of expression that arrive unlooked-for.

Because these patterns are not simply formed by prior narratives of selfhood but emerge in new encounters, they may be illuminated by practices of *hospitality,* where people risk meeting, contingently, as hosts and strangers. We do not see how Leclerc discovered Coulomb, but he did. They meet in the shrine as a soprano and contralto rehearse Pergolesi's *Stabat Mater* in the balcony. Strangers begin to collaborate around a text at once common and alien to them: common in that Jesus is a fragment in the cultural mélange they share, alien in that Jesus is also a point of resistance. The pattern of meeting and invitation is repeated with each player, and the integrity of their responses can be gauged, in part, by their receptivity and willingness to risk innovating together. Leclerc knows the old play needs reinterpreting, but his fear smothers any receptivity he might have to the interpretation offered by Coulomb.

The aspect of *contingency* appears in the contrasting hospital scenes. St. Mark's turns no patient away but is so overcrowded it can not treat Coulomb responsibly; he leaves still gravely ill, and when the efficient Jewish hospital later admits him, it is too late. Kenotic patterns of integrity are susceptible both to who comes to the encounter and to what circumstances develop. People in such patterns attempt to improvise personal and moral relations: as when the actors coalesce into a temporary family; as they resist Leclerc; and as the crowd follows them from station to station, interacting with them and becoming part of the performance. But there are no safeguards. In the interval of a second, the comic mood is silenced when Coulomb's cross is toppled. This introduction of the "accidental" into the film's reading of the passion narrative is a theological innovation. Traditionally, Christ dies for our sins, not our accidents.

Kenotic patterns of integrity include relations with moral norms and principles, which may be reconfigured and reinterpreted, critically and self-critically.

The view that kenotic patterns of integrity entail *receptivity* to contingent gifts and willingness *to innovate together* can, by itself, still seem a neutral consideration. True, "transformation," "receptivity," "openness," "ensemble," and "innovation" have quite positive connotations. But if pressed, we may find it hard to say *why* these phrases signify the good without introducing terms from other sources of discourse.

Recall that for Ricoeur, moral and ethical paradigms are embedded in language and lore; they are included in the liminal situations where persons discover themselves in encounters with others. We have seen how Arcand speaks of scriptures haunting him like echoes across time, particularly commands of love. In the "Passion on the Mountain," Coulomb lifts up sayings of Jesus that emphasize reversals of power, as demanded by principles of honesty and justice. "Distrust priests in long robes, pleased to be seen in public, who occupy the first rows in temples and the best seats at banquets, and who consume the inheritances of widows while intoning long prayers. . . ." Leclerc is in this audience, and Coulomb addresses him and his clerical associates directly, creating the potential for a social drama. "Those among you who would become great must be servants. those who would be first among you must be the slave of all" (131–32).

The imperative "texts" we encounter, along with persons and other cultural signs, may change us and our patterns with others, as we interpret and apply them. Words of compassion, justice, or respect for persons, as well as traditions behind such principles, are in the lore, prior to us. "Do unto others as you would have them do unto you." "Love your neighbor as yourself." "Play fair." "Be a good Samaritan." "Honor your father and mother." "Do not swear falsely." "The needs of the many outweigh the needs of the few, or the one." "Where your treasure lies, there your heart lies also." "Do no harm." "Help friends, harm foes." "Love your enemies." "The show must go on." Such maxims from various moral systems are not ostensibly consistent, and philosophical ethics tries to adjudicate them. But they do become configured, roughly or incompletely, in patterns of integrity, and can become occasions of conflict and entrapment.

At the beer commercial audition, directed by her now ex-boyfriend, Mireille falls victim to an implicit "standard practice" of exploitation, and Coulomb literally lashes out in moral outrage. Moral principles and imperatives can be "parts" to inhabit, and can entrap persons in too confined a drama of integrity. Coulomb is in such danger and is distressingly "out of character" when he strikes a woman who is one of the producers of the ad.[10] He tells the court psychiatrist that he is not of a violent nature but was angered by the "contempt" with which "actors, especially actresses" are treated, and that Mireille was "a friend whom I like very much" (140). His statement clearly juxtaposes the personal and the moral in a pattern of integrity. Yet his brutality is suggestive of how principles of morality can have a coercive, potentially violent subtext; the principle must be seen to win.[11] However, when he appears before the judge (played by Arcand himself, who evinces irony about the charade he presides over), Coulomb refuses the role of antagonist and pleads guilty, seemingly released from one possible integrity trap.

Leclerc is in quite another trap, and not one of integrity. "I am a bad priest," he tells Coulomb in Constance's apartment. And later, "I am crippled. . . . I do not know how to live" (155). Why is he "bad"? Not because the role of *a priest* is bad, nor because performing it *as a role* is bad, but because he performs it as a lie, with all the problems of harm to self and others that deception can entail. Sartre would say his deception is self-deception, or "bad faith." But here it is of an ironic sort, for Leclerc has probably read his Sartre, and Constance has forced some honesty on him. When Coulomb visits her, Leclerc is hiding in the bedroom. "Come out from in there," she says, "we are not playing a scene from Feydeau" (37). But they have been playing a farce; the new entrance of theater into their lives is offering them a way of stopping it.

Kenotic integrity is ethically receptive of other persons and other creatures, and is directed toward the interplay of persons with society and nature, polis and cosmos.

Arcand alludes to a scene from Brecht, in which a young monk proposes to quit astronomy because Galileo's discoveries will harm the faith of his poor parents. "How could they take it, were I to tell them that they are on a lump of stone ceaselessly spinning around a second-rate star."[12] *JM* rejects scientism when René questions the portentous tone of the Big Bang documentary, "Aren't a lot of questions left unanswered here?" (44). But in the film Leclerc does make an argument like the Little Monk's when he shows Coulomb a display of wheelchairs and crutches of people miraculously cured. "This is a collection of universal misery. The poor do not come here to learn the latest archeological discoveries from the Middle East; they come to be told that the Son of God loves and awaits them. . . . Most cannot afford Lacanian psychoanalysis" (152–53). But as Leclerc describes his father, who died unemployed and deranged, he implies that the main point of life is not really to imitate Christ but "to wait for death as comfortably as possible" (154). The question is why and where shall we live: In Leclerc's theater of bad faith, or in Coulomb's faith in a theater of inquiry?

We have seen that a crucial problem for conceptualizing kenotic integrity is its being so directed to suffering as to make one hostage to the other (sometimes said of Levinas's ethics) rather than a host and guest. Kenotic integrity would need to entail receptivity and mutuality, possibilities of enjoying (or delighting-in) as well as suffering-with-and-for-others. In this respect, "The Passion on the Mountain" is a tour de force, with a magic act, walking on water, cures and resurrections, a realistic crucifixion, and miraculous costume changes—against the backdrop of St. Joseph's Oratory and the glittering nighttime city. The spectacle obviously gives pleasure, and the TV and radio personalities fall over themselves trying to bask in its success.

The scriptural associations and parodies (e.g., the media lawyer qua Satan tempts Coulomb in Chez Charon, a skyscraper restaurant that overlooks Montreal: "This city can be yours!" he says) are not the only delights here. The boundaries between film and theater and between performers and audience are blurred as the crowd follows the players. The proximity of the audience allows for the calm exhortations of Jesus and the disciples to be just as affecting as their theater tricks. And the curtain call, in a vaulted grotto where the resurrection appearances also occur, is staged with care, showing how the players receive and are received by the spectators. Theatrical playing here is pointedly nondeceptive (the "smoke and mirrors" show) and mutually engaging. It entertains, moves, teaches, and creates time and space for critical questions and edification. The players' speeches before the curtain call juxtapose an ethics of kenosis with gestures to the authentic self:

> CONSTANCE: (*To an attentive spectator.*) It is for each to judge when the moment comes to choose one's path of salvation. You can ask no one but yourself. One must trust oneself with humility and courage. . . .
>
> RENÉ: Basically, our lives are very simple. They become insurmountably complex when one thinks only of oneself. . . . At the instant one thinks less about oneself than about the command to help others, life becomes perfectly simple. . . . (83)

Insofar as we "find ourselves" in patterns of kenotic integrity, we may also find we are "losing ourselves," moving into expansive relations of continuity and discontinuity between who we have been and are yet to be. We meet the ultimate horizons of integrity in moments when we find ourselves "at-one" among the historical and personal entanglements of joy and suffering, when we are emptied toward others, receptively.

Daniel Coulomb's "identifying" with Jesus is something the film sees in him more than he sees in himself, until near the end when the layers of the film's synchronic structure begin to merge. Before then, he is aware mainly of being an actor-director, who investigates his parts as best he can and defends his actors' privilege to perform them. Jesus is simply a "good subject," he tells the psychiatrist. Coulomb is not a self-intended "Christ figure" but an actor who discovers himself in performing with others. But this story takes him to unexpected places, and in the end, with the trauma to his brain, he is accidentally overtaken by the part he's been playing. The Apostles Creed says Christ "descended into hell" to speak to the denizens there. As Coulomb's brain swells he becomes delusional, and descends an escalator into the underground. There, he singles out people on the train platform for his apocalyptic message:

> When you see the abomination of desolation, if you are in the plains flee to the mountains. If on your balcony, do not go back in the house to take care of your affairs. If on the road, do not return home. (*He speaks louder to the passengers on the platform.*) Be sorry for those who are pregnant on that day. Pray that it does not fall in winter! (*He turns back to those near him.*) If people tell you, "The Savior is here," "The Savior is there," do not believe them. Do you hear? Do not believe them! False saviors ... false prophets ... the powers of heaven ... shaken ... neither the day nor the hour ... How surprised you will be ... the judgment ... watch ... (p. 175)

These words from Mark 13 are Daniel Coulomb's last words.[13] He collapses, Constance runs for help, and Mireille sits holding his head in a pose reminiscent of Mary Magdalene lamenting the body of Jesus taken from the cross, in Giotto's Arena Chapel frescoes.

The body, we have seen, is what makes a person unique in space and time. Yet the body is a pliable whole of discrete parts, and through transplant surgery these parts are available to others. In this way Arcand realizes a material possibility in retelling the Christ story that Martin Scorsese surprisingly rejects and Mel Gibson only hints at. In *The Last Temptation of Christ* (1988), temptation is overcome inwardly, gnostically, when Jesus wins his Manichean struggle between flesh and spirit and rejects the allure of married life. Salvation, then, is disembodied, despite images of Jesus removing his heart from his chest and turning wine into blood, and despite Christian boycotters offended by his dream of sexuality and domesticity. By contrast, whatever Gibson intended in Jesus' porous flesh and exuding blood, he implies a much greater interest in embodiment.[14] The blood goes everywhere: into the ground, the air, on everyone, and cannot be contained by the white linen Pilate's wife gives the two Marys to mop the red floor, after the endless flagellation scene.

If this *material association* of God and the world, mediated by blood and tissue, is implicit in Gibson, it is explicit in Arcand.[15] The surgery of harvesting Coulomb's organs is unsettling yet beautiful. Is this a resurrection? For his heart makes a man live and his corneas make a woman see. But Coulomb is not the messiah, his remains are cremated, his resurrection is deferred. The more precise referent is the Eucharist, for the body is indeed broken for others, and the blood is O-negative, "a God-send." Insofar as fragments of the body can be emptied and poured out, the harvesting of Coulomb is a literal instance of kenosis.

The relationship between the Christ who died on the cross and who appeared to others thereafter has been said to be one of "continuity and discontinuity."[16] In the Gospels, Jesus is sometimes recognized, sometimes not; untouchable, then touchable; here, then there, then gone again; seen and unseen.[17] When he appears to his friends, played by Mireille, Constance, and Martin, a hooded René must substitute for the risen Christ, since Coulomb needs time to climb off the cross to make the curtain call. So there is one part, and many bodies. The switch in actors hearkens to the mystery cycles where, as Beckwith emphasizes, many persons played Jesus at various locations on routes through the towns, which enhanced the sacramental significance of the Corpus Christi plays. Who we are—before and after we are transformed by our encounters with others or with new parts and responsibilities—is also a contingent mix of continuity and discontinuity. In this regard, the film has four endings:

1. Coulomb's pattern of integrity disperses into other patterns, those of the patients who receive his organs and the lives of the actors.

2. Of these, three give in to the temptation to create a *commercial avant-garde* theater company in Coulomb's name, as the lawyer (aka, Satan) proposes.

3. Mireille, however, leaves the lawyer's office in sad disgust and walks alone on Mont Royal, which may give the film a concluding impression of hopelessness. Her rejection of the "Daniel Coulomb Theater" implies there is little chance for kenotic integrity in corporate or institutional forms, and yet here the film may betray itself. There are in fact theater companies and film producers who do strive to be economically viable, without eclipsing their commitments to "artistic integrity." Indeed, the kind of acting and dramatizing that Coulomb and Arcand represent depends upon such communities.

4. The final image is of two women who had only passing encounters with Coulomb, the soprano and contralto we heard singing in the shrine when he first met Leclerc. Later at the audition they are there, lip-syncing a jingle—"We worship beer"—one of them in a bikini, dancing with a shirtless hunk. And now they are performing Pergolesi again, not in a sanctuary or a theater, but in the Metro station where Coulomb died. They sing from the *Stabat Mater,* whose Latin text Arcand quotes in the published screenplay, "When my body dies, let my soul not be refused

the glory of paradise" (188). Behind them is a poster of Pascal Berger, the actor in *The Brothers Karamazov* who called Coulomb a "real actor." His head has finally been hired to publicize a men's cologne, *L'Homme Sauvage,* "Wild Man." The French phrase is polyphonic, in which we hear tones of primitive nobility and authenticity without the artifices of culture. However, as a commercial icon in the subway, Berger's head is not really wild but mirrors our bondage to consumerism. Does the closing tableau offer only a choice between the meaningful Son of Man, of whom the women sing, and a meaningless Wild Man?

Yet recall that Berger was the John the Baptist figure. The Baptist was a wild man who ate grasshoppers and honey and dressed in camel hide, whose kenotic integrity was to allow his voice to be inhabited by another's voice (Isaiah) and to defer to another's voice (Jesus). To the moviegoer who notices any of this, if only subliminally, the face on the poster may call to mind *both* the face of Berger *and* the face of Coulomb, which it vaguely resembles. There is something disturbingly wild about kenotic integrity. We are most ourselves when not completely or only ourselves, but when we are living wild, with and for others, or as Stanley Hauerwas has happily put it, "out of control."[18]

Chapter XI

Who Is Guest, Who Is Host?

Hospitality and Strangers in Private Lives and The Cocktail Party

You don't hold any mystery for me, darling, do you mind? There isn't a particle of you that I don't know, remember, and want.

—ELYOT TO AMANDA, IN NOEL COWARD, *Private Lives*

Nobody likes to be left with a mystery:
It's so ... unfinished.

—EDWARD, IN T. S. ELIOT, *The Cocktail Party*

KENOTIC INTEGRITY EMERGES *through our capacities to perform parts—in life as in art—which we receive from others and do not completely make by ourselves.*

We recognize kenotic patterns of integrity in transformations of, yet in continuity with, prior narratives of identity. Such transformations of personal narrative may bring risk as well as enrichment, though not necessarily the risks of violent antagonism.

Patterns of kenotic integrity have a contingent gift-character and may be engendered or completed by others, be they strangers, friends, ensembles, or forms of expression that arrive unlooked-for.

These first traits of kenotic integrity have to do with contingencies: of the parts we encounter, of the narratives that shape identities, and of the patterns of integrity emerging in encounters. These patterns may have the contingency of gifts, destinies, calls, and the like.

The Cocktail Party (1949) is T. S. Eliot's best attempt to create verse drama after the "dead end" of *Murder in the Cathedral*. He had concluded that that play's topic and choral form were too distant from modern sensibilities to elicit a perception of serene and reconciling "order *in* reality."[1] If this self-criticism may also be read as recognition of the narrowness of moral patterns of integrity, then the later play attempts a larger pattern. Second, when Eliot revealed the source for *The Cocktail Party* to be Euripides' tragedy-with-a-happy-ending, *Alcestis,*[2] he brought into play the ancient theme of hospitality, which may subvert or even overcome the split between personal and moral integrity. The theme gave Eliot a proleptically postmodern leverage on the sort of West End comedy he wished to emulate and transcend, especially the confections of Noel Coward. Today Eliot's comedies are rarely performed and are mostly studied as ancillary to his poetry,[3] while Coward is credited with insight and poignancy few detected at the time, signaling a gay man's critique of gendered "normality."[4] However, by contrasting Eliot and Coward I suggest they were both concerned with paradoxes of hospitality and contingencies of integrity, in a culture where Shaw's "middle class morality" was showing its wear.[5] They were prospecting for versions of kenotic integrity.

The Integrity of "Flippancy"

The Coward play Eliot easily may have noticed was *Blithe Spirit* (1941).[6] As in *Alcestis,* where a wife returns from the dead via the agency of tipsy Heracles, Coward's chatty medium Madame Arcati conjures up the ghost of a writer's first wife. Eliot may have been impressed by the play's toast, "To *The Unseen,*" for in *The Cocktail Party,* Edward toasts the vaguely supernatural "Guardians." He would also be amused by Arcati's wistful lament about the decline of ritual and credulity. The "old bell and book method" of banishing ghosts "was quite effective in the old days of genuine religious belief but . . . I believe the decline of faith in the Spirit World has been causing grave concern" (64). But source hunting is not really the issue; it is the themes of love and marital hell that make *Private Lives* an issue for *The Cocktail Party.*

Consider another play that Eliot did mention, Sartre's *No Exit* (1944). There, hell is not a torture chamber but an eternally locked drawing room inhabited by two talkative women and a man who concludes, "Hell is—other people!"[7] Eliot said he was replying to Sartre via Edward Chamberlayne: "What is hell? Hell is oneself,/Hell is alone, the other figures in it/Merely projections" (98).[8] Comments on hell also circulate in *Private Lives*. Sybil insists on asking Elyot Chase, at the start of their honeymoon, about his feelings for his ex-wife, Amanda. Elyot: "She has some very good qualities." Sybil: "Considering the hell she's made of your life, I think you are very nice about it" (187). Amanda is also beginning a honeymoon, and minutes later when luck joins her with Elyot on the terrace outside their adjacent hotel rooms, they rationalize leaving their new spouses. "Think of the hell we'd lead them into if we stayed" (210). By the end of Act II, Elyot and Amanda are fighting again, and she denies any desire to remarry him: "I'd rather die in torment—" (233). When Elyot observes that in the eyes of heaven, they're still married ("Yes, dear, but we're not Catholics," 216), they reflect on their absence of faith.

> ELYOT: Don't you believe in anything?
> AMANDA: Oh yes, I believe in being kind to everyone, and giving
>   money to old beggar women, and being as gay as possible.
> ELYOT: What about after we're dead?
> AMANDA: I think a rather gloomy merging into everything, don't
>   you?
> ELYOT: I hope not; I'm a bad merger.

They speculate on the sort of afterlife they might choose; Amanda doubts she would opt for being young, "not if it meant having awful bull's glands popped into me." Elyot: "Cows for you dear. Bulls for me" (222). Such references to gender and oblivion are contextualized by absent transcendence.[9] Amanda and Elyot regret they cannot "believe" in anything. If her rejection of "youth" runs against cultural expectations then that is another way *Private Lives* and *The Cocktail Party* are comparable. She knows that youth is the illusion as well as the dream of Coward's "marvelous age," and Elyot thinks this age is "alright if you happen to be a specialist at something, then you're too concentrated to pay attention to all the other things going on. But for the ordinary observer, it's too much" (222). For convenience, I will gather Coward's critiques into three clusters concerning sex and knowledge, ethics and violence, and the relationship of privacy and performance.

Sex and Knowledge

During the symmetrical balcony dialogues, Coward looks askance at Victorian gender roles. Elyot tells Sybil—his conventional new bride who despises "sunburn" and "half-masculine" women, and who plans to "understand" Elyot and "manage him"—that "You're a completely feminine little creature, aren't you. . . . Everything in its place" (188). In the suite next door, Victor is posing as a "normal" man of "rugged grandeur" who vows to make Amanda happy "just by looking out for you" (193). But he finds her use of tanning oil frightening.

> VICTOR: I wish I knew you better.
> AMANDA: It's just as well you don't. The "woman"—in italics—
>   should always retain a certain amount of alluring feminine
>   mystery for the "man"—also in italics. . . .
> VICTOR: I'm glad I'm normal.
> AMANDA: What an odd thing to be glad about. Why? (195)

Elyot and Amanda do seem to toy with traditional expectations, as reflected in their choices of second spouses. Elyot tells Sybil his love for her is "wise[r] perhaps . . . and undramatic" and possibly "dull" (188). Amanda thinks she loves Victor "much more calmly" (193).

Coward's alternative to contained marital bliss is not exactly the "erotic friendship" that Milan Kundera portrays in *The Unbearable Lightness of Being* (1985), but it is comparable. Amanda and Elyot imply that what they really have is friendship-with-sex, where repartee is the metabolic rhythm and sex is an unreliable catalyst that may jolt or stop the rhythm. As their cozy banter in Act II verges on lovemaking, Amanda interrupts—"It's so soon after dinner," irritating Elyot, which irritates her. "You can't bear the thought that there are certain moments when our chemical, what d'you call 'ems, don't fuse together properly" (224). Such "love," she implies, is a little like original sin: "Selfishness, cruelty, hatred, possessiveness, petty jealousy. All those qualities came about in us just because we loved each other" (208). What sustains them is less a matter of passion than of aesthetic knowledge of one another. Elyot says he "knows" her every "particle" and so she is no "mystery" to him, and implies this lack of mystery is good. But Amanda says she is "sophisticated" and "far too knowing," which is what led to their violent fights. "I irritated him because he knew I could see right through him" (193).

The phenomenology of love in *Private Lives,* then, *apparently* discloses two people of equal intelligence and sophistication, brought by circumstance and chemicals into a relationship defined by perfect knowing, without note of difference. Yet they are different. Elyot is given more to anger and conventional sensibilities: "It doesn't suit women to be promiscuous." Amanda is more libertine: "It doesn't suit men for women to be promiscuous" (218). But for the most part they mirror one another. That love might involve other people around them, much less offspring, is ignored.

Victor claims to be normal. Amanda is "not so sure she is normal," though she has no "peculiar cravings for Chinamen or old boots, if that's what you mean. . . . I think very few people are completely normal really, deep down in their private lives."

> It all depends on a combination of circumstances. If all the various cosmic thingummys fuse at the same moment, and the right spark is struck, there's no knowing what one mightn't do. That was the trouble with Elyot and me, we were like two violent acids bubbling about in a nasty little matrimonial bottle. (195)

Of course if she *had* craved a Chinaman, or said, "like an acid and a base," the picture might be otherwise; but it is how Amanda and Elyot are like twins to each other that fascinates us and frustrates them. This thought should not be construed, however, as the critique of narcissism frequently leveled against same-sex relationships.[10] Are they narcissists?— quite likely. But it is a narcissism of their culture, which would also be pertinent of "normal" couplings, where each one finds in the other a reflection of unexamined expectations, such as Victor and Sybil project upon each other. Perhaps what Amanda and Elyot really suffer is *a lack of language* that embraces otherness, not an inability to embrace or know anyone other than themselves.

Moral Qualms and Ethical Aspirations

Amanda and Elyot wish to encounter life in "the moment," relying on whatever "honest" inspirations arise. This aspiration should not be dismissed as being without ethical substance, for it might release them from illusions of self-sufficiency. Elyot thinks "it's the true values of the situation that are really important. The moment we saw one another again we knew it was no use going on" (219). However, as they contemplate explaining their feelings and actions to their new spouses, they are not sure they can face it. Elyot: "We've got to decide instantly. . . . Go away together now, or stay with them, and never see one another again" (210–11).

We can take their self-analysis further. Life's moments of catalysis and responsibility are products of luck; their universe is a throwback to the Greek sense of luck (*tuchē*), as understood by Bernard Williams and Martha Nussbaum.[11] Elyot and Amanda admit they are each a "gambler."

"Chance rules my life" (194), she says. From time to time they become ill at ease and desire a clarifying sense of obligation. Amanda acknowledges she is prone to see "moral" things ("what one should do and what one shouldn't") "the wrong way around" (196). She tells Elyot she has a karmic dread of violating something "sacred." "We're being so bad, so terribly bad, we'll suffer for this, I know we shall" (211). She also worries, "We've certainly been pretty busy trying to justify ourselves" (219). In the meantime, they maintain long-nurtured grievances about their suspected and actual infidelities, which were part of what led them to divorce. But a more frightening provocation, depending on how it is played, is their violence. Knowing they are prone to smash gramophone recordings over their heads, they invent an anger-defusing shibboleth, "Solomon Isaacs," later shortened to "Sollocks" (another instance of fragmented moral discourse!), the utterance of which obligates them to stop shouting or talking for two minutes, though the rule becomes less effective the more it is invoked.

As distinct from the moral, the ethical way they embrace is that of "flippancy," in which they aim to live pleasantly, with sophisticated perception, for as long as possible, until the "worms pop out" (227). It is like Vivienne Bearing's understanding of "wit," a way of being ironic in the face of death. But in actual practice, flippancy operates as a private language for displacing grievances and can be experienced as cruelty, for even the flippant can be bothered by flippancy. And while Amanda and Elyot's banging and wrestling may be played comically—as a substitute for sex—we may find that the older the actors, the less comic the tantrums. In a 2001–02 revival of *Private Lives,* Lindsey Duncan (Amanda) and Alan Rickman (Elyot) were quite a few years older than the script implies, which resulted in their repartee being more intelligent but their actual blows more disturbing. Even so, Elyot intends his ethics of flippancy to skewer "manly" violence, a critique we might miss unless the actor lingers over it. In Act III, Sybil and Victor have arrived in Paris together and invaded the flat where Amanda and Elyot have resumed their long warfare, and Victor thinks he would like to duke it out with Elyot. Elyot's critique of Victor's posture sounds like he is talking about Europe between the wars: "all this belligerency is very right and proper and highly traditional, but . . . it won't get us very far."

VICTOR: To hell with all that.
ELYOT: I should like to explain that if you hit me, I shall certainly
    hit you, probably equally hard, if not harder. I'm just as strong

as you, I should imagine. Then you'd hit me again, and I'd hit
you again, and we'd go on until one or the other was knocked
out. (241)

It is true that Elyot says other things that undercut this high-mindedness.
But in spite of their claims against common morality and for living in
the moment, Amanda and Elyot look for ways to resist the chaos about
them. Flippancy takes on moral resonance as a hedge against violence.

> VICTOR: If you don't stop your damned flippancy, I'll knock your
>   head off.
> ELYOT (*raising his eyebrows*): Has it ever struck you that flip-
>   pancy might cover a very real embarrassment?
> VICTOR: In a situation like this, it's in extremely bad taste.
> ELYOT: No worse than bluster and invective. As a matter of fact,
>   as far as I know, this situation is entirely without precedent.
>   *We have no prescribed etiquette to fall back on.* I shall con-
>   tinue to be flippant. (238; my italics)

With "etiquette" and "flippancy," Elyot is seeking a paradigm, a virtue,
or a practice by which to comprehend the unprecedented confusion in
which the would-be spouses now find themselves.

Privacy and Performance

Amanda and Elyot are aware that "forgiveness" is also desirable. Elyot
tells Victor that if he still loves Amanda, then "you can forgive her, and
live with her in peace and harmony until you're ninety-eight" (242).
Elyot's statement reveals what he and Amanda want for each other, and
Private Lives is structured so that an implicit and impromptu ritual
transpires to release them from their impasse—indeed, a René Girard-
ian ritual in which primordial violence is transferred to new, probably
helpless victims. In Act III, Amanda has mustered enough poise to insist
they all four sit down to breakfast (the ritual); she and Elyot are not
speaking, and Sybil and Victor have been negotiating amicable divorces
from them. This awkward business, however, leads to Sybil and Victor
themselves trading insults and blows over coffee and brioche, as if married of course, so that Amanda and Elyot can observe what their chance
reunion has saved them from. With luggage in tow they quietly depart,
and in this liminal instant they are quite possibly happy.

The ending is delightful and leaves, as it should, all the ethical issues open. One of these is the relation of personal inwardness to outward manifestation, insofar as Amanda and Elyot have been watching reflections of themselves at a performance, in which Sybil and Victor imitate them. We have seen how performing, in a milieu that values sincerity and authenticity, is generally construed as a bad-faith pretense. And a problem of marriage in such a milieu is that to the extent it is a public performance, it would seem to confound the truth of private lives. Amanda and Elyot think that love means being able to see perfectly into the mind and habits of another, so that the playing out of roles, parts, or even etiquette should be inessential. On the other hand, as they now wonder how long their "ludicrous, overbearing love" might last, they do speak of love as a kind of performance.

> AMANDA: Shall we always want to bicker and fight?
> ELYOT: No, that desire will fade, along with our passion.
> AMANDA: Oh dear, shall we like that?
> ELYOT: *It all depends on how well we've played.*
> AMANDA: What happens if one of us dies? Does the one that's left
>   still laugh?
> ELYOT: Yes, yes, with all his might. (227; my italics)

Amanda and Elyot are happiest when they are entertaining each other, performing routines together, as when pretending to attend a dance with "the Grand Duchess Olga lying under the piano" and old Lady Bundle "blowing all those shrimps through her ear trumpet" (219). This blithe spirit of chatter will be echoed in *The Cocktail Party,* and on the basis of such playing there is some hope for Elyot and Amanda. Their fractious spats in Act II are interrupted not only by "Sollocks" but also by riffs and show tunes. After Amanda irritates Elyot about her chemicals not being ready to fuse, Elyot goes to the piano, and their ire dissipates. "*They sing several old refrains from dead and gone musical comedies finishing with the song that brought them together again in the first place*" (225). Each is attuned to how the other will play the parts chance gives them to play, though it is never clear they know why they should be hopeful.

> AMANDA: We should have said Sollocks ages ago.
> ELYOT: We're in love all right.

AMANDA: Don't say it so bitterly. Let's try to get the best out of it
    this time, instead of the worst. (218)

They are trying "to make the best of a bad job," as T. S. Eliot will say. Their private performances have critical integrity, exposing how gender roles can be imprisoning. To the extent their flippant repartee is mutual, it approaches being an improvisation that requires attending to each other as hosts and strangers. But it is not clear that their improvisations will take them beyond their own rooms, and thus their pattern of integrity is more centripetal than centrifugal. They pour into each other but do not imagine the good of their lives spilling into anyone else. Nor do they consider how they *are* mysterious to each other—although, when Elyot tells Amanda she holds no mystery to him, he qualifies it with, "do you mind?" (210). He knows, vaguely, that mystery would be good, not just Amanda's cliché about women being mysteries to men. While they have very little insight that what keeps them together are their theatrical capacities, we may see them in light of their intelligent performances and unacknowledged differences. If they entertain hope, Eliot wants to inquire into the reasons for such hope.

Hospitality and the "Two Ways"

If we delight in the reconciliation of Elyot and Amanda, it is likely because we enjoy their private performances. By contrast, Edward and Lavinia Chamberlayne in *The Cocktail Party* no longer improvise together while "listening to the gramophone" (96). Their furious repartee is unrelieved by self-deprecation. As with Amanda and Elyot, the expectation of perfect understanding is part of their "trap" (96), which leads to their inability to love or believe they can be loved, which creates a sense of unreality. Lavinia tells Edward she thought that if, by leaving, she "died" to him—"I who had been only a ghost to you"—he might be able to return to when once he was "real" (97–98). Edward is a barrister. He believes that she uses his status as part of the supporting cast for her aesthete salons. She in turn has cast him as a patient "on the edge of a nervous breakdown," and recommends a certain doctor. Edward needs no such advice.

I am simply in hell. Where there are no doctors—
At least, not in a professional capacity.

LAVINIA: One can be practical, even in hell:
     And you know I am much more practical than you are. (99)

The recommended doctor is the Unidentified Guest, later Sir Henry Harcourt Reilly, who turns up at a party Edward has canceled after Lavinia
leaves. But some guests have come anyway, including Edward's mistress
Celia; her admirer Peter, who is also Lavinia's lover; Reilly; and two
other irritating "Guardians," the busybody Julia and Alex from the foreign office. The latter three are secretly intervening in these lost lives,
trying to nudge them onto one or the other of two enigmatic "ways,"
which many of Eliot's critics have found irreconcilable. These ways can
be seen, however, as different ways of performing *xenia,* hospitality, a
theme Julia signals as she implicitly takes over the faltering party.

Edward, do sit down for a moment.
I know you're always the perfect host,
But just try to pretend you're another guest
At Lavinia's party. (17)

For a play rarely performed today, *The Cocktail Party* was successful
in 1949, flourishing with two interpretations of Reilly.[12] Alec Guinness
opened at the Edinburgh drama festival and later in New York; Rex
Harrison, perhaps in tones that he would later give to Henry Higgins,
played in London. Those recalling their voices can imagine how they
might have spoken here, when the Unidentified Guest first begins to
twist Edward's attitude about Lavinia's leaving him:

It will come to you slowly:
When you awake in the morning, when you go to bed at night,
That you are beginning to enjoy your independence;
Finding your life becoming cosier and cosier
Without the constant critic, the patient misunderstander . . .
And, turning the past over and over,
You'll wonder only that you endured it for so long. (28)

The speech illustrates one of Eliot's strategies, to translate the rhythms
of ordinary conversation into poetry unnoticed apart from the drama.[13]
Sometimes the verses intensify a character's expression of deeply compounded feelings by way of odd images and elusive meanings, and
sometimes they just do the necessary jobs of advancing the plot and the

repartee. One of the complaints about *The Cocktail Party* is that Eliot did these pedestrian jobs too well, that there is too much Coward and not enough poetry. If audiences have enjoyed its rare productions, critics have tended to treat it as an interesting failure. The most significant attacks have been directed to its form, to its thematic substance, and to the biographical contexts in which it was created:

Fractured Dramatic Arc   Eliot claimed that by using *Alcestis* as an armature, he introduced a mythic subtext analogous to the Christian structure that had been too visible in *Murder in the Cathedral*. The ways in which Euripides' characters are doubled or tripled has been treated well and at length by Virginia Phelan,[14] so a sketch of *Alcestis* is enough to show how Eliot uses Alcestis's return from Hades as a structure for Edward's, Lavinia's, and Celia's recoveries from spiritual death: Apollo has allowed King Admetus to postpone his death, provided he can find a willing substitute. He has approached others, including his parents, but none volunteer except his wife, Alcestis, who elicits his promise to mourn her death solemnly and never marry again. As the household settles into grief an old friend, Heracles, arrives unexpectedly, exhausted. Admetus cannot bear to send him away, so he welcomes him and tries to keep Alcestis's death a secret. But Heracles gets drunk, offends the servants, learns of the death, and full of remorse goes to fetch Alcestis from the underworld. If, as Richmond Lattimore suggests, the typical tragic hero is a person whose misfortune is due to one great "error," then Admetus is a man rewarded for a single virtue, his extraordinary hospitality.[15]

Eliot, in revealing his source, pointed to Reilly's behavior, but Julia and Alex are also figures of Heracles.[16] In Act II, Reilly begins guiding Edward and Lavinia toward a transformed but seemingly ordinary marital life. To Celia, however, distraught after Edward unexpectedly breaks off their affair, Reilly offers the choice of the other "way." Celia is his only patient with much depth of insight into her condition; she has a "sense of sin"—not of immorality, but of "emptiness" and "failure"—for which she feels a need to "atone." She now realizes that Edward and she were "strangers" who had merely "made use of each other," and wonders if we "can only love/Something created by our own imagination" (138). However, Celia can also envision an "exalted" love, a "vibration of delight/Without desire," an ideal from which, if meaningless, she wishes to be "cured" (139). This plea prompts Reilly to offer her the path he calls the "sanatorium," which for Celia will be a life of service at a nursing station in some faraway Kinkanja.

Celia's moment of self-diagnosis and choice is so compelling we want to see her again two years later in Act III, as a second cocktail party is about to begin. But Alex stuns us with news of her murder,[17] of how she had entered a religious order of nurses and was "crucified" while ministering to plague victims. If, as Peter says, Celia's death "knocks the bottom out of it" (174)—that is, if it interrupts the play's form as a comedy of mannerly adultery—then we have a dramatic problem. We must deal with this news, then return quickly to Edward and Lavinia waiting to meet their other party guests. It will be difficult to make this rupture and transition work theatrically, and Eliot himself thought that Act III was more an epilogue than an act.[18]

Misogyny   Given the destiny of Celia, another issue has threatened acceptance of Eliot's vision of hospitality: knowledge of his marriage to Vivienne Haigh-Wood and his dealings with other women, particularly his long friendship with Emily Hale. The troubled Vivienne was considered an albatross to Eliot.[19] But Lyndall Gordon's biography puts him in an ambiguous light, especially concerning his and Vivienne's brother's decision in 1938 to place her in an asylum, where she died in 1947. To the extent Edward and Lavinia reflect that history, their happy reconciliation and Celia's "sanatorium" can seem disingenuous. Moreover, Edward's rejecting Celia, at the moment he would be free to marry her, reflects Eliot's friendship with Hale. Gordon describes Hale's expectation of a proposal after 1947 and her great disappointment when Eliot married Valerie Fletcher in 1957. Thus, the sanctification of Celia can seem not the work of heathens from Kinkanja but Eliot's burden of personal guilt.

Violence   Celia's death is also troubling if it valorizes sacrificial violence. The issue is not the manner of her death, nor Reilly's answer to Lavinia's worry that her death made no difference: "Who knows / The difference [she] made to the natives who were dying / Or the state of mind in which they died?" (181). The issue is how Reilly can deem her death "triumphant" (186). He'd had a premonition, and the "only question . . . was, what sort of death?" (183). He could prepare Celia for choices, but the choice would be hers; however, this motif has been condemned as being too premeditated an arrangement of her murder. Gordon, who appreciates theological aspects of Eliot's work, speaks here of "sadism." "Bodies are women's creations," she writes; "we don't want to see them killed or tortured or throttled."[20] In other words, Celia as host is literally made hostage. But in his consulting room, Reilly did not necessarily imply that violence would be part of her "terrifying journey," with its "loneliness—and communion." Some who go to the sanatorium return to "lead very active lives/Very often, in the world" (142, 143). So her death would have been unexpected; the triumph, to Reilly, is that her suffering becomes a figure of atonement, "part of the design" (184). Nonetheless, the allusion to Thomas Becket may leave us wondering about the desirability of Eliot's "design."

The Two Ways   The path Edward and Lavinia choose is the counterpart of Celia's path, but to many the "two ways" defy reconciliation.[21] Reilly says the first way is enjoyed by all who are "reconcile[d] to the human condition," who no longer regret the loss of the vision that inspired them when young. They follow "the common routine," "avoid excessive expectation," appreciate the familiar "give and take" of life, are "tolerant of themselves and others." They

> Are contented with the morning that separates
> And with the evening that brings together
> For casual talk before the fire
> Two people who know they do not understand each other,
> Breeding children whom they do not understand
> And who will never understand them.
> CELIA: Is that the best life?
> REILLY: It is a good life. Though you will not know how good
>   Till you come to the end. But you will want nothing else,
>   And the other life will be only like a book
>   You have read once, and lost. In a world of lunacy,
>   Violence, stupidity, greed … it's a good life. (140–41)

As to "the other life," Reilly hesitates to describe it, but we have seen its contours in Celia. He then says, "Neither way is better./Both ways are necessary" (141). How can the two be equally good? Given the dreary connotations of "the common routine," "give and take," "excessive expectations," and the "breeding" of uncomprehending children, how can this choice be on a par with Celia's visionary life for others? And how, on such terms, can Lavinia and Edward be reconciled? Reilly thinks if they would stop accusing each other of their own faults they might see how their faults are the "bond that holds them together" (125). Lavinia is incredulous at this, but Edward thinks Reilly means "we must make the best of a bad job."

REILLY: When you find. Mr. Chamberlayne,
　　The best of a bad job is all any of us make of it—
　　Except of course, the saints—such as those who go
　　To the sanatorium—you will forget this phrase,
　　And in forgetting it will alter the condition. (126)

Below, I hope to show how this last line points toward a dynamic of hospitality that can—if anything can—roughly align the two "ways" in a kenotic pattern where the transformed meaning of "the best of a bad job" is really much better than "the best of a bad job."

The Limits of Naturalism　Before reconstructing that pattern, one more complaint should be mentioned. Possibly influenced by his dramatic collaborator, E. Martin Browne, Eliot wanted his secular plays to be performed naturalistically. This may have weakened otherwise strong theatrical intuitions. Katharine Worth applauds how Eliot's fragmentary play *Sweeney Agonistes* (1926) anticipated the minimalist dialogue and unanchored malice in Harold Pinter. And she thinks directors should ignore how Eliot and Browne diminished the Furies in *The Family Reunion* (1939), based on Aeschylus's Oresteia trilogy: make them, rather, terrifyingly objective. Likewise, she thinks *The Cocktail Party* "hints at the possibility of a 'black' theater coming out of the Coward formula."[22] I can imagine a stylized mise-en-scène, where unexpectedly colorful or obsessively black and white décor, with exaggerated late 1940s upscale fashions, could signal a confluence of spirituality and sexuality between the polite lines of adultery and fertility.

It can also be argued that those wanting more unity in Act III want the wrong thing. The revelation of Celia's death heightens the disruption of the ordinary world and confronts us with the link between violence and the sacred.[23] Does Christianity expose and overcome this link, as René Girard thinks, or does it deeply trade on it? Is Christian atonement the best or worst of a bad job? Conceivably, these are the kind of *questions* the play raises. Celia's death—along with Alex's report that natives erected a propitiating shrine to her (182)—is a disruption that *should* leave the actors and audience floundering for a while, raising the stakes on the play's proposal.

Playing as Guests and Hosts

Eliot's proposal is to envision our integral relations with others—including lovers, friends, and children—through the paradoxes of hospitality to strangers. Many things signal it. Edward says that on Lavinia's societal stage he felt like a butler; indeed, "Some of your guests may have thought I *was* the butler" (93). He does not grasp how there is nothing terribly bad in being taken for a servant, particularly if one carries it off well. Eliot took from *Alcestis* a vision of *xenia,* or hospitality, where "strangers" are expected to be both "guests" and "hosts," rather than "hostiles." Kenneth Reckford thinks Eliot invoked *xenia* to assert an ethic of life in the midst of death. The Greeks recognized that you gave the stranger something

> to eat and drink before asking questions (such as, was he a pirate or an honest merchant), and that your taking him in established, at least temporarily, a definite nexus of obligation between host and guest; for both become *xenoi,* and whoever failed in his duty would be punished by Zeus, the overseer of hospitality.[24]

Reckford considers how Eliot allows references to eating and drinking to become allusions to the eucharistic host, and how this invocation of hospitality brings the "two ways" into more evident coherence. I believe both of the two ways imply the self's *dispossession and repossession, through playing parts for and with others,* an implication to explore further.

Private Lives assumed that intimacy meant perfect knowledge, which would require private, self-sufficient knowing. In *The Cocktail Party,* hospitality relinquishes this assumption. Hospitality is etiquette, but not "mere" etiquette. It accompanies intimacy and distance. Eliot, writing before postmodern concerns with alterity, thought the code of hospitality offered ways of addressing modern alienation. Would we not do well to approach and dwell with others as guests and hosts? He does not deny that guests or hosts can become *hostile;* in fact, elements of hospitality might serve as a way of grasping the problem of hostility. Nor does he deny that "familiarity" is part of intimacy. But even in intimacy, there is familiarity and strangeness; and *xenia* can give a form to familiarity and strangeness, be it in bedrooms, courtrooms, or hospitals.

Reckford and Phelan, however, think Eliot used *xenia* in behalf of a "romantic" view of marriage derived from Heraclitus, in which spouses meet each day as interesting strangers.[25] And Phelan thinks Eliot was criticizing how the rootlessness of urban life corrupts the romance and pragmatism in an ideal marriage, while endorsing a "traditional" view in which spouses remain mysterious within established gender roles—as when the Chamberlaynes anticipate life in the country after their last party (where they can presumably be romantic and fertile). There is some truth in this. But there is a stronger sense in which the play's vision is not romantic. It was Schleiermacher who thought that we aim "to understand an utterance at first as well as and then better than its author."[26] This is what Amanda, Elyot, Lavinia, and Edward first assume, and Celia as well—but Eliot means to turn this assumption around. The only way we *can* understand one another is as guests and hosts, which requires another view of understanding: as a risky, even hyperbolic receptivity toward difference, irreducible to forms of sameness.[27]

Hospitality, then, is a *via negativa* of living and knowing: not only a way of martyrdom and mysticism, but a way of comprehending the ordinary. Knowledge of others comes under its purview, and knowledge of self. If we are "friends to ourselves," then we are also "strangers to ourselves"—a phrase from Julia Kristeva[28] for a condition Eliot would assess as part of being a finite creature; to be a "stranger" to oneself is part of what we are given to be, and thus is "good." Our "cure" must start with how we typically evaluate this strangeness as bad, and then prepare us for a new valuation. Thus, Reilly takes advantage of Edward's desire for "intimate disclosure to a stranger" (30); but he tells Edward not to rehearse his childhood, or produce dreams to analyze, nor even take overt action, but simply—like the Women of Canterbury—"do nothing. Wait." To Edward's fear this will make him seem ridiculous, Reilly advises, "Resign yourself to the fool that you are" (31). Edward confides how now that she has left, he can no longer picture Lavinia, as if he could not recollect her face. "And yet I want to get her back. . . . I must find out who she is, to find out who I am" (32). Edward is partly right and partly wrong, depending on what he means by "knowing."

If comprehensive hospitality does illuminate an intention of the play, we may still ask if this intention "works" theatrically. Eliot's text sometimes reflects the anti-theatrical prejudice that playing parts is imprisoning, as when Edward accuses Lavinia of forcing him into a pattern of bad faith. "You're still trying to invent a personality for me/Which will only keep me away from myself" (98). However, the discovery that he wants her back comes through impromptu theater, in which Reilly and the other Guardians are arranging entrances and encounters.

Those who berate Eliot for misconceiving psychiatry here miss the point: Reilly is a "doctor" but is never called a psychiatrist, and he intervenes in very un-psychoanalytic ways. In Act II he is more a Virgilian guide or Prospero figure.[29] With Julia and Alex he secretly arranges morality-as-hospitality plays for his patients, to alter their conditions in life. He will "remain the stranger," he tells Edward. "But . . . to approach the stranger/Is to invite the unexpected, release a new force. . . . It is to start a train of events/Beyond your control" (28), and also beyond Reilly's control. He confesses to Julia the risks involved in the choices he places before his patients, and Julia agrees: the Chamberlaynes "are stripped naked to their souls/And can choose, whether to put on proper costumes/Or huddle quickly into new disguises." As for patients like Celia, she asks, "what do we know/Of the kind of suffering they must undergo/On the way of illumination?" "You must accept your limitations," Julia tells Reilly (147, 148).[30]

Act III has a rhythm of *interruptions*,[31] which are both a challenge and an invitation to hospitality. For the act to work, this structure must remain apparent until the last resolving lines. It begins with Lavinia instructing the caterer. Edward interrupts by coming home early, worried she may be fatigued, and he compliments her dress. Their preparations are interrupted by the early arrivals of Julia and three uninvited guests she has "invited": Alex, Peter, and then Reilly. Celia should arrive next, and does not. So Alex's odd report of her death—he interrupts his own anecdote about monkeys, Christians, and cannibals—is an interruption of interruptions. Peter is devastated; after he leaves, Reilly reveals other aspects of Celia's death. And after he, Julia, and Alex depart, the Chamberlaynes are alone again, awaiting other guests.

This shape—expectation, interruption, expectation—must contribute to how the "party" is to be received as a metaphor for the *first* of the "two ways." The Chamberlaynes have over the last year become prudently extravagant. They have sent too many invitations, and more guests are coming than expected. One cannot simply give two parties, Lavinia explains, for everyone will think the other party is "more important" (155). The caterer is offering more food than the Gunnings, the rival party on this particular evening. As in Act I, the early guests—Julia, Alex, and Reilly—temporarily become hosts. So there is something profligate and kenotic about this party, and the Chamberlaynes now even have a Cowardesque humor about themselves.

EDWARD: I'm in good time, I think. I hope you've not been
     worrying.
LAVINIA: Oh no. I did in fact ring up your chambers,
     And your clerk told me you had already left.
     But all I rang up for was to reassure you …
EDWARD (*smiling*): That you hadn't run away?

LAVINIA: Now Edward, that's unfair!
     You know that we've given *several* parties
     In the last two years. And I've attended *all* of them. (154)

The Chamberlaynes have also begun to imitate the Guardians, as when they listen to Peter (Lavinia's former lover, we must remember) admitting he had been sustained by hope for Celia. He is a screenwriter, and while working in America, has hoped his success would win her into his life. Lavinia's reply sounds like Reilly, "What you've been living on is an image of Celia/Which you made for yourself, to meet your own needs" (178). Lavinia and Edward are on the verge of becoming Guardians, "Good Samaritans" (56), even "chamberlains."

However, with Alex's news Edward and Lavinia see themselves as responsible for Celia's death. Reilly's controversial judgment that her death was "triumphant" occurs during reflections on responsibility. Edward believes he himself has to be more responsible than "a band of half-crazed savages" (185).[32] But Reilly observes how none can bear judgment on all the unintended consequences of one's actions. "I often have to make a decision/Which may mean restoration or ruin to a patient—And sometimes I have made the wrong decision." Rather than blaming themselves, or thinking Celia's life was a waste, they should see it as a "triumph." "But I am no more responsible for the triumph—/And just as responsible for her death as you are" (186). Given this pattern of infinite and impossible responsibility,[33] the aptness of hospitality is again evident. Celia's "transhumanised" life among natives (147) is on a continuum with Edward's and Lavinia's lives: they are all playing as guests and hosts, as friends and strangers.[34]

Once all the Guardians leave, there should be a pause, perhaps uncomfortably long. Then Lavinia turns and asks Edward how she is looking. This introduces the last moment of the play, where the idea of "cocktail parties" is now required to carry sacramental and ethical meanings. Perhaps each light line could be played "on edge," to signal a heavier semantic load. Edward thinks she looks good, "I might almost say, your best. But you always look your best"—which echoes "the best of a bad job," a phrase they have forgotten, as Reilly predicted they would. She warns that no woman can believe that; "What you should have done was admire my dress."

EDWARD: But I've already told you how much I like it.
LAVINIA: But so much has happened since then. And besides,

> One sometimes likes to hear the same compliment twice.
> (189–90)

So much *has* happened since then. The flippancy of the last pages must be transmuted, to convey how much has changed since Alex arrived with his news. Earlier, Lavinia hints she has fatigue about this last party— "The best moment is the moment it's over" (157). Whereas now:

EDWARD: And now for the party.
LAVINIA: Now for the party.
EDWARD: It will soon be over.
LAVINIA: I wish it would begin.
EDWARD: There's the doorbell.
LAVINIA: Oh, I'm glad. It's begun. (190)

The business about Lavinia being tired yet looking fine in her dress prompted Eliot later to make another unscripted revelation, that Lavinia is pregnant; and in 1986, director John Dexter made sure her round tummy was noticeable on Edward's lines, "It's you who should be tired" (154) and "And you do need your rest now" (158).[35] This fertility would be important, obviously, and relates to the kenosis and hospitality we give to children we "breed" but never understand. It would also make the Chamberlaynes' eagerness to move to their "remote" summerhouse (158) seem less like private lives. The difficulty will be to shape the sentiment erupting from the audience when Lavinia enters with a prosthetic womb under her costume. Will it enhance or overshadow how hospitality has become the form of their mutual and limited understanding and of their love?

And will hospitality help reconceptualize the imagery of sacrifice associated with Celia? Perhaps, though not in a way that removes the difficulties, which are undeniably there. Christ's *suffering*—which for Eliot's Thomas connotes *acting* and *patience*—can be imagined as the *emptiness* of his body, his *host* wherein there would be room for strangers, friends, and enemies to be as hosts to one another. The logic of hospitality is one of contingency and excess. It is a generalizing concept, though its particularity in practice resists its generality; yet its excessive generality also resists the limits of particularity. There is the contingency that *these* guests may meet *these* hosts at *this* time in *this* place. There is also the excess that a bad guest or a bad host will need even more hospitality, and still more, which only few of us will be prepared to give. But the logic of hospitable excess also accompanies ordinary hospitality, where guests know when to leave, and good Samaritans pay their innkeepers, but still part company with "standing invitations" to return. So the way of the saint and the way of ordinary hospitality are both hospitable ways, and are patterns of kenosis and integrity. As for the saint's way, Celia's death would be a contingent rather than necessary part of "the design." Reilly says,

> I did not know that she would die in this way;
> *She* did not know. So all that I could do
> Was to direct her in the way of preparation.
> That way, which she accepted, led to this death.
> And if that is not a happy death, what death is happy? (183–84)

At other times we might imagine, Celia with her ensemble of lonely nurses must have enjoyed or delighted in the people she served. And perhaps on "some enchanted evening"—to be flippant about it—a stranger may yet ring the doorbell of the Chamberlaynes or the Chases and identify those unlikely couples as Guardians, even Samaritans on dangerous roads.

Chapter XII

Who Will Be My Neighbor?

Ethical Encounters and Moral Space in Caryl Churchill and Tony Kushner

HOSKINS: He's our fellow creature, and you're our fellow creature.
CLAXTON: You're God, you, you're God, no one's more God than you
if you could know it yourself, you're lovely, you're perfect—
BROTHERTON: No, I'm nobody's fellow creature.

> —CARYL CHURCHILL, *Light Shining in Buckinghamshire*

I've thought about it for a very long time, and I still don't understand
what love is. Justice is simple. Democracy is simple. Those things are
unambivalent. But love is very hard. And it goes bad for you if you
violate the hard law of love.

> —BELIZE, IN TONY KUSHNER, *Angels in America*

I suppose one would like something combustible at a party, something
catalytic, some fizz, each element triggering transformation in all
the other elements till all elements, which is to say, *guests,* are …
surprising to themselves and return home feeling less … less certain of
… those certainties which … *Because* of which, for example, powerful
antidepressants are consumed.

> —HOMEBODY, IN TONY KUSHNER, *Homebody/Kabul*

KENOTIC PATTERNS OF INTEGRITY *include relations with moral norms and
principles, which may be reconfigured and reinterpreted, critically and
self-critically.*

Kenotic integrity is ethically receptive of other persons and other crea-
tures, and is directed toward the interplay of persons with society and
nature, polis and cosmos.

These next two traits are occasions to ask how the moral and the ethical
are reconfigured in patterns of kenotic integrity. Recall that Ricoeur locates "the moral" in the larger context of "ethical" dialogue, witness, and
testimony in communities, where moral principles and personal relations
come together by way of wise, discerning practices. This view of practical wisdom is mutually kenotic. There is an implication that for Ricoeur
the moral *flows from and returns to* the ethical; this flow requires performance and improvisation, comparable to the practices of storytellers,
poets, and players. And while, for such practices, *eudaimonia*—happiness
or human flourishing—is possible, the realities of moral, personal, and
social conflict remain. With plays by Caryl Churchill and Tony Kushner,
I now want to ask, *how does the moral undergo kenosis in the midst of*
performances?

Three possibilities may be anticipated. First, moral principles are
configured in language, in hermeneutical and practical *encounters*. That
they are encountered means they may be reinterpreted or refused. Principles do not determine encounters; encounters contextualize principles.
Principles can guide or test practices but finally empty back into ethical
life together.

Second, moral norms and obligations can be like *roles or parts* one
bodily inhabits (as with Becket) or fails to inhabit (Elesin Oba). Theater
depicting moral dramas of integrity may implicitly invite the audience to
participate in the drama, as in Eliot, or ask the audience to question its
manner of participation, as in Brecht and Suzan-Lori Parks.

Third, moral principles may, with other markers, *mark the perfor-*
mance space of kenotic emptying. Recall that to juxtapose things is to
realize a "gap." Here, the gap is made by the proximity of principles to
lives, circumstances, ideas, and histories. This proximity is what Charles
Taylor and William Schweiker call "moral space,"[1] which would be an
aspect of Ricoeur's ethical realm. Moral space can also be a space of kenosis, where persons and parts empty into each other. Does moral space
itself undergo kenosis? Does time undergo kenosis? Does moral space in
the past pour into the present—or does the future somehow empty into
the present? What becomes of individuals in the space and time of kenosis? That we (1) *encounter principles*, that we (2) *inhabit them as parts*,
and that we (3) *move in moral spaces they mark*, are possibilities to be

seen in the plays of this chapter. With *Light Shining in Buckinghamshire* (1976) I am most concerned with encounter. The moral parts the characters play are crushed and the spaces they create are lost, except where we now dwell and become their witness.

Others, All in All: *Light Shining in Buckinghamshire*

Caryl Churchill writes as a socialist and feminist, and as a socialist she might be leery of so-called moral dilemmas. The worry that, say, *doing justice* and *creating art* are incommensurate goods might seem just a bourgeois muddle, when art may expose structures of suffering and injustice. But insofar as Churchill is a feminist, she does not elide the personal dimensions of integrity, for it is *persons* who are being crushed. Even so, do these Levellers, Diggers, and Ranters encounter one another as faceless "fellow creatures," or as individual faces?

The play documents people in the English Civil War (1642–51) who tried to "turn the world upside down." After reading it, we may be impressed more by its political critique than its theatrical delight, with its remote allusions and extracts from the 1647 Putney Debates (where Oliver Cromwell defended property rights). A production note urges directors not to have the same actors play the same parts "each time they appear." Rather, we are to enjoy the impression of many lives, seeking new alignments of love and justice. By the 1960s and '70s, those lives seemed made for our time, given the Ranters' proto-communism and notions of spouse sharing, partly on the grounds that spouses were not property.[2] But Churchill was more interested in how the English radicals interpreted their defeat in both millenarian and materialist terms, and in how views of property and sovereignty affected the status of selves and bodies. Thus, the device of blurring identities, by having actors exchange parts, fits with Ranter ideas. When, in 1997, I saw *Light Shining* staged by Amy Ludwig and the Blue Star Performance Company in a church hall in Chicago, Churchill seemed right. What mattered was an encounter with many voices, as the players attempted to recreate a distant moral space that would overlap our own.

In 1649 it was a space demarcated by conflicts over the apportionment of property, sovereign authority, and food. Gerrard Winstanley led some two score Diggers to St. George's Hill in Surrey to plant parsnips, beans, and carrots. "Take notice," a player announces, "that England is not a free people till the poor that have no land have a free allowance to dig and labour in the commons" (34). They express exhilaration and hope. And then the hope is crushed,[3] as players report how they were beaten, imprisoned, and their crops ruined. At risk of oversimplification, one can imagine the story's political spectrum in terms of how the English tried to juxtapose principles of property and sovereignty with bodily integrity.

On the right were *Royalists* and *Presbyterian Puritans.* In feudal theory, noble vassals owned their bodies and held land; however, as everyone's land and body belonged to the Crown, none enjoyed bodily integrity, and even Charles I lost his head. The Puritans opposed this system, and in 1640 controlled Parliament. They reflected how money and property flowed into a growing middle class, but as Calvinists they also envisioned a theocracy where only "the saints" or God's elect had sovereignty. In the center were the *Independents,* led by Cromwell. More religiously tolerant than the Puritans but also more militaristic, they purged Parliament of the Presbyterians and executed Charles. However, they linked suffrage to land ownership and thus continued to link bodily integrity with property. As Henry Ireton says in the Putney Debates, "The law of God doth not give me property, nor the law of nature, but property is of human constitution. I have a property and this I shall enjoy" (31).

Farther left are several groups. The *Levellers* insisted they had fought for universal manhood suffrage and fair apportionment (one man, one vote). Believing that God is in all things, and that all males are sovereign, they implied that bodily ownership is divinely authorized in every person. England was to be a "gathered nation" around these egalitarian principles. The *Diggers* or "True Levellers" also detached integrity from property, and held that uncultivated land should be held in common; Winstanley came to oppose private property generally. The *Seekers* expected Christ to return soon and render moot institutional religion; thus, they rejected church, clergy, and scripture in favor of what the Spirit revealed within every person. Most were pacifists. Finally, the *Ranters* are documented about the time the Levellers were defeated by Cromwell (1649). Claxton believed any person may share his or her body with anyone else. Such a mystical, antinomian, and materialist vision of all being one in Christ in effect dissolved bodily integrity in the opposite way feudalism did. Claxton: "We won't know our own faces" (59).

Thus *Light Shining in Buckinghamshire*[4] records the emergence of the radicals, then their dissolution by the Independents. In a sequence of scenes we see one woman persuade another, whose breasts are dry, to leave her infant at the mayor's doorstep. Then we witness a butcher face his wealthier customers: "Two rabbits, madam, is two shillings, thank you. And sir? A capon? Was yesterday's veal good? Was it? Good. Tender was it? Juicy? Plenty of it? Fill your belly did it? Fill your belly?" His cadence grows menacing—"You don't look as if you need a dinner. You look less like a man who needs a dinner than anyone I've ever seen"—then crescendos, "You've had your meat. You've had their meat. You've had their meat that can't buy any meat. You've stolen their meat. . . . You cram yourselves with their children's meat. You cram yourselves with their dead children" (45–46). His critique resembles that of Teiresias in *Antigone:* injustice done to the dead (denying them burial or cremation) or to the living (effectively starving them) amounts to a kind of cannibalism.

The Butcher and others are attempting to improvise moral roles in a social drama. In the scene "Cobbe Prays," a young man prays damnation on his Calvinist father, who ignores the poor near his property; he asks how he can receive a patriarchal blessing at the abundant family table, with "myself eating so quietly when what is going outside our gate?" (2). Later, "Two Women Look in a Mirror." They have been looting a manor house, find a mirror, and are pleased by how it can let you "see your whole body at once. . . . They [the owners] must know what they look like all the time. And now we do" (22). The women see themselves for the first time, but their discovery is ambiguous. Will they become trapped in a reflection of ownership, as do the Independents? Will they, in their reflections, become "the same" as others, or "other" than others? If they are the two women whom we later see adrift and starving, the question is moot: their new roles and new space will soon disappear.

What keeps *Light Shining* from being only about "crushing" are the eschatological and kenotic dimensions of Ranter ideology. Churchill employs Walt Whitman's "Song of the Open Road" to signal a creative moment in the audience's past that is realized in the radicals' future, "I will scatter myself among men and women as I go" (22). It was as if Whitman were emptying backward in time, into them, as when Cobbe is called to prophesy in London, or when the itinerant visionary, Jone [*sic*] Hoskins, is expelled from a congregation for answering back to a preacher, denying eternal damnation. She is rescued by Claxton, Captain of the Rant. His wife, however, is not pleased that he and Hoskins now believe in sharing spouses: anyone they are with, Hoskins says, "is Jesus Christ" (17). So Claxton takes to the open road, "gives" himself to many women, and becomes a visionary, knowing he "was in the midst of something."

> I have come to think there is no sin but what man thinks is sin. So we can't be free of sin till we can commit it purely. . . . [A]nd still my heart

pounds and my mouth is dry and I rush on towards the infinite nothing that is God. (37)[5]

"Nothing" is apparently the sublime "all in all," the Body of Christ, the Kingdom of God to come, when all differentiation is subsumed in sacred space and time. We see another momentary realization of this future in the penultimate scene, called "Meeting," where a few women and men gather at a public house. They share food, argument, and a pantheistic sacrament ("God's in this apple. . . . There's a man eats God," 51). Claxton recalls being a Seeker, thinking "the third age was coming" when "everything shone." But all this was betrayed by Parliament and Cromwell's New Model Army.

> And then I saw even the Seekers were wrong. Because while I
> was waiting for God, he was here already. So God was first in
> the king. Then in parliament. Then in the army. And now he
> has left all government. And he shows himself naked. In us.
> BRIGGS: We were the army of saints.
> CLAXTON: Let it go. Move on. God moves so fast now.
> HOSKINS: I try to be sad with you but I can't. . . . Now is just a
> strange time between Antichrist going and Christ coming, . . .
> So what's it matter now if we've no work and no food or can't
> get parliament like we want? . . . Christ will be here in his body
> like a man and he'll be like a king only you can talk to him.
> And he's a spirit too and that's in us and it's getting stronger
> and stronger. And that's why you see men and women shining
> now, everything sparkles because God's not far above us like
> he used to be when preachers stood in the way. . . . (52–53)

They do not agree on everything. Briggs, a Leveller, no longer thinks Christ will come. A Drunk protests God should "get down below on to earth. Live in my cottage. Pay my rent. Look after my children, mind, they're hungry" (60–61). Margaret Brotherton, who steals food and once left her baby in a ditch, has suffered too much to easily join this communion; she is certain she is damned, and does not think it good to be a "fellow creature." In the end, they do persuade her to be touched and share food.

Insofar as each voice is heard and none silenced, the "Meeting" is like Jürgen Habermas's regulative, utopian future scene of unrestricted conversation.[6] When it ends, the players sing from Ecclesiastes 5:12. The a cappella voices I heard in Chicago were beautiful, but in Brechtian fashion, we were not allowed to depart on notes of justice and wisdom. In the last scene, "After," the roles they assumed and the moral space they created are scattered. Hoskins believed Christ had come but "we missed it. I don't see how." Cobbe was tried for blasphemy and changed his name. Brotherton continued to steal. The Drunk enjoyed the new king's giveaways of bread and booze. Briggs, thinking he might reduce the price of corn by consuming less of it, learned to eat grass; people passed by and gawked at him, standing in a field. Claxton fled to the Barbados. He hears of strife in the faraway world, but for now his "great desire is to see and say nothing" (61–62).

Are these particular voices or one voice? The historical Abiezer Coppe recanted ambiguously; he saw little sense in martyrdom. Laurence Clarkson drifted from the Anglicans to the Presbyterians, then to the Baptists and Seekers, before being accused of Ranting; he died a debtor in a London jail.[7] Emigrating to the Barbados and "saying nothing" are moments Churchill took not from his life but from one Joseph Salmon, another Ranter.[8] The risk is to lose the particular "face of the other" (Levinas) in the apocalypticism of "all in all."[9] "When all things are subjected to [God], then the Son himself will also be in subjection under him, so that God will be all in all" (1 Corinthians 15:28). When all is in all, are there persons in particular? Is being lost in the depth and abyss of a divine or humane All a consummation devoutly to be wished, or not? Would such self-emptying amount to altruistic suicide, as it might seem for Briggs? Has kenosis eclipsed integrity, or do we see a kenotic integrity that transcends, without abolishing the personal and the moral? Churchill's mode of scattering the players and their parts surely celebrates kenotic integrity; yet it implicitly asks whether the theory and praxis of the radicals also put at risk the integrity of individual faces.

Emptying into Parts in a Morality Play: *Angels in America*

Tony Kushner also writes as a socialist and a gender activist, and if innovative roles are crushed in *Light Shining,* they are more effective occasions of political and personal change in *Millennium Approaches* and *Perestroika.* But at an academic panel in 2005, a sense of historical distance was noted between the 2004 HBO production and the years when the plays were first performed. Government silence about AIDS had ended. HIV was medically manageable in affluent societies. And Kushner's "Gay Fantasia on National Themes" could now seem "quaint" or "touching," even as the disease grew as a global threat. *Perestroika*'s last, metatheatrical lines also struck Kent Brintnall as "liturgical,"[10] when Prior Walter speaks to us from the Bethesda fountain in Central Park, by the statue of an angel of healing:

> The fountain's not flowing now, they turn it off in the winter, ice in the pipes. But in the summer it's a sight to see. I want to be around to see it. I plan to be. I hope to be.
> This disease will be the end of many of us, but not nearly all, and the dead will be commemorated and will struggle on with the living, and we are not going away. We won't die secret deaths any more. The world only spins forward. We will be citizens. The time has come. (II: 146)

He bids farewell—"Bye now./You are fabulous creatures, each and everyone"—dismissing us with Harold Bloom's translation of the Hebrew for *blessing*.[11] "*More Life*. The Great Work Begins." This benediction, Mark Edmundson had written a few years earlier, is "worthy of Tiny Tim."[12]

Angels in America is nothing if not a morality play. It celebrates the migratory desires of Mormons and European Jews, and seeks to transform moral space during an epidemic attacking intimacy and nonconformity. To judge it kitsch will likely irritate its fans, so Edmundson may have a point.[13] But if *Perestroika* earns its ending, it may be because in 1993, the HIV-inflicted were likely to be on both sides of the stage. Prior's blessing invited us to align ourselves with a future of progressive citizenship being realized at that moment in the theater. That bit of dialogue is set in 1990. Prior has survived for five years and has seen the Berlin Wall come down and the cold war end. Belize, Hannah, and Louis, who have been rather incommensurate persons, now enjoy political repartee. Prior interrupts them to speak to us directly. Phrases like "Bye now" and "You are fabulous creatures" seem part of an argot of gay communities, so it is arguable that the kitsch does not want us to forget or screen off—as Milan Kundera thinks kitsch does[14]—the disease, grief, guilt, and humor we have followed for six hours, but to *resist* the equation "Silence = Death." I want to focus not on the main stories—Louis's abandoning Prior, or Joe Pitt's affair with Louis, or Louis's involvement with Roy Cohn, or the post-"prelapsarian" Soviet mythology, or the reactionary Angels—except as they bear on three other characters: Hannah Pitt (Joe's widowed, Mormon mother), Belize (a black AIDS nurse, former drag queen), and Harper (Joe's Valium-addicted wife, who must deal with his self-loathing admission he is gay).

Hannah

The Mormons in *Angels* are counterparts to European Jews: both groups crossed the Atlantic or the continent, undergoing storied hardships, changing while resisting assimilation. While *Angels* obviously associates Jews with progressives and Mormons with conservatives, both are criticized for their intolerances, both provide some fun (the Mormon Visitors Center diorama and old Rabbi Isidor Chemelwitz, played by the actor playing Hannah), and both are implicitly celebrated for being "migratory." Even the Mormon diorama is taken seriously, when the wax Mother on the Conestoga wagon comes to life and says how people change:

> God splits the skin with a jagged thumbnail from throat to belly . . . and pulls till all your innards are yanked out and the pain! We can't even talk about that. And then he stuffs them back, dirty, tangled and torn. It's up to you to do the stitching.
> HARPER: And then get up. And walk around.
> MORMON MOTHER: Just mangled guts pretending.
> HARPER: That's how people change. (II: 77–78)

You change by pretending, but the pretending is real. After learning her son Joe is gay and Harper is missing, Hannah migrates from Salt Lake City to New York, and arrives at night in the snow, lost in the Bronx and looking for Brooklyn. There is no one to turn to for help but a psychotic bag lady, who slurps soup and talks to herself accusingly: "Feeding yourself, just feeding yourself, what would it matter, to you or to ANYONE, if you just stopped. Feeding. And DIED?" (I: 104). Most would hasten to another sidewalk, but Hannah listens, gathers up all her maternal authority, and demands directions to the Mormon Visitors Center. Her question snaps the woman's mind into clarity: "65th. and Broadway. . . . Go there all the time. Free movies. Boring but you can stay all day" (I: 105). Hannah makes a connection, recreating her moral role.

She responds similarly to Walter, whom she instructs on the nature of angels: they are "real" constructions of desire, belief, and prayer. "An angel is just a belief, with wings and arms that can carry you. It's naught to be afraid of. If it lets you down, reject it. Seek for something new" (II: 103). Hannah confirms, in her way, Belize's diagnosis, that the Angel is Prior's projection of a desire to stop the awful spiral of death and betrayal. In short, Hannah accepts a prophetic role that is role-transcending. She is probably lesbian, and is blessed by the departing, hermaphroditic Angel with an orgasm. Hers is one of the play's connecting figures, linking the Prior story, the Harper/Joe story, and the Angelic story. She is the better angel, and it seems Mormonism has well prepared her for "intermingling." If *Angels* is engaged in moral outreach, then Hannah also recapitulates connections among the gay, straight, religious, and secular strata of the audience.

Belize

If Hannah is moving toward the moral center of *Angels,* Belize is that center. After the flamboyant funeral of a "Great Glitter Queen," he pronounces: "Trailing sequins and incense he came into the world, trailing sequins and incense he departed it. And good for him!" (II: 33–34). Belize signals how *Angels* employs metatheatricality to serve ethical innovation, against roles imposed by illness, society, and ideology. Inasmuch as the villain Roy Cohn is also a histrionic self-fashioner, we must locate versions of "the good" in such self-fashioning, and Belize gives the clearest voice to the play's constellation of norms.

Belize redirects Prior Walter's false prophetic summons. If the "reactionary" call of the Angel is Prior's despairing projection of illness and abandonment (the Angelic message to humanity is, "You must stop moving!"),[15] then Belize's summons to him is genuinely other: "The world doesn't spin backward. Listen to the world, how fast it goes" (II: 47). We could also say that illness has narrowed Prior's conscience, made it "bad," in that the Angel brings him close to internalizing a maxim of evil. So Belize and later Hannah recall him to conscience and make him receptive to love, justice, and change, which animates his closing summons to us at the Bethesda fountain.[16]

Similarly with Louis: if we usually construe justice as "hard," and love as "soft," then Belize unsettles that dichotomy ("it goes bad for you if you violate the hard law of love"). Louis's inability to connect actual love with socialist "theory and praxis" is also identified by the Rabbi, who answers Louis's confessing question ("what does the Holy Writ say about someone who abandons someone he loves in a time of great need?") with a question of judgment, "Why should a person do such a thing? . . . The Holy Scriptures have nothing to say about such a person" (I: 25). The Rabbi also reminds him, "Catholics believe in forgiveness. Jews believe in guilt."

Belize, however, urges Louis to be receptive to forgiveness: to the "smell" (and in *Angels* smell, as in sex, mediates material kenosis, as the molecules of others empty into our passions, II: 30) of "Softness, compliance, forgiveness, grace" (I: 100). Much later, Belize recruits an incredulous Louis to say Kaddish over the warm body of dead Roy Cohn:

> He was a terrible person. He died a hard death. So maybe.... A queen can forgive her vanquished foe. It isn't easy, it doesn't count if it's easy, it's the hardest thing. Forgiveness. Which is maybe where love and justice finally meet. Peace, at least. Isn't that what the Kaddish asks for? (II: 122)

Belize's paradigm—that forgiveness meets justice and love—is not contradicted by his claim not to "understand" love. Nor by Roy's gleeful delusion he has tricked the ghost of Ethel Rosenberg into singing a lullaby for him. Nor by how Louis, until prompted by "Ethel," confuses the Kaddish with the Kiddush, the blessing over wine. Nor by Ethel's ending Roy's Kaddish with "V'imru omain . . . You sonofabitch" (II: 123). Forgiveness, comments Mary-Jane Rubinstein, is something "impossible." If only the *unforgivable* really need forgiveness (but, then, can they be *forgiven?*), then forgiveness must resist theoretical explanation and be practiced with its meanings suspended, under "erasure" (Derrida).[17] Forgiveness perhaps can be practiced as an *interrupting* of static roles of hostility, and Belize personifies such a practice. He also creates kenotic parts for others. Even Roy gives him a bottle of AZT, the new drug Belize suggested he use his clout to procure, to avoid double-blind experiments; upon his death, Belize steals the whole stash, saving Walter's life.

Harper

The only major figure Belize never meets is Harper, but the actor playing Belize also plays Mr. Lies, her hallucination from the National Organization of Travel Agents. And Harper meets Prior in a mutual dream, on the "threshold of revelation." She tells him, "Deep inside you, there's part of you, the most inner part, entirely free of disease" (I: 34). As Prior and Harper have not yet met, their encounter reflects an ontological desire for fusion, for a nonlocal mingling of consciousnesses and molecules.

Her ontology is opposite that of Roy—who sees the cosmos "as a kind of cosmic sandstorm in outer space [blowing] shards and splinters of glass" (I: 13)—and is also opposite that of the Angels. They have determined that God has abandoned Heaven, having thrown everything off the rails by creating humanity. Hence, the apparatchiks of Heaven want all movement and intermingling to cease. Harper's Valium puts her on a search for a better cosmos.

Her part-in-life has been stereotypical, a dull Mad Housewife. It is bad news enough to be trapped in a patriarchy; but to expect children from a husband who denies he's a "homo" has put her into paranoid, aimless dread. Except for her encounters with wax dummies in the Visitors Center, she is unreceptive to theatricality. When Joe pleads he has always struggled to keep his behavior "Decent. Correct. That alone in the eyes of God"—she rounds on him, "that's Utah talk, Mormon talk, I hate it, Joe . . ." (I: 40). Joe might have admitted, with Anouilh's Becket, that there is a "gap" in him, which outward vocational integrity (his second skin, signaled by his Mormon undergarment) might fill. But neither Kushner nor Harper can see much good in that. Our inner gaps must open outward; the outward must transform the inward. "Mormon talk" on Joe's lips is not transformed or transforming, as it might be for Hannah, but merely a lie, which he appears never to overcome.

Whether or not the weakest persona in *Angels,* Harper's attenuation makes her pliable and open to horizons made available by her inner travel agent. She wants to visit Antarctica and fix the hole in the ozone layer. Yes, this is crazy (she wanders snowy Brooklyn, "meets" an Eskimo and chews on evergreen trees, both rather unknown in Antarctica) but is also part of a liminality in which she can articulate a desire for *tikkun olam,* the mending of the world. At the end she does not join others at the fountain but has an epiphany on a jet across America under moonlight. Near the "ragged and torn" rim of ozone, on the threshold of revelation, "Souls were rising . . ."

> souls of the dead, of people who had perished, from famine, from war, from the plague, and they floated up, like skydivers in reverse, limbs all akimbo, wheeling and spinning. And the souls of these departed joined hands, clasped ankles and formed a web, a great net of souls, and the souls were three-atom oxygen molecules, of the stuff of ozone, and the outer rim absorbed them, and was repaired. (II: 141–42)

Harper also tells us, "Nothing's lost forever. In this world, there is a kind of painful progress, longing for what we've left behind, and dreaming ahead." Her vision of the dead rising to mend the ozone is ethically kenotic, while her faith in progress is susceptible to the kitsch critique. But if in *Light Shining* the good parts that people attempt to innovate in life are crushed, then in *Angels* those parts can be miraculously efficacious. In a morality play, parts can be both realistic and occasions of transcendence, much to the extent they are metatheatrical; for the audience is to locate itself *among* these parts, or even *in* these parts. Our ride with Harper beneath the ozone layer anticipates Kushner's invitation to follow the Homebody's migration to Kabul.

"It's Nice to Go Trav'ling": *Homebody/Kabul*

This lyric by Sammy Kahn could be a mantra for Tony Kushner. It says we can meet others in the world, while meeting ourselves, with all the risk and promise such meetings entail. To be sure, it is not always morally safe to go "traveling," not with that word's connotations of affluence, exoticism, even narcissism. It would be nice if theory and praxis could align, mark the way, and keep us in the roles of good neighbors. It would have been good if after the cold war a better millennium had approached. Past our own "culpable shores," there is simply too much to map, and so we lose ourselves, one way or the other, beyond the outer limits of moral space.

As its title implies, *Homebody/Kabul* is almost two plays that empty into each other. It begins with an hour-long monologue. An English lady, ensconced with antidepressants and secondhand, forgotten volumes, is reading to us from a guidebook. By the end of her discourse, she is ready to travel. We want to see her again; we never do. Then two people, apparently her husband and daughter, are in Kabul, Afghanistan, looking for her body. She has been reported slain, her body lost from the morgue; they never find it. The play may be perceived as a palimpsest, each side of the leaf bleeding into the other while remaining distinct. The monologue also has multiple layers bleeding into each other. One layer is the Homebody's declamation of adapted passages from Nancy Hatch Dupree's 1965 guidebook to Kabul.[18] A second motif recalls an Afghan man who sells hats and potpourri in a tiny London shop, which to her eye is an exotic portal to other worlds. She buys the unusual hats as favors for a party for her husband, an information technologist who has been promoted. But she notices the clean, diagonal edge of sliced-off fingers on the Afghan's hand, and imagines making love to him in Kabul. A third layer is her self-interrupting and other-interrupted stream of commentary. Through these layers of words, I suggest, she is moving from *narcissism* to *moral gnosis,* and from gnosis toward *ethical kenosis,* and the whole play reiterates this trajectory.

One possibility is that the trajectory is an allegory of a kenosis in which the self is utterly lost. This motion might be *tzimtzum,* the kabbalistic teaching that God, to make room for others and for freedom, contracts or withdraws, not unlike the lament of the *Angels in America.* To imitate divine love, should we not also disappear, to make room for others to be? Is that an implication of the Homebody's story? Another is that she has not disappeared. In any case, consider the first lines:

> "Our story begins at the very dawn of history, circa 3,000
> B.C...."
> (*Interrupting herself:*)
> I am reading from an outdated guidebook about the city of
> Kabul. In Afghanistan. In the valleys of the Hindu Kush
> mountains. A guidebook to a city which as we all know, has
> ... undergone change.
>   My reading, my research is moth-like. Impassioned, fluttery, doomed. A subject strikes my fancy. . . . (9)

These first-person pronouns, often possessive—"my reading," "as we know, "my fancy"—signal the narcissism she later acknowledges. Her interruptions, however, are not all projections. Sometimes "a subject," or bit of knowledge "strikes" her fancy. She is struck by "antilegomenoi," "castoff or forgotten knowledge" (18), or else by a person, "a subject." These interruptions lend credence to her flippant yet weighty assertion, "I love the world." If hermeneutical understanding is narcissism-risking-alterity, then the Homebody is a hermeneut par excellence. But is she alive or dead?

Kushner's play was, in part, occasioned by a local apocalypse,[19] namely the 1998 bombing of Khost, Afghanistan, ordered by Bill Clinton on the hunt for embassy bomber Osama bin Laden. How would the play have played if the line "the Taliban . . . they're coming to New York!" (83) had not been "eerily prescient" (a reviewer's phrase that bemused Kushner)?[20] Would it have been greeted as a fable of "orientalism," of the ways the West projects into the mirror of another culture and mistakes the returning reflection as knowledge of the other?[21] But after September 2001, *Homebody/Kabul* could only be seen in the glare of that encounter. Even so, the realism of the *Kabul* scenes is not as coherent as the themes of the *Homebody* monologue, assuming her performance can be as mesmerizing as Linda Emond's in both New York productions of late 2001 and 2004.

The Kabul story is a concoction of intrigues. Mrs. Ceiling, the Homebody, is reported killed by ruffians in Kabul. Perhaps she was caught outside without a burqa; or perhaps, as a westerner, she sparked rage after Clinton's attack. Her husband, Milton Ceiling, and daughter, Priscilla, listen to a horrible autopsy report and meet a seedy, sex-starved British official named Quango Twistleton (shades of Graham Greene and P. G. Wodehouse). Milton stays in his hotel smoking opium and telling Quango bad family secrets. But Priscilla searches the hospitals of Kabul, suspecting her mother may be alive after all. She is helped by a trusty native guide, Khwaja Mondanabosh, who claims to write poetry in Esperanto; he persuades her to carry his poems to London. She also meets the multilingual Pashtun librarian, Mahala, who wants help emigrating to England. Priscilla learns that for Mahala to cross the Khyber Pass (shades of Kipling), she will need British promissory papers (*Casablanca*'s letters of transit). Only Quango can provide these, and he offers to deliver them in exchange for sex with Priscilla who abruptly agrees, perhaps out of anger at her father.

Are we peering into puzzles within puzzles? Is Mrs. Ceiling dead, or has she converted to Islam, married an Afghan physician, while refusing now to see her daughter? This mystery is kept unresolved.[22] Does Khwaja really write Esperanto poetry? If so, do the poems conceal messages for London allies of the Northern Alliance? Is the scary mullah a spy among the Taliban, who facilitates Mahala's escape across the Khyber border? And if Mrs. Ceiling was murdered, did she die at the legendary grave of Cain near the spring, Cheshme Khedr, which Priscilla finds marked in her mother's guidebook? The stereotypicality of these plot devices is possibly the point; for while outraged by Taliban rule, Kushner means for us to see the effects of foreign entanglements and abandonments in Afghanistan. The issue is what normative perspective to bring to bear, given the disasters wrought by capitalists, Soviets, and fundamentalists. Kushner again offers the paradoxes of *hospitality* and *forgiveness,* norms seemingly more suited to person-space than nation-space.

As for hospitality: In the "Afterword" to *Homebody/Kabul,* Kushner recounts a tradition that Kabul was the one place in Cain's wanderings that did not reject him. Cain and Kabul met as guest and host, as if hearing the command "Do not kill." But their meeting meant that Kabul would forever be a strange attractor to chaos and killing. Kushner quotes a speech from an early draft: "But still it was a great mistake. Letting him stop here, burying him here. . . . They should have driven him away." Cain and Kabul make for a mix of violence and beauty so primordial that God should repent of it, and of this Kushner cites the Talmud: "Repentance preceded the world" (149).[23] In 2001, there was a primordial aura about Cain's grave, created by the Sufi hermit, or Marabout, who guards it. In 2003, the grave remained but the hermit was gone (at the Chicago Steppenwolf Theatre production, reflected in the revised edition). This made the scene easier to follow and gave more space for Priscilla and Khwaja; but no figure impresses holiness on the site, nor does Khwaja's short explanation of Cain and Kabul. True, that a mystic would guard a grave in a minefield is unlikely. And that his speeches had to be translated by Khwaja made it all too confusing, perhaps orientalist. Also, the revised scene is aguably more honest, for Cain is buried at Cheshme Khedr mainly in Kushner's imagination, and Khwaja professes to be uncertain about the grave.[24] Yet the Sufi had added a dimension now missing; and at Steppenwolf the scene seemed too cozy. Still, the structure of hospitality-and-hostility so crucial to *Homebody/Kabul* was preserved.

As for forgiveness: In the revision, Priscilla's anger about maternal neglect lessens. Originally, at the gravesite the Marabout implies that he sees Mrs. Ceiling's ghost. He offers Priscilla a prayer rug. She does not pray but agitates about her mother's "forgotten words," which have begun to infect her own voice: "Cosmolatry. Idolatrous worship of the world. Cosmognosis . . . the secret knowledge an animal has, a bird for example, which teaches them when to migrate and where to go." She is bitterly glad to leave her Mother "here. In Afghanistan" (115). As revised, Priscilla comes to Chesme Khedre looking for a "sign" from her mother. Kneeling at the grave, she wishes her mother, if alive, would at least write. "Kabul has changed me," she says (2004, 112). Khwaja tells her that Mrs. Ceiling has also changed, is a Muslim now—"I am a poet, it is not possible that I lie" (2004, 116)—and delivers a message that he says is from her mother:

> [Y]ou have suffered and will suffer more yet, she fears, because your heart which is a loving heart is also pierced through. She now prays to Allah who forgives all who sincerely repent, to forgive her and through her penitential loneliness, to forgive her daughter as well.

So Priscilla has been forgiven by her mother, or by Allah, or by Khwaja imitating her own best idea of her mother, and Priscilla is astonished, hurt but no longer angry. "Tell her I said good-bye" (2004, 116). A muezzin's call to prayer is heard, and Priscilla accepts from Khwaja more "poems." One of them is about a garden, death, and an angel, who speaks a "mother tongue," the language we learn through alms, *zakat*, the Pillar of Islam commanding us to "spend of what we love. . . . We give to one who has not" (2004, 118).

As in *Angels in America*, the Homebody's monologue contemplates the paradoxes of hospitality, and perhaps of forgiveness (although that theme only became prominent in the *Kabul* revision)—in a time when the moral risks of purporting to understand "the other" are felt acutely. But the Homebody's trajectory, from narcissism to kenosis via gnosis, implies a relinquishment of moral qualms we should have about *knowing or understanding* the other. In these apocalyptic times, she wants to say, *we must run the risks of uncertain knowledge.* She doesn't much like the guests she has invited to her husband's party, but hopes the Afghan hats may catalyze them, make them "fizz," transform, and become less certain of their certainties. "A party needs hats" (14).

The qualms she seeks to traverse are indicated by thoughts on "magic" and "touching," metonyms for knowledge and relationship. The items in the Afghan shop were created by people who once believed in magic, "as I do not, as we do not." Magic is "some combination of piety, joy, ecstasy, industry, brought to bear on the proper raw materials," which releases power that can be "enlisted in beneficent ways toward beneficent ends" (10). Magic's mix of piety and industry bespeaks its source and *telos* in desires for *eudaimonia*, human flourishing. The Homebody is playing with paradoxes: magic (signifying relationship) works associatively, by touching; but magic is lost when touched, or critically observed. Yet in our disenchanted time, reality is what "must suffer to be *touched*." This could allude to positivism, or to the magic of quantum reality: until the quantum is observed or touched, it is a cloud of possibilities, and upon being touched it loses possibilities. In being touched, is something corrupted? Does it lose its integrity, or gain it?

> Ours is a time of connection; the private, and we must accept this, and it's a hard thing to accept, the private is *gone*. All must be touched. All touch corrupts. All must be corrupted. And if you're thinking how awful these sentiments are, you are perfectly correct, these are awful times, but you must remember as well that *this* has always been the chiefest characteristic of the Present. . . . The Present is *always* an awful place to be. (11)

The Homebody lives in a cloud of knowing and unknowing: "almost nothing is known about the Hephthalites. . . . Perhaps more is known now . . ." (18). "I know nothing of this [man's] hand, its history . . ." (21). She surrounds herself with odd knowledge, which is why I suggest she is moving through gnosis, beyond narcissism. Kierkegaard might deem her obsessions not as an ethical but rather an aesthetic mode of life, of the kind he termed "reflective immediacy."[25] But that the Homebody is driven not just to *know* but *touch* others is signaled by: (1) the metatheatrical way she tells us how "my borders have only ever been broached by books. Sad to say. . . . Except once, briefly. Which is I suppose the tale I'm telling. . . . You must be patient" (12–13). (2) By her purpose in buying hats, to make her guests "surprising to themselves" (15). And (3) by a simple, declarative sentence, which concludes her long rehearsal of Afghan history: "Well. // *(She closes the guidebook and puts it down)* // Afghanistan is one of the poorest countries in the world" (22).

By moral gnosis, I mean she is on the way but not yet kenotic. She knows that avoiding knowledge is as culpable as knowing, and tells how a friend hesitates on the phrase "might do."

> "Off to the cinema, care to come?" "Might do." "Would you eat a potato plucked from that soil?" "Might do." Jesus wants you hot or cold, but she will hedge her every bet, and why should she not? (24)

Her friend is inert, stuck between anticipation and action, and the Homebody regards inertia as culpable, malevolent. Before she teleports to Kabul—"'Would you make love to a stranger with a mutilated hand if the opportunity was offered you?' 'Might do'" (29)—her monologue becomes a screed, and her voice and the milliner's merge into the voice of Every-Afghan: those who were with and against the Mujahideen, those stealing and stolen from, those believing in God, or terror, or in God *and* terror, concluding, "*you will never understand . . .*" (24). This could lead to moral paralysis, but the Homebody will not be confined. She does "love the world," she must touch it, and she assures us her love is not (or not only) narcissistic. She will abandon the safety of her kitchen, her "culpable shore" (27) and "go trav'ling." She will recite from the Persian poet Sa'ib-I-Tabrizi about the "strangeness and beauty" of the gardens of Kabul. "I love her," she and the poet say, because "knowledge and love both come from her dust" (29, 30).[26]

And in Kabul she vanishes, either torn apart (*Kabul* begins with an autopsy report by Dr. Qari Shah) or else into a new, discontinuous life (married to Qari Shah). Her story approaches the limit of kenosis, emptying into infinite moral space and is lost, never to return. It is not enough to judge her as presumptuously Western or neurotic, it is not enough to call her irresponsible. Anyone who follows a call of infinite suffering or desire may look like that, seen from safe and culpable shores. We love her or despise her, but like Milton and Priscilla we want to see her onstage again.

Instead, we see Mahala. The mutuality we want in kenosis may not be the mutuality we get. Milton and Priscilla improbably risk their lives to help Mahala leave Afghanistan. Why should Milton do this? It is made plausible when he and Mahala share metaphors. He thinks she knows of John Dewey, a pragmatist for whom soul and mind are "conjoined," dual. She believes, rather, in the Dewey Decimal system, which sorts out confusion and is pretty much what Afghanistan—a place of chaotic conjunctions of tribes and ideologies—needs. He thinks the information bundles or "duals" that he sends down electronic pathways are like her library system. She inquires, "And you shall ... make machine making to banish confusion?" (127). So they are in love.

The last scene, "Periplum" (Ezra Pound's word for a "tour" that returns to its beginning), is too brief to sort out all the loose ends, but is poetic in its compression. We are back in London, but now it is Mahala sitting here. She is not a collector of odd knowledge but a cataloguer, a sorter-out of many modes of knowing. She loathes the Taliban because they "like the communists" imposed a single system, whereas "The Dewey Decimal System is the only such system." "It provides no remedy," objects Priscilla. "Only it provides knowing," she replies, "and nothing more" (139). Priscilla is still unsure her mother is dead, and "Periplum" declines to provide resolutions. Mahala does say that the Mullah was a Mujahideen comrade with her family against the Russians. So Priscilla poses two hard questions, which reprise the Sartrean "dirty hands" dilemmas that underlie the play: did the Mullah, perhaps to keep his cover (but perhaps not) kill the Esperanto guide? Apparently so. And what about her mother? All Mahala will say—about the guide, the Mullah, the Esperanto messages, and implicitly about her mother—is qualified by, "I am lying, you think."

> I loathe the Taliban, they are my own people but I loathe them. You think I have lied to help bring from Afghanistan the poetry of Mr. Mondanabosh, which are not hymns of peace in dream language of universal brotherhood but military information for the Northern Alliance. (137)

How does the lie bear on Priscilla? That the Taliban required her mother's death? That the Northern Alliance required her death? That no one required her death? "I am lying, you think." A statement, not a question. Its antecedent is unknown, but its unmarked questions reverberate. What Mahala may or may not know must "go without saying," as they say, like infinite responsibility.

She does say she is "becoming Muslim again" and reading the Qur'an in Arabic, whose beauty "is inexpressible" (136). She has also been examining the "strange" books in the Homebody's house and tending her neglected garden. "A garden shows us what may await us in Paradise. . . . The rains are so abundant./In the garden outside I have planted all my dead" (139). What might this mean, the play's final line? As do many Christians and Jews, Muslims look for a resurrection of the dead, meaning they would live today as expectant participants in a new creation. But the fruits of Mahala's kenotic emptying and receptivity, and now Priscilla's receptivity—the fruits of their planting and tending both the living and the dead—are uncertain, unknown. Like Priscilla, we in the audience may have hoped to see the Homebody return to the stage, sitting with her books and talking. We are faced, instead, with another, *other than* the one we desired or hoped. What returns may be *other others,* other than those we expected for ourselves.

Coda: Questions from the Future

It is noteworthy that for Levinas, ethical existence does not begin with the realization "I can kill." Perhaps higher predators have a vague awareness of "I" or "we" in the sense of "there is not room for both of us" or "I can . . . eat, kill, copulate, seek shelter, flee," et cetera. But does a stalking tiger notice a gazelle gesturing for forbearance? My humanity begins with my surprise at hearing the prey pray, "Do not kill me." There are reservations to be made about this primal scene. Perhaps its imperative makes for too one-sidedly moral a conception of the ethical. Moreover, it is not clear that a view of the *good* can be grounded in a scenario of primal violence, even though Levinas and Kushner attempt to traverse this scenario, when Kabul and Cain welcome each other. But I would juxtapose with it another scene of primal mutuality: we become ethical selves as we hear another's word, *"Here, look, what do you make of this?"*—gesturing to something other, a creature, a color, or as Caryl Churchill suggests even a mirror to be shared, but in any case, something to be *named*. Would the hospitality implied in such an early word be *as* originary as "Do not kill me"? That is the question, or a question.

Another question: If we agree with Levinas and Ricoeur about the priority of the ethical, then can we *be with the future* ethically—since any future is contingent and does not now exist? First, if we can even *imagine* a future saying to us now, "Don't kill us" or "Look at this," we would be encountering the future as Thou, as *something like a person*. But is not this imagining merely analogical? Perhaps, but the whole idea of a person is analogical: a person is a "world," a "horizon," a "nexus of relations." The question requires imagining future generations living and suffering; to get that far takes us to the *moral* imperative, which already places us in relations of obligation with the future. A broader, *ethical* relation requires something more *mutual*, a mode of perception that is imaginative and performative. We can imagine that they in the future are addressing us "now"—out of their suffering and delight—saying to us, "We understand you in urgency and delight, as you spoke to us, and wrote to us in urgency and delight."

Is this too sentimental, as when we express "gratitude" for prior generations? Are we not complacent to imagine futures speaking in gratitude to us? But such complacency is transformed as we reflect upon the *judgments we have made* on past generations. When, *on behalf* of unborn Diggers, or Native Americans and Africans who would have descended from those lost in an American genocide or the Middle Passage, we lend our voices, hearing them say *now:* Why did you abandon us *then*?[27] If we can imagine future generations saying, "Do not abandon us," can we also imagine them beckoning, "Here, look at this" or, "If only we could show you this cure, or this form of governance, or this poem"? Just as today we hermeneutically invest texts and expressive events with meanings, and thereby keep the past under construction, can we discern futures investing our works and relations with meanings, making us responsible anew?

Chapter XIII

Where Will Fragments Be Held?

King Lear, *Kristian Levring, Robert Lepage,* *and* A Midsummer Night's Dream

> My face I'll grime with filth,
> Blanket my loins, elf all my hair in knots
> And with presented nakedness outface
> The winds and persecutions of the sky.
>
> —EDGAR, IN *King Lear* II.2.180–83

> They began to say words. Words made them forget. For a while they went around and said words without talking to each other. Henry listened.
>
> —KANANA, IN *The King Is Alive*

> Are all people who have disappeared hiding behind mirrors?
>
> —YOUNG JANA, IN *The Seven Streams of the River Ota*

> Bless thee, Bottom, bless thee! Thou art translated. (III.1.114)
>
> —QUINCE, IN *A Midsummer Night's Dream*

INSOFAR AS WE *"find ourselves" in patterns of kenotic integrity, we may also find we are "losing ourselves," moving into expansive relations of continuity and discontinuity between who we have been and are yet to be. We meet the ultimate horizons of integrity in moments when we find ourselves "at-one" among historical and personal entanglements of joy and suffering, when we are emptied toward others, receptively.*

This last trait brings to kenotic integrity ideas of atonement, less in the sense of substitution and sacrifice than in the English etymology of "at-one-ment." Fragments come into proximity, become *at one,* but without fusion or merger. Lives and ideas are imperfectly held: acknowledged, celebrated, healed, or lamented. At first, atonement, like kenosis, can seem a neutral category; who would not want to be "at one" with their desires? But some figures of atonement do not trade on zero-sum economies of winning and losing power. Perhaps when little atonements become ambiguous, it is because they are not *sufficiently* atoning. The logic of atonement implies more atonement, much as the logic of love implies more love.

While the question of this chapter begins with "where?" questions of "who" remain in play. Who will hold our fragments, if we cannot hold our own? How can we hold others' fragments when we cannot hold ourselves? Can we hold ourselves and others by *playing-at, playing-for,* and *playing-with*? Who will pick up the fragments of selves we drop? Would any ontological structure or theological conviction give us confidence that others will appear for us, perhaps to complete us, this time or next time? The question "where" arises from metaphors of emptying and emptiness. As others empty into us, then into our emptiness others may enter.

In *Lear,* the "where" can be a wilderness beyond Gloucester's castle, or the dizzying space below Dover's cliffs. In *A Midsummer Night's Dream,* it can be the forest where love and spite skew, the hall where rustic players play, or the bedrooms the fairies bless. In *The King Is Alive,* it is a desert in Namibia. In *The Seven Streams of the River Ota,* it is an urn and a kimono. Theater, then, is a possible place of emptiness, kenosis, and atonement. Here some who are lost or separated meet, and some unable to "play" are transformed in the meeting, and so can play again. They find and lose themselves, receiving and giving patterns of integrity.

Late Eclipses

For Shakespeare, human fragmentation and suffering frequently suggest a microcosm. Nature is at odds with itself as we are at odds. In *King Lear* (1605)—a pagan story with biblical resonances—this correlation is signaled by Lear's screaming at the "cataracts and hurricanoes" pouring upon the heath, and earlier when the bastard Edmund defames his legitimate brother Edgar. Gloucester has been duped, but even so he states how a chaotic cosmos imports to the integrity of persons and communities. "These late eclipses in the sun and moon portend no good to us. . . .

Love cools, friendship falls off, brothers divide: in cities, mutinies; in countries, discord; in palaces, treason; and the bond cracked 'twixt son and father" (I.2.103–9). We may sympathize with Edmund as he privately scoffs at this, at reading one's troubles in the stars (118–33). He thinks he has been unjustly severed from his inheritance, when bastardy is but the product of Nature, his "goddess," to whom "My services are bound" (1–2). But in saying this, observes Max Harris, he aligns with "nothingness,"[1] and we are appalled as he contemplates murder and treason, which in a monarchical world leaves all persons bereft.

We have seen how questions of integrity point ambiguously to wholeness and rightness. The integrity we want to ascribe to people is a complex aligning of embodied persons with moral limits and expansive ethical possibilities. But the normative character of integrity is difficult to conceptualize without recourse to other paradigms. What paradigms suggest themselves—forms of love, education, romance, vocational practices, and kenotic self-emptying—are also freighted with problems and questions. So when is kenosis right? Why is kenosis good?

I have noted how the paradigm of kenosis is *conceptually* dangerous, if turned into a system that is coherent without remainder. To this danger my response is that when we juxtapose ideas, considered as fragments, without presuming to know their wholeness, we make contingent spaces for others to enter. Others may bring knowledge, narratives, symbols, or models that might meet our own.[2] The structure and mode of these chapters hopefully represent such meetings-for-thought. I have also noted that kenosis is *ethically* dangerous, if it rationalizes subservience: when castes, races, classes, genders, faiths, et cetera, are deemed "fit" only to serve. My first reply is that another's *suffering presence* (which may call for our response) may be entwined with another's *eliciting or delighting presence* (which may empower our responses). Second, we may decide that the risk of becoming "hostage" to suffering (Levinas) is a risk we may take.[3] We may sometimes find ourselves utterly emptied in encounters with others, as in *King Lear*. Sometimes the others we host may also host us, as in *A Midsummer Night's Dream*. Both possibilities may be thickly entangled or entwined.

These occasions of mutuality cannot be guaranteed by moral principles or guides. Realizations of kenotic integrity remain contingent on how innovative are the juxtapositions *we make* (i.e., among desires and duties), and even more on how we *become juxtaposed* with other persons and events beyond our making. Our desires for wholeness may be met by indirection, when "we find ourselves when losing ourselves," as in playing other parts with other people. Losing, here, would mean relinquishing expectations of achieving by oneself wholeness.

When notions of theatrical kenosis are broached by theorists, it is almost invariably with suspicion. For Stephen Greenblatt (as for Harold Bloom) something like kenosis is a mode of "self-fashioning," or negotiated interests, or a sign of futility. Theater's moral good would be to "empty,"[4] or expose and deplete, all sorts of theatrical hocus-pocus that princes and clerics use to *maintain* their fleeting powers. Theater would be, then, a fraud that exposes fraud, which is his reading of *King Lear,* particularly of Edgar. But another view of kenosis would be that playing-as-another-for-another might be motivated to *restore* personality, family, and polis. We can see this in how Cordelia, Kent, the Fool, and Edgar assume roles of inferior, foreign, or empty status in compassion and civic duty—responding to a crisis where kingship and kinship have reached an impasse.

Cordelia

Cordelia's becoming the Queen of France is not ostensibly a diminishment in status. Nonetheless, it is a conversion from filial *impropriety.* When she says "nothing," rather than imitate formulas of love, it is usually accepted as a rejection of hypocritical playacting; she would occupy, Marjorie Garber writes, "the vanishing point of theatricality."[5] Yet her "sincere" way of playing at not-playing is in its way presumptuous. Lear's division of the kingdom occurs in a court ceremony,[6] and her silence evades the "duty" she claims to "obey." Moreover, her words are not disinterested. Lear is also presiding over a bizarre betrothal contest, and when Burgundy withdraws after Lear disinherits Cordelia (leaving her to magnanimous France) we might wonder if the motive for her famous declaration is to thwart a badly arranged marriage.

> You have begot me, bred me, loved me. I
> Return those duties back as are right fit,
> Obey you, love you and most honor you.
> Why have my sisters husbands, if they say
> They love you all? Haply, when I shall wed,
> That lord whose hand must take my plight shall carry
> Half my love with him, half my care and duty.
> Sure I shall never marry like my sisters
> To love my father all. (I.1.95–104)

Rather than following "duties," Cordelia has "obedience scanted," Goneril coolly notes (280). If Cordelia contributes to the king and kingdom's disintegration, then she must try to set it right. Her transformation will be kenotic, for she is made a *foreign* queen who in "patience and sorrow" (IV.3.16) becomes England's enemy in order to save it.[7] "Oh dear father," she thinks, "It is thy business that I go about" (IV.4.23–25). In keeping with such Christic echoes, she is hung; and in the "redemptive" performance tradition of this play, Lear holds her body in a pieta-like lament.[8]

Kent

It is Kent who first signals the pattern of playing a part of marginal social consequence to care for another's suffering. Lear has exiled him, but in loyalty this former king's counselor theatrically alters his appearance and affects the rough accent of a soldier or manservant; upon meeting Lear, he speaks in double entendres worthy of a court fool.

> KENT: I do profess to be no less than I seem; to serve him truly
>   that will put me in trust, to love him that is honest, to con-
>   verse with him that is wise and says little, to fear judgment, to
>   fight when I cannot choose—and to eat no fish.
> LEAR: What art thou?
> KENT: A very honest-hearted fellow, and as poor as the King.
>   (I.4.12–17)

On the heath, Kent ministers to Lear. Most of his other endeavors are not excessively Christic: he baits Oswald, for which he is put in stocks, and is a messenger and facilitator. But after Lear's death, when Albany offers Kent a share in the kingdom, he refuses: "I have a journey, sir, shortly to go;/My master calls me, I must not say no" (V.3.320–21), the kenosis of utter self-abnegation, suggestive of a classical, soldierly deputy who believes there is no more part to play.[9]

The Fool

The Fool mediates Lear to the audience[10] and is a comedian who rhymes truth to power under the cloak of wit. He dangerously offers foolery as a form of critical love for the King.

> LEAR: Dost thou call me fool, boy?

FOOL: All thy other titles thou hast given away; that thou wast
   born with.
KENT: This is not altogether fool, my lord. (I.4.141–44)

The Fool plays on the reversal of wisdom and foolishness and presses on
Lear the folly of dividing the kingdom, his "titles." "I had rather be any
kind o'thing than a fool, and yet I would not be thee, nuncle" (176–77).
And the nearer that Lear himself comes to playing the fool, the nearer he
comes to his humanity and kingship. When Edgar appears, disguised as
Poor Tom, the Fool diminishes, and empties out of the play (in III.6, he
leaves with Kent to carry Lear to Dover)—gone but for his associations
with Cordelia. It is hinted she had affections for the Fool, much as Hamlet had for Yorick. Lear, as he holds her dead body, says inexplicably,
"My poor fool is hanged." She would be another person into whom the
Fool has emptied.

Edgar

Edgar enters a wider horizon of self-and-otherness by emptying himself
into "nothing" for compassion's sake.[11] Nearly naked, filthy, he takes on
the "poorest shape" and so reduced, faces the chaos of nature. "Poor
Turlygod, poor Tom,/That's something yet: Edgar I nothing am" (II. 192).
Does he put on this mad part, with nakedness his costume and chased by
a "foul fiend," as a tactic of self-preservation, as Greenblatt thinks? "Edgar adopts the role of Poor Tom not out of a corrupt will to deceive but
out of a commendable desire to survive."[12] But it is more than that.

   Greenblatt explores how Edgar's theatricality imitates contemporary
polemics against "Popish" practices of exorcism. He styles himself as
one possessed, and at Dover pretends to see a demon flee when blinded
Gloucester falls from the "cliff." Edgar is playing on how theater was
a "metaphor and analytic tool" for exposing the ritual of exorcism.
Greenblatt infers that whenever Elizabethan theater gestured to sacred
rites, even sympathetically, their efficacy and meaning was evacuated or
"emptied out."[13] Indeed, even the skeptic's *claim that ritual is merely a
show,* when moved to the artificial commerce of the stage, is *itself* emptied of serious import. The result is *uncertainty,* not disbelief. Some in the
audience may well have construed the parody of exorcism in *Lear* to be
pro-Catholic, not anti-Catholic. However, Greenblatt believes the uncertainty that theater makes of ritual can be correlated with a cosmos bereft

of redemptive meaning. The resurrection "devoutly to be wished"—as when we see Lear holding the living, breathing boy who plays the dead Cordelia—would be precisely what we do not see.[14]

Here, I would redeploy Greenblatt's terms of deconstruction, to notice the *efficacies* of emptying. "Performance kills belief,"[15] but does it have to? Might not the transparent *performance* of ritual *make* its credibility? A ritual "emptied out" would be one that loosens its religious ligatures, so to speak, opening beyond its liturgical bonds.[16] Theater that acknowledges its theatricality—empties itself, shows its wires and mirrors—is not not-theater but theater that "deceives" without deceit; it can serve truthfulness. And ritual? Can showing the performative "truth of" the ritual—for example, that the biscuit is/is not Christ—also show "the truth," some aspects of which are believed to "set one free?" It is not only, as Tillich insists, that a true ritual is "self-negating."[17] To see its performative, enacted status is also to see its participatory character.[18]

As for Edgar, he has another reason to maintain his guise, even after knowing his father desires reconciliation. "Why I do trifle thus with his despair/Is done to cure it" (IV.6.33–34). To Albany he says he has come to know of Gloucester's miseries, "By nursing them, my lord" (V.3.180). Edgar assumes the "habit" and "semblance" of a madman in order to be his father's "guide." He has "Led him, begged for him, saved him from despair, [but] Never—O fault!—revealed myself unto him" (186–91). It is true that in staging the miracle of Gloucester's fall he is not without "fault," for his father is ready to embrace him. Does Edgar think a miracle might exorcise his despair? Or is he "motivated" only by Shakespeare's desire for a good theatrical effect? The effect is part of how we see Edgar transformed. He had been a naive, inept, albeit legitimate son, and Edmund easily took advantage of his "foolish honesty" (1.2.179). But as "nothing," his ethos has enlarged, as when at Dover, nearly naked,[19] he inhabits the Fool's role:

> LEAR: What hast thou been?
> EDGAR: A serving-man, proud in heart and mind, that curled my
>   hair, wore gloves in my hat, served the lust of my mistress'
>   heart.
> . . . .
> LEAR: Why, thou wert better in a grave to answer with thy un-
>   covered body this extremity of the skies. Is man no more than
>   this? (III.4.83–84, 100–101)

This one whom Lear calls "unaccommodated man," "a poor, bare, forked animal"—one in whom he recognizes his naked humanity and tears off his own "lendings" (105–6)—is not entirely pacific. Edgar has also become one who acts, killing Oswald and mortally wounding Edmund. After his long liminality is over, it is implied he will rule, and the Folio gives him the last word, "The weight of this sad time we must obey/Speak what we feel, not what we ought to say" (V.3.322–23). Does he endorse Cordelia's refusal to speak ceremonially? It would be fitting to praise her for she has died attempting to restore the King. But her negative profession of filial duty had *not* succeeded in saying what she felt. If Edgar (or Albany, in the Quarto) succeeds now, it is because he has *received feeling from the parts offered him* by "this sad time."

Lear

Lear is given two diagnoses: that his wits have become divided,[20] and that he is impatient. In the storm, he promises the Fool, "I will be the pattern of all patience,/I will say nothing" (III.2.37). Yet Kent tells Gloucester that the King's "wits have given way to his impatience" (III.6.4–5). Patience can be an integrity trait, related to endurance and constancy, but Lear's is impatience for nothingness. His "fast intent" is to "Unburdened crawl toward death" (I.1.35, 40). In the "Blow winds" speech (III.2) he is impatient for the end of the world. The Fool resists Lear's impatience: "If thou wert my fool, nuncle, I'd have thee beaten for being old before thy time" (I.5.38). Lear is old but not too old to be King. If to be a king and a father is to hold together the political and the personal, then Lear has lost his hold. To the raging elements he complains,

> Here I stand your slave,
> A poor, infirm, weak and despised old man.
> But yet I call you servile ministers
> That will with two pernicious daughters join
> Your high-engendered battles 'gainst my head. . . . (III.2.18–23)

If I have never harmed Nature, why does Nature fall on me and not my daughters? There can be no answer, not in a pagan or Christian cosmos, where rain falls on the just and unjust, except by inhabiting, stoically or graciously, a "pattern of all patience." But that requires wits, and Lear's are awash in the "tempest in my mind" (12). If you cannot hold yourself together, if your self is in pieces, what is left? Beyond patience, another possibility is that others may hold your pieces. And to do that, they may choose to take odd parts and improvise.

Such compassionate improvisation is a benefit of the world's being a "great stage of fools" (IV.6.179). This can be a metaphor of providential design, as in Calderón,[21] but also of how to live in the absence or tempestuous presence of such design. "Let me have surgeons,/I am cut to the brains," he exclaims at Dover. The "Gentleman" replies, "You shall have anything. . . . You are a royal one and we obey you" (188–89, 197). These ministries to Lear are transforming, but not finally so. How much of his mind is regained cannot be settled by the text alone.[22] His prayer outside the hovel in the storm can signal kenotic transformation, and it might be played as an effect of Kent's and the Fool's kindness. Lear prays that the "poor naked wretches" among his subjects be defended from the elements. "O, I have ta'en/Too little care of this." He hopes his care might turn the cosmos toward justice.

> Take physic, pomp,
> Expose thyself to feel what wretches feel,
> That thou mayest shake the superflux to them,
> And show the heavens more just. (III.4.33–36)

But this relief is only an interlude. Lear's most moving claims of identity come as his mind is most piecemeal: "I am the King himself," "every inch a king," "a king, my masters, know you that" (IV.6.84, 106, 196). The less certain of his kingship, the more certain he is of his humanity, as when he awakens to find Cordelia kneeling before him. He kneels instead to her. "No, sir," she says, "you must not kneel." Lear fears, however, "I am not in my perfect mind" (IV.7.59, 63). As he loses the integrity of self and world, others attempt to hold the pieces of his pattern.

Lear's fragmentation is not only a sign of the ragged integrity of even "strong" persons; it is also a sign of the protean nature that allows persons to take up other personae, the possibility that delights and troubles Hamlet. Lear's fragments may be held by those who assume other parts themselves; Edgar intuits that playing is required for his father's healing; Kent senses as much for Lear, and so also may Cordelia. Before the end Lear is able to tell her, "We two alone will sing like birds i'the cage." The words that follow can seem only the delusion of one who would repossess the daughter he lost. However, the world he imagines is not so narrow in its embrace of "the mystery of things." Given that they are imprisoned, its horizon is quite wide.

When thou dost ask me blessing I'll kneel down
And ask of thee forgiveness. So we'll live
And pray, and sing, and tell old tales, and laugh
At gilded butterflies, and hear poor rogues
Talk of court news; and we'll talk with them too—
Who loses and who wins, who's in, who's out—
And take upon's the mystery of things
As if we were God's spies. (V.3.10–17)

Then, when he holds her body against his own, he speaks a contradiction: "She's dead as earth. . . . Lend me a looking-glass;/If that her breath will mist or stain the stone,/Why then she lives" (259–61). Does he believe she lives when he holds a mirror and feather to her lips, and thinks it "stirs" to "redeem all sorrows" (263)? He dies asking, "Do you see this? Look on her: look, her lips,/Look there, look there!" (309–10). If in suffering, or in witness to suffering, language loses coherence, then saying contrary things can sometimes be truer than saying one thing. "Look there" invites us to be accountable to what Lear's life and language cannot complete.[23]

Others Who Play Lear

"To thine own self be true" was a harbinger of modern belief in the authenticity of, even the obligation of solitary self-expression. This belief is now so established that Edgar's plan to play and become "nothing" so as to "cure" or "nurse" Gloucester is all but incomprehensible. Was Shakespeare imagining something like homeopathy, imbibing a bit of the poison to effect a cure? This may be the strategy pursued in Kristian Levring's midrash on *Lear*.

Levring filmed *The King Is Alive* according to the minimalist code of the *Dogme* project, created by Danish directors Lars von Trier and Thomas Vinterberg. A lost tour bus runs out of gas near an abandoned mining town in the Namibian desert, without phone or radio and only canned carrots to sustain eleven passengers. One of them, Henry (David Bradley), is a wizened British stage actor turned Hollywood producer who happens to have memorized *King Lear*. He copies out the roles on the back of film script pages he has with him, and proposes they rehearse and perform *Lear* to keep sane. Their situation is terrible but not hopeless. An Australian bush veteran, Jack (Miles Anderson), imparts five rules for survival: conserve water, secure food, find shelter, stay visible, and keep your spirits up. He then walks into the desert to reach a distant village. The others occupy empty houses, dig latrines, collect dew for drinking water, and burn tires for a signal fire. They temporarily have food, and for their spirits there is Shakespeare and sex.

The King Is Alive would be skeptical about kenotic integrity engendered by theatrical play;[24] performing *Lear* has little to do with who lives or dies, or who becomes solicitous of others. The predicament has exposed fissures in their characters and relationships. Liz (Janet McTeer) thinks her husband Ray (Bruce Davison) is tired of her. Newly wed Amanda (Lia Williams) is learning that her Paul (Chris Walker) is a sexist pig (in a mad scene, he is reduced to oinking). Paul's father, Charles (David Calder), is also a pig, a well-exercised widower looking for a good lay. The brooding student from France, Catherine (Romane Bohringer), is too proud to play Cordelia among these yahoos and resents the perky American, Gina (Jennifer Jason Leigh), who enthusiastically accepts the part. Ashley (Brion James) is an alcoholic who plays Lear badly until he gets the DTs. And most are angry at the driver Moses (Vusi Kunene), whose broken compass got them lost. Henry is a Montaigne figure, one of Shakespeare's sources; he observes them, calls them "lost souls," and asks, "Is man no more than this?" Eventually, he must play Lear himself.

Henry never reveals a rationale for choosing "old Lear," but his comment about degeneration into a "fantastic striptease act of basic human needs" is telling. Suppose we were to ask him, "Why not *The Mikado?*" Or "Why not one of your movie scripts?" Or "Why not *A Midsummer Night's Dream*"? He might think them inappropriate; to survive spiritually in extreme abandonment, you should confront your situation with the honesty and insight *King Lear* provides. He recognizes that reversion to bestial greed is likely, and implies that *Lear* may help them transcend their individual despairs. He comes across as a dedicated director, seeking the best performances especially from the passengers with the least talent. He would represent kenotic integrity attempting, but largely failing, to elicit kenotic integrity in others.

While *Lear*'s characters do not parallel exactly those in *The King Is Alive,* Shakespeare does amplify their desires and fears. Some warm to their parts. Liz perfects a scene where Goneril kisses Edmund, played by Moses; she is obsessed with aging and childlessness and insists on rehearsing the kiss again and again to goad Ray into jealousy. Gina is a very small-time actor, who most wants the performance to come off. She persuades Charles to play Gloucester, which he will do only if she agrees to sleep with him, and she, who we infer has played other bad parts in her brief career, does, and thereafter humiliates Charles. So he puts on his best suit and hangs himself, but not before pissing on the dying Gina—dying because Catherine in jealousy has slipped this Cordelia spoiled carrots and poisoned her. So much for community theater.

What does turn these souls into something of a community is less playmaking than ritual. Deranged from watching Liz seduce Moses, Ray wanders into the dunes repeating, "My master calls me, I must not say no," and finds the corpse of Jack. (Why he has died is unclear.) They all go to bury him, and the procession they make becomes the first of two rites that transform the film into a less solitary allegory of existence. The other is the wake for Gina. In the windy night and glare of bonfires they hold her body and speak lines from *Lear* over her uncovered face. Henry: "She's dead as earth. . . . I might have saved her; now she's gone forever. / Cordelia, Cordelia, stay a little." And at this moment from out of the night Namibians arrive in trucks, a deus ex machina. The exhausted passengers are saved by strangers, who presumably have seen their fires.

Derrida likens "the desert"—where Hebrews received laws and hermits saw visions—to an ambiguous but originary site of sacrifice, difference, and meeting.[25] In the desert, those who have been marooned are encountered by unexpected others. The rescue is narrated in godlike detachment by an ageless African, Kanana (Peter Kubheka), from his battered, thronelike sofa: "From the desert came peace." How he has lived here apparently alone is never explained. He is puzzled by the daily rehearsals and watches them speak words "without talking to each other." He intuits the anti-theatrical prejudice, that such play is false or alienating.

> They ate a bit less every day. . . . Then they said the words the rest of the time. I don't know if the desert crept into their heads at night . . . but in the day it wasn't there. Together they said words. They still didn't say them to each other.

Henry wagers everything on the words of *King Lear,* yet it seems these words come only to express grief and guilt occasioned by what amounts to human sacrifice: Jack's death, Charles's suicide, and Gina's homicide. If the survivors do "say what we ought to say" well over Gina's body, it is more because violent death has given them articulacy, not the project of doing *Lear.* So the film reverts to naturalistic tragedy, and it doubts we can transcend the genes, neuroses, and power roles that ensnare us.[26] It desires, but finally cannot envision, the mutuality of kenotic integrity.

Urn and Kimono

We may find such envisioning when theatrical play becomes a way of putting the self-sufficient self under critique and also a way of "mending the world." In juxtaposing Robert Lepage with *King Lear*—in anticipation of *A Midsummer Night's Dream*—I am thinking of how Kent, Edgar, and the Fool cross hierarchical and social boundaries. Analogously, *The Seven Streams of the River Ota* (1994) travels across linguistic and cultural boundaries. We saw Lepage earlier, acting in Arcand's *Jesus of Montreal,* where his character narrated a film on the Big Bang and averred it left many questions "unanswered." Lepage's Quebecois company, Ex Machina, has created solo and ensemble pieces using a variety of performance styles and media to explore *translation* (in the senses of movement, change, and linguistic interpretation) as a metaphor of human contact and misprision. Also interesting, as the stories in *Seven Streams* develop, are old-fashioned and comedic separations-at-birth, incredible coincidences, and chance reunions.

The branches of the Ota flow through Hiroshima. Along them we follow sets of persons and their descendents from late 1945 to the 1990s, whose lives diverge, meet, and miss across generations and oceans. The players speak English, French, German, Dutch, Japanese, and Czech, translated by supertitles or by personae in the story; sometimes the translation connects, sometimes it creates misunderstanding. The seven-hour play employs Gagaku music, film, still photography, video, epic theater, Noh, Iaidō exercises, opera, Bunraku puppets, shadow boxes, mirrors, even a scene from Feydeau. Lepage says the work originated when, upon visiting Hiroshima, he was surprised to find a city renewed around motifs of interconnection, even of conjugality.[27] One of his surrogates and a framing character is Jana Čapek, a Czech Holocaust survivor who settles in Japan to study Zen. In martial arts attire, she tells us that in Iaidō,

> you don't have to measure up to someone else: the only adversary is yourself. To cut the ego with the sword is the ultimate combat. *The Seven Streams of the River Ota* is about people from different parts of the world who came to Hiroshima and found themselves confronted with their own devastation and their own enlightenment. For if Hiro-

shima is a city of death and destruction, it is also a city of rebirth and survival. (1)

Jana is a European Jew who goes to Japan presumably on Western terms and discovers there the West—not as her own projection, but a coincidence of history. In the Peace Memorial Park she sees the ruined dome designed by Jan Letzl, a Czech architect working in Japan early in the century.

> So, for me, facing that metallic skeleton was like being in front of a mirror. This empty shell was myself. Me, with my illusions, and all my past on my Jewish shoulders ... So I understood that my place was here, in Hiroshima. (106)

To encounter the self or the other requires *emptiness,* both in the literal sense of *space*—prewar Japan for Letzl, postexplosion Hiroshima for Jana—and of *room,* within or about oneself. Jana likens Letzl's dome to the Buddhist figure of the empty mirror, in which the self is not reflected. The play likens mirrors to places of encounter as well as reflection. What is most memorable to me is how the plot entanglements—involving lost parents and separated half-siblings, international lovers who meet or part in odd confluences, all hedged by different modes of art and suffering—attain ethical import via the innovation and rupture of theatrical forms.

Lepage can be as suspicious of theater as Shakespeare, but affirms collaborative theater-play as a better trope for existence than the myth of the solitary ego.[28] Critics have asked if his work is orientalist (the *Madame Butterfly* effect), or a critique of orientalism (a Brechtian *Butterfly* effect), or both. Some worry that the cultures and histories of suffering he treats (the Shoah, Hiroshima, AIDS) are reduced to iconic sameness.[29] Ex Machina's own metatheatrical critique is evident when a Quebec TV producer makes a travesty of interviewing Jana, whose Zen mastery has made her interesting. Another spoof is when a visiting Quebecois company performs Feydeau's farce, *La Dame de chez Maxim,* in Osaka, in Parisian French simultaneously translated into Japanese, and seen from backstage in the manner of Michael Frayn's *Noises Off.*

Theater is also implicated in the ambiguities of survival. Jana's escape from the Holocaust at age eleven was accomplished by a stage magician's magic mirror box on a train platform. As Jana reviews such events from her life—she watches them enacted behind two-way mirrors—she ponders how the vanishing of others has coincided with survival. Near the end of *Seven Streams,* in the role of Zen priest, she empties ashes from an urn into the sea, near the red torii arch at Miyajima. When I saw the play, I was uncertain whose ashes these were, for all the friends gathered here have losses to remember. I wondered if this was an image of release or resignation. Was it a Buddhist-informed recognition of rebirth and the illusions of desire, or a cliché about "coming to closure"? Later I wondered if my questions were the right questions.

Before the ritual of the urn was "The kimono dance." This kimono was to have been the wedding dress of a *hibakusha,* an atomic bomb–affected person we meet early in the play; her child by an American soldier is one of the stories we follow. In a carefully choreographed image, various characters appear, disappear, and reappear in the garment. To see several women and men passing through the silk folds of a single kimono is something like Kushner's image of souls rising to fill the hole in the ozone layer. The empty kimono is, as it were, larger on the inside than the outside. As the play's stories become integrated in its illuminated fabric, it briefly becomes an icon, wherein we witness lives being held in the spaces of other lives.

The Theater of Bottom's Head

Where will fragments be held? What sort of place is called for? Perhaps a place of witnessing and mending, a "theater of the world," the motif from Calderón that Balthasar enlists. Perhaps also a "theater of emptiness," Peter Brook's "empty space," where fragments are juxtaposed, where meetings and encounters occur. Perhaps also an "empty time," where the future might empty into the present and past, just as the past empties into the future. Perhaps a place and time where Lear and Cordelia can pray, laugh, and "sing like birds i'the cage" of blessing and forgiveness, but also of rival "sects" and court intrigues—"who's in, who's out"— and of "the mystery of things/As if we were God's spies" (V.3.15–18). If we shift these lines from their immediate context of "sacrifice" (implicitly Cordelia's sacrifice, upon which "The gods themselves throw incense," 20–21) and impending oblivion, they could also describe a kind of theater, where those on the stage and around it become momentarily *at one.*

The theater where fragments are *held* (not *fused, synthesized,* or *rationalized*) with their distances and gaps apparent, would then be a theater of *atonement,* or "at-one-ment" in the sense of solidarity with the living and the suffering.[30] Kushner, Churchill, and Lepage implicitly seek for such a theater, as would Shakespeare. If *Lear* speaks to politically "realist" places where social roles are mostly alienating and altruism barely survives, perhaps the earlier *A Midsummer Night's Dream* (1595) seeks for places where playing frees persons to be *with* and *for* others.

But there is danger in Athens. A bit like *Romeo and Juliet* (written about the same time), Egeus has forbidden his daughter Hermia, on pain of death, from marrying Lysander. She must marry Demetrius, who loves her but is loved by Helena, with whom he once dallied. The Duke, Theseus, senses something wrong in this, perhaps because he gets to marry his odd delight, an Amazon war-captive, Hippolyta. But by law he must uphold Egeus, although he commutes the alternative of marriage-or-death into marriage-or-nunnery. Theseus may also be thought to distract Egeus and Demetrius long enough for Hermia and Lysander to escape to the forest.[31] If the Athenian court is mostly a place of critique, where roles are exposed as alienating, the forest can be a carnevalesque place where limits are crossed and criticized and lives rearranged.[32]

To be sure, there is conflict in the forest as well. The fairy queen, Titania, has adopted an orphan child from India, which flares the ire of Oberon, the fairy king. He wants the child for himself, perhaps an expression of René Girard's "mimetic desire" or, as Louis Montrose suggests, anxiety about being dependent on a powerful wife.[33] Titania remarks for thirty-six lines upon how jealousy has disturbed nature and the lives of mortals (II.1.81–117), paralleling the "late eclipses" speech in *Lear*. Oberon is unmoved. With the aid of Puck he acquires a magic dew to make her dote on any creature she may see upon awakening—and also, as a benevolent afterthought, to make Demetrius love Helena. This supernatural horizon is at once jealous, gracious, and errant: its magic goes awry. Also in the forest are amateur players, "rude mechanicals" (III.2.9) who are rehearsing Ovid's tragic tale of Pyramus and Thisbe, which they hope to perform for Theseus and Hippolyta's wedding. Puck "translates" a player, Bottom the Weaver, into the form of an ass, to whose presence Titania will awaken and be delighted.

Theater, then, overlaps these places of critique and delight. After the lovers are sorted out, but before Bottom and company perform their play, Theseus and Hippolyta reflect on what they have learned of the strange activities in the woods. He warns that a poet's "imagination bodies forth/The forms of things unknown" and "gives to airy nothing/A local habitation and a name," and worries that these shapes will disseminate illusions.

Such tricks hath strong imagination,
That if it would but apprehend some joy,
It comprehends some bringer of that joy:
Or, in the night, imagining some fear,
How easy is a bush supposed a bear! (V.1.14–22)

It may seem Theseus expounds Plato's complaint about poetry lacking truth, to which Hippolyta replies with Aristotle, or the "allegory of the theologians,"[34] that imagination can disclose truth:

But all the story of the night told over,
And all their minds transfigur'd so together,
More witnesseth than fancy's images,
And grows to something of great constancy;
But howsoever, strange and admirable. (23–27)

Yet they both speak of the transforming work of poetic art, which in witnessing also creates. What is created? One answer would be that imagination bodies forth reality in the mind. Another would be that imagination, practiced onstage by players, creates *space* where lines are crossed, meetings occur, and fragmentary lives are held. This is why Edgar in *King Lear* and Henry in *The King Is Alive* would be insightful to suppose that the "nothing" of playing could actually "nurse" or atone, if this nothing were not mere nothing but an empty space for receptivity.

The supposition that Elizabeth attended *A Midsummer Night's Dream* when it was first performed at a wedding[35] gives us pause, for apart from fairy drops Bottom has little chance of making it with royalty in any realm. Shakespeare is bowing to the virgin queen—who was called "Amazon" and, as a woman who ruled men, was an anomaly[36]—and changing Apuleius's metamorphosis of a scholar into an ass, replete with bestiality, into a pleasant critique of social differentiation. Titania, aghast by "what visions I have seen" (IV.1.75) but now reconciled with Oberon, looks upon Bottom's ass-face that so delighted her: "O how mine eyes do loathe his visage now!" (78). So she exclaims, right after having *loved* Bottom with his "monstrous" ears and braying voice. But did we not see some unexpected good in their love play, though arranged in spite? If outside her bower Bottom is an ordinary artisan, then his translation into a donkey signals how he, the players, and the audience may be transported across the limits of their lives.

Of Bottom's ass-head: it was a theatrical mask fitted over the head,[37] and the shape-shifting must occur offstage (III.1.84–97). When it's time to change him back, Oberon instructs Puck to "take off this head" (IV.1.79). That the site of the change is his head is interesting for the embodiment of integrity. We can only partially objectify ourselves by perception; we can touch our face but cannot *see* it, not without devices. A mirror is such a device, yet one that distorts images, serves illusions, and cannot show the nexus of a particular life in time. But if mirrors cannot show our true faces, the witness of others can tell us how we are from time to time:

SNOUT: O Bottom, thou art changed! What do I see on thee?
BOTTOM: What do you see? You see an ass-head of your own do
   you? . . .
QUINCE: Bless thee, Bottom, bless thee! Thou art translated.
   (III.1.109–14)
TITANIA: I pray thee, gentle mortal, sing again:
   Mine ear is much enamour'd of thy note;
   So is mine eye enthralled to thy shape. . . . (132–34)
TITANIA: Come sit thee down upon this flowery bed,
   While I thy amiable cheeks do coy,
   And stick musk roses in thy sleek smooth head,
   And kiss thy fair large ears, my gentle joy. (IV.1.1–4)
BOTTOM [to Mustardseed]: . . . methinks I am marvellous hairy
   about the face; and I am such a tender ass, if my hair do but
   tickle me, I must scratch. (21–26)

Under Oberon's spell, Titania discerns the donkey's head as a human face, and she enlarges Bottom's own range of dreaming and acting. He, in turn, momentarily enlarges the creaturely possibilities she is prepared to envision and enjoy. Their charmed witness is analogous to how the mutuality of theatrical performing can help identify and explore patterns of kenotic integrity. And what they momentarily do for each other, Theseus will do for Bottom and his fellow rustics, who imagine themselves actors, and for their audience as well.

Bottom is the most imaginative of these players. He is "the best wit of any handicraft man in Athens" and "the best person too" (IV.2.9–11). Their day jobs recall the guilds of medieval pageants: Bottom the weaver, Flute the bellows maker, Snout the tinker, Snug the joiner, Starveling the tailor, Quince the carpenter. Quince is their impresario but he can hardly control Bottom, the ham who imagines he can take any part. Kevin Kline played him so in Michael Hoffman's 1999 film and also imagined him as a lonely, reflective individual (not as childlike as Montrose observes), and misunderstood in his enthusiasm. Bottom is inspired by an intuition for the compassion of playing. He begs "to play the lion too," but Quince worries he will terrify ladies. So Bottom says, "I will aggravate my voice . . . I will roar you as gently as any sucking dove; I will roar you and 'twere any nightingale" (I.2.76–78).

"Aggravate my voice" is a malapropism, a tiny genre that manifests how language and theater can transcend their makers' designs. What is bad about Bottom's notions of drama is from another angle good, as when Snout, sprinkled with plaster, performs the chink in the Wall, through which Pyramus and Thisbe whisper. When their play is finally staged, Wall is a hoot. But the chinks in their minimalist dramaturgy will one day be elevated by such avant-gardists as Brecht, Brook, Lepage, and LeCompte. Quince and Bottom's play is *Romeo and Juliet* in burlesque. Bottom: "*Thus die I, thus, thus, thus! / Now am I dead, Now am I fled; My soul is in the sky. . . . Now die, die, die, die, die*" (V.1.289–95). Flute as Thisbe taking her life over Pyramus is as silly; but another affecting moment in Hoffman's film is when Sam Rockwell drops his falsetto and speaks grief quietly, appreciating Shakespeare's restraining dialectic of realism and theatricality.

Bottom and Quince intend something serious and provoke mirth, and Theseus recognizes that the mirth should be redirected to good ends. What he means to convey to the players after their performance ("your play needs no excuse. . . .") is established when he tells Hippolyta why he hired this unlikely company. "For never anything can be amiss / When simpleness and duty tender it." Hippolyta is skeptical. So he relates an anecdote, which may have been Shakespeare's compliment to the gracious Queen Elizabeth who, when faced with awe-struck, "tongue-tied" subjects, would treat their stammers as if eloquent: "Out of this silence yet I pick'd a welcome" (V.1.100).[38] Theseus believes he has been such a Duke, who can hold the fragments of aggravated voices. The pattern of integrity he inhabits now gives room for others to inhabit. Egeus had behaved badly, and Theseus thwarted him—allowing tragic clouds to dissipate—not by relying on self-sufficient authority but by waiting, as it were, on gifts of providence or the fairies. His discernment and giving is not uncritical: he knew Egeus was harsh, and he knows Quince's actors are, frankly, terrible; Harold Bloom thinks Theseus is critical of theatrical play in contrast to Hippolyta.[39] Depending on how they are played, however, his critical jests make the audience's mirth more sympathetic than it would be otherwise, for Theseus is teaching them (and us) *to complete the good* that these players are attempting to create.

> HIPPOLYTA: This is the silliest stuff that ever I heard.
> THESEUS: The best in this kind are but shadows; and the worst
>   are no worse, if imagination amend them.
> HIPPOLYTA: It must be your imagination then, and not theirs.
> THESEUS: If we imagine no worse of them than they of them-
>   selves, they may pass for excellent men. Here come two noble
>   beasts in, a man and a lion. (V.1.207–12)

Do Theseus and Bottom ever meet in the full mutuality of kenotic integrity? *No,* and *probably not.* No, because "full mutuality" would be an abstract moral principle that can be enjoined in such meetings but is not by itself "meeting." Probably not, because however much Shakespeare's theater crosses boundaries, those boundaries remain edgy; we can hear a tone of condescension when Theseus generously tells Hippolyta:

> The kinder we, to give them [the players] thanks for nothing.
> Our sport shall be to take what they mistake:
> And what poor duty cannot do, noble respect
> Takes it in might, not merit. (V.1.89–92)

Here Theseus sounds a bit like Luther's God of justifying, unmerited grace, unless his "nothing" implies empty space for kenotic gifts. We may also hear patronizing tones as he congratulates them: "No epilogue, I pray you; for your play needs no excuse. . . . and [is] very notably discharged. But come, your Bergomask" (341–46). This speech could be played with congeniality and respect,[40] thus empowering the players, beckoning them to dance, and teaching the audience to respect them. Still, the witting slight is less generous than it might have been. Could there have been a good way to give Bottom the last word, along with Puck's closing plea?[41]

First, Puck

Now reconciled, Titania and Oberon instruct the fairies on how to "bless" and "consecrate" the sleeping lovers. Then Puck asks for applause and pardon for any offences these "shadows" (fairies and actors) may have given. After all, it was only "a dream"—but it is also a *promise:* "If you pardon, we will mend." Who will pardon, and what is at stake? *We* are to pardon. But are we to be priests, and has Puck put us in God's place? As for what is at stake, Oberon hints it is *suffering* and *theodicy*. "And the blots of Nature's hand / Shall not in their issue stand," meaning that the lovers' children will be safe from what contingencies—"mole," "hare-lip," and "scar"—may come in their "nativity" (395–99). But *where* will they be safe?

Lear and *Dream* are suggestive of how the kenosis of playing may address suffering. Playing-as-others, in art as in life, can be said to create or re-create emptiness, spaces of relative and temporary proximity, established in encounters. In emptiness, there can be *meeting space,* much as Edgar meets Gloucester and Lear. There can be *room* for personal fragments to be held and for thoughts and lives to mesh contingently. Disturbingly, there also dwell in such spaces those who do harm, and those who are living or dying in despair. At-one-ment in emptiness (here I am thinking both of "divine emptiness" and the particular, fragmented patterns of persons) does not mute the conundrums of theodicy, but makes more space for them to be spoken and heard. The question, "Why so much devastation and suffering, and then even more?" goes on and on.

To another question, does kenotic integrity logically *resolve* the cognitive disjunctions between personal and the moral integrity?—it does not. The disjunctions remain. But the "gap" betwixt and between juxtaposed persons and principles, relations and commitments, is more than a figure of speech, and more than a sign of insufficiency. It is also a zone of receptivity, where thoughts and stories might arrive to help complete our own. As a figure of our own emptiness (as relational and moral persons), the "gaps" of juxtaposition and encounter are where we may receive new patterns for integrity, as others may receive patterns from us. The gift of emptiness, then, gives us room; and yet, infinite room can fill us with dizziness and dread.

Now for Bottom

He is, thinks Bloom, "a very good man, as benign as any in Shakespeare,"[42] an observation to be mixed with Kevin Kline's witness to Bottom's solitude. His dream speech could serve as the play's last word. Awakening in the wood, his head restored, he calls for his cue, but no one is around to hear. So he reflects, amazed at his "most rare vision," his unutterable "dream," which in the fiction of the play was not a dream but an occasion in which he poured himself, lost himself, and experienced much that emptied into him:

> Methought I was—and methought I had—but man is but a patched
> fool if he will offer to say what methought I had. The eye of man hath
> not heard, the ear of man hath not seen, man's hand is not able to
> taste, his tongue to conceive, nor his heart to report, what my dream
> was. I will get Peter Quince to write a ballad of this dream: it shall be
> called 'Bottom's Dream', because it hath no bottom. . . . (IV.1.203–16)

Bottom alludes to Paul, who alludes to Isaiah (64:4). "The eye hath
not seen, and the ear hath not heard, neither have entered into the heart
of man, the things which God hath prepared for them that love him"
(1 Corinthians 2:9, Bishop's Bible, 1572). If Shakespeare knew verse 10
in Tyndale (1526) or the Geneva Bible (1576), he would have read how
"the Spirit searcheth all things, yea, the bottom of God's secrets."[43] To
take this mangling of Paul seriously need not detract from its humor.
"The joke searches out a long way," says Greenblatt, "to the solemnities
of the pulpit, to the plays that the professional acting companies took to
the provinces when Shakespeare was a boy . . . and perhaps to the young,
awkward Shakespeare himself, filled with visions his tongue could not
conceive and eager to play all the parts."[44] The allusion would mean that
Bottom's dream is both like his ass-head—a mask that literally has no
bottom—and "the heart of man," which in another sense has no bottom.
His dream, head, and heart are bigger on the inside than the outside.
They make a figure of kenotic emptying and reception, much like the
"house" filled with many "mansions" (John 14:2, in the King James Version), or Lepage's kimono, or Levring's rolls of play-text with their gaps
and indeterminacies, or the empty Globe Theater itself.

Bottom's head is a place of dreams, yes, but also a veritable theater,
where all may meet and be atoned, all-in-all, with room to spare. Theater can be an ephemeral sign of divine emptiness and expansiveness.[45]
As a figure of atonement, it would be a sign of the *more* that meets and
encompasses all things and nothing—as would the stage be such a sign,
on which the ballad of Bottom's dream will play.[46] He hopes to "sing
it in the latter end of a play, before the Duke. Peradventure, to make it
more gracious, I shall sing it at her [Thisbe's] death" (216–17). Could
this have been the last word? Perchance it would have been hard for the
Bard to weigh such terrible significance on Bottom. He is but one actor
in a play with so many epilogues it desires simply not to end. He requires
Peter Quince and so many others to hold these fragments in the integral
pattern of his eye, ear, hand, tongue, and heart.

On Integrity

Persons and Ensembles

And the Good Samaritan, he's dressing
He's getting ready for the show
He's going to the carnival tonight
On Desolation Row

—BOB DYLAN

The kinder we, to give them thanks for nothing.
Our sport shall be to take what they mistake:
And what poor duty cannot do, noble respect
Takes it in might, not merit.

—THESEUS, IN A Midsummer Night's Dream

I LEAVE THESE chapters with questions still waiting in the wings. How does kenotic integrity hold *critical appreciation of suffering* together with *delight,* in what Hamlet called "the beauty of the world; the paragon of animals"—both critique and delight being impulses that elicit artistic making? How is the moral held with the aesthetic and the personal? What relational view of the person does kenotic integrity give, in view of the emptiness in form? Have we only inverted the language of self-representation, making what is ordinarily good (e.g., sincerity, authenticity) bad, and what is ordinarily bad (histrionics, theatricality) good? And have we not lost our strong, coherent, and true selves? It is not clear how these questions can be settled by argumentative propositions; their meanings are better played and performed. But I hope the juxtaposed performances in these chapters have made space for "directions for thought," as Ricoeur would say. This postlude can be a reprise of such directions, with some new thematic variations.

Encountering Samaritans

So traveling on the road to Jericho, a Samaritan—an empty-yet-complex person—encounters another empty-yet-complex person, and is "moved with pity."

> He went to him and bandaged his wounds, having poured oil and wine on them. Then he put him on his own animal, brought him to an inn, and took care of him. The next day he took out two denarii, gave them to the innkeeper, and said, "Take care of him . . . I will repay you whatever you spend." (Luke 10:34–35)

The phrase "Good Samaritan" attaches an ethical attribution to a sign of identity. In the parable's context, Jews and Samaritans typically avoided one another. Most Samaritans were good, presumably, at the cultural project of being Samaritans. But our Samaritan is good because he assists a man, probably Jewish, implying some emptying of himself as Samaritan and a reconfiguring of identity-bearing expectations. Perhaps the wounded Jew would also be letting go of a strong hold on cultural identity, were he to accept aid from a Samaritan.[1] They both would be entering kenotic patterns of integrity.

Yet to make this theme of suffering and response *the* paradigm of kenotic integrity may miss a sense of delight in the play of form-and-emptiness. I have been asking if *response to the beckoning of form* is as ethical in meaning as is the *call of suffering*. Can the paradigm of kenosis hold in proximity both Bottom's delight in playing parts and Theseus's leading his court to fill the rustic "nothing" of the players? An objection comes to mind: a marked condescension in both stories, indicative of an asymmetry between host and guest. The Samaritan must literally descend to the man's place on the ground beside the road. And Theseus's "respect" may be lost in his tones of nobility. Yet perhaps it is unnecessary to arrange a perfect juxtaposition. Let us, instead, first return to the Samaritan. Were we to *stage* the parable, would its theatrical form contradict, then, its ethical import?

Possibly not, if the parables were always in their way theater, performed before a fractious audience.[2] The lawyer who prompts this parable may or may not be at odds with Jesus. "What must I do to inherit eternal life?" he asks. "Who is my neighbor?" Those in authority in Jesus' audience—scribes, Pharisees, Sadducees, priests, Levites—are often portrayed as seeking to discredit him. Others will enjoy how his performances skewer the privileged in behalf of the marginal: the blind and lame, widows, orphans, the poor, and those such as prostitutes, drunks, swineherds, Roman tax collectors, and Samaritans who are beyond the pale of the righteous. There might be militant Zealots here, impatient with parables when decisive action against Rome is needed; and eschatological Essenes, impatient that Jesus has not withdrawn to the desert to await the Last Days. But in the parables, the reign of God is not coming by palace revolt or desert apocalypse. John Dominic Crossan urges that the kingdom arrives to those who hear such a parable, *the moment they hear it.*[3] The parables occasion existential transformation: to those listening, the world is threatened, changed, or turned upside down. Jesus is playing to his audience, which becomes part of the act. Suspense is aroused. Will they arrest him? Will they applaud him? Will they push him over a cliff? Who is angered, ashamed, elated?

If the Samaritan instantiates moral dimensions of integrity, how does he do so? Does he recall the command to love his neighbor, or a similar moral or sacred norm? We are not told. Does he visibly align his body with the norm? Not initially. All we see is that he empties into the emptiness of a man lying by the road; only when he addresses the innkeeper does the alignment gain any wider public. We are told nothing more of this Samaritan, nor of the Jew and the innkeeper who trusted the Samaritan's promise. This ensemble scatters into intertextuality, "known but to God," as they say. At first, this drama seems liable to the ethical problems associated with kenosis (prelude to part IV). But notice that as the Samaritan leaves the injured man with the innkeeper, he is sharing the burden and goes on to other purposes. The Samaritan is not "hostage" to the man, though we never learn how either is transformed by the encounter. Yet the idea of encounter also has problems. How do we distinguish one sheer encounter from another, when encounters are moments that resist being typified by "content"?

I have suggested that encounters can have multiple (not just two) participants, and that moral principles may be among the participants, much as texts, memories, and voices may. In encounters, *principles can be met and reconfigured,* while *remaining clarifying patterns of shareable thinking.* Thus, Samaritans may be located approximately in specific, principled spaces. They followed traditions associated with Mount

Gerizim, not Jerusalem, and by the time of Jesus, Jews regarded them with increasing hostility; yet Samaritans were strict followers of the Pentateuch, though not the rest of the Hebrew scriptures.[4] So in the parable, when our Samaritan is moved to pity, his emotions would grasp Torah principles, some of which—such as offering hospitality to aliens and the distressed—have analogs in many cultures. Also, nothing marks the Samaritan as naive about the dangers of the road to Jericho. So his encounter would entail risk assessment, with the judgment that on this occasion, both the opportunity and the duty of hospitality override prudential caution. The Samaritan is also carrying oil and wine, which can salve wounds, and he has a donkey. So the deliberative aspects of the encounter would include his assessment that he has "effective means" to offer aid.

Principles, active in encounter as memories and voices, also become reconfigured and newly embodied. Again, we should imagine the parable's performative setting, where Jesus puts the audience in the awkward position of Jews being rescued by Samaritans. To follow the story is to risk a transformation of values. Those assumed good—the priest and Levite, who "by chance" pass by—fail to offer aid; the one assumed bad is now good. A listener's world would be threatened or transfigured by the performance, as he imagines his body in close proximity with the Samaritan rescuer. The parable is just as interesting in the dialogue where Luke places it. The lawyer, "wanting to justify himself," inquires about eternal life. Jesus answers by asking what the law says. One must love God and neighbor, the lawyer replies, and Jesus agrees. But the rejoinder—"And who is my neighbor?"—prompts the parable and then Jesus' next query, "Who proved to be the neighbor?"

Bottom's Face, the Samaritan's Masks

The answer Emmanuel Levinas gives is that the neighbor is any "face" we meet, which is always the face of suffering, whose plea, "Do not kill me," calls our humanity into existence. The ethical priority of the face can seem alien to theater, as if appealing to an authentic responsibility that precedes and finally precludes masks, roles, scripts, and so forth. Even so, we have seen that playing a part can be motivated by caring or healing, as in *King Lear*. If so, Levinas's motif of the "substitution" of oneself on behalf of the other is not necessarily anti-theatrical.[5] But his metaphor of the face has posed its own problems of universality and particularity.

Consider again the one who arrests the Samaritan's attention. "A man was going down from Jerusalem to Jericho, and fell into the hands of robbers, who stripped him, beat him, and left him half dead." The "face" is from one vantage *the* face, unmarked and undistinguished from different faces.[6] And indeed, in the parable we see nothing of this man, other than his suffering. We are not told explicitly that he is a Jew; in effect, he is "stripped" of cultural marks. Levinas might notice that he says nothing—it is suffering that speaks. But if Levinas denudes "the face," it is not because he would deny particularity but would not have particulars distract us from the primary call. However, does this account not risk losing the particular face of scars, blemishes, lines of aging and expression? Do we not also risk losing marks of gender, culture, and sociality? Does Levinas imply that as we attend to the details of actual faces we may be distanced from the primacy of suffering? If so, how would the particularities of a face's "mask" lessen the radicality of the command, "Do not kill me"? Would assessing the plea of the particular face, like Bottom's hairy ass-head, make it less a plea that obligates and more a nuanced and contingent plea-for-consideration? If so, the choice between mask and face would be a dichotomous choice.

However, a dialectical reading of mask and face is available. While the parable shows no actual faces, it does attend to roles, much like Peter Quince listing characters: Robbers, Priest, Levite, Innkeeper, and a Samaritan "traveler." It may ask the audience to take or identify with all these roles—shifting from the wounded man to the Levite, to the Samaritan, to the Innkeeper, et cetera. Details are specified: a road, a journey to Jericho, bandages, oil, wine, animal, inn, two denarii, a promise of more in repayment. Amid these details, the man is specified only as wounded, and this silence may enlarge the significance of the mise-en-scène surrounding him. The suggestion would be that persons are relations of accessibility and inaccessibility, context and event, mask and face.

But a dialectic of mask and face, in the style of Ricoeur, would not align one side with particularity and the other with universality; it would view both mask and face in respect to the limits and possibilities of embodiment. My bodily face *changes* in time, in aging, accidents, and experience; however, apart from horror films and odd surgical miracles, the face *cannot actually be exchanged*. I am in this sense not substitutable. Whereas a literal mask and its figurative counterparts—grooming, makeup, social and vocational roles, class, caste, gender—*can be exchanged*, with various degrees of difficulty. This difference is dialectical, insofar as culture and body intersect in persons. Thus, "masks" may affect my face, and my changing face over time affects how I expressively work through masks and parts with others.

The dialectic could be even more complex. We have noticed that, like Bottom, one can *touch* one's face, but one cannot directly *see* it without another's eye (or a device like a mirror or camera). My face, then, is *inherently my own,* yet is hard *for me* to objectify. Whereas a mask is something you and I can more easily gaze upon and objectify, it is *both mine and not mine,* because it is a cultural as well as personal construction. We could go a long way in defining a person as a dialectic of mask and face, which would have many psychological and social iterations, as in George Herbert Mead's distinction between the social "me" (closer to mask) and the active "I" (closer to bodily face),[7] or Balthasar's "role" (mask) and "mission" (face). For Ricoeur, face and mask would be analogous to *discourse,* that is, to the dialectic of event (closer to face) and meaning (closer to mask). To *meet the other* is to *meet the mask-and-face* and to follow the meanings that arise—not behind but *in front of the mask.* The mask would be a mode of expression and interpretation, through which the self receives itself with others.

Persons and Ensembles

However, mask and face make a rather settled dialectic and are not the only figures (for conceptualizing persons and integrity) that theater provides. In *A Midsummer Night's Dream* we find writ large what is implied in the parable, namely that the dramatic elements of encounter, imitation, dialogue, masks-and-faces, entrances-and-exits occur in ensembles. The ensemble is a motif that can show how kenosis is not confined to putative face-to-face, mask-to-mask, or face-to-mask relations. If Bottom, to extend Harold Bloom's praise of him ("a sublime clown and a great visionary," "a very good man, as benign as any in Shakespeare"),[8] receives a pattern of integrity, it is because he is moving at once *to complete others* and *to be completed by others,* with the ultimate limits of his horizons never finally in sight.

That Bottom's integrity has personal dimensions is easily elaborated; he seems opposite the Samaritan in this respect. He is a weaver, a committed yet misinformed actor, a dreamer and poet, a would-be lover of plays and creatures. Less obvious are the moral dimensions of his integrity. Yet it is in solicitude for the welfare of others that Bottom, were he to play the lion, would "aggravate" his voice and roar "as gently as any suckling dove." Here the gap in his grasp of the willing suspension of disbelief requires filling from those in the audience; and they, in turn, require the instructions of Theseus, which were revised by the aesthetics of Hippolyta, who considered how a story of "minds transfigur'd grows . . . into something of great constancy." The mutuality of kenosis extends deep into interior dimensions of Bottom's integrity, as dramatized in his soliloquizing on 1 Corinthians. Thus, we learn the limitless extent of his dream that "hath no bottom," filled by texts from Paul and Isaiah, anticipating its inscription by Peter Quince and its reception by the Duke. Bottom's vision, like his voice and his playing, is an ensemble. *And such juxtapositions of play and voice and vision can be thought to portray the person as an ensemble of relations and signs—and to portray integrity as the emptying of persons out of and into such ensembles, for the sake of delighting-in and suffering-with-and-for others.*

That last statement inevitably encounters the anti-theatrical prejudice. What the prejudice critically registers is, *at bottom,* not our culpabilities and propensity to "sin" (it does register sin, just not "at bottom"), but anxiety about finitude (which Kierkegaard thought precedes sin and creativity). We would like to believe we are whole, and that persons and principles can be all of one piece; but theater implicitly invites us to regard our wholeness and goodness as exceedingly complex creations. Our anxiety recurs in perennial accusations of theater as *hypocrisy, insincerity,* and paradoxically as both *denying and exalting* the strong, solitary, authentic self.

Hypocrisy

It is sometimes defined as feigning a virtue or belief one lacks. But this is odd when we observe how often we acquire virtues by imitating them. Does a performative view of integrity rehabilitate hypocrisy, turning a vice into a virtue?[9] Consider, rather, that the theater is a transparent situation as far as *feigning* is concerned. The problem arises in life, but even here we cannot always regard "real feigning" as wrong. To become a professional, including an actor, requires "faking" the profession until it "makes" the professional, an old bit of wisdom that also applies to other practices and vocations. There are also implications about *virtue* in that definition of hypocrisy, when the virtue a hypocrite feigns should itself be a "part" one ought to play. Hence, it is odd when the charge of hypocrisy attacks the virtue (or belief) as well as the feigner. To say, "I don't believe in politics because politicians only pretend to be honest," implicitly endorses the virtue of honesty and ought to search for honest political practices; but the charge of hypocrisy usually stops further conversation.

What is to keep a kenotic view of theater and of life from making a virtue of the alleged necessity of public hypocrisy? It has been suggested that in classic episodes of hypocrisy the pretence to virtue makes a victim of others.[10] In *Othello*, Iago feigns friendship in order to harm Othello. In *Angels in America,* Roy Cohn does not merely feign being straight but does so to suppress homosexuals, communist sympathizers, the poor, and the ill. So if hypocrisy really means harming others by feigning virtue, harming is the greater issue and is further removed from the dynamics of theatrical performance before a knowing audience. Moreover, the compromises and prudence required of politicians would be "hypocritical" mainly when used as a cover for doing harm to people over whom they have authority or power.

Insincerity

I have mentioned how in the Renaissance, geographic and economic mobility made social mobility—and the chance to change one's identity—a worry, which the virtue of sincerity addressed.[11] Polonius tells Laertes before he goes to France, *To thine own self be true.* However, if sincerity assumes we owe others an unmediated disclosure—without flippancy or reserve of thoughts, feelings, and attitudes—then theater tends to deconstruct discourse about this virtue. Polonius recommends sincerity as a practice, as a role to play, which seems odd. "Pretend to be sincere" is not normal advice (although "Try to be sincere" in effect asks us to play the part of sincerity). In common usage the advice "be sincere" almost unravels to falseness. Would theater similarly deconstruct the admonition to be *true*? Truth and honesty are of a parlance rich in awareness of the difficulty of knowing truth and speaking truthfully, of how truth can be hidden, contextual, ambiguous, paradoxical, and complex. In theater, truthfulness might well be the norm of sincerity, showing how sincerity is only meaningful as a part to discern and enact.

But theater also puts in doubt a kind of self-ownership that sincerity discourse can imply. If we largely know ourselves through the "masks" we perform with others, and with ourselves-as-other, then the pure self-ownership we may infer from Polonius is neither possible nor desirable. *Not possible:* there is "nothing" in back of masking but emptiness, although this emptiness need not be vacuous but, rather, a hospitable emptiness. Within our empty space of emerging possibilities, we cannot see ourselves except through all the particular parts, works, relations, and dreams that enter there. Some of these we make, but not one do we own, singularly or finally. *Not desirable:* if masks do not hide but *make* meaning, then a self apart from masks would suffer meaninglessness. So the relational self empties into and receives meanings from others—for better and worse, truthfully or not, justly or not, in love, indifference, and even bitterness—and thereby it meets "its self" coming to meet it. *One more oddity:* Polonius advises sincerity so that Laertes will not be false to people; but when the whole speech is examined, Polonius is proposing a shield against strangers. If a shield, then also a spear? Can sincerity also harm? The very frankness of Cordelia's "nothing" speech to her father may show the harm of subordinating one's other-relations to a perhaps unthinking notion of sincerity.[12]

Weak Self / Authentic Self

Another caveat to kenotic integrity is a double challenge, which warns that the emptying self is too "weak," yet is also an improvisational self that can claim imperious authenticity, like that of the Renaissance or Romantic genius. Paradoxically, in cultures influenced by Christianity, the figure of Jesus may stand behind both the weak, servant-of-suffering, which Nietzsche rejected, and the iconoclastic, poet-prophet that Nietzsche approved.

As to weakness, kenotic integrity takes as realistic the view that "to seek a self is to lose it" and "to lose a self" for others is perchance "to find" or receive it. These phrases make a multiple entendre. To seek a self could mean seeking a self so as to lose it (as in seeking a vocation in which to give or "lose" oneself), or to lose it in seeking to possess it (as in the irony of hubris). As to strength, kenotic integrity affirms reciprocal emptying and reception, provided that the return is contingent, ad hoc, and not a structure of necessity. Does the play of losing/finding mean that selves do not require prior, coherent, hence "strong" narratives? Kenotic integrity may agree that *selves are* only insofar as *they are narrative selves.* But past narratives are finite, fragmentary, distorted by rationalizations and pathologies, and need to be encountered anew and reconfigured. My past narrative-as-a-whole is, on the whole, simply *not there,* not unless it is given anew, and not only on past terms.

Against the objection that imitation negates authenticity, the paradigm of kenotic integrity is both imitative and innovative; it is a dialectic that may allow us to retrieve a better sense of authenticity, one in which the ensemble is as important as the individual improviser. This is where the figure of Jesus—who knows both John the Baptist and the "law and prophets" and who also enacts world-interrupting parables—informs and transcends our images both of the *itinerant troubadour* whose repertoire was highly generic and of the *poetic genius* who transforms generic forms. Each would enact the dialectic of imitation and innovation. For each, imitation is not static repetition but *receptivity* to persons, language, music, images, and ideas.[13]

Such receptivity begins to account for the prolific innovations of a Shakespeare, Blake, Virginia Woolf or, say, the Bob Dylan of Martin Scorsese's *No Direction Home* (2005) and Tod Haynes's *I'm Not There* (2007). In these films, the Dylan personae invent pasts and absorb other manners, musical forms, and moral-political "messages" and "causes" (to be sure, not words endearing to Dylan) from various singers and poets (such as Woody Guthrie and Arthur Rimbaud), which empty out into performances noted for their unaccountable innovations, which in turn are taken up by still more singers and "imitators." Kenotic integrity is relational. Relational selves can be those whose ensembles are tight-knit communities and families, or those whose ensembles are ever ahead of them and who require solitude. Jesus, while at times social, is no family man. Yet as "So alone" as Dylan is frequently shown to be in these films, he is nonetheless frequently seen in ensembles and indeed *is* an ensemble. In *I'm Not There*, several actors—Marcus Carl Franklin, Christian Bale, Cate Blanchett, Ben Whishaw, Heath Ledger, and Richard Gere—play figures representing different aspects of the fictionalized Dylan.

Relatively solitary paths into future ensembles, with and for others— and also paths of living and working together in relative anonymity in present ensembles—can be held in kenotic patterns of integrity. When Dylan's Good Samaritan dresses "for the show," is he dropping out, into a carnival world of grotesque abuse and horror? Or is he joining company among the least of those on Desolation Row, the singers and circus performers, and their interesting, marginal, sometimes nefarious entourage?[14] In kenotic patterns of integrity, the narratives of our past may return anew in our contingent futures, where we may receive others into our emptiness and where we may be received into theirs. Does this make for a person, self, or identity that is weak or strong? Kenotic integrity changes the import of such questions.

Credits

Notes

Preface

1. *Das Leben der Anderen* was written and directed by Florian Henckel von Donnersmarck, 2006, with Ulrich Mühe (Wiesler), Sebastian Koch (Dreyman), and Martina Gedeck (Sieland).

Introduction

The epigraph quotes Arthur Miller, *Death of a Salesman* (New York: Viking, 1949), 56. Shakespeare and Shaw are cited in later chapters. Excerpted drama texts are usually displayed (i.e., lined out and formatted) approximately as published and cited parenthetically by page or line number. The line abbreviations "l." and "ll." are used to indicate line numbers and avoid confusion with page numbers. In quoted matter, contracted ellipses (…) are part of the original text; expanded or normal ellipses (. . .) are my deletions. When my ellipses cover short portions of dialogue between speakers, to facilitate reading I have not always used the convention of a long line of points. When square brackets are part of quoted matter, I change them to another form, so all square brackets indicate my insertions.

1. See Stephen Carter, *Integrity* (New York: Basic Books, 1996). For analytic philosophical views of integrity, good places to begin are Lynne McFall, "Integrity," *Ethics* 98 (1987): 5–20, and Damian Cox, Marguerite La Caze, and Michael Levine, *Integrity and the Fragile Self* (Aldershot, UK: Ashgate, 2003).

2. Gabriele Taylor and Raimond Gaita, "Integrity," *Proceedings of the Aristotelian Society* 55 (1981): 143–76; for Gaita's response to Taylor, see 161–76.

3. The trait of wholehearted decisiveness also tends toward logical purity; see Harry Frankfurt, "Identification and Wholeheartedness," in his *The Importance of What We Care About: Philosophical Essays* (Cambridge: Cambridge University Press, 1988), 159–76.

4. Cheshire Calhoun discusses the management of conflicting social and normative elements of identity, including Maria Lugones on "Latina lesbians," in "Standing for Something," *Journal of Philosophy* 92 (1995): 235–60. Both possibilities (Latina and lesbian) are needed to describe such a person's "multitudinous being."

5. See Calhoun, "Standing for Something," and Cox et al.

6. John Rawls, *A Theory of Justice* (Cambridge: Harvard University Press, 1970), 519–20; italics mine.

7. See Ann Mongoven, "Impartiality as Practice," University of Virginia dissertation (Charlottesville, 1996). On moral integrity and willingness to keep commitments in adversity, see Mark S. Halfon, *Integrity: A Philosophical Inquiry* (Philadelphia: Temple University Press, 1989), 38–47.

8. Jody L. Graham, "Does Integrity Require Moral Goodness?" *Ratio* 14 (2001): 234–51.

9. Daniel Putman, "Integrity and Moral Development," *Journal of Value Inquiry* 36: 237–46, argues that integrity qualifies higher but not lower levels of development, as viewed by Carol Gilligan and Lawrence Kohlberg. The women whom Gilligan studied, in *In a Different Voice: Psychological Theory and Women's Development* (Cambridge: Harvard University Press, 1982, 1993), tended to value care over justice.

10. Iris Murdoch, *The Sovereignty of Good* (London: Routledge and Kegan Paul, 1970).

11. Susan Wolf, "Moral Saints," *Journal of Philosophy* 79 (1982): 419–39. Edward Lawry, "In Praise of Moral Saints," *Southwest Philosophy Review* 18 (2002): 1–18, praises them in terms of an ethics of virtue, not universal duties or obligations. On the conflict between seeming infinite obligations and finite personal interests and capacities, see William Schweiker, *Responsibility and Christian Ethics* (Cambridge: Cambridge University Press, 1995), 10–11.

12. Paul Ricoeur, *Oneself as Another,* trans. Kathleen Blamey (Chicago: University of Chicago Press, 1992), 338; see also David Bentley Hart in *The Beauty of the Infinite: The Aesthetics of Christian Truth* (Grand Rapids, MI: Eerdmans, 2003), 82. M. Jamie Ferreira unfolds a sense of mutuality in Levinas on hospitality and on the "infinite desire" for the other; see her "'Total Altruism' in Levinas's 'Ethics of the Welcome,'" *Journal of Religious Ethics* 29 (2001): 443–70, and "The Misfortune of the Happy: Levinas and the Ethical Dimensions of Desire," *Journal of Religious Ethics* 34 (2006): 461–83.

13. John Caputo, *Against Ethics: Contributions to a Poetics of Obligation with Constant Reference to Deconstruction* (Bloomington: Indiana University Press, 1993), 18. Edith Wyschogrod, *Saints and Postmodernism: Revisioning Moral Philosophy* (Chicago: University of Chicago Press, 1990), xxiv; to Wolf she replies that the saint's large regard for others is usually too interesting to be boring (286n.10).

14. Bernard Williams and Thomas Nagel use "moral luck" to describe the effects of chance on moral agency and evaluation; see essays in Daniel Statman, ed., *Moral Luck* (Albany: State University of New York Press, 1993).

15. Bernard Williams, "A Critique of Utilitarianism," in J. J. C. Smart and Bernard Williams, *Utilitarianism: For and Against* (Cambridge: Cambridge

University Press, 1973); see also Williams's "Persons, Character, and Morality" and "Moral Luck," in *Moral Luck: Philosophical Papers 1973–1980* (Cambridge: Cambridge University Press, 1981), 1–39. On how utilitarianism and deontology *can* envision personal integrity, see Sarah Conly, "Utilitarianism and Integrity," *Monist* 66 (1983): 298–311; Barbara Herman, "Integrity and Impartiality," *Monist* 66: 233–50; and Henning Jensen, "Kant and Moral Integrity," *Philosophical Studies* 57 (1989): 193–205. The latter think Kantian principles, seen as limit conditions, allow personal integrity; still, Williams does raise doubts about the articulacy of these philosophies in respect to persons.

16. Alasdair MacIntyre, *After Virtue,* 2nd. ed. (Notre Dame: Notre Dame University Press, 1984), especially 1–4, 27–34, 203–12, 242–43. For different critiques of MacIntyre, see Jeffrey Stout, *Ethics after Babel: The Languages of Morals and Their Discontents* (Boston: Beacon, 1988); and John Milbank, *Theology and Social Theory: Beyond Secular Reason* (Oxford, UK: Blackwell, 1990), 337–47.

17. Calhoun, 253–54.

18. Ruth W. Grant, *Hypocrisy and Integrity: Machiavelli, Rousseau, and the Ethics of Politics* (Chicago: University of Chicago Press, 1997), 16–17, 177–81. See Judith N. Shklar, *Ordinary Vices* (Cambridge: Belknap at Harvard University Press, 1984), 72–78.

19. On "weighing and balancing" moral principles, I am indebted to discussions in biomedical ethics, particularly James F. Childress, *Practical Moral Reasoning in Bioethics* (Bloomington: Indiana University Press, 1997).

20. Margaret Urban Walker, *Moral Understandings: A Study in Feminist Ethics* (New York: Routledge, 1998), 109; this discussion refers to her chapter 5, "Picking Up Pieces."

21. Ibid., 108.

22. See also Walker's, "Moral Luck and the Virtues of Impure Agency," in Statman.

23. Cox et al., *Integrity and the Fragile Self,* 41; italics mine.

24. Ibid., 7.

25. Jeffrey Stout, *Democracy and Tradition* (Princeton: Princeton University Press, 2004), 10.

26. See Susan E. Babbitt, *Artless Integrity: Moral Imagination, Agency, and Stories* (Lanham, Md.: Rowman and Littlefield, 2001), 134–35, 181–82, and *Impossible Dreams: Rationality, Integrity, and Moral Imagination* (Boulder, Colo.: Westview, 1996), 204–5.

27. Babbitt, *Impossible Dreams,* 24–29.

28. Jürgen Habermas, "On Hermeneutics' Claim to Universality," trans. Jerry Dibble, in *The Hermeneutics Reader: Texts of the German Tradition from the Enlightenment to the Present,* ed. Kurt Mueller-Vollmer (New York: Continuum, 1988), 294–319.

29. On imagination and construction, see Elaine Scarry, *The Body in Pain: The Making and Unmaking of the World* (New York: Oxford University Press, 1985), 161–80.

30. By this view, even when we refer to historical realizations of ideal practice, they, being in the past—hence, nonexistent—affect the present only via our imagining them now or in some future.

31. Schweiker, 33: "In all our actions and relations we are to respect and enhance the integrity of life before God." See Langdon Gilkey on human life and the integrity of natural process in *Nature, Reality, and the Sacred: The Nexus of Science and Religion* (Minneapolis, Minn.: Fortress, 1993), 150–52.

32. George Lakoff and Mark Johnson, *Metaphors We Live By* (Chicago: University of Chicago Press, 1980).

33. Walter Brueggemann, "A Neglected Sapiential Word Pair," *Zeitschrift fur die Alttestamentliche Wissenshaft* 89 (1977): 234–58. I am grateful to Esther Menn and Michael Satlow for assistance with Hebrew terms.

34. Jennifer L. Rike, "Loving with Integrity: A Feminist Spirituality of Wholeness," in *Spirituality, Ethics and Relationship in Adulthood: Clinical and Theoretical Explorations*, ed. Melvin E. Miller and Alan N. West (Madison, Conn.: Psychosocial Press, 2000), 150.

35. Most biblical citations are from the New Revised Standard Version (NRSV), copyright, 1989, Division of Christian Education of the National Council of the Churches of Christ in the USA.

36. The Greek Septuagint (LXX) translates *tam* as *akakia,* guilelessness, without bodily connotations.

37. See Cora Diamond, "Integrity," in *Encyclopedia of Ethics,* ed. Lawrence C. Becker (New York: Garland, 1992), and Jonathan Lear, *Open Minded: Working Out the Logic of the Soul* (Cambridge: Harvard University Press, 1998), 227–39. See also comments on integrity, ecology, holiness, and wholeness in Mark I. Wallace, *Fragments of the Spirit: Nature, Violence, and the Renewal of Creation* (New York: Continuum, 1996), 226.

38. E.g., A. C. Graham, *Disputers of the Tao: Philosophical Argument in Ancient China* (La Salle, Ill.: Open Court, 1989), 133.

39. On social and personal ordering, see David L. Hall and Roger T. Ames, *Thinking Through Confucius* (Albany: State University of New York Press, 1987), 156–68; on *cheng* (sincerity, absence of double-mindedness) extending to others and to "heaven," see Fung Yu-lan, *A History of Chinese Philosophy,* vol. 1, trans. Derk Bodde (Princeton: Princeton University Press, 1952), 129–30, 375–76; Benjamin I. Schwartz, *The World of Thought in Ancient China* (Cambridge: Harvard University Press, 1985), 405.

40. On performative aspects of Confucian concepts, see Herbert Fingarette, *Confucius: The Secular as Sacred* (New York: Harper and Row, 1972). However, Schwartz, 72, credits Confucius (*pace* Fingarette) with a discovery

of "the inner life of individuals." I am grateful to Robert Campany, Paul Groner, and Anthony C. Yu for assistance with Chinese terms.

41. On wholeness and plurality, see James Gutmann, "Integrity as a Standard of Valuation," *Journal of Philosophy* 4 (1945): 210–16. In German, no words—other than the borrowed *Integrität* and *Integer*—quite capture etymologically the whole/part and ethical connotations of integrity. *Redlichkeit* primarily connotes honesty in speech. Whatever has the quality of *Unverfalschtheit* is genuine, unadulterated, pure, not a false imitation. A person of *Unbescholtenheit* is respectable or chaste. To speak of personal wholeness, one might add *Ganzheit* to this semantic field.

42. Paul Ricoeur, *Interpretation Theory: Discourse and the Surplus of Meaning* (Fort Worth: Texas Christian University Press, 1976), 51.

43. See James F. Childress, "Metaphor and Analogy," in *Encyclopedia of Bioethics,* 2nd. ed., ed., Warren Thomas Reich, 5 vols. (New York: Macmillan, 1995) 3: 1765–73.

44. See Janet Martin Soskice, *Metaphor and Religious Language* (Oxford: Oxford University Press, 1985), 15.

45. Soskice observes that some but by no means all metaphors are those of conflicting predications, as Ricoeur may imply. See, as well, Frank Burch Brown, *Transfiguration: Poetic Metaphor and the Languages of Religious Belief* (Chapel Hill: University of North Carolina Press, 1983), 43–44.

46. Like Babbitt, Adam Zachary Newton, *Narrative Ethics* (Cambridge: Harvard University Press, 1995), 62–64, criticizes Nussbaum (see below) for privileging narratives of fine discernment, rather than stories of less articulate characters (e.g., Sherwood Anderson's *Winesburg, Ohio*).

47. Alasdair MacIntyre, "Epistemological Crisis, Dramatic Narrative, and the Philosophy of Science," *Monist* 60 (1977): 453–72.

48. See Richard Hornby, *Script into Performance: A Structuralist Approach* (New York: Applause Books, 1977, 1995), for a rejection of this dichotomy.

49. See Ricoeur on the conflict structure of metaphor, *Interpretation Theory,* 51, 68.

50. Peter Brook, *The Empty Space* (New York: Atheneum, 1968), 107–8.

51. Peter Shaffer, *Amadeus* (New York: Harper and Row, 1980, 1981), 57–58. See Max Harris on this passage in *Theater and Incarnation* (New York: St Martins, 1990), 33–34.

52. Frank Burch Brown, *Religious Aesthetics: A Theological Study of Making and Meaning* (Princeton: Princeton University Press, 1989), 16–19, 136–57.

53. Shaffer, 66.

54. MacIntyre and Ricoeur implicitly recognize the problem of moral inarticulacy about delight, as does Williams. Wyschograd (see 160) views narrative praxis as preceding moral concepts; her "postmodern saint" may be another candidate for the paradigms I am seeking.

55. Martha Nussbaum, Introduction to *Love's Knowledge* (New York: Oxford University Press, 1990), 3–6.

56. Newton, 8–14.

57. Daniel Boyarin, "Voices in the Text: Midrash and the Inner Tension of Biblical Narrative," *Revue biblique* 93–4 (1986): 581–97; see also Emil Fackenheim, *God's Presence in History: Jewish Affirmations and Philosophical Reflections* (New York: Harper and Row, 1970), 20–25, 69–92.

58. On narrative "gaps," see Wolfgang Iser, *The Act of Reading: A Theory of Aesthetic Response* (Baltimore: Johns Hopkins University Press, 1978), 169.

59. Miller, 56.

60. "Attestation" and trust in being a self, in Ricoeur, *Oneself as Another,* 21–22, reply to critiques of the Cartesian cogito. See Kevin Hart, *The Dark Gaze: Maurice Blanchot and the Sacred* (Chicago: University of Chicago Press, 2004), 122–23, commenting on Ricoeur, Levinas, and Blanchot.

61. Besides Brook, see Les Essif, *Empty Figure on an Empty Stage: The Theatre of Samuel Beckett and His Generation* (Bloomington: Indiana University Press, 2001), 15–27. On kenotic ontology, see Oliver Davies, *A Theology of Divine Compassion: Metaphysics of Difference and the Renewal of Tradition* (Grand Rapids, Mich.: Eerdmans, 2001), which may require a "stronger" self than I can affirm at the outset. "Unless we put ourselves at risk knowingly, with the self-awareness of a unified subject . . . , we do not put ourselves at risk at all. Rather, we are put at risk by forces extrinsic to the self" (9). I may be asking about the exclusiveness of these alternatives, between active and passive "risk."

62. See Elizabeth Burns, *Theatricality: A Study of Convention in the Theatre and in Social Life* (London: Longman, 1972); Erving Goffman, *The Presentation of Self in Everyday Life* (1959; Woodstock, N.Y.: Overlook, 1973); Kenneth Burke, *A Grammar of Motives* (New York: Prentice-Hall, 1945); Bruce Wilshire, *Role Playing and Identity: The Limits of Theatre as Metaphor* (Bloomington: Indiana University Press, 1982).

63. Ricoeur, *Oneself as Another,* contrasts *idem* and *ipse* in respect to self-identity, 2–3; see also Calvin O. Schrag, *The Self after Postmodernity* (New Haven: Yale University Press, 1997), 35–37.

64. Bert O. States's view of how characters overtly persist in a drama is similar to the sense I assign to *person:* "[C]haracter is what is always all there. There is never less of Hamlet or Horatio in one scene than in another," *Hamlet and the Concept of Character* (Baltimore: Johns Hopkins University Press, 1992), 19.

65. See Hans-Georg Gadamer on the "fore-structure of understanding" and "fusion of horizons" in *Truth and Method,* 2nd rev. ed., trans., ed. by Joel Weinsheimer and Donald Marshall, 265–71 (New York: Crossroad, 1989).

66. Burns, 129.

67. Lionel Abel, *Metatheatre: A New View of a Dramatic Form* (New York: Hill and Wang, 1963). See also Richard Hornby, *Drama, Metadrama, and Perception* (Lewisburg, Pa.: Bucknell University Press, 1986).

Prelude to Part I

The lines quoted are from the brochure for the Pearl Theatre Company, Shepard Sobel, Artistic Director, 1998.

1. See David Hapgood, *Year of the Pearl: The Life of a New York Repertory Company* (New York: Knopf, 1993), 5.

2. Emil Durkheim, *The Elementary Forms of the Religious Life,* trans. Joseph Ward Swain (1915; New York: Free Press, 1965), 62.

3. "Norms" and "principles" both speak to obligations that Ricoeur and others call *moral*. One could distinguish "principles" as linguistic and logical forms that specify "norms," presumed to be prior; e.g., "honesty" is the norm behind the principle, "do not lie (except when . . .)."

4. Ricoeur, *Oneself as Another,* chs. 7–9.

5. A list of principles based on usage in biomedical ethics; see Childress, *Practical Moral Reasoning in Bioethics,* 25–43.

6. Ricoeur's hermeneutics was a detour that became a main road of his phenomenological philosophy of the will. With *Freedom and Nature: The Voluntary and the Involuntary* (French, 1950)—the first movement of this project—he neared an impasse, which he explicated in the second movement, *Fallible Man* (English trans. of part 1 of *Finitude et culpabilité,* 1960). While thought can grasp the *possibility* that the will contradicts itself (Luther's bondage of the will), thought cannot *directly* grasp the sheer fact of fault. There is an indirect way around this impasse: actual fault is expressed in confession and testimony, types of discourse laden in myth, symbol, and metaphor; and such discourse is available for description and interpretation. So in *The Symbolism of Evil* (part 2 of *Finitude et culpabilité*) Ricoeur takes a long "detour" through hermeneutics, culminating in *Time and Narrative* (3 vols., English, 1983–85)—the point being that interpretation is a capability and activity of the self. Though a planned "poetics of the will" never appeared, the philosophy of the will continued, as in *Oneself as Another* (French, 1990). In *Memory, History, and Forgetting* (French, 2000), Ricoeur examines how mnemonic aspects of volition inform historical awareness. Ricoeur texts will be fully cited when first quoted. For a helpful recent analysis, see W. David Hall, *Paul Ricoeur and the Poetic Imperative: The Creative Tension Between Love and Justice* (Albany: State University of New York Press, 2007).

7. On the analogy between texts and meaningful actions, see Ted Klein's 1986 essay, "The Idea of a Hermeneutical Ethics," in *The Philosophy of Paul Ricoeur,* ed. Lewis Edwin Hahn (Chicago: Open Court, 1995), 349–66.

8. Ricoeur, *Oneself as Another,* 2–3.

9. Ibid., ch. 9: "The Self and Practical Wisdom: Conviction." For a succinct restatement of self-esteem and self-respect, see Ricoeur, *The Just*, trans. David Pellauer (Chicago: University of Chicago Press, 2000), ch. 1: "Who Is the Subject of Rights?"

10. Paul Ricoeur, *Interpretation Theory*, 71–95.

11. Ricoeur, *Oneself as Another*, 172 (italics in text). Hall, 94, notes that for Ricoeur, the moral is Kantian, the ethical is Aristotelian. But in principle, utilitarian principles would be included in moral "testing."

12. E.g., Pamela Sue Anderson, "Reclamation of Autonomy: Unity, Plurality, and Totality," in *Paul Ricoeur and Contemporary Moral Thought*, ed. John Wall, William Schweiker, and W. David Hall. (New York: Routledge, 2002).

13. E.g., Peter Kemp, "Narrative Ethics and Moral Law in Ricoeur," and John Wall, "Moral Meaning: Beyond the Good and Right," in Wall, Schweiker, and Hall. Kemp thinks the dialectic of the ethical (narrative) and the moral (principles) fails, and that Ricoeur should recognize there is no getting behind different levels of narrative. Wall believes Ricoeur needs a fuller account of the "narrative unity of life" and the "concept of the critical good" (60–61).

14. The Golden Rule (in several forms, such as "do not do to others what you would not want to happen to you") figures in many of Ricoeur's ethical discussions; he thinks John Rawls's procedural theory of justice as fairness tacitly assumes it, and he regards the Rule as an antisacrificial principle that resists an implication of utilitarianism, that some will need to be sacrificed for the greater good. See *The Just*, 37–39.

15. Martha Nussbaum, *The Fragility of Goodness: Luck and Ethics in Greek Tragedy and Philosophy* (Cambridge: Cambridge University Press, 1986), 7, 81, 221.

16. In his *Critique and Conviction: Conversations with François Azouvi and Marc de Launay*, trans. Kathleen Blamey (New York: Columbia University Press, 1998), 32, Ricoeur comments that he had always been "more attentive to the opposition between saint and sinner" than to his friend Mircea Eliade's "opposition between sacred and profane."

17. See Søren Kierkegaard, *The Concept of Anxiety*, trans. Reidar Thomte and Albert B. Anderson (Princeton: Princeton University Press, 1980), 32; and "'Original Sin': A Study in Meaning," trans. Peter McCormick, in Paul Ricoeur, *The Conflict of Interpretations*, ed. Don Ihde (Evanston, Ill.: Northwestern University Press, 1974), 274.

18. See Reinhold Niebuhr, "The Truth in Myths," in *The Nature of Religious Experience: Essays in Honor of Douglas Clyde Macintosh*, ed. J. S. Bixler (New York: Harper, 1937), and Niebuhr's *The Nature and Destiny of Man*, 2 vols. (New York: Scribners, 1941, 1943), 1:179–85, 251–60; see also Ricoeur, "'Original Sin.'"

19. See Paul Ricoeur, *The Symbolism of Evil,* trans. Emerson Buchanan (Boston: Beacon, 1967), 216–17; J. M. Bremer, *Hamartia: Tragic Error in the Poetics of Aristotle and in Greek Tragedy* (Amsterdam: Hakkert, 1969).

20. See my "Contingency, Tragedy, Sin, and Ultimacy: Trajectories in Langdon Gilkey's Interpretations of History and Nature," in *The Theology of Langdon B. Gilkey,* ed. Kyle A. Pasewark and Jeff B. Pool (Macon, Ga.: Mercer University Press, 1999).

21. Ricoeur, *Oneself as Another,* 249.

22. Ibid., 244, 245, largely in agreement with Nussbaum on *Antigone.*

23. Wall, 57.

24. Caputo, *Against Ethics,* 25.

Chapter 1

The epigraph quotes *Antigone,* trans. David Grene in *Sophocles 1,* ed. Grene and Richmond Lattimore (Chicago: University of Chicago Press, 1991), cited parenthetically by approximate Greek line numbers.

1. Halfon, *Integrity,* 38–47, and similar discussions create paradoxes. If the risks necessary to integrity are so great as to be supererogatory, would moral integrity somehow *not* be morally required? Conversely, might not integrity sometimes (as Ismene implies) require *avoiding* certain risks in order to uphold other obligations, say, to one's family? But if so, might such prudence sometimes involve more subtle risks, as to one's honor or to one's personal integrity?

2. See Christiane Sourvinou-Inwood, "Assumptions and the Creation of Meaning: Reading Sophocles' *Antigone," Journal of Hellenic Studies* 109 (1989): 134–48. Sourvinou-Inwood argues that an Athenian audience would bring little sympathy to Antigone—a woman defying both polis and house (*oikos*), since her uncle Creon was now by default its head—and would have granted Creon's authority to deny Polyneices religious burial, inasmuch as executed traitors were commonly "thrown into the pit." What is shown to be wrong is his violation of the cosmic order by leaving Polyneices' body *above ground,* offending the chthonic deities. While her marginalizing (on audience/reader response grounds) Antigone's claims about owing her bother a proper burial may seem tendentious, Sourvinou-Inwood's views of Antigone's disregard of sacral aspects of polis and *oikos,* and of Creon's *hamartia,* strike me as persuasive.

3. See Charles Segal, *Tragedy and Civilization: An Interpretation of Sophocles* (Cambridge: Harvard University Press, 1981). Myths and rituals, especially since Nietzsche's distinction between Dionysian dynamics and Apollonian form, have been interpreted as providing cultures with frameworks that control power, conflict, and chaos—realities that remain dormant in psyche and society. A culture's mythic structures, then, are like a clay pot holding simmering soup. Particular plays or epic poems (not them-

selves myths) are seen both to celebrate and also to interrogate the myths. The poets, in other words, expose both the heat in the "soup" and the cracks in the "pot." They do so, thinks James Redfield (following Aristotle against Plato), by putting the culture's values and norms under the stress of a complex *muthos* or plot. The play is like a hypothesis that asks, "What if?" What if a king was told he had killed his father and married his mother? How would he respond, whom would he believe, what would others believe about him, how would he rule, how would he understand himself? His story could be fashioned to show the pot cracking but not quite shattering. See Redfield, *Nature and Culture in the Iliad: The Tragedy of Hector* (Chicago: University of Chicago Press, 1975), chs. 1–2 on Aristotle and tragedy. See also Nussbaum, *The Fragility of Goodness,* which treats the tragedies as arguments with philosophers over the impact of contingency on virtue.

4. Patricia Jagentowicz Mills, "Hegel's *Antigone,*" in *Feminist Interpretations of G. W. F. Hegel,* ed. P. J. Mills (University Park: Pennsylvania State University Press, 1996), 59–88.

5. Mills argues that besides ignoring (1) sister-sister solidarity, Hegel also disregards (2) how Antigone's moral choice against Creon is courageous and *conscious,* not merely intuitive, (3) how she openly, without irony transcends her family without denying it, and thus realizes herself as particular, and (4) how her suicide completes a public act on behalf of the private sphere, rejecting Creon's assertion of the "right of the universal *over* the particular" (Mills's emphasis).

6. See G. W. F. Hegel, *Phenomenology of Spirit,* trans. A. V. Miller (London: Oxford University Press, 1977), 284. Mills and others notice how Hegel mistranslates (as "because") the conditional qualifier in *Antigone,* l. 924, thus implying that Antigone acknowledges error in asserting kinship against citizenship. However, Antigone means: *If* I am punished rightly by god's law, I'll soon know the truth after I die; but if Creon is guilty, may his suffering be no worse than he wrongly inflicts on me (see ll. 924–28, and Mills, 70).

7. Judith Butler, *Antigone's Claim: Kinship Between Life and Death* (New York: Columbia University Press, 2000), 77; italics mine. Jacques Derrida also criticizes Hegel, for treating the sister–brother relation as a transcendental exception to his system, in *Glas,* trans. John P. Leavey Jr. and Richard Rand (Lincoln: University of Nebraska Press, 1974), 151, 162–63.

8. Jean Anouilh, *Antigone* (Paris: La Table Ronde, 1946), 71–72, 89–90; my translations; see Lewis Galantiere's version in *Jean Anouilh,* vol. I: *Five Plays* (New York: Hill and Wang, 1958).

9. Anouilh, 95, 96. Antigone can only be referring to events in *Oedipus at Colonus,* not *Oedipus the King,* where Oedipus, after blinding himself in shame and rage, was hardly at peace.

10. Ibid., 115–16.

11. It is often reported that because the play's political substance was so ambiguous, both the Nazis and the French resistance fighters who saw it in Paris thought it supported their causes.

12. See Mary Douglas on "the abominations of Leviticus," in *Purity and Danger: An Analysis of Concepts of Pollution and Taboo* (London: Routledge, 1966), 41–57.

13. In the passages quoted, *philia*-related words are used for love, implying friendship and fraternity. But besides references to the bridal chamber, the Chorus's ode to *erōs* and Aphrodite (ll. 781–805) establish erotic connotations as well.

14. Scarry, *Body in Pain*, 109; see especially 14, 114–18.

15. Ibid., 178–79; while she does not explicitly link the bodily realization of the imagined Marshall Plan to analogical verification, it would seem implicit.

16. See Maurice Merleau-Ponty, *Phenomenology of Perception*, trans. Colin Smith (London: Routledge and Kegan Paul, 1962), 140. This 1945 work stands behind Ricoeur's philosophy of the will and a good many other phenomenological accounts of embodiment.

17. Nussbaum's trans., in *Fragility of Goodness*, 63. The Greek is transliterated from the Loeb ed., *Sophocles: Antigone, the Women of Trachis, Philoctetes, Oedipus at Colonus,* trans. Hugh Lloyd-Jones (Cambridge: Harvard University Press, 1994).

18. Howard Pickett offered this observation, suggestive of metatheatrical implications in the play.

19. See Lloyd-Jones at 1080–83. The cities may be those who joined Polyneices against Thebes.

20. See René Girard's theses about tragedy, culture, and sacrifice in *Violence and the Sacred,* trans. Patrick Gregory (Baltimore: Johns Hopkins University Press, 1977).

21. Michael Spingler, "Anouilh's Little Antigone: Tragedy, Theatricalism, and the Romantic Self," *Comparative Drama* 8 (1974): 228–38.

22. See Rawls's distinction in *A Theory of Justice*, 368–69.

23. See James F. Childress, "Appeals to Conscience," *Ethics* 89 (1979): 315–55; Childress observes that appellants to conscience perceive their integrity to be threatened by authorities whose requirements create intolerable moral dilemmas. All other arguments, short of appealing to the inviolability of conscience, have been ineffective; were the appellants now to acquiesce, their integrity would not withstand the judgment of their future selves. They say, "'I could not live with myself' . . . 'A man has to answer to himself first,'" etc. For such persons, according to Childress, conscience functions not as a moral authority (for they invest authority in paramount principles) but as a "personal sanction." That is, my conscience engages me in an interior dialogue or drama: it warns that my very self is in danger.

24. Childress thinks "the state must intend that conscience not be injured even to the extent of assuming some burdens and costs to prevent such injury," including protecting objectors to military service, jury duty, etc. (ibid., 331).

25. James F. Childress, "Nonviolent Resistance: Trust and Risk-Taking," *Journal of Religious Ethics* 1 (1973): 87–112; see also his "'Answering That of God in Every Man': An Interpretation of George Fox's Ethics," *Quaker Religious Thought* 15 (1974): 2–41.

26. Childress writes, "For Gandhi one's opponents should feel secure not because of their superior strength but because they discern an intention of non-harm in the resisters. . . . He insisted that if Indians could make Englishmen feel that 'their lives are protected against harm not because of matchless weapons of destruction which are at their disposal, but because Indians refuse to take the lives even of those whom they consider to be utterly in the wrong,' England's relationship to India would be completely transformed" ("Nonviolent Resistance," 97, quoting Gandhi).

27. Mary Whitlock Blundell, *Helping Friends and Harming Enemies: A Study in Sophocles and Greek Ethics* (New York: Cambridge University Press, 1989), 111–15.

Chapter II

The first epigraph quotes Jean Anouilh, *Becket, or, The Honor of God*, trans. Lucienne Hill (1960; New York: Riverhead, 1995), 34, cited parenthetically. The French is from *Becket ou l'honneur de Dieu*, ed. Bettina L. Knapp and Alba della Fazia (1959; New York: Appleton Century Crofts, 1969).

The second epigraph is from T. S. Eliot, *Murder in the Cathedral*, "With an introduction and notes by Nevill Coghill" (London: Faber and Faber, 1965). Cited parenthetically by line number, and by act number when needed for clarity. I will refer to "Thomas" in Eliot's play and "Becket" in other contexts.

1. Churchill quoted in Victor Turner, "Religious Paradigms and Political Action: Thomas Becket at the Council of Northampton," in *Dramas, Fields, and Metaphors: Symbolic Action in Human Society* (Ithaca: Cornell University Press, 1974), 60–97. Turner can be located among apologists for Becket, another being Anne Duggan, *Thomas Becket* (London: Arnold, 2004).

2. David Knowles, *Thomas Becket* (London: Adam and Charles Black, 1970), 139.

3. Frank Barlow, *Thomas Becket* (Berkeley: University of California Press, 1986), 86–87.

4. Barlow begins and ends his book on this theme, citing Peter of Celle's letter to John of Salisbury, ca. 1172, about the time John wrote an early biography of Becket. The first miracles were reported early in 1171, Thomas was canonized in 1173, and Henry's penance was in 1174.

5. Knowles, 169, reports that Becket came to view his struggle over the life of the Church to be "one which, like a tragic drama, could be resolved only by death."

6. See my "In Front of the Mask: The Priest in Contemporary Dramas of Integrity," *Word and World* 9 (1989): 372–81, and the chapter on Rolf Hochhuth in my *Tragic Method and Tragic Theology: Evil in Contemporary Drama and Religious Thought* (University Park: Pennsylvania State University Press, 1989).

7. For using Eliot's "pattern" to describe selves in relation to time and to others, I thank Judy Mae Cato, "Sea Drift: The Pattern of History in T. S. Eliot's *Four Quartets:* A Study of Eliot's Transformation of Wordsworth's Narrative Mode," University of Virginia dissertation, 1990.

8. Elder Olson, *Tragedy and the Theory of Drama* (Detroit: Wayne State University Press, 1966), 251–55. I write these observations in memory of Professor Olson, who taught the play vividly.

9. See Coghill, "Notes," 116–17, commenting on ll. 553–60.

10. In a prefatory note, Anouilh says his source was an 1847 history by Augustin Thierry. After learning of the mistake, he decided to leave the play as was. Turner observes that since Becket was admired by the English peasants, Anouilh was in a dramatic sense correct.

11. There is little or no history behind this subplot. Perhaps Anouilh noticed Thierry's racy comment that Becket shared Henry's "table, his games, and even his debaucheries," in *The Conquest of England*, vol. 2, trans. William Hazlitt (London: Dent, 1907), 61.

12. See Clifford Geertz, *The Interpretation of Cultures*, especially the chapters "Toward Thick Description" and "Religion as a Cultural System" (New York: Basic, 1973). In *From Ritual to Theatre: The Human Seriousness of Play* (New York: Performing Arts Journal Publications, 1982), 73, Victor Turner writes, "By paradigm I do not mean a system of univocal concepts, logically arrayed. I do not mean either a stereotyped set of guidelines for ethical, aesthetic, or conventional action." I read him implying that paradigms are prior to but not determinative of such systems, and, as well, render them less than stable.

13. Turner, ibid., italics mine.

14. All quotes from Turner on Becket are from "Religious Paradigms and Political Action." Carolyn Walker Bynum, in "Women's Stories, Women's Symbolism," in *Anthropology and the Study of Religion*, ed. Robert L. Moore and Frank E. Reynolds (Chicago: Center for the Scientific Study of Religion, 1984), 105–25, thinks his analysis is rather thin and derivative; I comment further on Bynum in a note in chapter IX.

15. Duggan, 25–27, in explaining why Becket did not immediately resign the chancellorship when consecrated archbishop in June 1162, notes that he did resign in August after receiving the *pallium*, insignia of his obedience to the pope and authority over other bishops.

16. See Alba Della Fazia, *Jean Anouilh* (New York: Twayne, 1969), 23–28.

17. I discuss Eliot's poetic-dramatic strategies and criticisms of his practice in chapter XI.

18. See my discussion of Elaine Scarry on "analogical verification" in chapter I.

19. Francis Fergusson, *The Idea of a Theater: A Study of Ten Plays and the Art of Drama in Changing Perspective* (Princeton: Princeton University Press, 1949), 215. E. Martin Browne in *The Making of T. S. Eliot's Plays* (Cambridge: Cambridge University Press, 1969), 44, has no ready answer to "What does Eliot mean by this moment?"

20. Jim W. Corder, *Uses of Rhetoric* (Philadelphia: Lippincott, 1971), 72–77, on Aristotle's "ethical argument" and Pope's image of climbing the Alps in his poem "An Essay on Criticism."

21. S. M. Halloran, "On the End of Rhetoric, Classical and Modern," *College English* 36 (1975): 621–30.

22. T. S. Eliot, *Poetry and Drama* (Cambridge: Harvard University Press, 1951), 26.

23. After filming the play, George Hoellering, in T. S. Eliot and Hoellering, *The Film of Murder in the Cathedral* (New York: Harcourt, Brace, 1952), felt the Knights' speeches "amused the audience instead of shocking them, and thereby made them miss the . . . point of the whole play" (xiv). Yet Hoellering may neglect how laughter need not be inconsistent with horrifying self-discovery. Browne, 60, says Eliot was surprised by a French production, where the speeches were frightening. "However much English audiences laugh at the scene," Browne observes, "it is well that this kind of menace should underlie its performance."

24. Apart from the sermon, Thomas has few liturgical lines, which often come at emotional peaks, as when he dies commending to the saints "my cause and that of the Church" (II.396). The Priests, in part II, mark the days between the sermon and the murder by carrying banners and meditating on the feasts of St. Stephen, St. John, and the Holy Innocents, which advances time but not action. Browne, 48, reports cutting this pageant when the play moved to London.

25. See Mircea Eliade on "the terror of history" in *The Myth of the Eternal Return, or Cosmos and History,* trans. Willard R. Trask (Princeton: Princeton University Press, 1954).

26. See William V. Spanos, *The Christian Tradition in Modern British Verse Drama: The Poetics of Sacramental Time* (New Brunswick, N.J.: Rutgers University Press, 1967), 88–89. Eliot also develops the "still point" metaphor in *Four Quartets.* See Louis L. Martz, "The Wheel and the Point: Aspects of Imagery and Theme in Eliot's Later Poetry," *Sewanee Review* 55 (1947): 126–47; Frank Burch Brown, *Transfiguration,* 56; and Michael Levenson, "The End of Tradition and the Beginning of History," in *Words in*

Time: New Essays on Eliot's Four Quartets, ed. Edward Lobb (Ann Arbor: University of Michigan Press, 1993), 158–78.

27. Katharine Worth wishes the panic, disgust, and alienation of the Chorus could be more theatrically realized than it was in Browne's production, along with the frightening imagery of cleansing the earth and air; see her "Eliot and the Living Theatre," in *Eliot in Perspective: A Symposium,* ed. Graham Martin (New York: Humanities, 1970), 148–66.

28. After the Knights' speeches, the clerics' prayers to St. Thomas (II.581–616) are not as effective as the doxology of the Chorus (ll. 618–50). I would reduce the Priests' prayers and let the Women assume a priestly task. Having them attend to the body apart from the Priests would be justified by the time after the murder when Thomas lay deserted, as reported by William FitzStephen. See Knowles, 148; Duggan, 214–15. I am appreciative of an engaging production at Princeton Theological Seminary in 2002, directed by Robert Lanchester.

29. See Duggan, 253–69.

30. Stanley Hauerwas and T. L. Shaffer, "Hope Faces Power: Thomas More and the King of England," *Soundings* 61 (1978): 456–79.

31. Robert Bolt, *A Man for All Seasons* (New York: Vintage, 1960, 1962), Preface, xi.

32. Ibid., 48.

33. See Peter Ackroyd, *The Life of Thomas More* (New York: Doubleday, 1998).

34. Ibid., 310.

35. See Stephen Greenblatt, *Renaissance Self-Fashioning: From More to Shakespeare* (Chicago: University of Chicago Press, 1980), 108–14.

Chapter III

Parts of this chapter, here much revised, appeared in a festschrift for Nathan Scott, in *Morphologies of Faith: Essays in Honor of Nathan A. Scott, Jr.,* ed. Mary Gerhart and Anthony C. Yu (Atlanta: Scholars Press, 1990).

The epigraph quotes from Wole Soyinka, *Death and the King's Horseman,* abbr. *DKH* (New York: Hill and Wang, 1975), 69. Available in a critical edition, ed. Simon Gikandi (New York: Norton, 2003).

1. *Keely and Du* (New York: Samuel French, 1993), by Jane Martin, probable pseudonym for Jon Jory; see Nancy Wick, "The Mystery of Jane Martin," *Columns* (March 2002; http://www.washington.edu/alumni/columns/march02/jory_martin.html).

2. See MacIntyre, *After Virtue,* 6–7. For a positive assessment of moral disagreement in diverse, modern society, see Jeffrey Stout, *Ethics After Babel: The Languages of Morals and Their Discontents* (Boston: Beacon, 1988), discussing abortion on 42.

3. For his cultural and educational background, see Wole Soyinka, *Ake: The Years of Childhood* (New York: Vintage, 1981), and Simon Gikandi's introduction to the critical edition of *DKH*. Soyinka grew up in a Nigerian Anglican family, where Yoruba traditions were an accepted presence.

4. See Gadamer, *Truth and Method,* 267–71. There has been controversy about Soyinka's valorization of the Yoruba worldview. Biodun Jeyifo, in *The Truthful Lie: Essays in a Sociology of African Drama* (London: New Beacon, 1985), 34, criticizes *DKH* for endorsing Elesin's honor: "the notion of honour (and integrity and dignity) . . . rests on the patriarchal, feudalist code of the ancient Oyo Kingdom, a code built on class entrenchment and class consolidation." Ketu H. Ketrak, however, thinks "Soyinka is surely questioning this kind of heavy communal demand which requires a man to sacrifice his life for the sake of some unspecified benefit to the community," in *Wole Soyinka and Modern Tragedy: A Study of Dramatic Theory and Practice* (New York: Greenwood, 1986), 89–90. Adebayo Williams defends the "utopian dimension" of Elesin's ritual, which contrasts with colonialist discourse, in "Ritual as Social Symbolism: Cultural Death and the King's Horseman," in *Soyinka: A Collection of Critical Essays,* ed. Oyin Ogunba (Ibadan, Nigeria: Syndicated Communications, 1994), 89–102. Derek Wright, 74–75, *Wole Soyinka Revisited* (New York: Twayne, 1993), also thinks Soyinka views Yoruba traditions as resources for cultural flourishing, postindependence; see Soyinka's "Who's Afraid of Elesin Oba?" in his *Art, Dialogue and Outrage: Essays on Literature and Culture,* ed., Biodun Jeyifu (Ibadan: New Horn Press, 1988), 110–31. But Wright points to inconsistencies in his mythic appropriation; some question its authenticity. Isidore Okpewho writes, "the tormented figure of the Yoruba god Ogun . . . cannot be separated from the trouble-torn personality of our poet-dramatist," in *Myth in Africa: A Study of Its Aesthetic and Cultural Relevance* (Cambridge: Cambridge University Press, 1983), 257.

5. Frank Rich did not think a 1987 New York staging by Soyinka at Lincoln Center overcame either the audience's incomprehension or the impression of "clash of cultures" (review of *DKH, New York Times,* March 2, 1987). But a 2009 Royal National Theatre production in London, directed by Rufus Norris, arguably did. To me it seemed that by casting the British with black actors in whiteface (as in the original 1976 production at the University of Ife), the joy of satire was increased—but not at the expense of issues of "understanding," which Jane later articulates. On the Ife staging, see Gerald Moore's review in Gikandi's Norton edition of *DKH,* 113–14. Of the 1987 New York production, Soyinka discerned "stages" of audience reception—in an interview by Laura Jones, published in Soyinka, *Art, Dialogue and Outrage,* 330–44.

6. Duro Ladipo, *Oba Wàjà,* in *Three Plays,* trans. Ulli Beier (Ibadan: Mbari Publications, 1964), 72. The text is reprinted in the Norton edition of *DKH*.

7. On Soyinka's diverse audiences, see Tundonu Arnosu, "The Nigerian Dramatist and His Audience: The Question of Language and Culture," *Odu* 28 (1985): 35–45; and Chuck Mike, *Soyinka as Director: Interview* (Ife: University of Ife, 1986). On theater performed between colonists and subjects, see Max Harris, *The Dialogical Theatre: Dramatizations of the Conquest of Mexico and the Question of the Other* (New York: St. Martins, 1993).

8. David Richards, on "Masks of Language" in *DKH,* in Gikandi, 196–207, these being excerpts from Richard's *Masks of Difference: Cultural Representations in Literature, Anthropology, and Art* (Cambridge: Cambridge University Press, 1994).

9. The 1946 date noted by both Ladipo and Soyinka is wrong; the incident happened in 1944–45. James Gibbs traces the error in "Elesin Oba, Who Stopped the Drums?" *Thisday* (Lagos, Nigeria), Oct. 8, 2000 (http://www.thisdayonline.com/archive.php). However, as neither Ladipo's opera nor the historical incident relate to the war, Soyinka is right to say he shifted the story to the World War II context; see also D. S. Izevbaye, "Mediation in Soyinka: The Case of the King's Horseman," in *Critical Perspectives on Wole Soyinka,* ed. James Gibbs (Washington, D.C.: Three Continents Press, 1980), reprinted in Gikandi, 141–51, at 149.

10. See Oludare Olajubu, "Iwi Egungun Chants—An Introduction," in *Critical Perspectives on Nigerian Literatures,* ed. Bernth Lindsfors (Washington, D.C.: Three Continents Press, 1975); and Margaret Thompson Drewal, *Yoruba Ritual: Performers, Play, Agency* (Bloomington: Indiana University Press, 1992), 90.

11. On ways *DKH* alludes to Yoruba myths without being explicit about them, see Obi Maduakor, *Wole Soyinka: An Introduction to His Writing* (New York: Garland, 1986), 267–81.

12. See Izebaye.

13. Richards, 200, identifies such a "half-child" as an *akibu,* which Soyinka explores in other works. An *akibu,* thinks Richards, is "a miraculous monstrosity, a destroyer of mothers and a symbol of cultural and political deformity in the nation." I am not sure that *DKH* regards the "unborn" child as a curse on the community, given the play's last line. Izevbaye, 142, implies the child could be seen as a mediator of transition.

14. For Soyinka on theater as transformation, see "The Fourth Stage (Through the Mysteries of Ogun to the Origin of Yoruba Tragedy)" (1969), revised in *Art, Dialogue and Outrage;* and his essays, "Morality and Aesthetics in the Ritual Archetype" and "Drama and the African World-View," in his *Myth, Literature and the African World* (Cambridge: Cambridge University Press, 1976), 1–60. See also Ann B. Davis, "Dramatic Theory of Wole Soyinka," in Gibbs, *Critical Perspectives,* 147–57, and Wright.

15. Wole Soyinka, "Drama and the Idioms of Liberation: Proletarian Illusions," in *Art, Dialogue and Outrage,* 42–60, at 45.

16. See Stephan Larsen, *A Writer and His Gods: A Study of the Importance of Yoruba Myths and Religious Ideas to the Writing of Wole Soyinka* (Stockholm: University of Stockholm, 1983).

17. On *orisa,* see Ulli Beier, *Yoruba Myths* (Cambridge: Cambridge University Press, 1980); J. Pimberton III, "A Cluster of Sacred Symbols: Orisa Worship Among the Igbomina Yoruba of Ilaangun," *History of Religions* 17 (1977): 1–28; Judith Gleason, *Oya: In Praise of the Goddess* (Boston: Shambhala, 1980); and Benjamin C. Ray, *African Religions: Symbol, Ritual, and Community* (Englewood Cliffs, N.J.: Prentice-Hall, 1976), 42–45, 52–59, 68–72.

18. Soyinka, *Myth, Literature and the African World,* 31.

19. Ibid., 30.

20. With Okpewho and Larsen, see Eldred D. Jones, *The Writing of Wole Soyinka* (London: Heinemann, 1973).

21. Soyinka, "The Fourth Stage," 21–22.

22. Beier, 34–36.

23. On Gadamer's neglect of "systematic distortion" as a limit to dialogical understanding, see Habermas in Mueller-Vollmer, and Paul Ricoeur, "Hermeneutics and the Critique of Ideology," in his *Hermeneutics and the Human Sciences: Essays on Language, Action, and Interpretation,* ed. and trans. John B. Thompson (Cambridge: Cambridge University Press, 1981). For a more social view of dialogical language and otherness, see Mikhail Bakhtin, "Discourse and the Novel," in his *The Dialogic Imagination,* trans. Caryl Emerson and Michael Holquist (Austin: University of Texas Press, 1981), which I discuss briefly in chapter VI.

24. Soyinka, "The Fourth Stage," 31–32. Henry Louis Gates interprets *DKH* as a classical tragedy of hubris, "Being, the Will, and the Semantics of Death" (1981), in Biodun Jeyifo, *Perspectives on Wole Soyinka: Freedom and Complexity* (Jackson: University Press of Mississippi, 2001), 62–76.

25. Robert Plant Armstrong, "Tragedy—Greek and Yoruba: A Cross-Cultural Perspective," in *Forms of Folklore in Africa: Narrative, Gnomic, Dramatic,* ed. Bernth Lindfors (Austin: University of Texas Press, 1977), 249. See Benjamin Ray, "'Performative Utterances' in African Rituals," *History of Religions* 13 (1973): 16–35, who would not limit the phenomenon in Africa to drama, fiction, or rituals.

26. See Drewal, 19–23.

27. Elesin, 61–73, calls Simon "ghostly one," "white man," "white one," "shadow," and "stranger"; whiteness refers more to Simon's ghostly insubstantiality than his race.

28. That iron is specified further signals that Elesin would integrate himself with Ogun. But another *orisa* here is Sango, god of thunder and kingship, who ostensibly hung himself before becoming an *orisa.* For Soyinka, Sango is more a sociopolitical, less a cosmic paradigm; he is god of electricity and

technology, "the tragic actor for the future age" ("The Fourth Stage," 28). In one myth, Sango jailed Obatala for seven years before they were reconciled. Until he kills himself, Elesin enchained resembles Obatala imprisoned.

29. Ricoeur, *Interpretation Theory,* 94–95.

30. On "instantiation," see Robert P. Scharlemann, "The Forgotten Self and the Forgotten Divine," in *The Critique of Modernity: Theological Reflections on Contemporary Culture,* ed. Ray Hart, Julian N. Hartt, Scharlemann (Charlottesville: University of Virginia Press, 1986), 55–92, at 70–71.

Prelude to Part II

The lines quoted are from *Hamlet,* ed. Ann Thompson and Ned Taylor, 3rd. Arden Shakespeare series, 2 vols. (London: Thomson Learning, 2006), vol. 1 (abbr. Arden3a), a critical edition of the 2nd. Quarto (Q2); however, "neither . . . a lender *be*" (not "lender, *boy*" in Q2) is from the 1st Folio. See my citation note in chapter IV.

1. Here, integrity can function similarly to conscience; see Gabriele Taylor, "Integrity," discussed in the Introduction; in chapter 1, see Childress, "Appeals to Conscience," especially on conscience as a personal sanction, 320–21.

2. Martin Dodsworth, *Hamlet Closely Observed* (London; Athlone, 1985), 297.

3. Lionel Trilling, *Sincerity and Authenticity* (Cambridge: Harvard University Press, 1972), 2.

4. Ibid., 13–16. See also Greenblatt, *Renaissance Self-Fashioning,* especially ch. 5. discussing *Othello* in terms of Iago's "improvisation of power."

5. Stephen Greenblatt, *Will in the World: How Shakespeare Became Shakespeare* (New York: Norton, 2004), especially ch. 2.

6. Trilling, 93–105. Grant, 58–59, thinks it anachronistic to attribute *authenticité* to Rousseau, for whom *integrité* and *honnêteé* are more common terms. Nonetheless, she observes, 87, that in *Emile* (1762) he thought bourgeois sincerity, with its bondage to social roles, involves persons in unconscious or naive contradictions between "doing" and "saying," inconsistent with integrity.

7. See Emmanual Levinas, *Otherwise than Being, or Beyond Essence,* trans. Alphonso Lingis (The Hague: Matinus Nijhoff, 1981), 143–45, which Paul Davies discusses in "Sincerity and the End of Theodicy: Three Remarks on Levinas and Kant," in *The Cambridge Companion to Levinas,* ed. Simon Critchley and Robert Bernasconi (Cambridge: Cambridge University Press, 2002), 161–87. Davies, and Howard Pickett in an unpublished paper on anti-theatrical and theatrical discourse in Levinas, note how Levinas reverses the usual view of sincerity as true to the inward self. I return to this theme in the postlude.

8. See Anne Righter, *Shakespeare and the Idea of the Play* (London; Chatto and Windus, 1962); Jonas Barish, *The Antitheatrical Prejudice* (Berkeley:

University of California Press, 1981); and Judy Kronenfeld, *King Lear and the Naked Truth: Rethinking the Language of Religion and Resistance* (Durham: Duke University Press, 1998).

9. Greenblatt, *Renaissance Self-Fashioning*, 227–29.

10. Richard Rorty, "Trotsky and the Wild Orchids," in *Philosophy and Social Hope* (London: Penguin, 1999), 8, 9: "I wanted to find some intellectual or aesthetic framework which could let me—in a thrilling phrase which I came upon in Yeats—'hold reality and justice in a single vision.'" He says he failed to find such a vision, describing how his temporary embrace of Platonism as a young man "had all the advantages of religion, without requiring the humility which Christianity demanded, and of which I was apparently incapable."

11. Jean Paul Sartre, *Being and Nothingness,* trans. Hazel Barnes (New York: Washington Square, 1956), 101–2. Stewart R. Sutherland, in "Integrity and Self Identity," *Philosophy,* suppl. vol. 35 (1996): 19–27, observes that "Sartre clearly had more luck with waiters than I do."

Chapter IV

The quote is from *Hamlet,* Arden3a. Citing Shakespeare is complicated by the earliest extant copies, now often treated as substantially different works. Most know *Hamlet* from editions or performances using or combining the 1604 Second Quarto (Q2) and the 1623 First Folio (F); recent critical editions have been based primarily on one or the other. There is some consensus that Q2 (the longest) would be closest to a draft by Shakespeare, probably used to print Q2 three years after *Hamlet*'s first performances. Harold Jenkins's Second Arden edition (London: Thomas Learning, 1983) (abbr. Arden2) was based on Q2 but includes some matter from F. Thompson and Taylor publish Q2 separately in the Arden3a volume, while editing both Q1 (the shorter, so-called bad quarto of 1603) and F in the Arden3b volume. I quote from Arden 3a, but occasionally incorporate F, indicated by "wF" (as in the epigraphs: in the first, the reference to the Clown is in F; in the second, I include F for clarity, "he but" rather than "a do").

1. Peter Brook's adaptation derived from his 1995 show, *Qui Est Là.* I am describing a performance of his *The Tragedy of Hamlet,* in Chicago, July 2001. It was developed in 2000, longer but with the same cast, at the Théâtre des Bouffes du Nord, Paris, described in Andy Lavendert, *Hamlet in Pieces, Shakespeare Reworked: Peter Brook, Robert Lepage, Robert Wilson* (Londen: Nick Hern Books, 2001), 227–41. In 2005, a film of the Paris *Tragedy of Hamlet* was released on DVD; while it captures the actors' interpretations, it lacks the lively theatrical values I witnessed and is not framed by the question "Who's there?" A documentary on the disc shows a scene before a live audience, more suggestive of how I saw it played.

2. Brook, *The Empty Space;* his chapters discuss "holy," "deadly," "rough," and "immediate" theater. David Wiles, *Tragedy in Athens: Performance*

Space and Theatrical Meaning (Cambridge: Cambridge University Press, 1997), 3–4, challenges Brook's metaphor of emptiness, pointing to how theatrical space, like sacred space, is defined, set apart, controlled, occupied, etc. Spaciousness and boundedness are, however, not mutually exclusive.

3. Brook ends the play by combining *Hamlet* I.1.165–66 with I.1.1. Gene Fendt also explores Bernado's "Who's there?" in *Is* Hamlet *a Religious Drama? An Essay on a Question in Kierkegaard* (Milwaukee: Marquette University Press, 1998), 79.

4. The Player's speech was declaimed in "Orghast," a language invented by Ted Hughes for an experimental play, *Orghast at Persepolis,* directed by Peter Brook in 1971. See Kenneth J. Cerniglia's review of the Seattle performance in *Theatre Journal* 54 (2002): 156–58.

5. Ricoeur, *Oneself as Another,* 19; Schrag, *The Self After Postmodernity,* 4.

6. See Milan Kundera's novel *The Unbearable Lightness of Being,* trans. Michael Henry Heim (New York: Harper, 1984), 248–51.

7. Harold Bloom, *Shakespeare: The Invention of the Human* (New York: Riverhead, 1998).

8. In their Introduction to Arden 3a, 59–74, Thompson and Taylor remind us of the ambiguities of "sources," and of how identifying them in Shakespeare is usually inferential.

9. See Stephen Greenblatt, *Hamlet in Purgatory* (Princeton: Princeton University Press, 2001), 195–96, 258–61.

10. See Bloom, 408–12. But one of the contingencies of composing and revising may have been the playwright's *reticence* to revise; see Ben Jonson's claim that Shakespeare reports "he never blotted out line," quoted in S. Schoenbaum, *William Shakespeare: A Compact Documentary Life,* rev. ed. (New York: Oxford University Press, 1987), 258–59.

11. Iser, *Act of Reading,* 165–72. See Frank Kermode, *The Genesis of Secrecy: On the Interpretation of Narrative* (Cambridge: Harvard University Press, 1979), 14–15.

12. Greenblatt, *Will in the World,* 323–24: "Shakespeare found that he could immeasurably deepen the effect of his plays . . . if he took out a key explanatory element, thereby occluding the rationale, motivation, or ethical principle that accounted for the action that was to unfold."

13. See Greenblatt's questions, *Hamlet in Purgatory,* 246, and Jenkins, Arden2, 122ff.

14. Greenblatt, *Hamlet in Purgatory,* 195–96, 256–57.

15. Bloom, 387, appears to accept the early-eighteenth-century writer, editor, and biographer Nicholas Rowe's report that Shakespeare himself played the Ghost. Wendy Coppedge Sanford, *Theater as Metaphor in* Hamlet, "the LeBaron Russell Briggs Honor Essay in English" (Cambridge: Harvard University Press, 1967), 7–25, identifies a pattern in which Hamlet and other characters function as "directors" in the play.

16. Ronald Knowles, "*Hamlet* and Counter-Humanism," *Renaissance Quarterly* 52 (1999): 1046–69.

17. Jenkins in Arden2, 457, thinks "taint not thy mind" concerns "Hamlet's attitude toward his mother." However, "this act" seems to refer to the injunction to deal with Claudius.

18. Fredson Bowers, "Hamlet as Minister and Scourge" (1955), reprinted in Bowers, *Hamlet as Minister and Scourge and Other Studies in Shakespeare and Milton* (Charlottesville: University of Virginia Press, 1989), 90–101. See also Dover Wilson, *What Happens in Hamlet,* 3rd. ed. (Cambridge: Cambridge University Press, 1960), 26–38 and *passim.*

19. Like Bowers, Fendt believes the Ghost commissions Hamlet to the not quite impossible task of seeking justice for Denmark. Fendt also notes, 116, that the Ghost does not explicitly require Hamlet to kill Claudius, although that is what revenge for murder would usually imply.

20. See Jenkins, Arden2, 433–34. Danish kings were chosen by provincial electors, English kings by inheritance; yet Mary, Elizabeth, and James in effect required "election" due to issues of succession. See F II.2, 250, when Rosencrantz and Guildenstern banter with Hamlet about "ambition." The issue is whether, before his father's death, Hamlet's election was anticipated.

21. Jenkins, Arden2, 523, against Bowers.

22. Bowers, 95, points to Richard III as a "scourge" on England for the murder of Richard II; a "minister" would be "Henry Richmond—the future King Henry VII," who defeats Richard III.

23. Fendt, 170.

24. See Jacques Derrida's comments on old Hamlet's ghost in *Specters of Marx: The State of the Debt, the Work of Mourning, and the New International,* trans. Peggy Kamuf (New York: Routledge, 1994), esp. 7; see also Richard Kearney, "Spectres of *Hamlet,*" in *Spiritual Shakespeares,* ed. Ewan Fernie (London: Routledge, 2005), 157–85.

25. Bowers, 96.

26. Goethe's Wilhelm Meister's Apprenticeship, quoted in Greenblatt, *Hamlet in Purgatory,* 229.

27. Bowers, 100, 101. Bowers thinks Hamlet's references to providence are not "lip-service or religious commonplace, but the very heart of the matter." Laertes has exposed Claudius's murder of Hamlet and homicide of Gertrude, and for this the Lords cry, "Treason, treason!" (V.2.307). It remains for Horatio to report the regicide of old Hamlet, but at most he is indirect about it (365).

28. Eleanor Prosser, *Hamlet and Revenge,* 2nd. ed. (1967; Stanford: Stanford University Press, 1971), x. Prosser in 1967 disagreed with Bowers on Elizabethan views of public revenge; her 1971 appendix on the limited duty to resist tyrants finds its application to *Hamlet* inconclusive.

29. Ibid., 33–34.

30. On this point, Prosser has company. See Roy W. Battenhouse, *Shakespearean Tragedy: Its Art and Its Christian Premises* (Bloomington: Indiana University Press, 1969), 239; but he does not think grace has transformed Hamlet by Act V. Recently, Jennifer Rust interprets the Ghost in terms of Protestant views of melancholy and loss of faith, "Wittenburg and Melancholic Allegory: The Reformation and Its Discontents in *Hamlet*," in *Shakespeare and the Culture of Christianity in Early Modern England,* ed. Dennis Taylor and David Beauregard (New York: Fordham University Press, 2003), 261–86.

31. In addition to Greenblatt's studies, see John Freeman, "This Side of Purgatory: Ghostly Fathers and the Recusant Legacy in *Hamlet*," in Taylor and Beauregard, 222–59. Jeffrey Knapp, in *Shakespeare's Tribe: Church, Nation, and Theater in Renaissance England* (Chicago: University of Chicago Press, 2002), aligns Shakespeare and Ben Jonson with Erasmian Christianity, a kind of free-church, inclusive Catholicism that was appreciative of the varied sorts of people who frequented theaters.

32. Prosser notices this, 133n.32, dissenting from Battenhouse's appeal to Dante's purgatory.

33. Ibid., 219.

34. Frank Kermode implies Prosser is trying to enforce a moralizing Christianity. See his "Reading Shakespeare's Mind" and Prosser's response, "Hamlet Brainwashed" (with a reply by Kermode), in *The New York Review of Books* (Oct. 12 and Dec. 21, 1967).

35. Greenblatt, *Hamlet in Purgatory,* 239; see 157, 204ff. He regards Shakespearean theater as a "cult of the dead" that addressed fear of boundaries between the living and dead. Fendt also implies the Ghost might be ambiguously vengeful *and* from purgatory, 112–18.

36. On morality restraining vengefulness, see R. Chris Hassel Jr., "'How Infinite in Faculties': Hamlet's Confusion of God and Man," *Literature and Theology* 8 (1994): 127–39, at 133.

37. René Girard, *A Theatre of Envy: William Shakespeare* (New York: Oxford University Press, 1991), 284. See also his *Violence and the Sacred.*

38. Bloom, 411.

39. See Fendt, 56.

40. Freeman, 245–46, on Catholic recusants using theater-like disguise as a survival strategy.

41. See David Bevington on "maimed rites." in *Action as Eloquence: Shakespeare's Language of Gesture* (Cambridge: Harvard University Press, 1984), 180–81.

42. See Wilson, 88–101, for whom the Ghost's and Hamlet's wild antics in the cellarage scene immediately prompt Hamlet to put on an antic disposition.

43. Jan H. Blits, *Deadly Thought: "Hamlet" and the Human Soul* (Lanham, Md.: Lexington Books, 2001), 7.

44. See Patrick Grant, "Imagination in the Renaissance," in *Religious Imagination*, ed. James P. Mackey (Edinburgh: Edinburgh University Press, 1986), 86–101, on *Hamlet*, 93–99; Prosser, 173, thinks the malign Ghost has challenged Hamlet "to define his own code."

45. Thus, the players mirror Shakespeare's political and economic situation. See Louis Montrose, *The Purpose of Playing: Shakespeare and the Cultural Politics of Elizabethan England* (Chicago: University of Chicago Press, 1996), 24–29, 50.

46. See Peter Brook, *Evoking Shakespeare* (London: Nick Hern, 1998), 30–31.

47. See the critique of *Hamlet* by Frater Taciturness, a pseudonym in Søren Kierkegaard, *Stages on Life's Way: Studies by Various Persons* (1845), trans. Howard V. Hong and Edna H. Hong (Princeton: Princeton University Press, 1988), 452–54. Fendt, 194–97, attempts to refute Taciturness's view (not SK's) that no drama can communicate one's inward relation to eternity.

48. Greenblatt, *Shakespearean Negotiations: The Circulation of Social Energy in Renaissance England* (Berkeley: University of California Press, 1988), 47, on Prince Hal's "theatrical improvisation" in *1 Henry IV*. While cognizant of delight in theatrical play, Greenblatt often finds it devolving into critiques of state theater. Here he captures a sense of the integrity of play in Falstaff, later betrayed by Hal. On power, Greenblatt is indebted to Pierre Bourdieu and Michel Foucault. See also Montrose on these issues.

49. Righter, 162; Jenkins, Arden2, 482.

50. See E. M. W. Tillyard, *The Elizabethan World Picture* (London: Chatto and Windus, 1958), 1–2; and Knowles, 1050–57, on coexisting optimistic and pessimistic views of humanity and creation, and on Montaigne and other sources for Hamlet's pessimism.

51. See Harold Bloom, *Hamlet: Poem Unlimited* (New York: Riverhead, 2003), 87, on Hamlet's "central statement."

52. See Montrose, 36–37, on how the confusion of social differences by players (who switched genders, status, roles, etc.) could threaten perceptions of religious and social order.

53. Hans Urs von Balthasar writes, "The ambivalent 'pleasure' of theatre going . . . is a mixture of a vigorous delight in transformation and curiosity as to what may unexpectedly emerge from such transformation," *Theo-Drama: Theological Dramatic Theory*, vol. I, trans. Graham Harrison (San Francisco: Ignatius, 1983), 261.

54. Jenkins's view, 479, that the First Player's Pyrrhus speech is not satirical can be confirmed in practice by Charlton Heston's performance of it in Kenneth Branagh's 1996 film, *Hamlet*.

55. The discussion of Shakespeare's views of theatrical imagination continues in chapter XIII.

56. See Grace Tiffany, "Anti-Theatricalism and Revolutionary Desire in *Hamlet* (Or, The Play Without the Play)," *The Upstart Crow* 15 (1995): 61–74, on how even the positive assessments of theater in *Hamlet* resonate with Puritan critiques of theater in England.

57. Stanislavski's "system," discussed in the next chapter, calls for actors to be motivated by *analogous* memories and emotions within themselves, not literally the same "motive."

58. See Battenhouse, 238; also Montrose, 102: "Claudius and Hamlet enact opposed and complementary courtly attitudes toward the theatre: At the same time that the monarch construes it as a means of diversion, his chiefest courtier construes it as a means of subversion."

59. Bloom, *Hamlet*, 9.

60. Fergusson, 98–142.

61. Knowles, 1062; Jenkins, 566, supplies sources from Seneca and here from Montaigne: "No man dies before his hour. The time you leave behind was no more yours, than that which was before your birth, and concerneth you no more."

62. On providence as a lure to freedom in Augustine, see Langdon Gilkey, *Reaping the Whirlwind: A Christian Interpretation of History* (New York: Seabury, 1976), 165.

63. J. M. Bremer, *Hamartia: Tragic Error in the Poetics of Aristotle and in Greek Tragedy* (Amsterdam: Hakkert, 1969). For an opposite view—of "role-playing" and *hamartia* as sin in *Hamlet*—see Battenhouse, 252–62, for whom Hamlet's improvising is demonic to the end.

64. Cautiously, Hassel, 138, also sides with the providential assessment of Hamlet in Act V. Tom F. Driver, *The Sense of History in Greek and Shakespearean Drama* (New York: Columbia University Press, 1960), 116–21, takes what was perhaps the straightforward view that Hamlet comes to realize he is under a providential command to avenge his father's murder.

65. See Scarry on bodily verification, discussed in chapter I.

66. Fergusson, 138–39, implies a providential reading of Fortinbras.

67. Greenblatt, *Will in the World*, 136–42.

68. Knapp, 54: Prospero "reveals himself to his enemies, kenotically, in the guise of the resurrected Christ" and in the end "aligns himself with a 'sociable' or 'fellowly' Christian theology that refuses to disown 'flesh and blood.'"

69. *The Tempest*, ed. Virginia Mason Vaughan and Alden T. Vaughan, 3rd Arden Shakespeare series (London: Thomson Learning, 1999).

70. Righter, 203–4, notices the participatory phenomenology of theater in *The Tempest*, but casts it in terms of resignation. The Jacobean court masque celebrated the confusion of actors and spectators, a confusion

characterizing Prospero's island-stage. "As Prospero's explanation [of the masque] reaches its end, the audience in the theatre seems to lose its identity. Life has been engulfed by illusion. The spectators in the playhouse are no different in quality from Ferdinand and Miranda; they are actors, for the moment silent, who watch a play within a play."

Chapter V

The first epigraph quotes Henrik Ibsen, *A Doll House,* in *Ibsen: Four Major Plays: Volume I,* rev. ed., trans. Rolf Fjelde (New York: Signet, 1965, 1992), 108; unless indicated, quotes are from here. For some passages, Peter Watts's translation in *The League of Youth, A Doll's House, The Lady from the Sea* (Harmmondsworth, UK: Penguin, 1965) and William Archer's mostly literal translation in *Ibsen's Prose Dramas,* vol. 1 (London: Walter Scott, 1890) are cited.

The second epigraph quotes from *The Seagull,* trans. Paul Schmidt, *The Plays of Anton Chekhov: A New Translation* (New York: Harper Perennial, 1999), 118.

1. On Konstantin's motivations toward his mother here, see David Magarshack, *Chekhov the Dramatist* (London: Lehman, 1952), 195. On the theatricality of most of the play's characters, see Peta Tait, *Performing Emotions: Gender, Bodies, Spaces in Chekhov's Drama and Stanislavski's Theatre* (Aldershot, UK: Ashgate, 2002); and Clara Hollosi, "Chekhov's Reactions to Two Interpretations of Nina," *Theatre Survey* 24 (1983): 117–26.

2. Emil Zola quoted in *Seeds of Modern Drama,* vol. 3, ed. Norris Houghton (New York: Dell, 1963), 15; I remain grateful to Bill Davis of Eureka College for this source.

3. August Strindberg, "Author's Foreword," in *Six Plays of Strindberg,* trans. Elizabeth Sprigge (New York: Anchor, 1955), 61. Quotes from *Miss Julie* and *Dream Play* are from this source.

4. See Karl Jaspers, *Strindberg and Van Gogh: An Attempt at a Pathographic Analysis with Reference to Parallel Cases of Swedenborg and Hölderlin,* trans. Oskar Grunow and David Woloshin (1922; Tucson: University of Arizona Press, 1977), 84, where "doubt" and "sensitivity to pressure" define Strindberg's struggle to express truth despite debilitating delusions. I discuss Gaita in the Introduction.

5. Strindberg, "Authors Note," 193.

6. See Paul Tillich's accounts of the expressionist impulse in art in his *Theology of Culture,* ed. Robert C. Kimball (London: Oxford University Press, 1959), 74.

7. See Tom F. Driver, *Romantic Quest and Modern Query: A History of the Modern Theatre* (New York: Delacorte, 1970), 216.

8. Quoted in Michael Meyer's Preface to his translation of Henrik Ibsen, *Brand,* fwd. W. H. Auden (New York: Doubleday Anchor, 1960), 17; quota-

tions are from this translation. Meyer reports Strindberg saying that Brand had "the voice of Savonarola" (the fifteenth-century Italian Catholic reformer). Auden discusses the integrity of the genius (Peer Gynt) and that of the apostle or reformer (Brand), and problems of "directly" dramatizing these roles.

9. Meyer, 14. Brand was based on a theological student Ibsen knew, Christopher Bruun, as well as on the revivalist G. A. Lammers, and on Ibsen himself (Meyer, 14).

10. Driver, *Romantic Quest and Modern Query*, 161.

11. Bernard Shaw, *The Quintessence of Ibsenism*, 2nd. ed. (New York: Bretano's, 1917), 53.

12. "If we take the words as a judgment pronounced upon Brand, the play is weakened in structure. However, if we take them in some other way, . . . the play becomes a highly ambivalent account of the destructive power of genius. Brand's genius, however, is not that of intelligence or of artistic imagination but of ethical purity," Driver, *Romantic Quest and Modern Query*, 180–81. The *deus caritas* "answer is demonstrably not the poet's but a rejoinder designed to reveal the tragic dimensions of an absolute will," Balthasar, *Theo-Drama* I: 206n.6.

13. Balthasar, 210.

14. Harry Haun quoting Nicholas Martin (who directed Kate Burton), in "Redefining Hedda," *Playbill* 117.10 (Oct. 2001): 22.

15. See June Schlueter's description of hilarious Monty Python skits on the fate of Nora, "How to Get into *A Doll House:* Ibsen's Play as an Introduction to Drama," in *Approaches to Teaching Ibsen's* A Doll House, ed. Yvonne Shafer (New York: Modern Language Association of America, 1985), 63. See also Austin Quigley's chapter on the play in his *The Modern Stage and Other Worlds* (New York: Methuen, 1985).

16. Richard Hornby, *Script into Performance*, 158, supports intensifying symbols in Ibsen and describes directing a production that made the door sound like "the slamming of a bank vault."

17. See Fjelde on translating *Et Dukkehjem* as *A Doll House,* rather than "a doll's house," xxiv.

18. Hornby, 162, regards Nora as a romantic. She has leapt from the sensuous aesthetic (with attendant hypocrisy) not to the ethical (of which Torvald would be a parody) but to a place where she might become something of a romantic poet or philosopher. On religion and the limits of the ethical, see David Tracy, *Blessed Rage for Order: The New Pluralism in Theology* (Chicago: University of Chicago Press, 1975, 1996 ed.), 102–3.

19. In 1880 German and Austrian producers solicited Ibsen for a final reconciliation scene based on Nora's shame at leaving her children, which he provided against his better judgment.

20. See Tom Stoppard's introduction to his adaptation, *The Seagull: A New Version* (London: Faber and Faber, 1997), ix.

21. Konstantin's "new forms" echoes Chekhov, whose style in *The Seagull* was a departure for him. But autobiographical ingredients are distributed among several characters; Trigorin, Konstantin, and Dorn reflect different aspects of Chekhov's writing. See Donald Rayfield, *Chekhov: A Life* (London: HarperCollins, 1997), 352–53.

22. Magarshack, 42: the difference between Chekhov's plays of "direct" and "indirect action," such as *The Seagull,* is that the former show "life as it is" while the latter glimpse, as well, "life as it should be." Konstantin, then, rejects strict naturalism (as did Chekhov) but also Chekhov's indirect reform of naturalism (i.e., the imperative to show life as it is *and* as it should be).

23. See Richard Gilman, *Chekhov's Plays: An Opening into Eternity* (New Haven: Yale University Press, 1995), 84.

24. On the parallel between Konstantin's play and his character, see Robert Louis Jackson, "Chekhov's *Seagull:* The Empty Well, the Dry Lake, and the Cold Cave," in *Chekhov: A Collection of Critical Essays,* ed. Robert Louis Jackson (Englewood Cliffs, N.J.: Prentice-Hall, 1967), 99–111.

25. Tatyana Shchepkina-Kupernik, quoted in David Magarshack, *Chekhov: A Life* (Westport, Conn.: Greenwood, 1952), 288.

26. Ronald Hingley, *A New Life of Anton Chekhov* (New York: Knopf, 1976), 221, 222; however, Levkeyev did appear that evening in another more conventional comedy following Chekhov's play (Magarshack, *Chekhov: A Life,* 293).

27. Constantin Stanislavski, *My Life in Art,* trans. J. J. Robbins (1924; New York: Theatre Arts Books, 1948), 356.

28. Hingley, 245.

29. See Magarshack, *Chekhov: A Life,* 339, and Tait, 109.

30. Stanislavski, *My Life in Art,* 358–59.

31. See Balthasar, 252.

32. Driver, *Romantic Quest and Modern Query,* 85.

33. Stanislavski, *My Life in Art,* 404, 405–6; italics mine.

34. Hornby, *Script into Performance,* 47–48.

35. In "The System and Methods of Creative Art," in *Stanislavski on the Art of the Stage,* trans. David Magarshack (New York: Hill and Wang, 1961), the actor cannot separate "his worldly 'I' from his actor's 'I.' . . . How does one acquire this singleness of purpose which comes as a result of one's love of art and one's self possession? Can it be achieved just because I say to the actor, Think in this way! . . . Only the actor whose development proceeds along harmonious lines can, quite independently and through his own acquired experience, raise himself step by step to a wider consciousness" (118, 119). However, in acting one is "purged of 'self.' . . . By means of the exercises according to my system, the studio must bring about this renunciation of 'self' and the switching over of the actor's entire attention to the conditions supplied by the author or composer so as to reflect in them the truth of the passions" (115).

36. Driver, *Romantic Quest and Modern Query,* 83.

37. In *My Life in Art,* 458–67 (ch. 48, "The Beginnings of My System"), Stanislavski tells of traveling to Finland in the summer of 1906 to sort out all he had learned of acting and directing.

38. Friedrich Schleiermacher, *Hermeneutics: The Handwritten Manuscripts,* trans. James O. Duke and Jack Forstman (Missoula: Scholars Press, 1977), 150, 112, 113.

39. Stanislavski, "System and Methods of Creative Art," 127.

40. Stanislavski, *My Life in Art,* 461.

41. Balthasar, I: 289.

42. Ibid.

43. But neo-orthodox critiques are being challenged; see *Barth and Schleiermacher: Beyond the Impasse?* ed. James O. Duke and Robert E. Streetman (Philadelphia: Fortress, 1988); Bruce L. McCormack, "What Has Basel to Do with Berlin: Continuities in the Theologies of Barth and Schleiermacher," *The Princeton Seminary Bulletin* 23 (2002): 146–73.

44. Process theologians, drawing on Alfred North Whitehead, are twentieth-century examples. The uses of existentialism and German idealism in Rudolf Bultmann and Paul Tillich are ambiguous examples, since they *do* grant authoritative primacy to key New Testament themes.

45. E.g., Bultmann and Mircea Eliade (myth), Tillich (symbol), Amos Wilder, Sallie McFague, and Janet Soskice (metaphor), Susan Handelman and Daniel Boyarin (midrash). Most critics of the alleged "translation" strategy, such as Karl Barth, would place Bultmann and Tillich among the translators; but I disagree that translation-as-substitution was primarily what they were doing.

46. "Redescription" or "renarration"—the latter a term I owe to a University of Virginia dissertation by Brantley Craig (Charlottesville, 2007)—indicates how such projects involve creative interpretation.

47. George Lindbeck, *The Nature of Doctrine* (Philadelphia: Westminster, 1984), drawing on Clifford Geertz and the ethnographic mode of "thick description." See also sympathetic criticism of Lindbeck and Geertz in Kathryn Tanner, *Theories of Culture: A New Agenda for Theology* (Minneapolis: Fortress, 1997).

48. E.g., theologians such as Barth, Hans Frei, and Stanley Hauerwas; in Judaism, see Michael Wyschogrod, Jon Levenson, and Peter Ochs.

49. Balthasar, I: 413.

50. Ibid., 19. Ben Quash applies especially this theme from Balthasar in his *Theology and the Drama of History* (Cambridge: Cambridge University Press, 2005), 4.

51. Balthasar, 45–48, 68–69, 481–87, 645–48. See Quash, 64.

52. MacIntyre, *After Virtue,* 174–89, on "goods internal to a practice."

53. See James Lindemann Nelson, "The Secular Problem of Evil and the Vocation of Medicine," in *Pain Seeking Understanding: Suffering, Medicine,*

and Faith, ed. Margaret Mohrmann and Mark Hanson (Cleveland: Pilgrim Press, 1999).

54. See Ben Quash, "The Theo-Drama," in *The Cambridge Companion to Hans Urs von Balthasar,* ed. Edward T. Oakes and David Moss (Cambridge: Cambridge University Press, 2004), 143–57.

55. See Robert P. Scharlemann, *Reflection and Doubt in the Thought of Paul Tillich* (New Haven: Yale University Press, 1969).

56. Driver, *Romantic Quest and Modern Query,* 11, quoting a translation by James Kirkup.

57. Ibid., 348.

58. Ibid., 388, 389. For an interesting criticism, namely, that Driver focuses "on the negative side of a pluralistic universe at the expense of the positive side," see Quigley, 261.

59. See Tom F. Driver, "The Twilight of Drama: From Ego to Myth," in *Humanities, Religion, and the Arts Tomorrow,* ed. Howard Hunter (New York: Holt, Rhinehart, and Winston, 1972), 74–100, an essay that elaborates on his conclusion about the closure of modern drama.

60. Driver, *Romantic Quest and Modern Query,* 348; italics mine.

61. Tom F. Driver, *The Magic of Ritual: Our Need for Liberating Rites that Transform Our Lives and Our Communities* (San Francisco: HarperSanFrancisco, 1991).

Chapter VI

The epigraph from *Pygmalion* (1912) is from Bernard Shaw, *Androcles and the Lion, Overruled, Pygmalion* (New York: Bretanos, 1916), 197; Shaw's italics; his spelling and punctuation reforms are retained in the quotations. I am grateful to Vanessa Ochs and also to Frank Burch Brown and the Association of Disciples for Theological Education, as well as to Robert Jenson and members in residence at the Center of Theological Inquiry in 2002, all of whom responded to earlier versions of this chapter.

The second epigraph is excerpted from Willy Russell, *Educating Rita* (Harlow, Essex, UK: Longman, 1985), 48.

The third epigraph quotes from John Guare, *Six Degrees of Separation* (New York: Vintage, 1990), 107, 108.

1. *My Fair Lady,* music by Frederick Loewe, book and lyrics by Alan Jay Lerner, vocal score, rev. ed. (1956; New York: Chappell/Intersong, 1969), 90.

2. Jeff Lundon interviewing Kitty Carlisle Hart, National Public Radio's *Weekend Edition,* Saturday, July 15, 2000. See Julie Andrews, *Home: A Memoir of My Early* Years (New York: Hyperion, 2008), 195–96.

3. Directed by Lewis Gilbert, screenplay by Willy Russell, 1983.

4. The film shows this scene and does try to dramatize Rita's experience of class dislocation.

5. The first production of *Pygmalion* was given in Vienna in 1913, in German.

6. Richard Huggett, *The Truth about* Pygmalion (New York: Random House, 1969), 76. Details about the production are from this source and from Michael Holroyd, *Bernard Shaw,* vol. 2 (New York: Random House, 1989).

7. From the 1938 version of *Pygmalion,* in *The Portable Bernard Shaw,* ed. Stanley Weintraub (New York: Viking, 1977), 424; Shaw's italics.

8. Arnold Silver, *Bernard Shaw: The Darker Side* (Stanford: Stanford University Press, 1982), 270–79.

9. In Ovid's *Metamorphoses,* Book 10, Pygmalion sculpts a female figure and is so smitten by its beauty he prays for the ivory to come to life. His prayer is granted, and tradition later calls her Galatea; they have a child—suggesting that Venus has rewarded his piety. Idolatrous knowledge is a theme of *Frankenstein;* another is the monster's suffering; the medium is not ivory but dead flesh. In Shaw, the medium is human speech. See Geoffrey Miles, ed., *Classical Mythology in English Literature: A Critical Anthology* (London: Routledge, 1999), 332–33, 340, 344, referring to Frankenstein, Shaw, and Russell. See also J. Hillis Miller, *Versions of Pygmalion* (Cambridge: Harvard University Press, 1990), 1–12, though he omits Shaw.

10. While "the rain in Spain" precipitates in the 1938 film and in *MFL,* it falls in no version Shaw published. The revised play, with new scenes Shaw wrote for the film, does include Higgins coaching Eliza on her vowels: "Say a cup of tea" (Weintraub, 373). Guare alludes to this when Trent Conway coaches Paul, "Say bottle of beer" (see below).

11. Jacques Derrida, *Monolingualism of the Other; Or, the Prosthesis of Origin,* trans. Patrick Mensah (Stanford: Stanford University Press, 1996).

12. Jean Reynolds, *Pygmalion's Wordplay: The Postmodern Shaw* (Gainsville: University Press of Florida, 1999), notes that while Higgins is "[l]ogocentric to the core" (110), Shaw's views of language are congenial to Derrida's, and are aligned more with Eliza than Higgins. However, this judgment must be weighed against egalitarian statements of Shaw's that excessively elide difference, as I indicate below. Reynolds is helpful in appreciating Shaw's self-fashioning—the "G.B.S." persona—and his views of the paradox of acting. See Shaw's "Acting, by One Who Does Not Believe in It" (1889), in his *Platform and Pulpit,* ed., Dan H. Laurence (New York: Hill and Wang, 1961), 12–22; the actor is most "real" onstage when realizing himself in a good part, but can be false on or offstage when assuming conventional roles.

13. In *My Fair Lady,* this episode occurs at the Ascot races.

14. The novel, Mikhail Bakhtin claims, exemplifies how after the Renaissance, "heteroglossia" could be shaped by authors or, as he says, "dialogized." See his *The Dialogic Imagination,* 291–97. Harris, in *The Dialogical*

Theatre, applies Bakhtin to theater, showing how scripts or scenarios are offered to "others" to be performed and interpreted—not only other actors but also by those with other concerns and social interests—sometimes with subversive and enlightening effects.

15. Turner, *Dramas, Fields, and Metaphors* (discussed in chapter II) and also *From Ritual to Theatre,* 32–35, on the more open-ended "liminoid" (as opposed to "liminal") character of passages in modern society. In Bynum's critique of Turner, in "Women's Stories, Women's Symbolism," the question is whether liminality is a mode of meaning needed by those entrenched in power, or a mode of escape for those who struggle against such power. Shaw portrays Eliza as emerging meaningfully out of the liminality Higgins arranges, though she does not emerge as Higgins intends. Bynum would possibly be more interested in Act V, where Eliza struggles against Higgins; Mrs. Higgins says, in effect, that she has no use for the liminality of meaningful transformation, because she cannot afford its consequences.

16. See Anselm L. Strauss, *Mirrors and Masks: The Search for Identity* (Glencoe, Ill.: Free Press, 1959), whose social-pyschological views on language and rhetoric would complement Bakhtin's.

17. On Shaw's socialism and reform of language, see Reynolds. See also William Irvine, "Shaw, the Fabians, and the Utilitarians," *Journal of the History of Ideas* 8 (1947): 218–31; and Mary Peter Mack, "The Fabians and Utilitarianism," *Journal of the History of Ideas* 16 (1955): 76–88.

18. That Shaw subtitled the play "a romance" gave some license to the endings he did not like. On the romanticist strain in Shaw, see Driver, *Romantic Quest and Modern Query,* 249–82.

19. See Shaw's 1933 Preface to *On the Rocks.* Extermination is also implied at the end of his 1935 play about Judgment Day, *The Simpleton of the Unexpected Isles.*

20. See the fifth part of Shaw's *Back to Methuselah* (1921). On how his sometime admiration of Mussolini, Hitler, and especially Stalin related to his socialism and creed of "creative evolution," see Gerard A. Pilecki, *Shaw's Geneva: A Critical Study of the Evolution of the Text in Relation to Shaw's Political Thought and Dramatic Practice* (The Hague: Mouton, 1965).

21. Williams, "Critique of Utilitarianism," 108–18, and *Moral Luck,* 1–39.

22. See Nussbaum, *Love's Knowledge;* Charles Taylor, *Sources of the Self: The Making of Modern Identity* (Cambridge: Harvard University Press, 1989); Ricoeur, *Oneself as Another,* chs. 7–9.

23. See articles collected in Statman, *Moral Luck.*

24. Williams, *Moral Luck,* 22–26. Erik Erikson describes Shaw undergoing an analogous experience of withdrawal from Ireland for England, where he emerged into a new identity as a writer, socialist, dramatist, in *Identity, Youth, and Crisis* (New York: Norton, 1968), 142–50.

NOTES TO PAGES 161–173   *377*

25. Even if, say, an Augustinian vision can theoretically comprehend various goods, holding duty and desire in a single thought remains a difficult
task. See Richard Rorty, "Trotsky and the Wild Orchids," 9.

26. The italics are phrases Paul interpolates into J. D. Salinger, *The Catcher
in the Rye* (1945; New York: Bantam, 1964), 90. The passage he is "quoting"
actually reads, "but what scares me most in a fist fight is the other guy's face.
I can't stand looking at the other guy's face, is my trouble. It wouldn't be so
bad if you could both be blindfolded or something. It's a funny kind of yellowness, when you come to think of it, but it's yellowness all right. I'm not
kidding myself." I am not guessing at Guare's intention here, only Paul's.

27. Dan Barry, "About New York; He Conned the Society Crowd but
Died Alone," *New York Times,* July 19, 2003; Barry reports Hampton
claimed to have written a Harvard course paper on "Injustices in the Crimi-
nal Justice System."

28. Wassily Kandinsky, *Concerning the Spiritual in Art,* trans. M. T. H.
Sadler (New York: Dover, 1977).

Prelude to Part III

The first epigraph quotes from Samuel Beckett, *Waiting for Godot: A
Tragicomedy in Two Acts* (New York: Grove, 1954), 37b–38a. The edition
numbers only the verso pages; I cite verso as "a," recto as "b."

The second epigraph is excerpted from Isaac Asimov, *The Gods Themselves* (New York: Doubleday, 1972), 92.

1. See Martin Esslin, *The Theatre of the Absurd* (London: Eyre and Spot-
tiswoode, 1962), 37, and Essif, 64.

2. William Mueller and Josephine Jacobsen, "Samuel Beckett's Long Saturday: To Wait or Not to Wait," in *Man in Modern Theater,* ed. Nathan A.
Scott Jr. (Richmond: John Knox, 1965), 76–97.

3. David H. Hesla, *The Shape of Chaos: An Interpretation of the Art of
Samuel Beckett* (Minneapolis: University of Minnesota Press, 1971), 144:
"[t]he real call of conscience is not Pozzo's cry for help" but is recognized
in "the soundless image of two men helping a third. . . . The image is all but
lost in the business that precedes and follows it. It is there, and then gone.
But it is the moment to which the whole of the play leads, and which, in its
simplicity and purity, stands in judgment on the meaningless waiting. . . ."

4. Maurice Merleau-Ponty, *The Visible and the Invisible, Followed by
Working Notes,* ed. Claude LeFort, trans. Alphonso Lingis (Evanston:
Northwestern University Press, 1968), 149.

5. On capability and belonging, Merleau-Ponty, *Phenomenology of Perception,* 137–47. See also Richard M. Zaner, "Body: Embodiment: The
Phenomenological Tradition," *The Encyclopedia of Bioethics,* 2nd. ed.,
ed. Warren Reich, vol. 1 (New York: Macmillan Library Reference, 1995):
293–99. For a fuller discussion, see Zaner, *The Context of Self: A Phenom-*

enological Inquiry Using Medicine as a Clue (Athens: Ohio University Press, 1981).

6. See "Personal Identity and Individuation" and "Bodily Continuity and Personal Identity" in Bernard Williams, *Problems of the Self: Philosophical Papers, 1956–1972* (Cambridge: Cambridge University Press, 1973).

7. John B. Barrow and Frank D. Tipler, *The Anthropic Cosmological Principle* (Oxford: Clarendon, 1986), 615.

8. Derek Parfit, *Reasons and Persons* (Oxford: Clarendon, 1984, 1987), 279. See Douglas Hofstadter, *I Am a Strange Loop* (New York: Basic, 2007), 301–12; he credits Parfit's teleporter-to-Mars scenario to Daniel C. Dennett, "Introduction," in *The Mind's I: Fantasies and Reflections on the Soul,* ed. Hofstadter and Dennett (Toronto: Bantam, 1981).

9. Paul Ricoeur, *Oneself as Another,* 138.

10. Ibid., 132.

11. Ibid., 168: "In a philosophy of selfhood like my own, one must be able to say that ownership is not what matters. What is suggested by the limiting cases produced by the narrative imagination is a dialectic of ownership and of dispossession, of care and carefreeness, of self-affirmation and of self-effacement. Thus the imagined nothingness of the self becomes the existential 'crisis' of the self."

12. Paul Tillich, *Dynamics of Faith* (New York: HarperCollins, 1957), 40–44.

13. Zaner, "Body," 297. See also Drew Leder, *The Absent Body* (Chicago: University of Chicago Press, 1990).

Chapter VII

Parts of this chapter appeared in a festschrift for my mentor: *Literature, Religion, and East/West Comparison: Essays in Honor of Anthony C. Yu,* ed. Eric Ziolkowski (Newark: University of Delaware Press, 2005). I am grateful to William Barr and the Association of Disciples for Theological Discussion, who responded to an early version of the essay.

The first epigraph is from *Philoctetes,* in *Sophocles 2,* trans. David Grene (Chicago: University of Chicago Press, 1957), ll. 83–84; line numbers and Greek phrases from *Sophocles: Antigone, The Women of Trachis, Philoctetes, Oedipus at Colonus,* Loeb Classical Library, ed. and trans. Hugh Lloyd-Jones (Cambridge: Harvard University Press, 1994).

The second epigraph quotes Seamus Heaney, *The Cure at Troy: A Version of Sophocles'* Philoctetes (London: Faber and Faber, 1990), 44.

1. Sophocles may reflect his own crisis of integrity after voting to establish the tyranny of the Four Hundred. W. M. Calder III, "Sophoclean Apologia: *Philoctetes,*" *Greek, Roman and Byzantine Studies* 12 (1971): 153–74, agrees the author is the Sophocles in Aristotle's *Rhetoric* 3.18.

2. Oscar Mandel, *Philoctetes and the Fall of Troy* (Lincoln: University of Nebraska Press, 1981). On the absent Lemnians, see Oliver Taplin, "The

Mapping of Sophocles' *Philoctetes*," *Bulletin for the Institute of Classical Studies* 34 (1987): 69–77.

3. See Thomas M. Falkner, "Containing Tragedy: Rhetoric and Self-Representation in Sophocles' *Philoctetes*," *Classical Antiquity* 17 (1998): 25–58.

4. How they elicit our belief depends on vexed questions: whether the text is consistent that both the man *and* his bow are required, and that he must be *persuaded*. Some contend that Odysseus and Neoptolemus never doubt they must trick Philoctetes into accompanying them. But to explain away all the textual incongruities in terms of deception weakens Neoptolemus's discovery that Philoctetes is as important as the bow and reduces his awakening compassion. Others say the text is inconsistent, or that Odysseus suppresses the terms of the prophecy, or that the aporias would go unnoticed in performance. Odysseus seems one to ignore or rationalize what he knows and fears, that the oracle requires a cooperative Philoctetes, not just his bow. Odysseus may or may not be bluffing when he threatens to abandon him again, but never grasps that Philoctetes must come willingly to Troy.

5. See Meredith Clarke Hoppins, "What Happens in Sophocles' 'Philoctetes'?" *Traditio* 37 (1981): 1–30; Richard Hamilton, "Neoptolemus' Story in the *Philoctetes*," *American Journal of Philology* 96 (1975): 131–37; and Anthony J. Podlecki, "The Power of Words in Sophocles' *Philoctetes*," *Greek, Roman and Byzantine Studies* 7 (1966): 233–50.

6. See Podlecki; Oliver Taplin, "Significant Actions in Sophocles' *Philoctetes*," *Greek, Roman and Byzantine Studies* 12 (1971): 25–44; for opposite views see Hamilton and Calder.

7. Martha Nussbaum, "Consequences of Character in Sophocles' *Philoctetes*," *Philosophy and Literature* 1 (1976): 25–53. Mary Whitlock Blundell, in "The Moral Character of Odysseus in *Philoctetes*," *Greek Roman and Byzantine Studies* 28 (1987): 307–29, doubts Odysseus is motivated by the common good.

8. Mary Whitlock Blundell, "The *Phusis* of Neoptolemus in Sophocles' *Philoctetes*," *Greece and Rome* 35 (1988): 137–48; John Gibert, *Change of Mind in Greek Tragedy* (Göttingen: Vandenhoeck und Ruprecht, 1995), 146–47.

9. Blundell, *Helping Friends,* 203.

10. *Hegel On Tragedy,* ed. Anne and Henry Paoluci (New York: Harper and Row, 1962), 33.

11. Edmund Wilson, *The Wound and the Bow* (New York: Oxford, 1947); Drew Leder, "Illness and Exile: Sophocles' *Philoctetes*," and Sidney F. Parham, "Philoctetes' Wound," in *Literature and Medicine* 9 (1990): 12–20; David B. Morris, *The Culture of Pain* (Berkeley: University of California Press, 1991), 148–55. Bryan Doerries translates and arranges scene readings from *Philoctetes and Ajax* in his "Theater of War" project, performed to elicit therapeutic testimony and conversation from veterans, their families,

and the public; see Patrick Healy, "The Anguish of War for Today's Soldiers, Explored by Sophocles," *New York Times,* Nov. 12, 2009.

12. William F. May, *The Patient's Ordeal* (Bloomington: Indiana University Press, 1991), 15–35, writing on the burn injury of "Dax" Cowart.

13. Scarry, *Body in Pain,* 5.

14. Gotthold Ephraim Lessing, *Laocoön: An Essay on the Limits of Painting and Poetry,* trans. Edward Allen McCormick (Baltimore: Johns Hopkins University Press, 1984), 8. On staging pain, see Peter D. Arnott, *Public Performance in the Greek Theatre* (London: Routledge, 1989), 68, 139; Oliver Taplin, *Greek Tragedy in Action* (Berkeley: University of California Press, 1978; Mandel, plates 1–4; Segal, *Tragedy and Civilization,* 334–35.

15. Jacques Vidal-Naquet, "Sophocles' *Philoctetes* and the Ephebia," in Jean-Pierre Vernant and J. Vidal-Naquet, *Myth and Tragedy in Ancient Greece,* trans. Janet Lloyd (New York: Zone, 1988), 161–79.

16. R. P. Winnington-Ingram, *Sophocles* (Cambridge: Cambridge 1980), 284–85. On other ambiguities in Neoptolemus's character and destiny, see Taplin, "Mapping"; Deborah Roberts, "Different Stories: Sophoclean Narrative(s) in the *Philoctetes,*" *Transactions of the American Philological Association* 119 (1989): 161–76.

17. On Neoptolemus's questions I am grateful to colleague Marcia Day Childress, who discusses *Philoctetes* in medical humanities seminars.

18. Ismene Lada-Richards, "Neoptolemus and the Bow: Ritual *Thea* and Theatrical Vision in Sophocles' *Philoctetes,*" *Journal of Hellenic Studies* 117 (1997): 179–83.

19. Seamus Heaney, in an interview by Harry Eyres, *Times* (London), April 2, 1991. See also Cedric Whitman, *Sophocles: A Study of Heroic Humanism* (Cambridge: Harvard University Press, 1951), 178.

20. Heaney, 44, paraphrasing l. 813.

21. Segal, *Tragedy and Civilization,* 307.

22. See Joe Park Poe, in *Heroism and Divine Justice in Sophocles' Philoctetes* (Leiden: Brill, 1974), 49.

23. See Daniel Tobin, *Passage to the Center: Imagination and the Sacred in the Poetry of Seamus Heaney* (Lexington: University of Kentucky Press, 1999), 276.

24. Hugh Denard, "Seamus Heaney, Colonialism, and the Cure: Sophoclean Re-visions," *Performing Arts Journal* 22(3) (Sept. 2000): 1–18.

25. In Eyres, Heaney says, "I think everyone in Northern Ireland has both an Odysseus and a Neoptolemus inside them. Odysseus is the solidarity figure, who speaks in the first person plural on behalf of the tribe. But there must also be the first person singular, the Neoptolemus, who says 'yes, but you must also abide by a strict personal morality.' "

26. See Tobin. See also Jefferson Hunter, "The Borderline of Poetry," *Virginia Quarterly Review* 68 (1992): 801–8; John Herington, "The Song of the Bow," *New Criterion* 11 (1992): 73–75.

27. Heaney, in Eyres. Denard observes how leaders such as Mary Robinson (president of Ireland, 1990–97) and Bill Clinton have quoted Heaney's choruses, seeking a postcolonial vision and discourse for Northern Ireland.

Chapter VIII

The first epigraph quotes from Suzan-Lori Parks, *Venus* (New York: Theatre Communications Group, 1997), 4. Parks's spelling and punctuation reflect accents and speech patterns.

The second epigraph quotes from Bernard Pomerance, *The Elephant Man* (New York: Grove Weidenfeld, 1979), 3.

The third epigraph quotes from Margaret Edson, *Wit: A Play* (New York: Faber and Faber, 1993, 1999), 35.

1. The Merrick chapter in Frederick Treves, *The Elephant Man and Other Reminiscences* (London: Cassell, 1923), is also in Ashley Montagu, *The Elephant Man: A Study in Human Dignity* (New York: Dutton, 1979). Both Pomerance and the 1980 David Lynch film (apparently unrelated to the play) cite these sources. Michael Howell and Peter Ford, *The True History of the Elephant Man* (London: Allison and Busby, 1980), reprints Treves, but appeared when the disorder was thought to be neurofibromatosis. See J. A. Tibbles and M. M. Cohen Jr., "The Proteus Syndrome: The Elephant Man Diagnosed," *British Medical Journal* 293 (1986): 683–85.

2. On a future community of discourse as a regulative ideal, see Habermas in Mueller-Vollmer.

3. See, for example, Stephen Jay Gould, "The Hottentot Venus," in *The Flamingo's Smile* (New York: Norton, 1987), 291–305, and the title poem in Elizabeth Alexander, *The Hottentot Venus*, Callaloo Poetry Series vol. 9 (Charlottesville: University of Virginia Press, 1990). Since the play, the biography of Baartman and the cultural history of "the Venus" have been explored by Clifton Crais and Pamela Scully in *Sara Baartman and the Hottentot Venus: A Ghost Story and a Biography* (Princeton: Princeton University Press, 2009). Parks's *Venus* is severely criticized as exploitive in Jean Young, "The Re-objectificatie and Re-commodification of Saartjie Baartman in Suzan-Lori Parks' *Venus,*" *African American Review* 31 (1997): 699–708. But her Brechtian strategies of implicating the audience are appreciated in Harry J. Elam Jr. and Alice Raynor, "Body Parts: Between Story and Spectacle in *Venus* by Suzan-Lori Parks," in *Staging Resistance: Essays on Political Theater,* ed. Jeanne Colleran and Jenny S. Spencer (Ann Arbor: University of Michigan Press, 1998), 265–82; and Deborah R. Geis, *Suzan-Lori Parks* (Ann Arbor: University of Michigan Press, 2008), 77.

4. Such a vaudeville, *The Venus Hottentot, or the Hatred of Frenchwomen,* played in Paris in 1814–15, overlapping when Baartman was exhibited; see T. Denean Sharpley-Whiting, *Black Venus: Sexualized Savages, Primal Fears, and Primitive Narratives in French* (Durham: Duke University Press, 1999), 32–41. The play is translated by the author in an appendix.

5. Teresa Dowell-Vest says the Jefferson consideration was part of the context for deciding to produce *Venus* in Charlottesville, Va., in a Live Arts play program (2001).

6. Steven Jay Gould, *The Mismeasure of Man* (New York: Morton, 1981), 53, on BBs and the methods of Samuel George Morton. On the Baron Georges Cuvier and other French anatomists who examined—without empathy or anything resembling romantic affection—and later dissected Baartman, see Gould, "Hottentot," and Crais and Scully, 131–36, 139–42, 144.

7. It is not clear that anything like this occurred; Treves did think Merrick had a romantic streak that shadowed his life (Montagu, 32). Kendal is a composite of women acquainted with Merrick.

8. Donne's meditations on his life-threatening illness of 1623 are discussed in William B. Ober. "John Donne as Patient: *Devotions upon Emergent Occasions*" and Murray D. Arndt, "Distance on the Look of Death," *Literature and Medicine* 9 (1990): 21–37, 38–49. Arndt draws comparisons between the *Devotions* and the "Holy Sonnets."

9. Rudolf Otto, *The Idea of the Holy,* trans. John W. Harvey (1923; London: Oxford University Press, 1950), 12–19, 31–40.

10. See Jennifer A. Gage, "The Moral Universe of Complementary and Alternative Medicine (CAM): A Cultural-Theological Reading of Mind-Body Interventions," University of Virginia dissertation (Charlottesville, 2004).

11. On Aeschylus and Sophocles, see Ricoeur, *Symbolism of Evil.* On theodicy, see my "Holding Fragments," in Mohrmann and Hanson.

12. See Richard Rorty, *Contingency, Irony, and Solidarity* (New York: Cambridge University Press, 1989), 73–74.

13. Vivian on 50 cites her "former student," Richard Strier, "John Donne Awry and Squint: The 'Holy Sonnets,' 1608–1610," *Modern Philology* 86 (1989): 357–84. Among Strier's points are that Donne often failed to assimilate theologically or poetically his professed Calvinism, that in some sonnets he succeeded, and that Sonnet 5 was one time when he *deliberately* made a bad theological argument (ll. 1–8) for the sake of irony, although the wish to be forgotten by God is distressing. "A Calvinist sense of sin has banished merit as a way to salvation, but nothing—or rather, nothingness—has replaced it. Donne finds it difficult to accept being saved as a sinner, and he cannot convincingly imagine being free from sin" (384).

14. Edson may imply that the sonnet's conclusion is singly ironic and means for its readers to realize they should ask God to remember them. She might, however, regard "sin" (rather than the poet) as the object of "forget," which would affect how we should take the last lines. Helen Gardner admits the end of Sonnet 5 seems "facile," but notes precedents in scripture, in Donne's sermons, and in George Herbert where "forgetting" can be a metaphor for "forgiving." See John Donne, *Divine Poems,* ed. Helen Gardner, 2nd. ed. (Oxford: Clarendon, 1978), xxx, 68.

15. See Martha Greene Eads, "Unwitting Redemption in Margaret Edson's *Wit*," *Christianity and Literature* 51 (2002): 241–54.

16. See interview material with Edson and actor Carmen Roman, in Penelope Mesic, "Breathing Lessons," *Chicago* Magazine (June 2001): 48–50.

Chapter IX

The first epigraph is from Euripides, *The Bacchae*, trans. and intro. William Arrowsmith, in *Euripides 5*, The Complete Greek Tragedies (Chicago: University of Chicago Press, 1959), ll. 1279–81.

The second quote is from Richard Schechner, *Environmental Theater* (1973; New York: Applause, 1994), 145.

The third epigraph is from Mary Zimmerman, *Metamorphoses: A Play*, "Based on David R. Slavitt's translation of *The Metamorphoses of Ovid*" (Evanston: Northwestern University Press, 2002), 60. When Zimmerman uses or combines Slavitt's lines with her own, I indicate this parenthetically. See Slavitt (Baltimore: Johns Hopkins University Press, 1994).

1. Elinor Fuchs, *The Death of Character: Perspectives on Theater after Modernism* (Bloomington: Indiana University Press, 1996).

2. Ibid., 71–74 and *passim*. See Keir Elam, *The Semiotics of Theatre and Drama* (London: Methuen 1980); and Mark Fortier, *Theory/Theatre: An Introduction*, 2nd. ed. (London: Routledge, 2002), 19–36.

3. See chapter IV, on Driver.

4. Antonin Artaud, *The Theatre and Its Double*, trans. Marie Caroline Richards (New York: Grove, 1958). See Jacques Derrida, "The Theater of Cruelty and the Closure of Representation," in *Writing and Difference*, trans. Alan Bass (Chicago: University of Chicago Press, 1978), 232–50. Max Harris, in *Theater and Incarnation* (New York: St. Martins, 1990), 40–41, warns against reducing Artaud's theory to "pure abstraction," for he was aiming at a sense of archetypal reality.

5. Fuchs, 170.

6. See Stanton B. Garner, *Bodied Spaces: Phenomenology and Performance in Contemporary Drama* (Ithaca: Cornell University Press, 1994), 30.

7. In Aristophanes' comedy, the *Thesmophoriazusai*.

8. René Girard, *Violence and the Sacred*, 134.

9. Arrowsmith, "Introduction," in *Euripides 5*, 143. David Kovacs, introducing his translations in new Loeb Classical Library editions, doubts Euripides was a religious skeptic, despite comments in Aristophanes; see *Euripides: Cyclops, Alcestis, Media* (Cambridge: Harvard University Press, 1994), 22–32.

10. Valdis Leinieks, *The City of Dionysos: A Study of Euripides' Bakchai* (Stuttgart and Leipzig: B. G. Teubner, 1996), 49–50.

11. In another myth, Dionysus is born of Zeus and Persephone, and angry Hera has the Titans dismember him; Zeus places his heart in Semele's womb, from whence Dionysus's rebirth.

12. See Simon Goldhill, *Reading Greek Tragedy* (Cambridge: Cambridge University Press, 1986), 262–64. Kovacs thinks Teiresias criticizes those such as Pentheus who despise religion generally not just Dionysian religion; *Euripides: Bacchae, Iphigenia at Aulis, Rhesus* (Cambridge: Harvard University Press, 2002), 7–8.

13. D. J. Conacher, in *Euripidean Drama: Myth, Theme, and Structure* (Toronto: University of Toronto Press, 1967), 58, thinks the *Bacchae* was innovative in depicting Dionysian religion "as a universal phenomenon: man's periodic need of release from the rational and the commonplace, and of return to the elemental springs of life by means of his emotions."

14. See William Hunter Shephard, *The Dionysus Group* (New York: Peter Lang, 1991); and Performance Group, *Dionysus in 69*, ed. Richard Schechner (New York: Farrar, Straus and Giroux, 1970), no pagination, abbreviated PG; the latter is a photographic record with script and comments by Schechner and Group members.

15. Shephard, 152–54.

16. Ibid., 216.

17. Richard Schechner, *Performance Theory* (London: Routledge, 1988, 2003), 15.

18. See PG and Shephard on the ecstasy dance and caress. On the ritual negotiation of power, see Catherine Bell, *Ritual Theory, Ritual Practice* (New York: Oxford University Press, 1992), especially on the "ritual body," 94–117.

19. Shephard, 172.

20. David Kovacs argues that Pentheus's desire *to see* is directed toward religious ecstasies, not sexual behavior, in *Euripidea Tertia* (Leiden: Brill, 2004), 129–30,

21. Schechner, *Environmental Theater*, 126.

22. Ibid., xi; see also Schechner's "Drama, Modern," in *The Encyclopedia of Religion*, ed. Mircea Eliade (New York: Macmillan, 1984), and his *The Future of Ritual: Writings on Culture and Performance* (London: Routledge, 1993).

23. Froma Zeitlin, a classicist who saw the play, does not think it acknowledged its implications of a "'fascism of liberation and violence,'" in her essay, "*Dionysus in 69*," in *Dionysus Since 69: Greek Tragedy at the Dawn of the Third Millennium*, ed. Edith Hall, Fiona Macintosh, Amanda Wrigley (Oxford: Oxford University Press, 2004), 75.

24. I am grateful to Howard Pickett for this question.

25. George Devereux, "The Psychotherapy Scene in Euripides' *Bacchae*," *Journal of Hellenic Studies* 90 (1970): 35–48.

26. Euripides, 216; Arrowsmith fills a gap in the extant play, based on manuscript fragments.

27. Story theater involves telling while playing stories or folktales, especially to bring out political subtexts, as in Brecht. See Paul Sills, *Story The-*

atre: Adapted for the Stage (London: Samuel French, 1971), and Sills, *Story Theater: Four Shows* (New York: Applause, 2000).

28. Ben Brantley, review of *Metamorphoses, New York Times,* Oct. 10, 2001.

29. My description is based on the text and on two productions in New York. The Second Stage Theatre, in Oct. 2001, used a proscenium stage; the play reopened on a thrust stage at Circle in the Square, in March 2002.

30. Frank Burch Brown, at a meeting of the Association of Disciples for Theological Discussion (2001); what follows is inspired by his most helpful response to my discussions of kenosis.

31. Paul Tillich, *Systematic Theology,* vol. 3 (Chicago: University of Chicago Press, 1963), 137.

32. See prelude to part IV.

33. Dante, *The Inferno* 25, ll. 64–69, trans. John Ciardi, *The Divine Comedy* (New York: Norton, 1961). See ll. 94–108 for more of the imagery of bestial transformation and violation.

34. For Augustine, evil is the privation or corruption of the good, and has no substantial existence.

35. See Brown, *Transfiguration,* 87.

36. See Erich Auerbach on Dante's "figural" view of history and eternity in *Mimesis: The Representation of Reality in Western Literature,* trans. Willard R. Trask (Princeton: Princeton University Press, 1953), ch. 8.

37. Zimmerman cites material from Rainer Maria Rilke's poem "Orpheus. Eurydice. Hermes."

38. The myth is in Apuleius, *Metamorphoses* (or *The Golden Ass*) 6. Zimmerman may echo Edith Hamilton, *Mythology* (New York: Little, Brown, 1942), 34: "So it all came to a most happy end. Love and the Soul (for that is what Psyche means) had sought and, after sore trials, found each other; and that union could never be broken."

Prelude to Part IV

1. I do not assume that *doulos* (slave) in Philippians 2:7 recalls the suffering and then exalted servant in Isaiah 52:13–53:12. The servant likely refers to Israel, and Paul may be alluding to a Hellenistic divine man, or to views of Adam. See Morna D. Hooker, *Jesus and the Servant* (London: S.P.C.K., 1959), 120–21, 147–48, 158–63; see others cited below. The parallels are in "emptying" and "pouring" as other-directed movements, and in the appraisals of such emptying as "exaltation."

2. Geertz, 89–90, where "sacred symbols function to synthesize a people's ethos . . . and their world view."

3. Donald Lopez, *Prisoners of Shangri-la* (Chicago: University of Chicago Press, 1998).

4. See Stout on MacIntyre, Hauerwas, and other "new traditionalists" in *Ethics After Babel.*

5. See Childress, *Practical Reasoning in Bioethics,* 25–43.

6. In *I and Thou,* trans. Walter Kaufmann (New York: Scribners, 1970), 57, Martin Buber speaks of three spheres of relation: with persons, nature, and "spiritual beings" (*geistige Wesenheiten*). The latter include forms of art, language, and action that "speak" to us; see Steven Kepnes, *The Text as Thou: Martin Buber's Dialogical Hermeneutics and Narrative Theology* (Bloomington: Indiana University Press, 1992), 23.

7. Paul Ricoeur treats these aspects of memory ("evoked" and "searched" or "recalled") dialectically in *Memory, History, and Forgetting,* trans. Kathleen Blamey and David Pellauer (Chicago: University of Chicago Press, 2004), 26–30.

8. There may be neutral if not positive connotations to "pouring." When Rebekah "pours out" (*pi'el*) water from a pitcher into a trough (Gen. 24:20), the Greek Septuagint (LXX) translates the verb as *eksekenosen*. However, the word's literal meaning, "to make bare," is also said of wombs, another negative image. LXX translates a related verb (*hiph'il*) in Isa. 53:12 as *paredothē* ("handed over"), but it could also be rendered *eksekenosen*. In English, Isaiah is commonly translated, "he poured out himself" (NRSV following the King James Version, KJV, "he poured out his soul"). Paul speaks of himself "being poured out [*spendomai*] as a libation" (Phil. 2:17).

9. Jeffrey Hopkins objects to views of "absolute emptiness" applied to Tibetan Buddhism, in *Meditation on Emptiness* (Boston: Wisdom Publications, 1983, 1996), 16. See also Shubert Ogden's criticisms of Masao Abe's relating Christian kenosis to Kyoto school Buddhist views of *sunyata* (emptiness, nothingness), in *The Emptying God: A Buddhist-Jewish-Christian Conversation,* ed. John B Cobb Jr. and Christopher Ives (Mary Knoll, N.Y.: Orbis, 1990), 125–34. Janet Gyatso cautions against absolute emptiness in "Compassion at the Millennium: A Buddhist Salvo for the Ethics of the Apocalypse," in *Thinking Through the Death of God: A Critical Companion to Thomas J. J. Altizer,* ed. Lissa McCullough and Brian Schroeder (Albany: State University of New York Press, 2004), 147–67.

10. See Daphne Hampson, *Theology and Feminism* (Oxford: Blackwell, 1990), 155; Catherine Keller expresses similar reservations in her response to Abe, in Cobb and Ives, 102–15. Marta Frascati-Lochhead analyzes several feminist appropriations of kenosis in *Kenosis and Feminist Theology: The Challenge of Gianni Vattimo* (Albany: State University of New York Press, 1998). Sarah Coakley answers worries about kenosis "swallowing the other" in "Kenosis: Theological Meanings and Gender Considerations," in *The Work of Love: Creation and Kenosis,* ed. John Polkinghorne (Grand Rapids: Eerdmans, 2001). esp. 204–9, and in "*Kenosis* and Subversion: On the Repression of 'Vulnerability' in Christian Feminist Writing," in *Swallowing a Fishbone? Feminist Theologies Debate Christianity,* ed. Daphne Hampson (London: S.P.C.K., 1996).

11. Gianni Vattimo, *Beyond Interpretation: The Meaning of Hermeneutics for Philosophy,* trans. David Webb (Stanford: Stanford University Press, 1994), 48–54.

12. See Ferreira's discussions of Levinas on desire, cited in the Introduction. On the mutuality of kenosis in literary art, see Alphonso Lingis, "Kenosis," in McCoullough and Schroeder.

13. Harold Bloom, *The Anxiety of Influence: A Theory of Poetry* (London: Oxford University Press, 1973), 77–92.

14. I do not know if Bloom ever makes this argument; he might think that Paul, the "original" New Testament writer, knew too little of the actual "poetry" of Jesus to be anxious about it.

15. Thomas J. J. Altizer, *The Gospel of Christian Atheism* (Philadelphia: Westminster, 1966), 62–75.

16. See Malcolm Jeeves, "The Nature of Persons and the Emergence of Kenotic Behavior," in Polkinghorne, 66–89.

17. See Oliver Davies, especially ch. 2, "The Compassionate Self."

18. Donald G. Dawe, *The Form of a Servant: A Historical Analysis of the Kenotic Motif* (Philadelphia: Westminster, 1963), 29–31; Hans Urs von Balthasar, *Mysterium Paschale: The Mystery of Easter,* trans. Aidan Nichols (1990; Grand Rapids: Eerdmans, 1993), 23–36. A "veil" can conceal and reveal. In the KJV, it translates the torn "curtain" (*katapetasma*) of the temple in Matthew 27:51 and the "curtain of flesh" in Hebrews 10:20, where Christ's flesh alludes to the temple curtain. But "veil of flesh" can also connote clothing or disguise. Athanasius speaks of Christ taking the form of a slave and "putting on flesh," *Against the Arians* I.11.43. Augustine, in a sermon on John 5:19, speaks of Christ "clothed in flesh," alluding to John 1:14 and to Jesus being born of Mary; see also *On the Trinity* I.7, where he uses *habitus* for "form" or "fashion" in Phil. 2:7. Calvin uses the veiling to speak of the hiddenness of Christ's divinity, *Institutes* II.13.2. And Karl Barth speaks of the impossibility of knowing the Son apart from his humanity: "His form as a man is regarded and described rather as the concealing [*Verhüllung* = veiling, disguising] of His true being . . . ," *Church Dogmatics,* 4 vols. in 13 part-volumes, trans. G. W. Bromiley (Edinburgh: T and T Clark, 1936–75), 4.1 (1956): 163. However, here "veiling" probably has to do with un-concealment: the Son is recognized through the veil of flesh and is constituted as Son through incarnation. See Bruce L. McCormack, "Karl Barth's Christology as a Resource for a Reformed Version of Kenoticism," *International Journal of Systematic Theology* 8 (2006): 243–51. I am grateful to Paul Dafydd Jones for this Barth passage.

19. See discussions in D. M. Baillie, *God Was in Christ* (New York: Scribner's, 1948); Dawe; Lucien Richard, *Christ: The Self-Emptying God* (New York: Paulist, 1997); Thomas R. Thompson, "Nineteenth Century Kenotic Christology: The Waxing, Waning, and Weighing of a Quest for a Coherent

Orthodoxy," in *Exploring Kenotic Christology: The Self-Emptying of God,* ed. C. Stephen Evans (Oxford: Oxford University Press, 2006), 74–111.

20. See McCormack, "Karl Barth's Christology"; Paul Dafydd Jones, "Karl Barth on Gethsemane," *International Journal of Systematic Theology* 9 (2007): 148–71; and Lucien Richard, "Kenotic Christology in a New Perspective," *Eglise et Theologie* 7 (1976): 5–39. See also Jürgen Moltmann, "God's Kenosis in the Creation and Consummation of the World," and Keith Ward, "Cosmos and Kenosis," in Polkinghorne, *Work of Love.*

21. I am grateful to Petra Harvey, who explores the person-to-person ethical implications of *Theo-Drama* in an unpublished paper on Levinas and Balthasar.

22. See Balthasar, *Mysterium Paschale,* 30, and *Theo-Drama,* vol. 4 (1994): 331. McCormack and Jones discuss whether a similar logic of participation can be understood in Barth, and I am indebted to Jones for conversations about this interpretation.

23. Gordon D. Fee, in "Philippians 2:5–11: Hymn or Exalted Prose," *Bulletin for Biblical Research* 2 (1992): 29–46, questions the preexisting hymn theory. He argues for Pauline composition and observes where kenotic-like statements of obedience to God occur elsewhere in Paul.

24. Donald G. Dawe, "A Fresh Look at the Kenotic Christologies," *Scottish Journal of Theology* 15 (1962): 337–49.

25. See Graham Ward, "Kenosis, Death, Discourse and Resurrection," in Lucy Gardener, David Moss, Ben Quash, and Graham Ward, *Balthasar and the End of Modernity* (Edinburgh: T and T Clark, 1999), 23.

26. See P. R. Martin's translation in *Carmen Christi: Philippians ii. 5–11* in *Recent Interpretation and in the Setting of Early Christian Worship* (Cambridge: Cambridge University Press, 1967), 38. His reading of "name" (*onoma*) as "rank" in verse 9a would be supported by David Seeley, "The Background of the Philippians Hymn," *Journal of Higher Criticism* 1 (1994): 49–72, a study of Jewish and Roman political ideology.

27. James D. G. Dunn, *Christology in the Making: A New Testament Inquiry into the Origins of the Doctrine of the Incarnation* (Philadelphia: Westminster, 1980), 114–21.

28. Richard, 59, commenting on Ernst Käsemann, "A Critical Analysis of Philippians 2:5–11" (1950), trans. Alice F. Carse, *The Journal for Theology and Church* 5 (1969): 45–88, at 61 (also published as *God and Christ: Existence and Province,* ed. Robert W. Funk [New York: Harper and Row, 1969]).

29. Richard B. Hays, *The Moral Vision of the New Testament: Community, Cross, New Creation* (San Francisco: HarperSanFrancisco, 1996), 29. Similarly, see Morna D. Hooker, *From Adam to Christ: Essays on Paul* (Cambridge: Cambridge University Press, 1990), 89–93.

30. Knapp, *Shakespeare's Tribe,* 27.

31. See Ricoeur, *Oneself as Another,* 21–23, and ch. 10.

32. See Les Essif, *Empty Figure on an Empty Stage: The Theatre of Samuel Beckett and His Generation* (Bloomington: Indiana University Press, 2001), 15; however, Essif is less interested in "filling" than with emptiness itself as a condition of both mind and reality.

33. See Jean-Luc Marion, *God Without Being: Hors Texte,* trans. Thomas A. Carlson (Chicago: University of Chicago Press, 1991).

34. Søren Kierkegaard, *The Concept of Anxiety,* trans. Reidar Thomte and Albert B. Anderson (Princeton: Princeton University Press, 1980), 45, 61; see Reinhold Niebuhr, *The Nature and Destiny of Man,* vol. I: *Human Nature* (New York: Scribner's, 1941), 251.

35. See Moltmann's discussion of Lurianic kabbalah, in Polkinghorne, *Work of Love,* 137–51.

36. Robert Jenson, *Systematic Theology,* vol. 1, *The Triune God* (Oxford: Oxford University Press, 1997), 226. KJV renders John 14:2, "In my Father's house are many mansions."

37. See Douglas R. Hofstadter, *Gödel, Escher, Bach: An Eternal Golden Braid* (New York: Vintage, 1979), 56.

38. See Ephesians 1:23, and Brian Schroeder, "Absolute Atonement," in McCollough and Schroeder, on the fortuitous English etymology of reconciling at-one-ment, 66. See also "all in all" in 1 Corinthians 15:28.

39. See William Schweiker, "Time as Moral Space: Moral Cosmologies, Creation, and Last Judgment," in *The End of the World and the Ends of God: Science and Theology on Eschatology,* ed. John Polkinghorne and Michael Welker (Harrisburg: Trinity Press International, 2000).

40. See Robert W. Funk, *Parables and Presence: Forms of the New Testament Tradition* (Philadelphia: Fortress, 1982), 34.

41. John Dominic Crossan, *In Parables: The Challenge of the Historical Jesus* (New York: Harper and Row, 1973), 64–66. Crossan puts it even more starkly: good and bad are "reversed" in the parables; the hearer's world is "turned upside down," which *is* the eschatological challenge of the historical Jesus. I discuss this parable as theatrical drama in the postlude.

Chapter X

The quoted dialogue is from Denys Arcand, *Jésus de Montréal* (Quebec: Boréal, 1989), abbr. *JM,* 70; rough translations are mine. This text is the screenplay, written and directed by Arcand.

1. "Second Shepherds' Pageant," *Everyman and Medieval Miracle Plays,* ed. A. C. Cawley (London: Dent, 1956).

2. See the discussion of Elaine Scarry in chapter I.

3. Sarah Beckwith, *Signifying God: Social Relation and Symbolic Act in the York Corpus Christi Plays* (Chicago: University of Chicago Press, 2001), 63–64.

4. Harris, *Theater and Incarnation,* 82; O. B. Hardison, "Drama: Western European," *The Encyclopedia of Religion,* ed. Mircea Eliade (New York:

Macmillan, 1987); Rosemary Woolf, *The English Mystery Plays* (London: Routledge and Kegan Paul, 1972), 190–93; V. A. Kolve, *The Play Called Corpus Christi* (Stanford: Stanford University Press, 1966), 139–40,173.

5. Beckwith, 10–15.

6. Ibid., 59, 134–57. The phrase "hocus pocus" may be a parody of the Latin "*hoc est enim corpus meum*," referring to the Eucharistic host. On *JM*, see 174–80.

7. Arcand, Preface, 7–8. The last reference probably refers to Les Mystère des Voix Bulgare, a vocal group featured on the soundtrack.

8. For an account of how *JM* "subverts the passion play," see Lloyd Baugh, *Imaging the Divine: Jesus and Christ-Figures in Film* (Kansas City, Mo.: Sheed and Ward, 1997), 119–22.

9. Mark 13 may allude the apocalyptic "son of man" in Daniel 7:13. W. Barnes Tatum thinks Daniel Coulomb's first name alludes to the relationship of Mark to Daniel; see Tatum, *Jesus at the Movies: A Guide to the First Hundred Years* (Santa Rosa, Calif.: Polebridge, 1997), 183–86.

10. The same producer who wants "the head" of the actor associated with John the Baptist.

11. E.g., John Milbank, 279; see also Williams, "Moral Luck."

12. Bertolt Brecht, *Galileo,* English version by Charles Laughton (New York: Grove, 1966), 83.

13. There are a few scenes in the published script not in the film, one that gives Coulomb an uncanny ability to shame an Italian pizza maker into giving the actors free pizzas. In the ambulance, his last words urge Constance to pay the pizzeria when she has some money (176), alluding to the last words of Socrates, "I owe a cock to [the god] Asclepius."

14. Alison Milbank appreciates the blood and porous materiality, reviewing *The Passion of the Christ,* in *The Declaration,* March 18, 2004, an independent newspaper at the University of Virginia (Charlottesville).

15. I am grateful to a discussion of Jesus movies with Dennis Smith and members of the Association of Disciples for Theological Discussion, 2004.

16. Michael Welker, "Resurrection and Eternal Life: The Canonic Memory of the Resurrected Christ, His Reality, and His Glory," in Polkinghorne and Welker.

17. Beckwith, 75–80, on the paradox of "he is risen; he is not here."

18. Stanley Hauerwas, *Community and Character: Toward a Constructive Christian Social Ethic* (Notre Dame: Notre Dame University Press, 1981), 11.

Chapter XI

The first quote is from Noel Coward, *Private Lives* (1930), in *Three Plays: Blithe Spirit, Hay Fever, Private Lives,* introduction by Philip Hare (New York: Vintage, 1999), 210.

The second quote is from T. S. Eliot, *The Cocktail Party* (San Diego: Harcourt, Brace, 1950), 29.

1. T. S. Eliot, *Poetry and Drama* (Cambridge: Harvard University Press, 1951), 26, 31, 43–44.

2. Ibid., 38. Before Eliot gave this lecture, none suspected the *Alcestis* connection.

3. There were revivals of *The Family Reunion* by the Royal Shakespeare Company in 2000 and of *The Cocktail Party* in 1997 and 2001 at the Edinburgh "Fringe" festival, and in New York in 2010. On British director John Dexter's production of *The Cocktail Party* at the Phoenix Theatre in London in 1986, see Randy Malamud, *T. S. Eliot's Drama: A Research and Production Sourcebook* (New York: Greenwood, 1992), 119.

4. See Sean O'Connor on *Private Lives* in *Straight Acting: Popular Gay Drama from Wilde to Rattigan* (London: Cassell, 1998), especially 111–21.

5. See Worth, "Eliot and the Living Theatre," on thematically serious relations between Coward's and Eliot's drama.

6. Eliot saw his close friend Emily Hale perform in *Blithe Spirit* in 1946; Lyndall Gordon, *T. S. Eliot: An Imperfect Life* (New York: Norton, 1999), 409.

7. Jean-Paul Sartre, *No Exit and Three Other Plays*, trans. Stuart Gilbert (New York: Vintage, 1946, 1955), 47.

8. Eliot told his director, E. Martin Browne, that he was replying to Sartre, reported in Browne's *The Making of T. S. Eliot's Plays* (Cambridge: Cambridge University Press, 1969), 233.

9. O'Connor, *Straight Acting,* in reference to the collapse of Mrs. Moore's faith in *A Passage to India,* places Elyot and Amanda in "the modernist universe of Conrad, Eliot, and Forster" (118). One could add, here, Dorothy L. Sayers, whose shell-shocked aristocrat, Lord Peter Wimsey, invokes "the sacred duty of flippancy" as he investigates a displaced corpse in *Whose Body* (1923).

10. Karl Barth at times viewed each gender as completing the other, and homosexuality as a sort of self-sufficient idolatry that refused created, heterosexual otherness; see *Church Dogmatics* III.4 (1961): 165–66. However, see David Matzko McCarthy, "The Relationship of Bodies: A Nuptial Hermeneutics of Same-sex Unions," in Eugene F. Rogers Jr., ed., *Theology and Sexuality: Classic and Contemporary Readings* (Oxford: Blackwell, 2002), 212–13: "Gay men and lesbians are persons who encounter the other (and thus discover themselves) in relation to persons of the same sex. . . . Homosexual and heterosexual desire follow along the same path insofar as both seek fulfillment through difference." See also Rogers's own essay, "Sanctification, Homosexuality, and God's Triune Life," in the same volume.

11. See Nussbaum. *The Fragility of Goodness.* See also my discussions of Williams and "moral luck," in the Introduction and elsewhere.

12. Malamud, 116.

13. Eliot, *Poetry and Drama,* 14–15. See also David E. Jones, *The Plays of T. S. Eliot* (Toronto: University of Toronto Press, 1960), 127; and Spanos, 188–91.

14. Virginia Phelan, *Two Ways of Life and Death:* Alcestis *and* The Cocktail Party (New York: Garland, 1990), one of the most detailed studies of the two plays and their criticism.

15. Lattimore, in his Introduction to *Alcestis,* in *Euripides 1,* ed. David Grene and Richmond Lattimore (Chicago: University of Chicago Press, 1955), 4.

16. Other *Alcestis* characters are divided as well; see Phelan, 9. Admetus is also Peter; Heracles is Reilly, Julia, and Alex. On Reilly also being Pheres (Admetus's father), see Kenneth J. Reckford, "Heracles and Mr. Eliot," *Comparative Literature* 16 (1964): 1–18, at 2.

17. See Helen Gardner, "The Comedies of T. S. Eliot," *Essays by Divers Hands* 34 (1966): 55–73, esp. p. 72. Gardner criticizes Eliot here; but the use of messengers to report horrible actions was a convention of Greek tragedy, and it contributes to this play's structure of interruptions.

18. Eliot, *Poetry and Drama,* 38. Criticism of the play's dramatic structure often blends into criticism of the "two ways"; see Phelan, 220–30; Denis Donoghue, *The Third Voice: Modern British and American Verse Drama* (Princeton: Princeton University Press, 1959, 127–29.

19. Virginia Woolf referred to Vivienne as a "bag of ferrets," Gordon, 283.

20. Ibid., 418; Gordon also quotes reviewer Susannah Clapp's reaction to *The Cocktail Party* at the 1997 Edinburgh Festival: "The ending is . . . repugnant, condemning an inconvenient girlfriend to a grisly death . . . which is represented as a moral triumph."

21. Phelan, 220. See Nathan A. Scott Jr., "T. S. Eliot's *The Cocktail Party:* Of Redemption and Vocation," *Religion in Life* 20 (1951): 274–85; William Lynch, "Theology and the Imagination," *Thought* (Spring 1955): 61–86. Harris, *Theater and Incarnation,* 104–6, thinks the play "represents a certain strand of Christian thought that advocates resignation and heroic suffering."

22. Worth, 163. The Coward play she has in mind is *Design for Living* (1933), which is even more critical of gender roles and marriage than *Private Lives.*

23. On this view, Eliot should have rejected Browne's advice to cut some description of Celia's crucifixion. Alex had said her body was painted with juice that attracted ants; Browne, 226.

24. Reckford, 3.

25. Ibid., 11: "We shall not here discuss Eliot's incipiently romantic idea of marriage, except to note it is largely founded on the neo-Heraclitean idea of strangeness—a wife who changes into a new person becomes unattain-

able and perhaps an object of longing even in marriage." However, I do not think the play implies that spouses should possess each other.

26. Friedrich Schleiermacher, "Hermeneutics," in *Hermeneutics and Criticism, and Other Writings*, trans. Andrew Bowie (1819; Cambridge: Cambridge University Press, 1998), 23.

27. See Gadamer, 219: "It is enough to say that we understand in a *different* way, if we understand at all." For hyperbolic implications of hospitality, see Jacques Derrida, *Of Hospitality: Anne Dufourmantelle Invites Jacques Derrida to Respond,* trans., Rachel Bowlby (Stanford: Stanford University Press, 2000). See also John Caputo and Michael J. Scanlon, eds., *God, the Gift, and Postmodernism* (Bloomington: Indiana University Press, 1999).

28. Julia Kristeva, *Strangers to Ourselves,* trans. Leon S. Roudiez (New York: Columbia University Press, 1991), 1–3.

29. On Reilly as a guide, like Virgil in Dante's *Divine Comedy,* see Nathan A. Scott Jr., "The Theatre of T. S. Eliot," in *Man in the Modern Theatre,* ed. Scott, 13–39. On Reilly's relation to Prospero in *The Tempest,* Phelan cites C. L. Barber, "The Power of Development … In a Different World," in F. O. Mattheissen, *The Achievement of T. S. Eliot* (New York: Oxford University Press, 1958), 235.

30. When Julia, Alex, and Reilly are alone, it is apparent they are equals in the role of Guardians.

31. See Ann P. Brady, "The Alchemy of Humor in *The Cocktail Party,*" in Jewel Spears Brooker, *Approaches to Teaching Eliot's Poetry and Plays* (New York: MLA, 1988), 179–82.

32. Spanos, 224, thinks accepting responsibility for Celia's death helps the transformation of Edward and Lavinia's relationship enough to mitigate the discontinuity of the "two ways."

33. This view of responsibility touches ideas of karma in the Bhagavad-Gita, which interested Eliot and contemporary writers, such as E. M. Forster, *A Passage to India,* ch. 19. On "impossible" obligations, see John Caputo, *Against Ethics,* and *On Religion* (London: Routledge, 2001).

34. Gardner, 65, treats the cocktail party as prelude to a meal, a symposium, or a "banquet of love," followed by the "Great supper, in the house of many mansions, [where] there will be places not only for 'the soldier saints' [like Celia] . . . but also for those who have in various ways lived a 'good life', and learned . . . to 'bear the beams of love' and exchange forgiveness."

35. Eliot referred to Lavinia's pregnancy in a letter to Geoffrey Faber in 1949, excerpted in T. S. Eliot's *The Cocktail Party,* ed. Nevill Coghill (London: Faber and Faber, 1974), 192; on Dexter's direction, see Malamud, 119, Gordon, 418–19.

Chapter XII

The dialogue is from Caryl Churchill, *Light Shining in Buckinghamshire* (1978; New York: Theatre Communications Group, 1985), 58–59.

The second quote/epigraph is from Tony Kushner, *Millennium Approaches,* Part I of *Angels in America: A Gay Fantasia on National Themes,* 2 vols. (New York: Theatre Communications Group, 1992–1996), 100. Part II is *Perestroika,* rev. ed. (1996). References to each play are cited by part (I or II) and page.

The third quote is from Tony Kushner, *Homebody/Kabul* (New York: Theatre Communications Group, 2002), 15; references are to this edition unless the revised edition (2004) is noted.

1. Charles Taylor, 28. See also Schweiker, "Time as Moral Space."

2. On the left wing of the English civil war, see Christopher Hill, *The World Turned Upside Down: Radical Ideas During the English Revolution* (London: Temple Smith, 1972); A. L. Morton, *The World of the Ranters* (London: Lawrence and Wishart, 1970); and Nigel Smith, *A Collection of Ranter Writings from the 17th. Century* (London: Junction, 1983). It is an interesting question as to whether the Ranters existed or were created by hostile audiences then, and sympathetic audiences now. J. C. Davis, in *Fear, Myth and History: The Ranters and the Historians* (Cambridge: Cambridge University Press, 1986), argues that Morton and Hill hope to find in English history a time when the protestant ethic (individualism rationalizing the unequal distribution of goods) might have been avoided (24, 133–34). Davis thinks they depend on seventeenth-century polemicists, whose writings do not show that the Ranters were a sect or even a loose organization but, instead, were a "sensation" or "myth." This myth was projected by moralizers and even would-be sympathizers (e.g., Quakers and Diggers) to deflect attacks on themselves. Only Laurence Clarkson held "core" Ranter beliefs, and not all of them at any one time: materialist pantheism, the reality of Christ in all persons, the denial of sin, all amounting to a "practical antinomianism" (25). Davis thinks Abiezer Coppe (also referred to as Cobbe) was a Leveller with little in common ideologically with Clarkson. While Davis tends to reduce Hill and other Ranter champions to their Marxist ways of reading of history, he seems right to notice how they agree that the Ranters were not a distinct movement.

3. Geraldine Cousin, *Churchill: The Playwright* (New York: Methuen, 1989), 20, on a diagram by Churchill suggesting a dramatic structure: "rigidities- movement- joy- crushings- disillusion."

4. A "Digger pamphlet" provides the title according to Churchill; however, Hill, 94, assigns it to Levellers writing in 1648, before Winstanley's work.

5. See Laurence Clarkson's retrospective and recanting pamphlet of 1660, *The Lost Sheep Found* (Exeter: The Rota, 1974), 6–27; most of the text is available in Smith.

6. Habermas, 315.

7. Morton, 142, reports that Clarkson converted again to become a follower of Ludowick Muggleton, and died in jail in 1667.

8. Hill, 176, quoting from Joseph Salmon, *Heights in Depths and Depths in Heights,* available in Smith, 215–16. Similarly, "Cobbe Prays" (1–2) is apparently based on Clarkson's memory of avoiding his father's blessing, as well as on Coppe's penchant for swearing.

9. See chapters by Edith Wyschogrod ("Crucifixion and Alterity"), Brian Schroeder ("Absolute Atonement"), and Alphonso Lingis ("Kenosis"), in McCollough and Schroeder. These essays explore relations between Altizer's theology and Levinas's ethics.

10. Kent Brintnall, "Shifting Contexts for Grief and Rage: Watching *Angels in America,*" part of a panel on *Angels* at the American Academy of Religion meeting in Philadelphia, Nov. 19, 2005.

11. On Harold Bloom and "blessing," see Kushner, II: 7, 154–55.

12. Mark Edmundson, *Nightmare on Main Street: Angels, Sadomasochism, and the Culture of Gothic* (Cambridge: Harvard University Press, 1997), 173.

13. For Edmundson, *Angels* seeks to unite late-twentieth-century Gothic sadomasochism with Romanticism or Emersonian transcendentalism. He thinks this uniting would be good were it pulled off, but it was not; and that the desire for "more life" is what unites Cohn and Belize is regarded by Edmundson as merely Kushner's bow to "complacent transcendence" (e.g., kitschy interest in Angels).

14. See Kundera on kitsch, 251, as screening awareness of mortality.

15. On the angel, see James Fisher, *The Theater of Tony Kushner: Living Past Hope* (New York: Routledge, 2002), 54. It pays homage to Paul Klee's painting *Angelus Novus,* which Walter Benjamin, "Theses on the Philosophy of History" in his *Illuminations,* trans. Harry Zohn (New York: Schocken, 1968), 257–58, calls, "the angel of history," blown backward into the future by a "storm" "we call progress." He thinks it looks on the accumulated "wreckage" of history, and would "awaken the dead, and make whole what has been smashed." Kushner's angel fits better a poem Benjamin quotes, "Gruss vom Angelus" by Gerhard Scholem: "My wing is ready for flight / I would like to turn back. / If I stayed timeless time, / I would have little luck."

16. On conscience and prophecy, see Paul Ricoeur, "The Summoned Subject in the School of the Narratives of the Prophetic Vocation," in his *Figuring the Sacred: Religion, Narrative, and the Imagination,* trans. David Pellauer (Minneapolis: Fortress, 1995), 262–75.

17. See Mary-Jane Rubinstein, "Of Ghosts and Angels: Derrida and Kushner on the Impossibility of Forgiveness," another paper for the Kushner panel at the Philadelphia AAR meeting, 2005.

18. Nancy Hatch Dupree, "in collaboration with Ahmad Ali Kohzad," *An Historical Guide to Kabul,* 2nd ed. (Kabul: Afghan Tourist Organization 1972); 1st ed., 1965 (by Nancy Hatch Wolfe). Kushner follows the order of

her essay "The Story of Kabul," takes short phrases and a poem from it, and captures her "voice."

19. See Tod Linafelt and S. Brent Plate, "Apocalypse Now and Then: Living Beyond the End of the World," paper at the American Academy of Religion meeting in New Orleans, Nov. 1996. There are, in "local apocalypses," survivors who remain haunted by memory and testimony.

20. Kushner, "Afterword," *Homebody/Kabul;* a blurb credits the phrase to Michael Kuchwara. Kushner also says his revisions do not reflect 9/11 or subsequent wars in Afghanistan and Iraq.

21. See Edward Said, *Orientalism* (New York: Pantheon, 1978).

22. Kushner says that while composing the play in longhand, he was sure Mrs. Ceiling was dead; but as he typed the draft she seemed to him alive, in Mel Gussow, "Write It, Stage It, Tweak It: Tony Kushner Continues to Tinker with 'Homebody/Kabul,' " *New York Times,* Sept. 9, 2002.

23. Kushner cites the Babylonian Talmud, Nedarin 39B.

24. Jason Zinoman, "Theater: Excerpt; Homebody/Kabul," *New York Times,* May 9, 2004, reports that Kushner considered the original scene "confusing." As for the grave, Kushner could have read in Dupree (1972, 114) that the spring, Cheshme Khedr, is associated with a white-bearded prophet who appears "to the lost and needy," and that both Hindus and Muslims venerate the site. But she does not say it is Cain's grave; this appears to be Kushner's invention.

25. See Søren Kierkegaard, *Either-Or,* vol. 1, Preface by "Victor Eremita," trans. David F. Swenson and Lillian Marvin Swenson (Princeton: Princeton University Pres, 1944), 9.

26. Dupree, vii–x, comments on Sa'ib-I-Tabrizi's poem "Kabul."

27. Toni Morrison's novel *Beloved* explores the sort of ethical question that arises "from the future," in respect to imagining the stories of those lost in the "Middle Passage."

Chapter XIII

Sections on Shakespeare and Levring, here revised, appeared in *Literature and Theology* 19 (2005): 159–80, an issue edited by Jennifer Geddes. The Lepage discussion revises comments in my essay in *Evil After Postmodernism: Histories, Narratives and Ethics,* ed. Geddes (London: Routledge, 2001) and another essay in Polkinghorne and Welker. The title recalls my chapter, "Holding Fragments," in Mohrmann and Hanson. For promptings from these editors I am grateful.

The first dialogue extract is from *King Lear,* ed. R. A. Foakes, 3rd. Arden Shakespeare series (London: Thomson Learning, 1997). *King Lear* is extant in the First Quarto of 1608 and First Folio of 1623, different enough that some editors now treat them as distinct plays. But Foakes, 119, revives the view of a single play that underwent some but not drastic revisions, variously reflected in both texts; he generally follows F, with some Q readings as well.

The second epigraph is from *Dogme 4: The King Is Alive*, directed by Kristian Levring (Zentropa Entertainment, 2000). The film is in English and Swahili with subtitles, which I have quoted.

The third quote is from Robert Lepage and Ex Machina, *The Seven Streams of the River Ota* (London: Methuen, 1996), 49.

Quince's quote is from *A Midsummer Night's Dream*, ed. Harold Brooks, 2nd. Arden Shakespeare series (London: Thomson Learning, 1979); the text is based on the First Quarto of 1600.

1. Harris, in *Theatre and Incarnation*, 128, identifies four readings of nature within *Lear*: Edmund aligns with nature's nothingness; Lear and Gloucester lose their Aristotelian faith in a nature correlated with social stability; Cordelia, Edgar, Kent, and Albany would resist nature's nothingness through decisive moral action ("to heal . . . insanity and despair"); but the death of Cordelia suggests that nature remains indifferent to the ethical good. I am intrigued by whether the play's moments of indeterminacy give any of these readings a final status, and whether room remains for a kenotic view of emptying.

2. See Paul Ricoeur, "Whoever Loses Their Life for My Sake Will Find It," in *Figuring the Sacred*, 284–88, where he applies Matt. 16:25 to the limits of secular and religious knowing.

3. See Oliver Davies, 44 and *passim*. See also Stanley Hauerwas, *Suffering Presence: Theological Reflections on Medicine, the Mentally Handicapped, and the Church* (Notre Dame: Notre Dame University Press, 1986).

4. See Stephen Greenblatt, *Shakespearean Negotiations*, particularly the chapter "Shakespeare and the Exorcists," 94–128.

5. Marjorie Garber, *Shakespeare After All* (New York: Pantheon, 2004), 656.

6. Foakes, 37–38.

7. Frank Brownlow, "Richard Topcliffe: Elizabeth's Enforcer and the Representation of Power in *King Lear*," in *Theatre and Religion: Lancastrian Shakespeare*, ed. Richard Dutton, Alison Findlay, and Richard Wilson (Manchester, UK: Manchester University Press, 2003), 161–78, reads *Lear* as retrospectively critical of tyrannous aspects of Elizabeth's rule; he notes that "Cordelia's invasion of England backed by a French army realizes one of the worst nightmares of Elizabeth and her Privy Council" (168).

8. See citations in Foakes, 34–35. Christic associations, ironic or not, should neither be discounted nor exaggerated. Foakes describes an earlier, rival "King Leir," which was more overtly redemptive; but if Shakespeare's is more tragic, that does not obliterate these allusions.

9. Kent, here, may carry out Horatio's "Roman" impulse to drain his chief's cup of poison.

10. The Fool is thus also comparable to Horatio, thinks Bloom, *Shakespeare*, 494.

11. See Jonas Barish, *The Antitheatrical Prejudice* (Berkeley: University of California Press, 1981), 129. On Edgar's popularity, see Foakes, 46, 112; on Edgar as actor, see William R. Elton, King Lear *and the Gods* (San Marino, Calif.: Huntington Library, 1966), 87.

12. Greenblatt, *Shakespearean Negotiations*, 121.

13. Ibid., 126.

14. See ibid., 124–25.

15. Greenblatt, 109; see 116: "Where there is no pretense to truth, there can be no *imposture* . . . ; 126: "But if false religion is theater, and if the difference between true and false religion is the presence of theater, what happens when this difference is enacted in theater?" I am grateful to Howard Pickett for alerting me to "emptying" language in Greenblatt.

16. See Caputo, *On Religion*, 31.

17. Tillich, *Dynamics of Faith* (1957; New York: Perennial Classics, 2001), 112.

18. Recall in chapters I and II how performatives realize or effectuate the referent in being performed.

19. On Edgar and apparel, see Judy Kronenfeld, King Lear *and the Naked Truth: Rethinking the Language of Religion and Resistance* (Durham: Duke University Press, 1998), 90–91.

20. Lear, then, is not senile but unwise; then he becomes divided. See Foakes's note on I.1.40.

21. See Balthasar on Calderón's *Great Theatre of the World*, in *Theo-Drama* 1:164–65.

22. E.g., Lear is a player in the mock trial (III.6), where he imagines dispensing justice upon his daughters. But the trial has the taint of revenge, does not advance the story, and is not in F.

23. For less hopeful views of Lear, see Harris, *Theater and Incarnation*, 132, and Paul Fiddes's essay, "Taking Death Seriously," in *The Promised End: Eschatology in Theology and Literature* (Oxford: Blackwell, 2000), 53–75, which glosses a number of lines I gloss. He thinks that despite Christic and other reconciling images, Lear remains "a 'very foolish, fond old man' (IV.7.60). This tragedy cannot be forced into the Christian sequence of life through death. . . . Lear is not redeemed, but he does *learn*" (64; Fiddes's italics). I do bring *Lear* closer to such a sequence; but as the sequence relates to kenosis, it also touches on Fiddes's sightings of humanity "reduced to absolute zero" (61), which also apply to the film *The King Is Alive*.

24. Levring thus contrasts with Cynthia Scott's 1990 film *The Company of Strangers*, about seven elderly women and a black driver who get along fine after their bus fails in the wilds of Canada.

25. Jacques Derrida, "Faith and Knowledge," trans. Samuel Weber, in Derrida, *Acts of Religion,* ed. Gil Anidjar (New York: Routledge, 2002), 55.

26. See Raymond Williams, *Modern Tragedy* (London: Chatto and Windus, 1966), 69–71; Terry Eagleton, *Sweet Violence: The Idea of the Tragic* (Oxford: Blackwell, 2003), 130–31.

27. Robert Lepage, *Connecting Flights: In Conversation with Rémy Charest,* trans. Wanda Romer Taylor (New York: Theater Communications Group, 1998), 86.

28. On the collaborative creation of *Seven Streams,* see Aleksandar Saša Dundjerović, *The Theatricality of Robert Lepage* (Montreal: McGill-Queens University Press, 2007), 123–52; on authoritarian directing, see Lepage, *Connecting Flights,* 57–59.

29. See Jennifer Harvie, "Transnationalism, Orientalism, and Cultural Tourism: *La Trilogie des dragons* and *The Seven Streams of the River Ota*" (119–42), and Sherry Simon, "Robert Lepage and the Languages of Spectacle," in *Theater sans Frontières: Essays on the Dramatic Universe of Robert Lepage,* ed. Joseph I. Donohoe Jr. and Jane M. Koustas, 224. (East Lansing: Michigan State University Press, 2000).

30. For a historical and constructive account of atonement, see Robert Jenson, *Systematic Theology,* vol. 1: *The Triune God* (New York: Oxford University Press), 181–93. My interest was sparked by Jane McAvoy's provocative *The Satisfied Life: Medieval Women Mystics on Atonement* (Cleveland: Pilgrim, 2000). On solidarity and atonement, see Jürgen Moltmann, *The Crucified God,* trans. R. A. Wilson and John Bowden (New York: Harper and Row, 1973), 190–95. On the atonement's etymology and importance to Altizer, see Brian Schroeder, "Absolute Atonement," in McCullough and Schroeder, 65–87.

31. Theseus may do this despite telling Hermia, "To you your father should be as a god" (I.1.47). René Girard, however, in *A Theatre of Envy,* 168–73, sympathizes with Egeus's impatience with Hermia's changing desires, for she once jilted Demetrius for Lysander. But that Demetrius had made at least a show of love for Helena would be something an informed Duke would know.

32. See Montrose, *The Purpose of Playing,* 200, on Puck as "a promoter of carnivalesque inversions." The second half of his book is devoted to *Dream.* Harris also frames the last chapter of *Theater and Incarnation* with *Lear* and *A Midsummer Night's Dream.*

33. Montrose, 134–35. See Girard, 55; "mimetic desire" wants something only because another desires it.

34. J. A. Bryant, *Hippolyta's View: Some Christian Aspects of Shakespeare's Play* (Lexington: University of Kentucky Press, 1961), 4–9, applying distinctions in Dante and Aquinas.

35. See Brooks, lv–vii; Montrose doubts this conjecture, but he thinks "the pervasive *cultural* presence of the Queen was a condition of the play's imaginative possibility" (160; my italics).

36. Garber, 216.

37. Brooks notes how Shakespeare could have read Reginald Scot's 1584 account of how one could put a real "asses head upon a man's neck and shoulders," lx, 148.

38. Ibid., lxvi–lxvii, on V.100–105.

39. Bloom, 169–70.

40. As Derek Godfrey played him in Peter Hall's 1968 Royal Shakespeare Company film (VHS).

41. See Montrose, 199–202, on how Puck, not Theseus is given the meta-theatrical "last word." Harris, 143, sees in Puck's "Lord, what fools these mortals be!" (III.2.115) "a judgment not on humanity as such, but on humanity's pretentions," exemplified by the players and lovers.

42. Bloom, 152.

43. Garber, 233; R. W. Dent, "Imagination in *A Midsummer Night's Dream*," *Shakespeare Quarterly* 15 (1964): 115–29, at 121.

44. Greenblatt, *Will in the World*, 36.

45. On emptiness, see my "Moving in the Disjunction: Langdon Gilkey, Secularity, and the Emptiness of God," *American Journal of Theology and Philosophy* 28 (2007): 137–60.

46. Montrose, 193, detects in Bottom's use of Paul "an inverse relationship between the temporal hierarchy of wealth and power and the spiritual hierarchy of wisdom and virtue." See also Greenblatt, *Shakespearean Negotiations*, 127, on the transforming, "hollow round space" of the Globe Theater.

Postlude

The first epigraph is from Bob Dylan, *Lyrics, 1962–2001* (New York: Simon and Schuster, 2004), 181.

1. See Funk, 34.

2. Crossan, *In Parables*, reconstructs the "original" parables of Jesus, apart from their placements in the Gospel narratives. For my purposes it is unnecessary to separate this parable from Luke's context of "who is my neighbor?" For Jesus and Luke, the parable is both an action and a transformation of conventional morality; in both contexts, the parable is theatrical when its rhetorical setting is imagined. See also comments on Crossan in the prelude to part IV.

3. Crossan, 32, 66; a parable's performance instantiates, or brings into play God's reign.

4. Prior to this period, antagonism by Jews toward Samaritans seems not to have been as great as later portrayed. See R. J. Coggins, *Samaritans and*

Jews: The Origins of Samaritanism Reconsidered (Oxford: Basil Blackwell, 1975), and Ingrid Hjelm, *The Samaritans and Early Judaism* (Sheffield, UK: Sheffield Academic Press, 2000).

5. Levinas, *Otherwise than Being*, 113–18. Pickett identifies the theatrical import of substitution in an unpublished paper on Levinas's use of face, mask, and other theater-related terms. On Levinas, see also Oliver Davies, 129–36, 139–41.

6. Ibid., 88: "The face of a neighbor . . . escapes representation; it is the very collapse of phenomenality." In the next sentences and on 90 Levinas mentions the face's "nudity," "aging," and "wrinkles," but these reinforce its weakness and nonphenomenality. In "Ethics as First Philosophy," trans. Sean Hand and Michael Temple, in *The Levinas Reader*, ed. Sean Hand (Oxford, UK: Blackwood, 1989), 75–87, he writes: "The proximity of the other is the face's meaning, and it means from the very start in a way that goes beyond those plastic forms which forever try to cover the face like a mask of their presence to perception. But the face always shows through these forms" (82–83). In *Ethics and Infinity: Conversations with Philippe Nemo*, trans. Richard A. Cohen (Pittsburgh: Duquesne University Press, 1986), 86, Levinas speaks of "an essential poverty in the face; the proof of this is that one tries to mask this poverty by putting on poses, by taking on a countenance."

7. George Herbert Mead, *Mind, Self and Society*, ed. Charles W. Morris (Chicago: University of Chicago Press, 1934, 1962), 173–78.

8. Bloom, *Shakespeare*, 151, 152.

9. See my discussion of Ruth Grant in the Introduction.

10. I am again grateful to discussions with Pickett for this consideration. See Skhlar, *Ordinary Vices*, on cruelty.

11. Lionel Trilling, *Sincerity and Authenticity*, discussed in the prelude to part II.

12. See Shklar on sincerity, 58–67.

13. See Jean-Luc Marion on the "constituted witness" to the "saturated phenomenon," in *Being Given: Toward a Phenomenology of Givenness*, trans. Jeffrey L. Kosky (Stanford: Stanford University Press, 2002), 216–19.

14. See Mark Polizzotti, *Highway 61 Revisited* (New York: Continuum, 2006), 134–36. The song's reference to "postcards of the hanging" alludes to the 1920 abduction from jail and mob lynching of three black circus hands (arrested for rape on doubtful evidence) in Duluth, Minnesota, where Bob Dylan would be born in 1941. Polizzotti also discusses Dylan's childhood interest in circus and theatrical performers; he sees in the song a nightmarish "Baedeker of Hell," whose "characters seem to lead mysterious alternate lives, to perform darker functions on the side."

Index

Abe, Masao, 386nn9–10
Abel, Lionel, 25
Ackroyd, Peter, 72
Aeschylus, 182, 213, 382n11; *Oresteia* trilogy, 42, 68
aesthetics: in Anouilh's *Becket,* 55, 60–61; in avant-garde theater, 224–26; in Coward's *Private Loves,* 272; and ethics or morality, 17, 64, 148, 252, 333, 349n52, 364n10; and integrity, 18; in Kierkegaard, 126, 130, 306, 371n18; in Shakespeare, 114, 339; in Soyinka, 81, 361n14. *See also* delight (aesthetic response); form; Hamlet, as paradigm; participation; representation (mimesis)
Albee, Edward, *Who's Afraid of Virginia Woolf,* 80
alienation or distancing effect (*Verfremdungseffekt*), 198, 200, 220, 221, 230, 238
Altizer, Thomas J. J., 246, 248, 395n9, 399n30
Ames, Roger T., 348n39
Anderson, Pamela Sue, 352n12
Anderson, Sherwood, 349n46
Andrews, Julie, 25, 147–48, 374n2
Anouilh, Jean: *Antigone,* 44–45, 49, 52, 384n9; *Becket, or The Honor of God,* 55, 60–65, 300, 357nn10–11
Ansky, S., *The Dybbuk,* 231
Antigone, as ethical paradigm, 19, 30, 34–37, 39, 43, 51–52, 54–56, 58, 73, 129, 148. *For the play or character see also under* Anouilh, Jean; Sophocles, *Antigone*
anti-theatrical prejudice, xii, 17, 117, 128, 148, 202, 284, 322, 336, 339, 363–64n8, 369n56
Apuleius, *Metamorphoses* (*The Golden Ass*), 327, 385n38

Arcand, Denys, *Jesus of Montreal,* 21, 252, 255–67, 323
Aristophanes, 222, 383n9
Aristotle, 13, 33–34, 67, 352n11, 358n20, 397n1; on poetry and drama, 19, 58, 118, 186, 189, 220–21, 327, 353–54n3
Armstrong, Robert Plant, 84
Arndt, Murray D., 382n8
Arnosu, Tundonu, 361n7
Arnott, Peter D., 380n14
Arrowsmith, William, 222–23, 224, 228, 384n26
Artaud, Antonin, 145, 221, 383n4
Asimov, Isaac, 171, 176, 178
Athanasius (of Alexandria), 387n18
atonement, 21, 70, 249–52, 281, 282, 311–12, 325, 332, 395n9
Auden, W. H., 370–71n8
audience participation. *See* participation
Auerbach, Erich, 385n36
Augustine (of Hippo), 23, 117, 179, 232, 246, 377n25, 385n34, 387n18
Austin, J. L., 66
authenticity. *See under* integrity
autonomy, 9–10, 30, 205, 244. *See also* respect for persons (principle)

Baartman, Saartjie (Sara or Sarah), 198, 199, 200, 205, 381nn3–4, 382n6. *For the character, see also* Parks, Suzan-Lori, *Venus*
Babbitt, Susan E., 11–12, 349n46
Baillie, D. M., 387–88n19
Bakhtin, Mikhail, xv, 156, 362n23, 375–76n14, 376n16
Balthasar, Hans Urs von, xv, 122, 128, 248, 325, 368n53, 371n12, 372n31, 387n18, 388n21, 398n21; on "role" and "mission," xv, 97, 141–44, 338
Barber, C. L., 393n29

Larry D. Bouchard is an associate professor of religious studies at the University of Virginia.

DATE DUE
